INTERNET VALUATION

Internet Valuation

THE WAY AHEAD

JOHN BRIGINSHAW

palgrave

First published 2002 by
PALGRAVE
Houndmills, Basingstoke, Hampshire RG21 6XS and
175 Fifth Avenue, New York, N.Y. 10010
Companies and representatives throughout the world

PALGRAVE is the new global academic imprint of St. Martin's Press LLC Scholarly and Reference Division and Palgrave Publishers Ltd (formerly Macmillan Press Ltd).

ISBN 0–333–94960–9

This book is printed on paper suitable for recycling and made from fully managed and sustained forest sources.

A catalogue record for this book is available from the British Library.

Library of Congress Cataloging-in-Publication Data

Briginshaw, John.
Internet valuation : the way ahead / John Briginshaw.
p. cm. — (Finance and capital markets series)
Includes bibliographical references and index.
ISBN 0–333–94960–9
1. Corporations—Valuation. 2. Electronic commerce. 3. Internet industry—Finance. I. Title. II. Series.

HG4028.V3 B65 2002
658.15—dc21 2002025180

Editing and origination by
Aardvark Editorial, Mendham, Suffolk

10 9 8 7 6 5 4 3 2 1
11 10 09 08 07 06 05 04 03 02

Printed in Great Britain by
Antony Rowe Ltd, Chippenham and Eastbourne

To Sheila and Diane, RIP

Contents

List of Figures

List of Tables

Preface

Warren Buffett[1] once suggested that if he were running a course in valuation, he would set a final exam question asking students to value an internet company. Any student who gave an answer would fail! This oft-quoted view on internet valuation is more attractive than ever but unfortunately not everyone can be as sanguine as Mr Buffett about the problems of valuing these stocks – however difficult the task, many of us are called upon to undertake it.

This book is intended to assist those people attempting to value internet stocks, and tackles this at a number of levels. We start from the bottom. Part I is a quite straightforward 'how to' intended to help the reader to build valuation models for internet firms. First we introduce a bare minimum of valuation theory in about a dozen pages (which many readers will be able to omit). The second chapter gives the Amazon.com case study data. The third chapter gives some basic grounding in accounting to help the reader understand where to find data within the accounting statements: the Amazon.com accounts are used as an example. This chapter ends with an appendix on accounting issues for internet companies, which readers can dip into as needed. We include an extended, step-by-step example of evaluating valuation parameters and then building a spreadsheet valuation model for Amazon. Our main methodology in Part I (and, indeed, throughout the book) is discounted cash flow (DCF) analysis. This first part is intended to impart three key learnings:

- how to determine the values of key parameters from past data
- how to build a flexible spreadsheet model to value an internet firm
- how the 'end result' equity valuation is produced by the model, using DCF.

Two key issues in Part I are 'taken on trust' at that point. The first is the cost of capital or the discount rate that goes into the model, together with the wider issue of why we use the DCF model. The second is the determination of the strategic outlook for internet firms.

Part II of the book addresses more advanced topics in the valuation of internet firms. These include the choice of a cost of capital and the 'meta problem' of a choice of method for calculating cost of capital. Methods considered are the capital asset pricing method (CAPM), the Fama French 4 factor model and reverse determination of the cost of capital. Other topics in this section include market efficiency and real option valuation techniques. We justify our use of the DCF paradigm for valuing firms. We also consider the 'comparables method' – that is, the use of ratios such as price/sales multiples and price per user values. We present qualitative and quantitative evidence in opposition to the comparables method. Unless different firms possess an unlikely level of 'comparability', this method is doomed to failure.

Part III of the book discusses the strategic outlook for internet and e-commerce firms, and how to cope with the changing environment for these firms. Gaining strategic understanding is a vital element of the valuation task – without understanding how to detect which firms have a 'good' strategy (one which will create a sustainable competitive advantage over other companies and therefore produce profits above and beyond the cost of the capital invested), the valuation task is a hopeless one. This part includes examples of how to apply classic strategic frameworks such as the 'five forces' and the 'value chain' to internet firms. These powerful frameworks, devised by Michael Porter of the Harvard Business School, are relevant both to new economy and to old economy firms. We continue our example of Amazon, and study the strategic position of the company using these frameworks. We consider the product life cycle, as it relates to new economy firms and their products. We survey other internet-based strategic models which have been advanced, for example network effects. We also look briefly at the outlook for various types of internet firm, and for broadband and mobile commerce.

Part IV rounds off the book by considering a couple of applications of valuation: the valuation of non-public equity, and the valuation of internet firms undergoing mergers and acquisitions (M&A). We also consider the increasingly important issue of valuing an e-commerce operation's contribution to overall firm value.

This last example demonstrates our inclusive attitude to the discussion of internet valuation. A common definition of an internet company has been that it should derive 50% or more of its revenue from activities related to the internet. However, we expect an increasing proportion of e-commerce activity to be carried out by non-pure-play internet firms.

INTENDED AUDIENCE

The natural reader for this book is a graduate equity analyst embarking on his or her first day at an investment bank. He or she is told to 'value an internet company,' and is thrown this book. If we have done our job, this book should enable such an analyst to get up to speed quickly and to produce a valuation model that he or she understands and that produces sensible numbers. Other likely readers are students of valuation, either at a college or studying by themselves, and other people interested in valuing internet firms.

This is probably the wrong book for the curious non-professional who owns a small number of shares in an internet firm, since it requires some investment of time to learn techniques rather than offering 'a view' on internet valuation and on the values of individual internet companies. Also, readers who have already spent some time valuing internet firms may already be using many of the techniques we discuss here.

NO MAGIC FORMULA

We have an important confession to make at this point: there is no 'magic formula' to value internet firms, neither in this book nor in any other. Fundamental analysis, however challenging, is the investor's only tool in valuing these companies. In this way we can build a solid valuation foundation for the use of internet technology in enhancing efficiency and creating shareholder value. This is, as it has always been, the way ahead for the internet investor.

WEBSITE

Please check the book's website:

www.internet-valuation.com/palgrave

which provides useful extra resources, notes and errata. A copy of the book is required to login.

Note

1 Some sources attribute this comment to Charlie Munger, Buffett's long-time colleague.

Acknowledgements

This book emerged out of my executive course on Internet Valuation for Euromoney Training, which I taught several times between May 2000 and April 2001, and my jointly authored article in the March 2000 issue of *Business Strategy Review* (*BSR*) on Valuing Internet Companies. I wish to thank my *BSR* co-author, Professor Chris Higson of the London Business School, for his tireless mentorship. Although we published this paper at the height of the dot-com mania, we managed to maintain a sense of historical perspective that makes this paper one of the less ridiculous outputs of that difficult time: for this, Chris must take a good deal of the credit.

I have benefited from the advice of colleagues on the Berkeley PhD program, especially David Tien, Guohua Jiang and Bokhyeon Baik; and also from the wonderful faculty at the Haas School and from exposure to the many scholars who visit and present at Berkeley. Special thanks go to Nick Wood of Metropolitan Venture Partners and Vimal Patel of Alliance Ventures for reading through Chapter 16, and to David Tien, Janet Jato and Ash Alankar for reading through key sections. Thanks also to: Stephen Rutt and Andrea Hartill of Palgrave; Andrew Nash (for copy-editing); and Linda Norris and colleagues at Aardvark Editorial.

Finally, I thank Janet for all her help and affection.

JOHN BRIGINSHAW
Berkeley, California

List of Abbreviations

ADSL	Asynchronous Digital Subscriber Line
A/P	accounts payable
APT	Arbitrage Pricing Theory
ARN	Accounting Research Network
ASB	Accounting Standards Board (UK)
ASP	Application Service Provider
B2B	business-to-business
B2C	business-to-consumer
B2E	business-to-employee
BCA	best case analysis
BOA	beginning operating assets
CAPM	capital asset pricing method
CARA	constant absolute risk aversion
CBOE	Chicago Board Options Exchange
CBOT	Chicago Board of Trade
CCA	continuing case analysis
CD	certificate of deposit
CEO	chief executive officer
CFA	cash-flow analysis
CFO	chief financial officer
cHTML	compact hypertext markup language
COGS	cost of goods sold
CRRA	constant relative risk aversion

CRSP	Center for Research in Securities Prices
DCA	discontinuity analysis
DCF	discounted cash flow
DJIA	Dow Jones Industrial Average (a share price index)
DSL	Digital Subscriber Line
EBITDA	Earnings Before Interest, Taxes, Depreciation and Amortization
EITF	Emerging Issues Task Force (US)
eps	earnings per share
ERP	equity risk premium
ESOP	employee stock option plan
EVA	economic value added
FASB	Financial Accounting Standards Board (US)
FCA	funding crunch analysis
FCC	Federal Communication Commission
FCF	free cash flow
FD	full disclosure (US SEC policy)
FF	Fama and French four-factor model
GAAP	Generally Accepted Accounting Principles
GDP	gross domestic product
GPS	Global Positioning System
HR	human resources
HTML	hypertext markup language
IAS	International Accounting Standards
IPO	initial public offering
ISDN	Integrated Services Digital Network
ISP	Internet Service Provider
kb/s	kilobits per second
LAN	local area network
LBO	leveraged buyout
LBS	location-based services
LNVOD	limited video (nearly) on demand
LSE	London Stock Exchange
LTCM	Long Term Capital Management
LVOD	limited video on demand
M&A	mergers and acquisitions
MBA	Master of Business Administration
MBO	management buyout
MRP	market risk premium

NA	no (risk-free) arbitrage
N/A	not applicable
NASDAQ	National Association of Securities Dealers Automated Quotations
NICs	National Insurance Contributions
NLB	'nice little business'
NM	not meaningful
NOL	net operating loss
NPV	net present value
NVOD	near video on demand
OA	other assets
OAS	options are (a form of) salary
OCA	other current assets
OCL	other current liabilities
OLS	ordinary least squares (regression analysis)
OP	option premium
P2P	path to profitability
P&L	profit and loss
PC	personal computer
PDA	personal digital assistant
PDC	personal digital cellular
PE	price/earnings (ratio)
PEACS	Euro convertible subordinated notes
PEAD	post earnings announcement drift
PFME	'perfect foresight' market efficiency
PHS	personal handy system
POM	'plain old mortar'
PR	public relations
P/R	price/revenue (ratio)
QECAP	quoting engine and customer acquisition portal
QoS	quality of service
R&D	research and development
RIV	residual income valuation
ROA	real options analysis; return on assets
RoBOA	return on beginning operating assets
RoCE	return on capital employed
RoCEL	return on capital employed limitation
SA	strategic analysis
SCM	supply-chain management

SD	standard deviation
SEC	Securities and Exchange Commission (US)
SG&A	selling, general and administrative costs
SKU	stock keeping unit
SME	small-to-medium enterprise
TCP	Transport Control Protocol
TFA	tangible fixed assets
TSCSREG	times series cross-section regression
TTM	trailing twelve months (PE ratio)
TVOD	true video on demand
UCLA	University of California at Los Angeles
UITF	Urgent Issues Task Force (UK)
UNC	University of North Carolina
VC	venture capital; venture capitalist
VOD	(true) video on demand
WACC	weighted average cost of capital
WAP	wireless application protocol
WCA	worst case analysis
WML	wireless markup language
xDSL	extended (definition of) DSL
XML	extensible mark-up language

PART I

The Basics

CHAPTER 1

Basic Valuation Theory

WHY INVESTORS BUY STOCKS AND SHARES

Investors are prepared to pay for stocks or shares because these shares give them a right to participate in the future earnings or cash flows of the companies issuing those shares. If a company issues 1,000,000 shares, an investor buying 10,000 of those shares will have the right to 1% of the company's future dividends, earnings and cash flows. The concept that buying a share gives the investor partial ownership of a company's *assets* is exactly equivalent to this. This is because a company's assets are priced in the marketplace on the basis of their ability to generate earnings and cash flows.

INTERNET FIRMS: ARE THEY DIFFERENT?

Internet firms are different from old-economy firms in that many internet firms have no current earnings. However, the reason why investors buy internet shares is the same as the reason they buy 'normal' shares – they wish to participate in the future earnings of the company. Most likely, the investors buy the shares because they feel that the earnings that the firm will generate in the future will more than reward them for the risks they take in buying the stocks. For this reason, internet shares are valued using the same underlying method as those of normal shares. *Projections of future cash flows* are made, and it may well be that the first one or two years of the projection may show negative or marginal cash flows. However, for internet firms the differences are in execution rather than in theoretical approach:

- more careful and painstaking analysis of the internet companies' past history and future prospects is required
- more caveats have to be borne in mind with regard to potential discontinuities and their effect on the future value of the internet firm
- a lack of accounting data may force reliance on non-accounting or non-financial data, which may be less reliable or more open to interpretation
- even with painstaking and careful analysis of past history and future value drivers, valuations are likely to be more prone to error than valuations of conventional firms
- while old-economy firms tend to have capital structures consisting of debt and equity, new economy firms possess capital structures in which equity predominates, together with some contingent claims (mainly employee share options and convertible debt).

VALUATION USING THE 'GREATER FOOL THEORY'?

The *greater fool theory* is not a valuation method: it has been proposed as an explanation of high internet stock prices during 1998–2000. It is also relevant to the perceived tendency of asset markets to go into periods in which asset prices rise very rapidly, before falling even more rapidly. This tendency is termed the *asset price bubble phenomenon*, because in rapidly 'blowing up' and almost instantly 'popping', the path of asset prices resembles a bubble. The internet stock price rises in 1998–March 2000 are now generally seen as an example of an asset price bubble. Previous examples of asset price bubbles are the tulip bubble in seventeenth-century Holland (see Dash, 1999), the South Sea bubble, the US stock market boom of the 1920s, the US growth stock craze of 1959–61, the high-tech boom of the early 1980s (Shiller, 1989) and the biotech boom of 1989–91.

The greater fool theory suggests that some investors purchase stocks not for reasons of intrinsic value – that is, they do not buy shares to participate in future earnings – but because they believe they will be able to sell them in the future to a 'greater fool' for a higher price. In an asset price bubble, the asset price embarks on a sustained upward movement, and investors come to depend on this upward movement, and abandon attempts to value the underlying cash flows of the asset or security (except possibly for cursory or unsupportable valuation exercises which serve as a method of rationalizing their pre-existing desire to purchase). Instead investors simply buy the asset, which in turn fuels the rise of asset prices. Investors then hope to find a 'greater fool' to sell the overvalued asset on to.

At some point the asset bubble 'bursts'. The cause of this bursting process is not well understood, but one explanation may be that the pressure of buying is exceeded by pressure from previous buyers seeking to crystallize their profits, and by short sellers. 'Bad news' by key companies in a stock bubble has been known to precipitate collapse, as has other general economic information which investors may have been fixating on. (The recent obsession with the comments of Alan Greenspan may be an example of this tendency for investors to fixate on certain information items.) However, it is worth noting that while these events may cause the bursting *process*, the bursting itself is not a sensible response to changes in fundamentals (for example projected future earnings or future economic growth) but a reflection of the end of an anomalous period of overpricing, during which asset prices have 'lost touch' with fundamentals. Underscoring this point, the bursting of asset price bubbles may also occur at times of little or no 'news'. This was the case for the bursting of the internet bubble, and for the bursting of the stock price bubble in 1929.

MARKET VALUE AND INTRINSIC VALUE

There are two values for any share or stock:

- the market value of the stock
- the intrinsic value of the stock.

The *market value* is easy to identify by looking in the financial pages or by accessing an online quote service such as www.quote.com. However, what we really want is not today's or yesterday's market value, or even the 'real time quote' value, but some information on *tomorrow's* market value.

This is the reason for the importance of the *intrinsic value* of a stock. Intrinsic value is the value of the future cash flows that the stock will provide. If an investor holds the stock for an indefinite period of time, this is the value that will accrue to him or her. Simple mathematical formulae enable us to transform predictions of future cash flows over the next several years into an estimate of the stock's intrinsic value today. These formulae comprise the DCF methodology. DCF enables us to value cash flows which we expect the company to pay in the future and to compare them directly to cash flows which occur today.

The intrinsic value is the value of the *future* cash flows from a company *expressed in today's money*. Therefore it is the maximum amount of money a sensible investor will pay for a share of the stock. Any valuation method is an attempt to calculate the *intrinsic* value, which is then used to predict the future *market* value. Market values and intrinsic values may diverge widely (for example, if there is an asset price bubble as discussed above), but in the long run market value will be close to intrinsic value. This is because there is no reason for investors to buy stocks except to obtain future cash flows – stocks have no aesthetic appeal, or other intangible benefits. Therefore, as the future plays out, investors will increase their holdings in shares which have intrinsic value greater than the current price (thereby putting upward pressure on stock prices), and decrease their holdings in shares which do not, causing market prices to tend towards intrinsic values.

In summary, fundamental analysis yields an estimate of the intrinsic or fundamental value of a stock or share. It does this by determining the potential of the firm to generate cash flows. This projection comes from past financial data on the firm's performance or, failing that, from predictions of the firm's future operating parameters ('fundamentals'). Projections that 'there will be a big market' or that 'this is like a new industrial revolution' are interesting, but irrelevant to valuation unless we can estimate their effect on the future revenues and margins of the companies we are valuing. If the calculated intrinsic value is less than the current market value, the stock is a poor investment and should be sold. If the calculated intrinsic value is more than the current market value, the stock is a good investment and should be bought.

There is one big problem with intrinsic value. Because working out intrinsic value requires predicting the future, intrinsic value cannot be calculated precisely, but can only be estimated approximately. However, since there is no reliable method for 'calculating' future market value, use of intrinsic value analysis is the only choice we have.

HOW DO WE VALUE FUTURE CASH FLOWS FROM COMPANIES?

The key question is how to compare future cash flows with current cash resources. The action of investing is fundamentally a 'swapping' process. When the investor buys a share, he or she is swapping money in the pocket or bank account today for the right to share in profits or cash flows tomorrow or later in the future. Put simply, there are two 'problems' with these cash flows, two ways[1] in which they are 'inferior' to having money to spend today:

- they are in the future
- they are risky.

VALUING PAYMENTS FROM SAFE INVESTMENTS

Dealing with these problems in turn, the first problem is that the cash flows we hope to receive from the shares are *in the future*. Given the choice of money now or money in the future, we will prefer money now, if for no other reason than that we can earn a small amount of extra interest on the money we receive now, which we cannot earn on the money we receive in the future.

To consider this problem alone, let us suppose we knew of a firm that was not risky – that is, the company could predict its earnings accurately and pay them all out. An investment in this company would be exactly like a savings account or certificate of deposit (CD), and could be valued in the same way.

For example, suppose prevailing interest rates are 5%, and SafeCompany Ltd offers to sell a share which will pay back £110 next year (for sure). This share would be worth £110/1.05 = £104.76. To see why this is true, think of swapping the £104.76 now for £110 in one year. This is a fair swap because £110 is the most one could earn from a competing investment.[2]

Applying this idea over a longer period, what would the sensible investor pay for a share in OtherSafe, Inc., which is issuing shares guaranteed to pay $110 in two years? To solve this question, let us consider the competing investment, supposing again that prevailing interest rates are 5%. Let us consider investing $100 for two years. At the end of the first year the investment would be worth $105. At the end of the second year, we would earn interest on the $100 and also on the $5 of interest from the first year. The result at the end of year 2 would be $105 × 1.05 = $110.25, or $100 × 1.05 × 1.05, or $100 × 1.05^2.

Another way of saying this is that the *discount factor* for a two-year investment at a 5% interest rate or discount rate is $1/1.05^2 = 0.90703$. That is: to work out how much a payment in two years' time is worth today (using a 5% discount rate), we need to multiply the future value by 0.90703. So we would pay $99.77 ($110 × 0.90703) for an investment in OtherSafe.

The general formula for the value of a cash flow of C in n years at an interest rate of r is:

$$\text{present value of C in } n \text{ years} = \frac{C}{(1+r)^n}$$

Two things should be noted. First, in the calculation of '1 + r', the interest rate or discount rate (r) should be converted to a decimal number – for example 6% will become 0.06, meaning that 1 + r has the value 1.06. Second, because we are using the concept of arbitrage, the r that 'matters' is the interest rate of *competing* investments, not the interest rate advertised by the company or bank.

VALUING PAYMENTS FROM RISKY INVESTMENTS

Investments can be risky in two ways. The most common perception of risk in an investment is that there is a risk that investors will 'lose their money'. An example of this would be a saver who invests in an account at a bank which fails: the interest promised would not be received, and the investor would lose his or her principal.

The other way in which an investment can be risky is if the returns from the investment are uncertain from the start. An investment in the shares of a company is an example of this. Some companies pay *dividends* in cash to shareholders, which are a portion of the earnings or profits that the firm make in a year. However, internet firms rarely do this (neither do most growth or early-stage firms). For the shareholder in an internet firm, there is no guarantee of a payment of 3% or 5% such as there is from a bank account. There is also no likelihood (at any rate, not yet) of receiving a quarterly or semi-annual dividend of 0.2% × 1% of the value of the shares, such as would be expected by a shareholder in AT&T or BT. The money that a shareholder in an internet firm makes will depend on whether the market valuation of the firm rises over time. This, in turn, is dependent on the future earnings and prospects of the firm. The possibility exists that returns will be low, and the further possibility exists that (if the firm goes bankrupt) the investor will lose all his or her money. Of course, the possibility also exists that the firm will do very well, and the shareholders will then share in this prosperity.

How can we convert these simple observations into a valuation method for risky investments? Well, although firms provide very uncertain returns, it is still possible to evolve estimates of what future profits they may make, and from these estimates of profits work out what returns to expect from the shares. It also seems sensible that if an investor is asked to choose between a safe investment and a risky investment, such as a share, he or she will want *higher returns* from the risky investment. In order to reflect this, we use the *same formula* as we use to value payments from safe investments, but we add a *risk premium* to the value of r. For a safe investment r would typically be 5%. For a risky investment r would be 10% or more. Also, since companies do not advertise or even discuss expected returns or payments from their shares, we once again calculate the risky r from the returns on competing investments, choosing investments that are as similar as possible to the ones we are trying to value.

Let us look at an example:

An investor already has a large collection of investments in a variety of firms. A friend offers her an investment in a property scheme that the friend has developed.

He expects to sell the scheme in two years for $1.3m. The investor is aware that this type of property investment has typically returned 10% in the past. What price should she pay for a 1% share?

The price one would pay for a 1% share is the present value of 1% of $1.3m at a discount rate of 10%, for example:

$$\frac{C}{(1+r)^n} = \frac{0.01 \times \$1.3\text{m}}{(1+0.1)^2} = \frac{\$13{,}000}{1.21} = \$10{,}744$$

One would try to get away with less (depending on how good a friend he is!) but, assuming that past returns are a good estimate of expected returns, $10,744 would be a fair price.

Note that the $1.3m is what the developer *expects* to sell the project for. If the investor knew that the project would be sold for $1.3m in two years, the project would be risk-free. But she does not know whether the ex-post cash received when the developer sells the property will be less than $1.3m, or more: $1.3m is simply his best estimate. Similarly, if we were to say that the expected return from shares in Amazon.com is 15% over the next year, and then wait a year and see what the return actually was, the actual return might be 20% or even minus 5%, because of the uncertainty inherent in shares. The return could be plus several hundred per cent, as it was for Amazon in 1998, or minus 75%, as it was for the firm in 2000. Clearly, past returns do not always provide easy guidance for what discount rate we should use!

Going back to our property example, we can see that the calculation of the $10,744 value for the share in the property project is influenced by two numbers – the future value of the project ($1.3m) and the discount rate (10%). If the potential investor is unsure of the $1.3m (perhaps her friend has been somewhat optimistic in the past) and feels it is 'risky' in the vernacular sense, the temptation is to reflect this extra risk by using a discount rate of, perhaps, 20%. However, this temptation should be resisted: instead, the $1.3m number should be adjusted downwards, perhaps by gathering more information on property values. 'Fudging' the discount rate produces a meaningless number as present value and, if comparing projects or firms, penalizes those for which projections are not optimistic as well as those for which they are. Companies which seem to have vulnerable forecasts or which seem to require unbelievable growth to gain 'traction' should have cash flows projected forward realistically and then have those cash flows discounted at a fair rate. This is preferable to accepting 'best case' financials and trying to make up for it by using a high discount rate.

But what is a fair discount rate?

THE 'CAPM' MODEL OF CALCULATING THE DISCOUNT RATE FOR A COMPANY'S EQUITY

We discuss the calculation of discount rate (which is also called *cost of capital* or *hurdle rate*) in detail in Chapter 5. This section gives a practical guide to calculating cost of capital using the most widely used method, which is called the *CAPM (capital asset pricing model).*

In our example of valuing a risky investment we were required to estimate the discount rate for the investment, which we were able to do because we had been given information on typical returns in that industry (property). But what about estimating cost of capital or discount rate for an internet company for which there may not be many (or any!) similar companies with which to compare? What about trying to obtain a discount rate for a company or industry which has no 'track record' to look at? What we would like is to have some shortcut measure of how risky the firm is – because the more risky it is, the greater the return the investor will require from it.

The shortcut method is the CAPM. This is a method which measures the risk of a stock by looking at how volatile the stock's returns are, relative to the returns of the market. The measure of volatility relative to the market is called the firm's β. The β for a firm can be obtained from a number of websites, for example www.bloomberg.com. Once β has been obtained, the discount rate, r, can be obtained using the following sequence of equations:

$$r = r_f + \text{risk premium}$$

That is, the cost of capital can be obtained by adding a risk premium to the safe or *risk-free rate*. We call the risk-free rate r_f, to distinguish it from the cost of capital for the 'risky' firm, r. The risk-free rate can be obtained from several sources, including www.cnnfn.com in the USA and www.FT.com in the UK.[3] Over the past few years this has varied between just below 2% (2002) and 6%. Figure 1.1 shows the changes in the risk-free rate (13-week treasuries) in the USA between 1980 and late 2001.

Although the risk-free rate declined sharply in late 2001/early 2002 to low values, it has been above 10% as recently as the early 1980s. Because the 2001/2002 declines have been a result of monetary policy in response to the possible onset of recession and to the economic threat resulting from terrorist activities, we do not expect these low levels to persist. At early 2002, *a sensible estimate of short-term risk-free rates over the medium term is 4%.*

$$r = r_f + \text{risk premium} = r_f + \text{MRP} \times \beta$$

The risk premium is obtained by multiplying the market risk premium (MRP), the expected return of the average equity, by the β, which measures the relative riskiness of the firm.

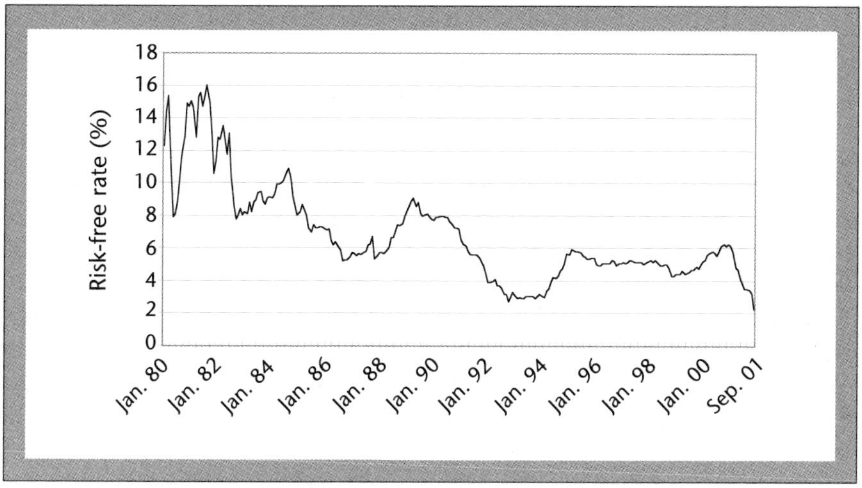

Figure 1.1 Changes in the risk-free rate for 13-week US treasuries

$$r = r_f + \text{risk premium} = r_f + \text{MRP} \times \beta = r_f + (r_m - r_f) \times \beta$$

The MRP is equal to r_m, the expected return of the market, minus r_f, the risk-free or safe rate of return. We will discuss in Chapter 5 how the MRP can be calculated. For the moment, *we will use an MRP of 5% for the US and the UK*. This is inspired by the calculations of Dimson et al. (2001), who calculated the MRP over 100 years of data in several countries, yielding numbers for the geometric mean of 4.7% in the UK and 5.6% in the USA. These researchers looked back at the detailed stock data, worked out the returns on the stock market for each year, and subtracted the short-term risk-free return (bills) to obtain the MRP for each year. These were combined to form an average of the MRP for the last century. We believe that this historical MRP is a reasonable estimate of the future MRP and can be used to calculate discount rates for stocks.

For most firms β is close to 1. Internet firms have typically had higher β values, generally of 1–2, and sometimes as high as 3. Therefore, the CAPM typically produces estimates of the discount rate for internet firms of 10–20%.

DEFINITION OF CASH FLOW FOR COMPANIES

So far in this chapter we have talked directly about valuing cash flows. However, we now define how cash flow is measured in practice for companies. Cash flow, or *free cash flow* (FCF), is the amount of cash which is produced by the operating assets of the firm in any one period and which is available to the investors. This is the cash received from customers as revenue, minus the costs expended and assets bought in the period, minus taxes:

FCF = cash flow from operations – net investment in assets – cash taxes

where cash flow from operations = earnings or profit – increase in working capital + add-back of depreciation and other non-cash items

We will discuss much of this terminology when reviewing the accounts of Amazon.com in the next chapter. For the examples we talk about in this chapter, there are no assets, so the calculation of cash flow is simply that cash flow is equal to profit: that is, revenues minus costs. In accounting, *assets* (tangible things that are used for the longer term, such as buildings, computers and desks) are treated differently from *costs* like raw materials or electricity. They are not directly subtracted from profit, but the cost is taken gradually over the useful life, shared out as *depreciation* in each year the company owns the assets. However, if one needs more assets to run the business, that uses up cash and decreases cash flow. For the moment that is the key understanding needed from the equations above.

CAPITAL STRUCTURE OF COMPANIES AND THE CALCULATION OF THE WACC

The majority of internet companies are financed only by *equity* (shares, stock) rather than by *debt* (loans, paper). The source of a company's financing gives rise to its *capital structure*. A company financed entirely by equity has a simple capital structure. Its assets are balanced (financed) precisely by its equity. Its *balance sheet* (the part of the accounts where the capital structure is noted down) would look like this:

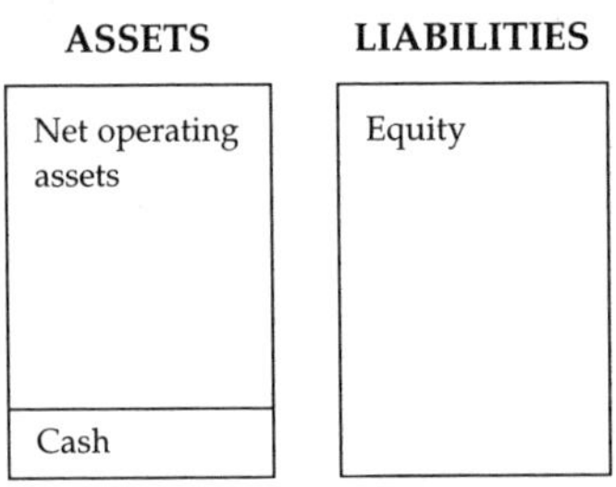

In any valuation exercise, the value of *operating assets* is the key unknown. The value of *cash* is known, because cash in the balance sheet, bank account or pocket is freely interchangeable. Therefore if we value the net operating assets by valuing the future free cash flows, and then add the known value of cash, we obtain the value of quoted equity. Note that there is no need to take the future value of the cash: today's value is adequate, because we do not expect the firm to be able to generate extra value from investing its cash – we expect it to generate value only from using its operating assets. Also the issue of discount rate is simplified, provided the amount of cash is small. We can estimate the cost of equity capital, *r*, from the CAPM, and if cash is a low percentage of total assets, then the appropriate discount rate for cash flows from the operating assets is also *r*. If cash or other low expected-return assets (such as government bonds) form a large proportion of the business financed by the pure equity, then the operating assets would require a higher discount rate than *r*.

Some companies are financed by both debt and equity. This means that their capital structure and the risk-adjusted discount rate for the cash flows from their operating assets cannot be simply calculated from the CAPM. First of all let us consider a simple case, in which cash is exactly balanced by debt or borrowings:

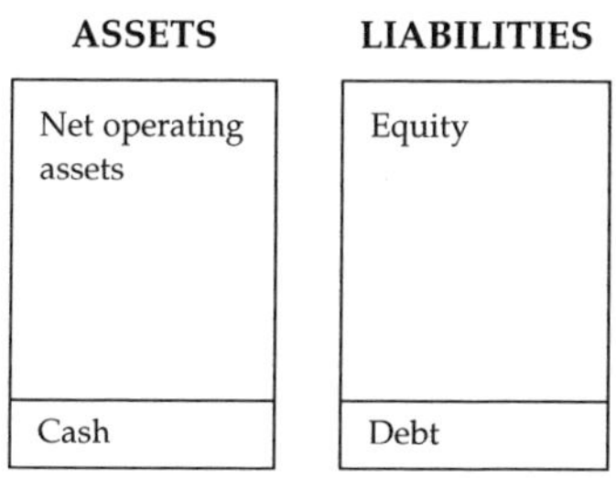

In this case the presence of debt is irrelevant to valuation, provided that debt and cash are equal at market value. The company is simply establishing some financial flexibility funded by debt, the operating assets (funded by discounting future cash flows) are equal to the equity value, and *r* is a suitable cost of capital for discounting the free cash flows from operating assets.

A final, more complex case is when debt is greater than cash:

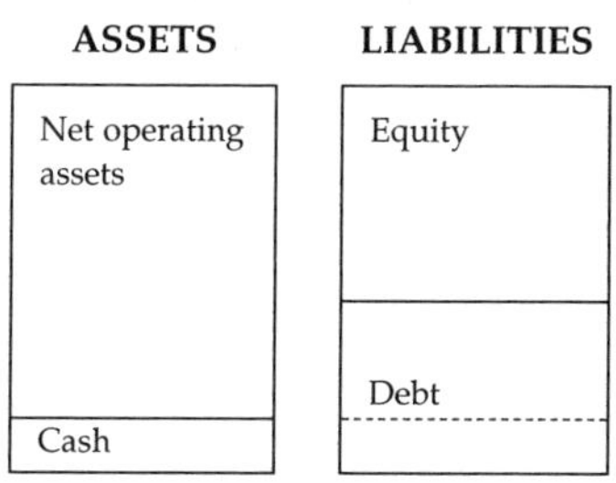

Ignoring the portion of debt offset by cash, we obtain a simplified capital structure in which net debt is equal to debt minus cash:

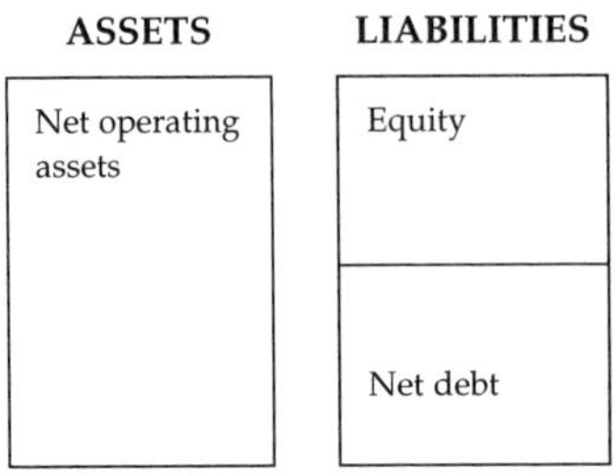

In this case the influence of net debt is too large to ignore. If the debt has an expected return, r_{Debt}, of just above the risk-free rate (an expected return of perhaps 1% over risk-free, or 5%) and if the CAPM estimates that the cost of equity capital, r, is perhaps 11.5% (for a $\beta = 1.5$ stock), then this tells us that the expected return of the operating assets – that is, their *cost of capital* – is somewhere in between. This logic is formularized by the *weighted average cost of capital*, or *WACC*, formula. The simple WACC formula gives the discount rate to be applied to cash flows from operating assets for a part equity- and part debt-financed company:

$$\text{simple WACC} = r_{\text{Debt}} \frac{D}{V} + r \frac{E}{V}$$

where D = value of debt
E = value of equity
$V = D + E$ = value of company.

Note that the above formula is calculated in exactly the way its name suggests: it is an average of the cost of capital of the two parts of the capital structure, weighted according to the proportion that each one forms of the company's value. However, there is one small complication. If the company is paying taxes, it receives a tax benefit of debt, in a roundabout way. This is because interest on debt is tax-deductible – that is, it is taken out of the profits of the company before the Inland Revenue (UK) or Internal Revenue Service (US) calculates the profits to be taxed. To reflect this, the after-tax WACC formula becomes the following:

$$\text{WACC} = r_{\text{Debt}} (1 - T_c) \frac{D}{V} + r \frac{E}{V}$$

where T_c = the (corporate) tax rate.

Since most firms pay taxes, this WACC formula is the one normally used. For internet companies to have value, they will have to make profits in the future, so this standard WACC formula is still relevant for these companies. (The WACC for a company which will *never* make profits is immaterial, since the company value will be zero.) However, internet company debt can be quite risky, so its inclusion in the calculation may not depress the WACC much below the cost of equity capital. For example, Amazon.com's convertible debt tracks changes in its stock price very closely, and since the firm is unlikely to be in a tax-paying position for several years, the equity discount rate is used as the WACC.

VALUATION EXAMPLE

Let us now move to a slightly more complex illustrative example of a valuation.

> www.Knightswhosayni.biz (KWSN) is a quoted website selling Monty Python paraphernalia. For the year just ended yesterday (the first year of operations), KWSN has sales of £1.5m and costs of £2m. It expects growth of 50% in revenues for five years. Its cost structure is as follows:
>
> - £1m of costs are for website, buildings (rented) and staff
> - £1m of costs for last year were for obtaining Monty Python memorabilia and for packing and posting these.
>
> The website, buildings and staff are expected to be able to handle all the sales for the next five years without additional annual costs for these elements. Unit costs for procuring and shipping the products are expected to be constant.
>
> At the end of the five years the owners will seek to sell to Disney, AOL Time Warner or some other large media player for a ten times earnings multiple.
>
> The firm has no debt or cash and has an equity β of 2. The tax rate is 30% and tax is paid immediately at the end of the year. There are no depreciating assets.
>
> **Required:** What is the value of Knightswhosayni.biz?

Step 1: Project revenues and costs

We extract the following data from the above problem:

- Each year's revenue is 1.5 times the previous years.
- There is a fixed cost element for buildings and so on of £1m (fixed because it stays the same irrespective of the volume shipped).
- There is a variable cost element, which last year was £1m (future: 67% of sales.

Table 1.1 KWSN: projected data for years 1–5

	£m	£m	£m	£m	£m	£m
Year	*0*	1	2	3	4	5
Revenues	***1.50***	**2.25**	**3.38**	**5.06**	**7.59**	**11.39**
Fixed costs	*1.00*	1.00	1.00	1.00	1.00	1.00
Variable costs	*1.00*	1.51	2.26	3.39	5.09	7.63
Total costs	***2.00***	**2.51**	**3.26**	**4.39**	**6.09**	**8.63**
Pretax profit	***–0.50***	**–0.26**	**0.11**	**0.67**	**1.51**	**2.76**

We project these predicted data forward, to find pre-tax profits (see Table 1.1). (Year 0 data is shown in italic. These are not included in the present value calculation because they are in the past.)

Step 2: Calculate tax

We extract the following data from the problem:

- The company has a net operating loss carry-forward of £0.5m from the first year of operations. This means that under US or UK tax law it will not pay any tax on the first £0.5m of profit which it makes.
- There is no depreciation in this company: all costs are on a cash basis (this simplifies the tax calculation and means that *profits are the same as free cash flows* in this idealized example).

Table 1.2 KWSN: projected post-tax profits (cash flows) for years 1–5

	£m	£m	£m	£m	£m	£m
Year	*0*	1	2	3	4	5
Pretax profit	***–0.50***	**–0.26**	**0.11**	**0.67**	**1.51**	**2.76**
Accumulated NOLs	***0.50***	0.76	0.64	N/A	N/A	N/A
Profit liable for taxation	*N/A (loss)*	N/A (loss)	0	0.03	1.51	2.76
Taxation (30%)	***0***	**0**	**0**	**0.01**	**0.45**	**0.83**
Post-tax profits	***–0.50***	**–0.26**	**0.11**	**0.66**	**1.05**	**1.93**

- The tax rate is 30%.

Using the pre-tax profits from Step 1, we calculate the *NOLs* (*net operating losses*) in the future and the tax payable, to find post-tax profits, which are equal to cash flows (Table 1.2).

Step 3: Calculate the terminal value

We extract the following data from the problem:

- The company will be sold as a going concern in five years.
- The price will be ten times the year 5 earnings.

We multiply the post-tax earnings for year 5 (calculated in Step 2) by 10 to find the price for which the business will be sold in year 5. This is called the *terminal value* for the firm. The terminal value, together with the year 5 post-tax earnings, give the total cash flow received in year 5:

Terminal value = 10 × £1.93m = £19.3m
Total cash flow in year 5 = £21.24m (rounding)

Step 4: Discount the years 1–5 cash flows back to today, and sum them

- Only future cash flows are included.
- The discount rate using the CAPM is 14% ($r = r_f + \text{MRP} \times \beta = 4\% + 5\% \times 2$)

Present value of year 1 cash flow	$= -0.26/1.14$	$= -0.23$
Present value of year 2 cash flow	$= +0.11/1.14^2$	$= +0.09$
Present value of year 3 cash flow	$= +0.66/1.14^3$	$= +0.45$
Present value of year 4 cash flow	$= +1.05/1.14^4$	$= +0.62$
Present value of year 5 cash flow	$= +21.24/1.14^5$	$= +11.03$
Total present value		£11.97m

Answer: The current value of KWSN is £11.97m.

Notes

1 In the case of shares in unquoted companies there is a third way, in that they are also *illiquid* – that is, the shares cannot be traded on the market without driving the price away from the buyer or seller. We discuss this issue further in Chapter 16.

2 This is a very simple example of arbitrage pricing. *Arbitrage* is the process of seeking profits by buying one investment and selling a similar or related investment. In an efficient capital market these profits will be close to zero.

3 As a matter of convention in this book, the risk-free rate is taken as the return on the shortest available government security, typically a 3-month T-bill. Some other texts calculate the risk-free rate as the longer term bond rate of interest, because the underlying firm has a long life and because long bond rates tend to be less susceptible to short-term fluctuations in interest rates. This method works well, provided the MRP used is the market rate of return minus the return on bonds rather than bills. Dimson et al. (2001) give both MRPs.

CHAPTER 2

Case Study: Valuing Amazon.com

INTRODUCTION

The following case study gives some information about Amazon.com, Inc., together with some supporting and related documentation on other similar or comparable firms.

This information will allow readers to construct an Excel spreadsheet to value the company.

SETTING THE SCENE

It is February 2002, and Amazon.com has recently reported its audited results for 2001. For the full year, the company recorded a pro forma loss of $45m (Year 2000: $317m; pro forma loss excludes goodwill amortization, losses in associates and certain other charges) on revenues of $3.12bn (Year 2000: $2.76bn). However, under US GAAP, losses were $0.57bn (Year 2000: $1.4bn). At the same time, the company announced a small net profit for 4th quarter 2001 ($35m pro forma, $5m GAAP). The historical accounts for the company are shown in Appendix 2.1.[1]

Disclaimer: While every effort has been made to ensure the correctness of the information in this case study, no guarantee of truthfulness is made or implied. The case study has been prepared entirely from publicly available information as a basis for discussion rather than to illustrate either effective or ineffective handling of an administrative situation. It is not endorsed and has not been checked by Amazon.com, Inc., or any other company, and does not constitute a statement of strategy or a statement about valuation by that firm.

Figure 2.1 Stock price chart of Amazon.com (AMZN)

Note: $20 per share = $7.433bn market capitalization

In common with other internet e-commerce players, Amazon.com has suffered a precipitous fall in share price and in public and investor confidence. The company's stock value peaked at $40bn on 10 December 1991 but has since declined to approximately $4.8bn. The firm's stock price performance is shown in Figure 2.1.

Time named Amazon's CEO (Jeff Bezos) Man of the Year in December 1999, and there was widespread enthusiasm for the company amid investors and stock analysts at that time. However, 2001 has brought a much harsher public relations environment, with speculation that the company may not survive far into the future, and the firm is variously referred to as 'Amazon.con, Amazon.toast, Amazon.bomb and my favourite, Amazon.org, because we're clearly a not-for-profit,' according to the ever-jovial Bezos. However, the company's performance in the 4th quarter of 2001 gave enthusiasts hope that it might be turning the corner into profitability.

BACKGROUND AND FUNDING

Amazon.com was founded by Jeff Bezos in July 1994. Bezos was formerly a senior vice president at D.E. Shaw, a Wall Street hedge fund firm; and prior to his banking career, he graduated in Electrical Engineering and Computer Science from Princeton University.

After a period of website and other development, the company commenced serving customers in July 1995. Initially the firm was funded by capital from Jeffrey P. Bezos and other sources. In June 1996, the firm raised venture capital funds from Kleiner Perkins of approximately $7.8m (source: Kleiner Perkins website and Amazon.com S-1 filing). The firm's first public market funding came in May 1997, when it raised $54m from sales of common stock at a stock price of $18. The stock's first day bounce was a comparatively modest (compared to some future IPOs) 31%. At the close of business on 14 May 1997, the IPO date, the outstanding common stock was valued at $560m.

As shown in the company's historical accounts (see Appendix 2.1), Amazon.com grew rapidly. It placed an emphasis on optimizing logistics, recruiting distribution and merchandising experts from leading US retailer Wal-Mart, among others. The company emphasized growth over profitability, and was therefore unable to fund growth from internally generated funds, and had to raise substantial funds. Subsequent to its IPO, Amazon mainly raised money through the debt or convertibles markets. On 29 December 1997 the company concluded a $75m, three-year credit facility (led by Deutsche Morgan Grenfell, Inc.). On 5 May 2000 Amazon raised $326m from the sale of senior discount notes, a debt instrument which would pay interest from the year 2003. Following this the company raised money from convertible bond issues. On 28 January 1999, Amazon sold $1.25bn (raised from $500m to meet investor demand) 4.75% Convertible Subordinated due 2009. And on 16 February 2000, Amazon sold €690m of its 6⅞% Convertible Subordinated Notes due 2010 (mainly in the European convertible markets). As of 31 December 2001 the company reported cash and cash equivalents of $540.3m (the company also owned marketable securities of $456.3m).

LINES OF BUSINESS

Amazon commenced business as an online bookstore in July 1995. It added music in June 1998, DVD/video sales in November 1998, Amazon auctions in March 1999, zShops (hosting of online stores for merchants) in September 1999, and home improvement, electronics and software in November 1999. During the year 2000 the company added further stores, including cars (partnership with Greenlight.com), kitchen, health and beauty (partnership with drugstore.com), outdoor, tools, and Amazon outlet (discounted and/or reconditioned branded goods). In February 2001, in what was seen as a policy shift, the company was quoted as saying it would no longer sell unprofitable items. However, at February 2002 there had been no clear sign of a downsizing in the firm's product offering. In fact the firm continued to add new 'stores',

Table 2.1 Timeline of stores opened by Amazon.com

Date	Store	Date	Store
16 Jul. 95	Books	2 May 00	Kitchen and housewares
11 Jun. 98	Music	19 May 00	Home living (with living.com) (now closed)
15 Oct. 98	International (amazon.co.uk and amazon.de)	23 Aug. 00	Cars (with greenlight.com)
1 Nov. 98	DVD	4 Oct. 00	Camera and photo
17 Nov. 98	Video	28 Nov. 00	Cell phones
17 Nov. 98	Gifts and gift certificates	28 Dec. 00	Outlet
13 Jan. 99	Toys and games (with ToysRUs from September 2000)	18 May 01	In theatres
		23 May 01	Baby and baby registry (with ToysRUs)
30 Mar. 99	Auctions	2 Aug. 01	Borders.com co-branded
13 July. 99	Electronics	22 Aug. 01	Corporate accounts
30 Sep. 99	zShops (small stores can market from Amazon's website)	29 Aug. 01	Computers (with Ingram Micro and others)
		11 Sep. 01	Target (with Target Corporation, Minneapolis)
9 Nov. 99	Software		
9 Nov. 99	Tools and hardware	26 Sep. 01	Travel (with expedia.com and others)
9 Nov. 99	Computer and video games		
5 Apr. 00	Outdoor living	30 Oct. 01	Magazine subscriptions (with Synapse Services)
17 Apr. 00	Health and beauty (with drugstore.com)		

although many of these were in partnership with other companies. The full timeline of stores added is shown in Table 2.1.

Information on the segment breakdown of fiscal year 2001 sales (as provided by the company) and the potential market size of major product lines is shown in Table 2.2.

In order to leverage its web-based storefront, Amazon.com accelerated its partnership activity from early 2001 onwards. The company's precise revenue sharing arrangements with partners have not generally been disclosed by the company. The partnerships and any revenue disclosure are shown in Table 2.3.

INVENTORY AND FIXED ASSETS

The CEO of Amazon.com originally sited the company in Seattle, to be close to the largest wholesale books warehouse in the world, that of Ingram books, in Oregon. Originally the company only stocked 2000 out of the 1 million books it offered for sale (Ghemawat and Baird, 1998). However, in 1998–99 the

Table 2.2 Amazon.com sales (US only): full year 2001

	Amazon full year 2001 sales (US) ($m)	US market (2000, $m p.a.)	Projected growth in US market (2000, % p.a.)	World market (2000, $m p.a.)
Books	1689	28,800	4.4	86,400
Music	*	13,700	7.2	38,700
DVD/video	*	9,600	7	26,700
Toys	**	22,600	6.6	62,800
Electronics	547	57,000	8.7	57,000
Software		5,000		12,000
Home improvement	**	400,000	4.1	
Auctions, zShops, marketplace, and so on	225***	****		
All US retail		2,600,000		

* Music, DVD and videos are combined with books
** Toys are combined with electronics
*** Revenue for all services
**** Not identifiable

Sources: Company reports, Morgan Stanley, ING Barings, Prudential, Forrester Research. All figures except those in the first column are estimated.

Table 2.3 Amazon.com: partnerships

Date	Store	Partner	Revenue disclosure (if any)
17 Apr. 00	Health and beauty	drugstore.com	
23 Aug. 00	Cars	greenlight.com	
19 Sep. 00	Toys and games	ToysRUs	
23 May 01	Baby and baby registry	ToysRUs	
23 Jul. 01	AOL	AOL Time Warner	AOLTW makes $100m investment in Amazon stock
2 Aug. 01	Borders.com co-branded	Borders.com	
20 Aug. 01	Electronics (in-store pick-up)	Circuit City	
29 Aug. 01	Computers	Ingram Micro (order fulfilment for new computers), Essex Technology Group, Overstock.com and TechSmart, Inc. (refurbished computers)	
11 Sep. 01	Target	Target, Inc.	'Under the five-year strategic alliance, Amazon.com will receive per unit fees and annual fixed fees' (amounts undisclosed)
26 Sep. 01	Travel	expedia.com (Microsoft), hotwire.com, National Leisure Group	
30 Oct. 01	Magazine subscriptions	Synapse Services	

Table 2.4 Amazon.com: distribution centres (December 1999)

Location	Date acquired	Square footage (maximum)
Seattle, Washington	Inception	93,000
New Castle, Delaware	Nov. 97	202,000
Fernley, Nevada	Jan. 99	322,560
Coffeyville, Kansas	Apr. 99	750,000
Campbellsville, Kentucky	May 99	770,000
Lexington, Kentucky	May 99	600,000
McDonough, Georgia*	Jun. 99	800,000
Not announced	2000	1,500,000

*The firm announced the closure of the McDonough, Georgia, facility in January 2001.

company began to open distribution centres, investing a total of $300m (Fogarty, 1999). The company's inventory levels also rose, to enhance control and prevent stock outs. Prudential Securities (1999) estimated that, once the planned 5m square feet of distribution space is complete, the company would have the capacity to ship $10bn of merchandise annually. The distribution centres planned at December 1999 are listed in Table 2.4.

The facilities are all leased under operating leases. Applicable costs of these facilities were included in marketing and sales costs. Meeker (2000) estimated that the fulfilment cost component of sales and marketing cost was 16% of sales in 1999Q4 and 15% of sales in 1999Q3. This compares to a value of 10% of sales in 1998Q4, before the distribution centre build-up was in full swing.

OPPORTUNITIES

Amazon is frequently rumoured to be in negotiations for an e-commerce alliance, particularly with Wal-Mart Stores, Inc. Amazon has an agreement with ToysRUs to assist ToysRUs with online marketing of its products. Also, in summer 2001 the company negotiated alliances with AOL, Target and Circuit City. The alliance with AOL will mean that Amazon and AOL will partner to offer shopping services.

Furthermore, within specific market sectors Amazon and other online retailers may be better placed than offline retailers. One example of this is in the recorded music market, where digitally downloadable music is a specific sub-segment that online retailers would be likely to dominate. This and other similar innovations (such as digitally downloadable e-books) are dependent for widespread take-up on increased bandwidth. The progress in rolling out high-bandwidth connections has been slow in the USA, but Jupiter Communications forecasts (in Fogarty, 2000) that the number of internet subscribers connected by a high-bandwidth connection (cable, xDSL, ISDN) will reach 10.5m in 2002 from 1m in 1998.

The company continues to explore partnerships with other firms. The company has also introduced specific customer-facing customization initiatives such as 'My Store', which offers a tailored page to customers, and corporate accounts, which enable corporates and organizations to pay in arrears for goods and services. The company has tailored 'speciality stores' for key providers and for key markets such as that for Christian products (www.amazon.com/christian).

The company was accused of going even further by trialling customized prices (based on demographics or location) in September 2000. However, Amazon denied this and stated that it had carried out random pricing tests (that is, not adjusted for demographics) on DVDs to gauge the influence of discounts on revenues (that is, to test the shape of the 'demand curve'); it refunded $21,000 to customers who had suffered as a result of the trial. However, this clearly shows that Amazon has extensive capability to tailor prices, possibly by customer, country, time of day, time of year, and so on.

THREATS

Competition is extremely fierce in online retailing. Despite Amazon's well-recognized brand name and excellent reputation for customer service, the company does not charge premium prices for delivered goods in comparison to store-bought (offline) or delivered (other online) goods. Besides focused online retailers, leading offline retailers are considered likely to concentrate on the online market to maintain revenue and earnings growth, which are essential to their stock market ratings (Table 2.5).

Table 2.5 Amazon.com's competitors

	Books	Music	Toys
Online	Bn.com Buy.com Books-a-million.com	CDNow/Columbia House GetMusic.com Bn.com	FAO.com
Offline	Barnes & Noble, Inc. Borders Group Wal-Mart Costco	Tower Records Virgin HMV Wal-Mart	Wal-Mart ToysRUs Kmart Target Stores

In line with a long-term tax advantage of the US mail-order industry, state sales taxes (2–10% of sales) are only payable in states where the company is based. This means that Amazon.com customers can order sales tax-free in the US, except residents of Washington state. This tax advantage may be reviewed if online sales increase, but it is thought unlikely that it will be withdrawn.

Finally, low stock market ratings may affect the company's ability to raise financing for future growth, or even to gain credit to conduct its day-to-day business.

POSSIBLE COMPARATOR COMPANIES

Accounts for possible comparator companies are given in Appendix 2.2. These may enable readers to determine a likely steady-state margin and asset needs for the business.

Note

1 The historical quarterly and annual results are included in the spreadsheet casedata.xls, in the sheets 'QUARTERLY' and 'ANNUAL' respectively. This spreadsheet is downloadable from www.internet-valuation.com/palgrave.

APPENDIX 2.1: HISTORICAL ACCOUNTS OF AMAZON.COM

Table 2.6 Amazon.com: annual

Note: **Figures in $Thousands**	**31 Dec. 95**	**31 Dec. 96**	**31 Dec. 97**	**31 Dec. 98**	**31 Dec. 99**	**31 Dec. 00**	**31 Dec. 01**
Net sales	511	15,746	147,758	609,996	1,639,839	2,761,983	3,122,433
Cost of sales	409	12,287	118,945	476,155	1,349,194	2,106,206	2,323,875
Gross profit (loss)	102	3,459	28,813	133,841	290,645	655,777	798,558
Marketing and sales	200*	6,090*	38,964*	133,023*	413,150*	179,980	138,283
Fulfilment						414,509	374,250
Product development	171	2,313	12,485	46,807			
Technology and content					159,722	269,326	241,165
General and administrative	35	1,035	6,573	15,799	70,144	108,962	89,862
Stock-based compensation					30,618	24,797	4,637
Amortization of goodwill and other intangibles					214,694	321,772	181,033
Impairment-related and other						200,311	181,585
Merger and acquisition related costs, including amortization				50,172	8,072		
Total operating expenses	406	9,438	58,022	245,801	896,400	1,519,657	1,210,815
Income (loss) from operations	–304	–5,979	–29,209	–111,960	–605,755	–863,880	–412,257
Interest income	1	202	1,898	14,053	45,451	40,821	29,103
Interest expense			279	26,639	84,566	130,921	139,232
Other income, net					1,671	–10,058	–1,900
Non-cash gains & losses, net						–142,639	–2,141
Net interest income (expense) and other				–12,586	–37,444	–242,797	–114,170
Income (loss) before equity in losses					–643,199	–1,106,677	–526,427
Equity in losses of equity–method investees/other					–76,769	–304,596	–40,850
Net income (loss)	–303	–5,777	–27,590	–124,546	–719,968	–1,411,273	–567,277
Weighted average shares outstanding	340,794	271,860	259,812	296,344	326,753	350,873	364,211
Year end shares outstanding	261,990	286,200	287,244	318,534	345,155	357,140	373,218

* Also includes fulfilment

continued

Table 2.6 *continued*

Note: **Figures in $Thousands**	**31 Dec. 95**	**31 Dec. 96**	**31 Dec. 97**	**31 Dec. 98**	**31 Dec. 99**	**31 Dec. 00**	**31 Dec. 01**
Abbreviated balance sheet							
Tangible fixed assets	57	985	9,265	29,791	317,613	366,416	271,751
Intangible assets	0	0	0	186,377	730,144	255,325	79,749
Investments	0	0	0	0	371,462	92,250	28,359
Cash and marketable securities	996	6,248	125,066	373,445	706,188	1,100,522	996,585
Other current assets	31	892	12,269	50,809	305,990	260,607	211,335
Other assets	0	146	2,406	8,038	40,154	60,049	49,768
Total assets	1,084	8,271	149,006	648,460	2,471,551	2,135,169	1,637,547
Current liabilities	57	4,870	42,318	160,891	724,613	958,379	906,422
Other long term liabilities							
Debt	0	0	78,202	348,824	1,480,660	2,144,041	2,171,125
Equity (preference and convertible)	0	0	0	0	0	0	0
Equity (ordinary)	977	3,401	28,486	138,745	266,278	–967,251	–1,440,000
Total liabilities	1,084	8,271	149,006	648,460	2,471,551	2,135,169	1,637,547
Dupont relationship							
Operating assets	–19	–2,847	–18,378	114,124	1,040,750	76,268	–265,460
Operating margin	–59.5%	–38.0%	–19.8%	–18.4%	–36.9%	–31.3%	–13.2%
Operating asset turnover	NM	NM	NM	5.35	1.58	36.21	NM
Return on operating assets	NM	NM	NM	–98%	–58%	–1133%	NM
Other indicators							
Revenue growth		2981%	838%	313%	169%	68%	13%
Inventory days (basis revenues)	12.2	13.2	22.2	17.7	49.1	23.1	16.8
Accounts payable minus other current assets days (revenues)	60.8	58.7	72.7	55.1	84.1	52.8	44.1
Fixed assets (% revenues)	11%	6%	6%	5%	19%	13%	9%

Table 2.7 Amazon.com: quarterly

	30 Sept. 99	31 Dec. 99	31 Mar. 00	30 Jun. 00	30 Sep. 00	31 Dec. 00	31 Mar. 01	30 Jun. 01	30 Sep. 01	31 Dec. 01
Net sales	355,777	676,042	573,889	577,876	637,858	972,360	700,356	667,625	639,281	1,115,171
Cost of sales	285,300	588,196	445,755	441,812	470,579	748,060	517,759	487,905	477,089	841,122
Gross profit	70,477	87,846	128,134	136,064	167,279	224,300	182,597	179,720	162,192	274,049
Fulfilment expenses							98,248	85,583	81,400	109,019
Marketing expenses							36,638	34,658	32,537	34,450
Marketing, sales and fulfilment expenses	86,555	179,424	140,111	129,813	138,342	186,223				
Product development expenses	44,608	57,720	61,244	67,132	71,159	69,791	70,284	64,710	53,846	52,325
General and administrative expenses	18,512	26,051	26,045	28,468	26,217	28,232	26,028	22,778	21,481	19,575
Merger and acquisition and invest related costs	99,481	84,386								
Stock-based compensation	11,789	14,049	13,652	8,166	4,091	–1,112	2,916	2,351	–2,567	1,937
Amortization of goodwill and other intangibles			82,955	80,413	79,194	279,521	50,831	50,830	41,835	37,537
Restructuring or merger expenses			2,019	2,449	11,791		55,512	58,650	3,994	4,681
Impairment-related expenses (non-cash)							58,748			
Total operating expenses	260,945	361,630	326,026	316,441	330,794	562,655	399,205	319,560	232,526	259,524
Income (loss) from operations	–190,468	–273,784	–197,892	–180,377	–163,515	–338,355	–216,608	–139,840	–70,334	14,525
Interest income	12,699	8,972	10,126	10,314	9,402	10,979	9,950	6,807	6,316	6,030
Interest expense	21,470	–18,508	27,621	33,397	33,809	36,094	33,748	35,148	35,046	35,290
Net interest income (expense)	–6,612	–9,536	–17,495	–23,083	–24,407	–25,115	–23,798	–28,341	–28,730	–29,260
All other (mainly loss from equity method investees)			–93,038	–113,724	–52,602	–197,929	6,275	–178	–70,810	19,822
Net income (loss)	–197,080	–283,320	–308,425	–317,184	–240,524	–561,399	–234,131	–168,359	–169,874	5,087

Table 2.8 Amazon.com: quarterly balance sheet

Summary Balance Sheet	09/30/98	12/31/98	03/31/99	06/30/99	09/30/99	12/31/99	03/31/00	06/30/00	09/30/00	12/31/00	03/31/01	06/30/01	09/30/01	12/31/01
Tangible Fixed Assets	23,821	29,791	60,600	156,333	221,243	317,613	334,396	344,042	352,290	366,416	304,179	292,422	288,373	271,751
Intangible Assets	213,064	178,638	187,194	741,865	705,932	730,144	647,192	596,778	520,470	255,325	204,420	152,895	111,061	79,749
Investments	582	7,740	0	106,020	196,317	371,462	422,324	299,976	164,476	92,250	51,042	36,952	25,347	28,359
Cash & Marketable Securities	337260	373445	1442965	1144237	905685	706188	1008881	907621	900024	1100522	642973	608969	668100	996585
Other current assets	37,397	50,809	82,313	112,721	174,383	305,990	262,068	259,019	263,061	260,607	212,737	200,388	202,176	211,335
- *of which: inventories*	19,772	29,501	45,236	59,387	118,793	220,646	172,257	172,360	163,880	174,563	155,562	129,035	130,739	143,722
other	17,625	21,308	37,077	53,334	55,590	85,344	89,811	86,659	99,181	86,044	57,175	71,353	71,437	67,613
Other Assets	7,590	8,037	39,912	37,038	36,239	40,154	54,882	53,294	54,306	60,049	54,804	53,410	51,311	49,768
TOTAL ASSETS	619,714	648,460	1,812,984	2,298,214	2,239,799	2,471,551	2,729,743	2,460,730	2,254,627	2,135,169	1,470,155	1,345,036	1,346,368	1,637,547
Current liabilities	98,771	160,891	194,399	268,071	344,895	724,613	551,182	589,892	641,884	958,379	585,405	629,903	612,144	906,422
- *of which: accounts payable*	60,046	113,273	133,018	165,983	236,711	463,026	255,797	286,239	304,709	485,383	257,411	257,976	236,992	444,748
interest payable	0	10	0	23,960	10,045	24,888	15,812	41,213	35,056	69,196	16,720	43,833	41,635	68,632
other	38,725	47,608	61,381	78,128	98,139	236,699	279,573	262,440	302,119	403,800	311,274	328,094	333,517	393,042
Other long term liabilities														
Debt	341,179	348,824	1,541,048	1,459,097	1,474,979	1,480,660	2,152,944	2,149,262	2,099,910	2,144,041	2,138,161	2,145,064	2,188,218	2,171,125
Equity (Preference and Conv)														
Equity (Ordinary)	179,764	138,745	77,537	571,046	419,925	266,278	25,617	-278,424	-487,167	-967,251	-1,253,411	-1,429,931	-1,453,994	-1,440,000
TOTAL LIABILITIES	619,714	648,460	1,812,984	2,298,214	2,239,799	2,471,551	2,729,743	2,460,730	2,254,627	2,135,169	1,470,155	1,345,036	1,346,368	1,637,547
Dupont Relationship														
Operating Assets	183,683	114,124	175,620	885,906	989,219	1,040,750	1,169,680	963,217	712,719	76,268	241,777	106,164	66,124	-265,460
Operating Margin	-27.0%	-17.6%	-19.0%	-39.0%	-53.5%	-40.5%	-34.5%	-31.2%	-25.6%	-34.8%	-30.9%	-20.9%	-11.0%	1.3%
Operating Asset Turnover	2.30	5.35	4.65	1.15	1.23	1.58	1.64	2.27	3.46	36.21	11.95	28.05	45.06	N.M.
Return on Operating Assets	-62%	-94%	-88%	-45%	-66%	-64%	-57%	-71%	-89%	-1260%	-369%	-588%	-496%	N.M.
Other Indicators														
Revenue Growth (quarterly basis TTM)	38%	44%	34%	24%	20%	35%	17%	14%	13%	12%	5%	3%	0%	5%
Relevant annualised sales (TTM)	423,061	609,996	816,264	1,014,664	1,216,743	1,639,839	1,920,085	2,183,584	2,465,665	2,761,983	2,888,450	2,978,199	2,979,622	3,122,433
Inventory days (basis quarterly revenues)	11.7	10.6	14.1	17.2	30.5	29.8	27.4	27.2	23.5	16.4	20.3	17.6	18.7	11.8
Accounts payable minus other current assets days (basis quarterly revenues)	25.2	33.2	29.8	32.7	46.5	51.0	26.4	31.5	29.4	37.5	26.1	25.5	23.6	30.9
Fixed Assets (%TTM Revenues)	6%	5%	7%	15%	18%	19%	17%	16%	14%	13%	11%	10%	10%	9%

Table 2.9 Amazon.com: segmental

Segmental disclosures (2000 10K405)

	1998 ($)	1999 ($)	2000 ($)	2001 ($)
Revenues, *of which*	**609,819**	**1,639,839**	**2,761,983**	**3,122,433**
US Books Music DVD	588,013	1,308,292	1,698,266	1,688,752
Early stage US		163,804	682,642	772,307
International	21,806	167,743	381,075	661,374
	(%)	(%)	(%)	(%)
Revenue growth year-on-year	313	169	68	13%
US Books Music DVD		122	30	–0.6%
Early stage US			317	13%
International		669	127	73%
	($)	($)	($)	($)
Gross profit, *of which*	**133,664**	**290,645**	**655,777**	**798,558**
US Books Music DVD	128,710	262,871	417,452	453,129
Early stage US		–7,801	160,889	205,273
International	4,954	35,575	77,436	140,606
Segment gain/(loss), *of which*	**–61,032**	**–352,371**	**–317,000**	**–45,002**
US Books Music DVD	–35,534	–31,000	71,441	156,753
Early stage US		–242,148	–243,371	–98,643
International	–25,498	–79,223	–145,070	–103,112
Other non-cash operating expenses	**–48,023**	**–253,384**	**–546,880**	**–367,255**
Net interest expense and other	**–12,586**	**–37,444**	**–242,797**	**–124,693**
Equity in losses of equity-method investees	**–2,905**	**–76,769**	**–304,596**	**–30,327**
Net loss	**(124,546)**	**(719,968)**	**(1,411,273)**	**(567,277)**

APPENDIX 2.2: POSSIBLE COMPARATOR COMPANIES

Table 2.10 Barnes & Noble (BKS): accounting data ($m)

	9 Jan. 94	8 Jan. 95	27 Jan. 96	1 Feb. 97	31 Jan. 98	30 Jan. 99	29 Jan. 00	3 Feb. 01
Revenues	1,337	1,623	1,977	2,448	2,797	3,006	3,486	4,376
Cost of sales and occupancy	874	1,050	1,269	1,569	2,019	2,143	2,484	3,170
Gross profit	463	573	708	879	778	863	1,002	1,206
Selling and administrative expense	263	311	377	456	540	577	651	813
Rental expenses	120	147	182	225				
Depreciation and amortization	29	37	48	60	77	88	112	145
Pre-opening expenses	9	9	12	18	13	9	7	8
Impairment charge	0	0	0	0	0	0	0	107
Restructuring charge	0	0	124	0	0	0	0	0
Operating profit (loss)	42	69	–35	120	147	189	232	134
Interest, net	0	0	0	38	0	0	0	0
Other income	0	0	0	0	0	–8	10	–113
Earnings before tax	16	46	–63	81	110	157	219	–33
Provision for income taxes	9	20	–10	30	45	64	90	19
Net earnings (loss)	8	25	–53	51	53	92	124	–52
Abbreviated balance sheet								
Tangible fixed assets	190	244	320	435	482	510	568	566
Intangible assets	138	134	97	93	90	87	298	359
Investments	0	0	0	0	0	82	241	137
Cash and marketable securities	138	55	9	12	13	31	24	26
Other current assets	408	558	839	855	965	1,057	1,217	1,429
Other assets	21	35	50	51	41	40	66	40

Table 2.10 *continued*

	9 Jan. 94	8 Jan. 95	27 Jan. 96	1 Feb. 97	31 Jan. 98	30 Jan. 99	29 Jan. 00	3 Feb. 01
Total assets	896	1,026	1,315	1,447	1,591	1,808	2,414	2,557
Current liabilities	364	458	622	614	713	772	923	935
Non-debt long term liabilities	13	20	31	46	62	107	213	178
Debt	190	190	262	330	285	249	432	667
Equity (preference and convertible)	0	0	0	0	0	0	0	0
Equity (ordinary)	329	358	400	456	532	679	846	778
Total liabilities	896	1,026	1,315	1,447	1,591	1,808	2,414	2,557
Dupont relationship								
Operating assets	381	493	653	774	804	897	1,254	1,419
Operating margin	3.2%	4.2%	–1.8%	4.9%	5.3%	6.3%	6.7%	3.1%
Operating asset turnover	3.51	3.29	3.03	3.16	3.48	3.35	2.78	3.08
Return on operating assets	11.1%	13.9%	–5.4%	15.5%	18.3%	21.0%	18.5%	9.4%
Other indicators								
Revenue growth	23%	21%	22%	24%	14%	7%	16%	26%
Inventory days (basis revenues)	100.1	113.5	136.8	109.3	111.3	114.9	115.5	103.4
Accounts payable minus other current assets days (revenues)	57.1	59.5	58.6	37.5	45.3	46.9	50.8	32.7
Fixed assets (% revenues)	18%	18%	20%	22%	20%	18%	19%	16%

Table 2.11 Borders Group (BGP): accounting data ($m)

	23 Jan. 94	22 Jan. 95	28 Jan. 96	26 Jan. 97	25 Jan. 98	24 Jan. 99	23 Jan. 00	28 Jan. 01
Revenues	1,371	1,511	1,749	1,959	2,266	2,595	2,999	3,271
Cost of sales (including occupancy)	1,031	1,127	1,302	1,438	1,634	1,859	2,148	2,354
Gross margin	340	384	447	521	632	736	851	917
SG&A	281	333	374	410	485	558	674	736
Pre-opening expense	3	6	7	7	7	8	8	6
Asset impairment and other write downs	0	0	63	0	0	0	0	36
Goodwill amortization	7	7	206	1	2	3	4	3
Restructuring costs and other	143	19	3					
Operating income (loss)	–93	44	–200	103	138	167	166	135
Interest expense	1	1	5	7	7	16	18	13
Income (loss) before income tax	–94	43	–205	96	131	151	148	122
Income tax provision	–38	22	6	38	51	59	58	48
Net income (loss)	–61	21	–211	58	80	92	90	44
Abbreviated balance sheet								
Tangible fixed assets	200	244	244	289	374	494	558	562
Intangible assets	249	260	39	40	110	107	123	94
Investments	0	0	0	0	0	0	0	0
Cash and marketable securities	30	237	36	43	65	43	42	59
Other current assets	506	580	705	804	953	1,091	1,157	1,276
Other assets	21	36	29	36	33	33	36	56
Total assets	1,006	1,357	1,053	1,212	1,535	1,768	1,916	2,047

Table 2.11 *continued*

	23 Jan. 94	22 Jan. 95	28 Jan. 96	26 Jan. 97	25 Jan. 98	24 Jan. 99	23 Jan. 00	28 Jan. 01
Current liabilities	458	554	483	604	755	855	891	974
Non-debt long term liabilities	79	55	29	25	50	56	68	68
Debt	11	16	68	36	132	140	152	159
Equity (preference and convertible)	0	5	0	0	0	0	0	0
Equity (ordinary)	458	726	472	511	598	715	803	846
Total liabilities	1,006	1,356	1,052	1,176	1,535	1,766	1,914	2,047
Dupont relationship								
Operating assets	439	510	504	504	665	812	913	946
Operating margin	–6.8%	2.9%	–11.4%	5.3%	6.1%	6.4%	5.5%	4.1%
Operating asset turnover	3.12	2.96	3.47	3.89	3.41	3.20	3.28	3.46
Return on operating assets	–21.2%	8.6%	–39.7%	20.4%	20.8%	20.6%	18.2%	14.3%
Other indicators								
Revenue growth	16%	10%	16%	12%	16%	15%	16%	9%
Inventory days (basis revenues)	116.2	127.7	133.3	137.6	141.7	143.6	131.3	134.1
Accounts payable minus other current assets days (revenues)	57.0	56.6	56.6	57.1	67.7	76.6	62.3	61.4
Fixed assets (% revenues)	15%	16%	14%	15%	17%	19%	19%	17%

Table 2.12 Wal-Mart (WMT): accounting data ($m)

	Jan. 93	Jan. 94	Jan. 95	Jan. 96	Jan. 97	Jan. 98	Jan. 99	Jan. 00	Jan. 01
Revenues	55,985	67,985	83,412	94,749	106,146	119,299	139,208	166,809	193,295
Cost of sales	44,175	53,444	65,586	74,564	83,663	93,438	108,725	129,664	150,255
Gross profit	11,810	14,541	17,826	20,185	22,483	25,861	30,483	37,145	43,040
SG&A	8,321	10,333	12,858	14,951	16,788	19,358	22,363	27,040	31,550
Operating profit	3,489	4,208	4,968	5,234	5,695	6,503	8,120	10,105	11,490
Interest on debt	143	331	520	692	629	555	529	756	1,095
Interest on capital leases	180	186	186	196	216	229	268	266	279
Income before income taxes	3,166	3,691	4,262	4,346	4,850	5,719	7,323	9,083	10,116
Total provision for income taxes	1,171	1,358	1,581	1,606	1,794	2,115	2,740	3,338	3,692
Income before minority interest	1,995	2,333	2,681	2,740	3,056	3,604	4,583	5,745	6,424
Minority interest	0	0	0	0	0	78	153	170	129
Cumulative effect of accounting change	0	0	0	0	0	0	0	–198	0
Net income	1,995	2,333	2,681	2,740	3,056	3,526	4,430	5,377	6,295
Abbreviated balance sheet									
Tangible fixed assets	9,793	13,176	15,874	18,894	20,324	23,606	25,973	35,969	40,934
Intangible assets	0	0	0	0	0	0	0	9,392	9,059
Investments	0	0	0	0	0	0	0	0	0
Cash and marketable securities	12	20	45	83	883	1,447	1,879	1,856	2,054
Other current assets	10,186	12,094	15,293	17,248	17,110	17,905	19,253	22,500	24,501
Other assets	575	1,151	1,607	1,316	1,287	2,426	2,891	632	1,582
Total assets	20,566	26,441	32,819	37,541	39,604	45,384	49,996	70,349	78,130

Table 2.12 *continued*

	Jan. 93	Jan. 94	Jan. 95	Jan. 96	Jan. 97	Jan. 98	Jan. 99	Jan. 00	Jan. 01
Current liabilities	5,106	5,760	8,091	8,656	10,339	13,319	15,756	20,395	22,288
Non-debt long term liabilities	207	322	411	400	463	809	716	759	1,043
Debt	6,494	9,606	11,591	13,398	10,634	10,815	10,613	22,082	22,316
Equity (preference and convertible)	0	0	0	0	0	0	0	0	0
Equity (ordinary)	8,759	10,753	12,726	15,087	18,168	20,441	22,911	27,113	32,483
Total liabilities	20,566	26,441	32,819	37,541	39,604	45,384	49,996	70,349	78,130
Dupont relationship									
Operating assets	15,241	20,339	24,272	28,402	27,919	29,809	31,645	47,339	52,745
Operating margin	6.3%	6.2%	6.0%	5.6%	5.4%	5.5%	5.9%	6.1%	6.0%
Operating asset turnover	3.67	3.34	3.44	3.34	3.80	4.00	4.40	3.52	3.66
Return on operating assets	23%	21%	21%	19%	21%	22%	26%	22%	22%
Other indicators									
Revenue growth	26%	21%	23%	14%	12%	12%	17%	20%	16%
Inventory days (basis revenues)	64.4	62.3	63.8	63.6	56.4	52.2	46.6	44.6	41.3
Accounts payable minus other current assets days (revenues)	21.3	17.4	20.5	20.0	22.1	23.6	21.2	22.8	22.7
Fixed assets (% revenues)	18%	20%	20%	22%	22%	23%	22%	25%	25%

Table 2.13 Target (TGT): accounting data ($m)

	29 Jan. 94	28 Jan. 95	3 Feb. 96	3 Feb. 97	31 Jan. 98	30 Jan. 99	29 Jan. 00	3 Feb. 01
Total revenues	19,233	21,311	23,516	25,371	27,757	30,951	33,702	36,903
Cost of sales	14,164	15,636	17,527	18,628	20,320	22,634	23,029	25,295
Gross profit	5,069	5,675	5,989	6,743	7,437	8,317	10,673	11,608
SG&A	3,158	3,614	4,043	4,289	4,532	5,077	7,490	8,190
Taxes other than income taxes	343	373	409	445	470	506		
Depreciation and amortization	515	548	594	650	693	780	854	940
Operating profit	1,053	1,140	943	1,359	1,742	1,954	2,329	2,478
Interest expense, net	–446	–426	–442	–442	–416	–398	–393	–425
Restructuring expense				134				
Earnings before income taxes and extraordinary charges	607	714	501	783	1,326	1,556	1,936	2,053
Provision for income taxes	232	280	190	309	524	594	751	789
Net earnings before extraordinary charges	0	434	311	474	802	962	1,185	1,264
Extraordinary charge from purchase and redemption of debt	0	0	0	11	51	27	41	0
Net earnings	375	434	311	463	751	935	1,144	1,264
Abbreviated balance sheet								
Tangible fixed assets	5,947	6,385	7,294	7,467	8,125	8,969	9,899	11,418
Intangible assets	0	0	0	0	0	0	0	0
Investments	0	0	0	0	0	0	0	0
Cash and marketable securities	321	147	175	201	211	255	220	356

Table 2.13 *continued*

	29 Jan. 94	28 Jan. 95	3 Feb. 96	3 Feb. 97	31 Jan. 98	30 Jan. 99	29 Jan. 00	3 Feb. 01
Other current assets	4,190	4,812	4,780	5,239	5,350	5,750	6,263	6,948
Other assets	320	353	321	482	505	692	761	768
Total assets	10,778	11,697	12,570	13,389	14,191	15,666	17,143	19,490
Current liabilities	2,702	3,181	3,341	3,878	4,283	4,801	5,352	5,444
Non-debt long term liabilities	536	582	623	630	720	822	910	1,036
Debt	4,435	4,697	5,141	5,041	4,698	4,708	5,019	6,491
Equity (preference and convertible)	368	321	319	321	310	292	0	0
Equity (ordinary)	2,737	3,193	3,403	3,790	4,460	5,311	5,862	6,519
Total liabilities	10,778	11,974	12,827	13,660	14,471	15,934	17,143	19,490
Dupont relationship								
Operating assets	7,219	8,064	8,688	8,951	9,257	10,056	10,661	12,654
Operating margin	5.5%	5.3%	4.0%	5.4%	6.3%	6.3%	6.9%	6.7%
Operating asset turnover	2.66	2.64	2.71	2.83	3.00	3.08	3.16	2.92
Return on operating assets	15%	14%	11%	15%	19%	19%	22%	20%
Other indicators								
Revenue growth	7%	11%	10%	8%	9%	12%	9%	9%
Inventory days (basis revenues)	47.4	47.6	46.9	43.6	42.8	41.0	41.2	42.0
Accounts payable minus other current assets days (revenues)	28.4	29.8	31.0	29.4	28.7	29.9	31.3	27.9
Fixed assets (% revenues)	31%	30%	31%	29%	29%	29%	29%	31%

CHAPTER 3

Amazon.com: Accounting Review

CASE MATERIALS

Chapter 2 sets out the Amazon.com valuation case. A *case* means that we have gathered together relevant facts on Amazon.com in a written document to assist readers in studying the topic of its valuation. Although the history of the firm is interesting, the digestion and analysis of the accounting numbers is probably the most vital area. These are the main evidence that we call upon in our key task, which is to value the net operating assets of the business.

COMPANY ACCOUNTING STATEMENTS ARE KEY INFORMATION

Company accounting statements, including the income statement, the balance sheet, the cash flow statement and the notes, show the past financial performance of a company in a prescribed format. This prescribed format is the result of the application of a number of accounting and reporting rules that together are termed the GAAP (*Generally Accepted Accounting Principles*). These rules are defined and updated by standard-setting bodies, the FASB (Financial Accounting Standards Board) in the USA and the ASB (Accounting Standards Board) in the UK. Each body has a task force that attempts to respond quickly to emerging or urgent issues in company accounting. This is the Emerging Issues Task Force (EITF) in the USA, and the Urgent Issues Task Force (UITF) in the UK.

Although past performance is unlikely to continue into the future, accounting statements provide key evidence to help us estimate what future performance will be. For example, if a company is growing its revenues by 50% this year then – in the absence of fresh product launches, marketing campaigns or changes in the underlying marketplace for its product – it is unlikely to grow revenues by *more* than 50% next year. If an e-tailer is holding a large amount of inventory or stock this year to ensure that it can deliver to customers then, unless it has a game-plan in place for decreasing those inventory levels, they are likely to persist as a proportion of revenues.

These understandings hold in the new economy and, in fact, are frequently exacerbated. For example, an early stage firm can record enormous percentage growth from a very small base, particularly by using deep discounting, by selling to 'friendly firms', or by appealing to early adopters. However, this rapid initial growth will tend to decline over time as a percentage of previous period revenues.

It is a truism that, ideally, the holding of inventory or stock is to be avoided by firms. Inventory of raw materials, intermediate products or finished goods is cash invested in physical goods lying around in warehouses or offices. This is cash which does not pay interest and which would be better to be in shareholders' hands (where they can invest it in more equity or more savings or debt certificates, depending on their risk tolerances). However, the instance of a *stock out*, whereby a firm cannot deliver a product or cannot deliver it in time (because it is out of stock), is inimical to brand development. Customers experimenting with the new delivery method record the experiment as a failure relative to their expectations. This has caused many e-commerce firms to increase their inventory levels as a proportion of sales, over time.

Nor is this understanding limited to e-commerce firms. Certain high bandwidth internet providers have poor reputations for customer service. In order to cut costs they economize on customer support technicians. Therefore they 'stock out' of the customer support resource at peak times, causing long waits, customer dissatisfaction and eventually customer defections. Other internet service firms, such as ISPs (internet service providers), web hosting companies and providers of other internet-related services can also stock out of the customer support resource, or of key bottleneck human resources needed to register or set up new accounts, to provide services or to fix problems with their system. Even the most highly regarded internet firm, AOL, stocked out of modem connections shortly after introducing its unlimited use plan in 1996–7.

REVENUES, COSTS AND ASSETS

The running of a business is a complex process. New markets have to be identified. Marketing campaigns have to be designed and 'buzz' has to be generated. The appropriate staff have to be hired, motivated and compensated. Needed hardware has to be bought, and then content and scripts (to give the Web page the ability to react to customer input) have to be added. The linking of back-end databases to the front-end scripts is also an essential stage.

While the business is a complex animal, the representation of the business for the purposes of financial analysis is straightforward. In order to serve customers, an infrastructure of some kind has to be built up. To do this the firm buys assets and incurs costs to make those assets into a business which can serve customers. These assets and costs are funded by issuing securities, which are the balancing liabilities of the early company. Revenues begin to be received from customers. It is perfectly normal for firms to spend some amount of costs before they receive revenues, but over time cash flows from revenues must comfortably exceed the cash flows expended on costs and in buying necessary assets. This is necessary in order to provide investors in the firm's securities with adequate returns on their investment. Cash flow valuation summarizes these cash inflows and outflows into a single measure of cash flow for the year. These are then discounted back to give the value of the company.

In summary, then, the drill for projecting company financials is as follows:

1. Project the revenues for future years.
2. Project the costs for future years, using an understanding of:
   - How much of the costs are fixed (do not vary with revenues).
   - How much of the costs are variable (do vary with revenues).
3. Estimate what assets will be required to allow the company to service the customers who will be paying revenues.

WHAT WE CAN FIND IN THE COMPANY ACCOUNTS

The main statements in the company accounts are:

- the *income statement* (sometimes called the 'statement of operations', called the profit and loss or 'P&L' in the UK)
- the *balance sheet*
- the *cash flow statement*.

For the version in the case material, we processed the data slightly to make it compatible with earlier years, so in this chapter we look at the original source data from the company's annual report, the 10K or 10K405 filing.[1] This is a public document held at the SEC. At the time of writing it can be obtained from a number of online services, for example www.edgar-online.com and www.freeedgar.com. (The line numbers have been added, to aid easy reference.)

As a preamble, let us recall that our reason for examining the statements is quite focused. We are seeking information which will enable us to predict future cash flows. We are seeking to be informed about the *future* by looking at the *past history* of what cash flows the company has received from customers (revenues, in the income statement), what cash flows it has paid to suppliers (the various costs in the income statement) and what its asset needs have been in the past (which we find by analysing the balance sheet). The accounting statements are well suited but not ideally suited to helping us in our task. Their main unavoidable disadvantage is that they look at the past, not the future. A secondary disadvantage in using the past accounting statements as a predictor of the future is that some of the payments and items are more likely to persist in the future than others. For example, a merchandising company will not be able to avoid spending money to buy merchandise for resale ('cost of goods sold' in the income statement), but whether a company that has spent cash on acquiring other companies will continue its acquisition activity is a strategic judgment which managers will make.

Income statement

Interestingly enough, even though we are doing cash-flow valuation, we don't make that much use of the cash-flow statement. (This statement is useful for certain purposes, such as summarizing financing cash flows and showing cash flow consequences of acquisitions, investments and asset purchases.) This is because it is not sufficiently detailed to give us the full breakdown of information needed. We make more use of the balance sheet and, especially, the income statement (Figure 3.1). The income statement gives information on the main positive cash flows; those received from customers in return for goods and services; and part of the negative cash flows, the costs incurred in serving the customers. The income statement ends with the earnings or loss for the year, which is the accounting judgment of whether the firm has generated value for equity holders.

Let us now step through the income statement, taking particular note of how the 'line items' relate to likely future cash flows.

Lines 1–10

Lines 1–10 are title lines.

Figure 3.1 Amazon.com: income statement

Amazon.com, Inc.
Consolidated statements of operations
(in thousands, except per share data)

Years ended December 31

		2001	2000	1999	1998
11	Net sales	$ 3,122,433	$ 2,761,983	$ 1,639,839	$ 609,819
12	Cost of sales	2,323,875	2,106,206	1,349,194	476,155
14	Gross profit	798,558	655,777	290,645	133,664
15	Operating expenses:				
16	Fulfilment	374,250	414,509	237,312	132,654*
17	Marketing	138,283	179,980	175,838	
18	Technology and content	241,165	269,326	159,722	46,424
19	General and administrative	89,862	108,962	70,144	15,618
20	Stock-based compensation	4,637	24,797	30,618	1,889
21	Amortization of goodwill and other intangibles	181,033	321,772	214,694	42,599
22	Restructuring-related and other	181,585	200,311	8,072	3,535
24	Total operating expenses	1,210,815	1,519,657	896,400	242,719
26	Loss from operations	(412,257)	(863,880)	(605,755)	(109,055)
27	Interest income	29,103	40,821	45,451	14,053
28	Interest expense	(139,232)	(130,921)	(84,566)	(26,639)
29	Other income (expense), net	(1,900)	(10,058)	1,671	–
30	Other gains (losses), net	(2,141)	(142,639)	–	–
32	Net interest expense and other	(114,170)	(242,797)	(37,444)	(12,586)
34	Loss before equity in losses of equity-method investees	(526,427)	(1,106,677)	(643,199)	(121,641)
35	Equity in losses of equity-method investees, net	(30,327)	(304,596)	(76,769)	(2,905)
37	Loss before change in accounting principle	$ (556,754)			$ (124,546)
38	Cumulative effect of change in accounting principle	(10,523)			
40	Net loss	$ (567,277)	$ (1,411,273)	$ (719,968)	$ (124,546)
42	Basic and diluted loss per share:				
43	Prior to cumulative effect of change in accounting principle	$ (1.53)	$ (4.02)	$ (2.20)	$ (0.92)
44	Cumulative effect of change in accounting principle	(0.03)	–	–	–
46	Basic and diluted loss per share	$ (1.56)	$ (4.02)	$ (2.20)	$ (0.92)
48	Shares used in computation of basic and diluted loss per share	364,211	350,873	326,753	296,344

* Includes marketing

Line 11: Net sales

Net sales or *revenue* (also called *turnover, sales* or *'the top line'*) is a key driver of value. Revenue is shown only on the income statement. Revenue can be viewed as the cash received from customers in exchange for goods and services supplied by the business. It does not exactly correspond to cash received from customers if some customers have delayed-payment plans (for example, business customers usually have a 30- or 60-day grace period before paying for goods or services bought), but the relationship is close, extremely close in the case of *business to consumer* (*B2C*) companies. B2C companies, unlike companies with mainly business customers, receive payment from credit card companies at about the time the consumer's order is placed.[2]

The income statement in the 2000 10K405 gives us three years of revenues, so we can see the revenue growth rates in that time. Note the 'explosive' growth in revenues in the three-year time period, growth by a factor of 4.53 (2000 sales are 4.53 times larger than 1998), or growth of 353% over the 1998 revenue (2000 sales minus 1998 sales are 353% of 1998 sales). There are two things to note straight away. First, growth is not synonymous with share value. It is easy to grow a company's revenue by selling products below cost – we are not saying that that is what is happening here, but valuers must be alive to the risk. The second point is rather more subtle. Let us do a couple of quick calculations about the growth. Growth by a factor of 4.53 equates to growth by a factor of 2.13 per year. (This is calculated from $\sqrt{4.53} = 2.13$ or $4.53^{1/2} = 2.13$. As another example: if we were breaking out sales growth over three years to a yearly growth, we would take the three-year factor and raise to the power of 1/3.) Yet growth between 1999 and 2000 was only by a factor of 1.68 (68% growth), whereas between 1998 and 1999 growth was by a factor of 2.69 (169% growth) – a pattern of *declining* growth. We will return to this topic later but, for now, think about the following two questions. What is likely to have happened in the year 2001? Second, what type of error would we introduce if we assumed that the 1999–2000 growth rate would continue for the next five years? Incidentally, always think in terms of growth by factors rather than by percentage growth rates (for example growth by a factor of 2.69 not 169% growth), as the former are easier to use in calculations.

Line 12: Cost of sales

Costs are the resources the business has to expend to provide customers with the goods and services for which the customers pay revenues. The income statement breaks down costs into two main categories. The first cost category is *cost of goods sold* or *cost of sales*. These terms have become synonymous and their strict meaning is that they are the cost of inventory that the business has sold to customers. This clearly has most meaning in the case of e-commerce merchandising firms which possess physical inventory and sell it to customers. However, in some firms, especially service firms (which do not require any physical inventory), the cost of sales may include some non-physical inventory costs of serving the customer, such as the purchasing of bandwidth by ISPs to allow their customers to access the internet (for example AOL). Another example is the e-commerce consulting firm Razorfish, which breaks out project personnel costs (costs of personnel being billed to clients or available for billing) separately from other personnel costs (that is, staff who would not be expected to be billed even if the firm were operating at capacity, such as top management, the press office, and the like).

The method of analysing cost of sales is to calculate it as a percentage of sales, and then to see how it changes over time (is the company we are looking at getting better or worse?) and to see how it compares with other similar companies (how does the company compare with other companies?). However, one of the problems with these comparisons is the different definitions of cost of sales used by various companies.

For example, Amazon has been criticized for classifying 'fulfillment costs' (defined in Amazon's 2000 10K405 as 'costs incurred in operating and staffing our fulfillment and customer service centers, including costs attributable to receiving, inspecting and warehousing inventories; picking, packaging and preparing customers' orders for shipment; credit card fees; and responding to inquiries from customers') as operating costs rather than cost of sales. In this way Amazon ensures that the first indicator of firm profitability, the **gross profit on line 13** (revenues minus cost of sales), is strongly positive. The decision by Amazon has been approved by their auditors, so it is within the discretion of companies to classify their costs between these two areas of the income statement – that is, there is nothing dishonest about it. However, it points up the difference between the *accounting* purpose of cost of sales (the accounting purpose is that cost of sales should include any costs that help inventory to have value, whether sold or not) and the purpose to which *analysts* try to put cost of sales (that is, as a proxy for 'variable costs', costs that tend to rise in step with sales). It demonstrates that cost of sales and, by implication, gross profit are not very useful quantities for the analyst, because of the flexibility companies have in defining them. Specifically, cost of sales is not a good proxy for variable costs, since many costs stated 'below' cost of sales also have variable components.

Lines 15–24: Operating costs

The second cost category is variously called *operating costs, selling general and administrative costs, other costs* or sometimes even *overhead*. Although it does not sound like a great term, the best term of these four is 'other costs'! These other costs include all of the costs expended on running the business other than the costs of inventory and any other costs included in cost of sales. The method of analysing these is similar to the method of analysing cost of sales: we express the different cost quantities as a percentage of sales, and see how they behave over time and how they compare with similar companies. We also look at the total of these costs and how that behaves over time. Are they rising with sales or staying constant? This gives us further clues as to how they will behave in the future, as sales increase further.

The normal categories within other costs are sales and marketing costs and general and administrative costs. As can be seen, Amazon breaks down other costs into six line items:

Line 16 : Fulfilment costs represent distribution costs incurred in operating and staffing distribution and customer service centres. This includes cost of receiving inbound goods, packing and shipping product, credit card fees, and costs to answer customer queries.

Line 17: Marketing cost is the cost of advertising, promotional and public relations expenses, including the cost of the company's marketing and sales staff.

Line 18: It also breaks out *technology and content* costs from other costs to show how much is being spent on developing its website and other 'assets'. Technology and content is defined as 'principally ... payroll and related expenses for development, editorial, systems and telecommunications operations personnel and consultants; systems and telecommunications infrastructure; and costs of acquired content, including freelance reviews'. There are two issues to mention here. First, it is interesting to note that this spending has accelerated in the years to 2000. Early theorists on the internet expected these costs to be relatively constant over time as an initial investment in a fixed amount of technology (the web storefront) was visited by an increasing number of shoppers. In practice web storefronts have required constant updating and upgrading to maintain revenue growth and to pique consumer interest. The second issue to note is that it might be difficult to compare this spending with the spending of an 'offline' retailer, which would not have such a reliance on its internet storefront or such a high proportion of spending (Amazon spent an average of 9.5% of sales on technology and content during 1998–2000). The only suitable method in doing this will be to add together 'other costs' and compare them with the other costs of offline retailers. In this way the technology costs of Amazon (virtual storefront) will be compared with the costs which substitute for those costs in high street stores, such as property and store costs (physical storefront).

Line 19: *General and administrative* is the 'everything else' category in which costs for the general management of the company are disclosed. The 10K405 defines it as 'payroll and related expenses for executive, finance and administrative personnel, recruiting, professional fees and other general corporate expenses'.

Note: Up until this point (line 19) all of the line items have a pretty direct relationship to cash flow and are extremely informative of how future cash flows are likely to pan out. After this point the line items are very relevant to determining the future of the business, but do not have a simple direct relationship to cash flows.

Line 20: *Stock-based compensation* is the notional expense that the company recognizes as a cost in the income statement. By 'notional' we mean that there is no cash paid out by the company at this time. Much of the expense is related to the employment of managers who joined Amazon from acquired companies. Part of the money paid to buy the acquired companies is deemed to be part of the ongoing pay-packet of the key employees.

Line 21: *Amortization of goodwill and other intangibles* is another notional cost linked with acquisitions. At the time any company buys another company the purchase price is not included as a cost, because we expect the company to get some longer term benefit from the purchase, so it does not help us to get a fair view of the year's profit to lump all that acquisition cost into the one year. The cost is therefore spread out as 'amortization'.[3] Both this cost and that on line 18 might seem not to belong in the income statement, and indeed they do not correspond to any *current* cash flow. They are routinely ignored in analysts' future projections. However, they do point up that part of the company's growth has been financed by acquisitions. These acquisitions were funded with shareholder's cash (that is, 'real money') when the acquisition took place – and the presence of the amortization is the accounting way of saying: 'This money the shareholders spent acquiring companies – we ought to be seeing some rewards for that!' The best way to view these line items is that they indicate to us that the company has had a level of acquisition activity, and *if this level of acquisition activity continues we have to project the future costs of that activity*. If on the other hand we are assuming that the company will *not* acquire any more firms, then we can forget about projecting these acquisition-related costs, but we ought to *assume a slower rate of growth* than we would do otherwise.

Line 22: *Restructuring related and other:* This category is composed partly of non-cash items such as 'write-downs' of goodwill and other assets (it was wholly composed of non-cash items in 1998–2000) and partly of cash costs of downsizing and of continuing to pay lease costs on premises which are no longer needed. To find out the breakdown between cash and non-cash items, the reader has to refer to the notes to the 10K. We discuss an example of such a note in Appendix 3.1 (in the discussion on 'Understanding Pro Forma Accounting'). It should be noted that even non-cash write-downs of acquired businesses should not be ignored just because they are non-cash. They may be a bad signal about the company's acquisition skills for the future.

Line 24: This sums the operating costs.

Line 26: Operating profit

The *operating profit* is one of the key numbers in the income statement (and indeed in the whole accounts). It is the revenues minus the cost of sales minus the other costs. It is the profit earned before any payments to security holders, so it is before interest on debt, and it is also before tax. (It also excludes profits and losses from 'equity method investees', meaning companies that Amazon has a sizeable (20–50%) equity stake in, but that are not parts of Amazon the company – these profits and losses are noted in line 35.)

The operating profit is particularly important for our purposes. This is because we use it as a starting point for our calculation of the free cash flow from the operating assets to equity and debt. In order to convert operating profit to free cash flow, we have to carry out the following procedure:

1. subtract taxes
2. adjust for the cash used up by investing in new operating assets such as fixed assets (machinery) and inventory (stocks) – which we find from the balance sheet below
3. add back depreciation and some other non-cash items (*depreciation* is the smoothed-out accounting representation of spending on operating assets, especially fixed assets: if we did not add this back we would be double-counting the fixed asset spend)
4. carry out any other adjustments for non-repeating cash flows such as acquisitions, other income and so on, depending on our future projections of these cash flows.

(*Note:* We will talk more about these details later).

Lines 27–8: Interest

These lines track the *interest* received from securities that the company owns and interest paid to those who own debt securities in the company. Some of this expense may be non-cash: for example if the company issues a 'zero coupon' bond that rolls up interest to the end of the payment agreement, to be paid all at once, then the interest payable will need to include interest in the current year to give a fair view of profit. However, it should all be viewed as 'real money'.

Line 29: Other income/expense (net)

This encompasses any costs which do not fit in anywhere else in the accounts and which are not large enough individually to warrant their own categories.

Line 30: Other gains (losses), net

This line item encompasses any other non-cash gains or losses. In this case the 10K (pages 30–1) shows that these losses are related to foreign currency gains and losses, and to impairment losses on equity investment. Interestingly enough, some foreign currency gains and losses had previously been taken direct to balance sheet as other comprehensive loss, but due to a new accounting standard were reclassified as impairment losses on equity. Impairment losses are due to perceived declines in the value of firms Amazon bought smaller stakes in (between 20–50%) with the aim of making money on the investment.

Line 32

Line 32 sums lines 27–30.

Line 34

Line 34 shows the profit (loss) from operations minus the costs totalled in line 32.

Note: If the company were profitable, the *taxation* line would appear at this point in the income statement.

Line 35: Equity on loss in equity-method investees

We have already discussed impairment losses from the companies Amazon has invested in. These impairment losses come about because the company looks at the investments and what it paid for them, and decides they are not worth that much any more. However, each of these investee companies is also putting out reports showing profit and loss, and the investing company's (in this case Amazon's) shareholders 'own' part of that *current year* profit or loss. Suppose firm X, in which Amazon holds 20% of the equity, loses $100m: Amazon must report 20% of that loss here (together with any impairment loss) – that is, $20m. Because earnings are after tax, the equity in losses appears here rather than further up the income statement.

***Line 40: Net loss** (one day, it is hoped, annual profit will go here!)*

Net loss is calculated by subtracting the loss in equity investees (line 35) from the loss before losses in equity investees (line 30). This is the accounting estimate of 'how well shareholders have done' this year. It is a fairly conservative estimate, since accounting is conservative. For example, we talked about impairment losses above: let's suppose that the value of our equity investments goes up – how would this be reflected in the income statement? Well, interestingly enough, it wouldn't. The increase in value of the equity investments would not be reflected until Amazon either:

- sells the investments
- makes money (profits) from them.

and in the latter case only gradually, according to the profits Amazon makes. What we mean by conservative is that accounting tends to produce the representation *least likely to overstate* asset values and profits. In other words, if a sum of money is included in earnings, the shareholders should be able to depend on it – the company should have executed all the transactions required to obtain the profit. That makes earnings a tough yardstick but an important one.

Note: If the company were paying cash *dividends*, the spending on these would be here.

Lines 42–48: Earnings per share calculation
This is the calculation of the profit or loss on an individual share, obtained by dividing the earnings (line 40) by the number of shares in the issue (line 48) to get the *earnings per share* (line 46). 'Diluted' means that the earnings are divided not just by the shares in the issue, but by all other shares that might get issued (such as shares that the managers have 'options' on, which is a type of employment deal whereby managers can obtain cheap shares if the company does well – see also Chapter 7). However, this is not applicable for a company making a loss, because the loss per share would be lowered, which is counter-intuitive (option holders take up their options to participate in future earnings, not current losses).

Balance sheet

The purchase of assets also results in negative cash flows (that is, cash flows exiting the company). The amount of assets a company owns at the end of each period (year, half year or quarter) is noted in the *balance sheet*. The balance sheet breaks down the assets into categories. There are fixed assets such as machinery or computer hardware, intangible assets such as goodwill (see below), and current assets such as stock (inventory), trade debtors (accounts receivable), and cash.

The change in each of these types of asset is the key measure of the cash flow associated with them. This can be measured by comparing balance sheets from two succeeding periods or by looking at the *cash flow statement* which shows the movement in different asset classes. The assets of the company must be funded by an equal amount of *liabilities*, which are claims on the company's assets. Some of the liabilities come about in the course of everyday business; examples of this are trade *creditors* (accounts payable), which is simply the term for money owed to suppliers, and *taxes* payable. However, especially for an early stage company, the bulk of liabilities are investments in the company by *equity holders* (people who have bought shares in the company) or by *debtholders* (people who have issued loans to the company). These securities directly fund most of the assets of the early stage firm.

We now look at the individual line items in the Amazon.com balance sheet (Figure 3.2).

Lines 1–10

Lines 1–10 are title lines.

Lines 11–26

Lines 11–26 show the *assets* of the business. For each dollar of assets there must be a dollar of *liability*: that is, the balance sheet shows the assets the business owns, and all the 'claims' on these – the debt holders and the accounts payable (suppliers, called trade creditors in the UK) have a claim on the business, and the equity holders have a subordinated or 'junior' claim (after the debtholders). These claims are shown in lines 28–53.

Line 13: Cash and cash equivalents

Line 13 shows *cash and cash equivalents*. This is cash held in Amazon.com bank accounts, plus securities that are immediately convertible into cash. Examples of the latter would be investments in short term US government bills. Since these are financial assets (and not likely to generate any net present value), they are netted off against the debt and excluded from the calculation of enterprise value.

Line 14: Marketable securities

Marketable securities are securities that are tradable in a liquid market but not immediately convertible into cash. This could encompass a wide range of securities from longer term tradable debt instruments to quoted equities. (Amazon states on page 24 of its 10K405 that marketable securities in 2000 include at least $36m of equities (2001: $13m).)

Line 15: Inventories

Inventories (*stock* in the UK) is the value of the physical stock owned by the company for further processing and subsequent sale to the customer. The inventory is valued at cost – what was paid for it – not at the value it can be

Figure 3.2 Amazon.com: balance sheet

Amazon.com, Inc.
Consolidated balance sheets
(in thousands, except per share data)

	December 31		
	2001	**2000**	**1999**
ASSETS			
Current assets:			
Cash and cash equivalents	$ 540,282	$ 822,435	$ 133,309
Marketable securities	456,303	278,087	572,879
Inventories	143,722	174,563	220,646
Prepaid expenses and other current assets	67,613	86,044	79,643
Total current assets	1,207,920	1,361,129	1,006,477
Fixed assets, net	271,751	366,416	317,613
Goodwill, net	45,367	158,990	534,699
Other intangibles, net	34,382	96,335	195,445
Investments in equity-method investees	10,387	52,073	226,727
Other equity investments	17,972	40,177	144,735
Other assets	49,768	60,049	40,154
Total assets	$ 1,637,547	$2,135,169	$2,465,850
LIABILITIES AND STOCKHOLDERS' DEFICIT			
Current liabilities:			
Accounts payable	$ 444,748	$ 485,383	$ 463,026
Accrued expenses and other current liabilities	305,064	272,683	176,208
Unearned revenue	87,978	131,117	54,790
Interest payable	68,632	69,196	24,888
Current portion of long-term debt and other	14,992	16,577	14,322
Total current liabilities	921,414	974,956	733,234
Long-term debt and other	2,156,133	2,127,464	1,466,338
Commitments and contingencies			
Stockholders' deficit			
Preferred stock, $0.01 par value:			
Authorized shares–500,000			
Issued and outstanding shares–none	–	–	
Common stock, $0.01 par value:			
Authorized shares–5,000,000			
Issued and outstanding shares–373,218 and 357,140	3,732	3,571	3,452
Additional paid-in capital	1,462,769	1,338,303	1,194,369
Deferred stock-based compensation	(9,853)	(13,448)	(47,806)
Accumulated other comprehensive loss	(36,070)	(2,376)	(1,709)
Accumulated deficit	(2,860,578)	(2,293,301)	(882,028)
Total stockholders' deficit	(1,440,000)	(967,251)	(266,278)
Total liabilities and stockholders' deficit	$1,637,547	$ 2,135,169	$2,465,850

sold for. However, in the event that the value of inventory *falls below* the price paid for it, the company has to 'write it down'. This is to maintain the conservative nature of accounting. For example, Amazon has experienced some inventory writedowns. Rising inventory uses up cash, therefore the cash flow related to inventory is calculated as last year's inventory minus this year's. So, if last year's is more than this years, we have a *positive* cash flow (cash is being 'freed up' because we have decreased inventories); if we have larger inventory this year than last, we have a *negative* cash flow. The usual method of evaluating a company's inventory performance is to calculate inventory as a percentage of sales or to calculate how many 'days' of inventory the company is holding. This is usually approximated to:

$$\text{stock days/inventory days} = \frac{\text{inventory}}{\text{sales}} \times 365$$

(Strictly speaking, the denominator should be cost of goods sold, but the approximation above is in more common use.)

Once the inventory as a percentage of sales has been calculated, we observe how it changes over time and compare it to those for other similar firms. Looking at this very restricted amount of data (only three years), we can see that Amazon has improved its inventory performance markedly (from 13.4% of sales to 4.6% of sales), decreasing inventory while increasing sales by nearly 70%. We would need to study a longer history or, in this case, at least look at the detail and in the quarterly reports to understand what the precise pattern of inventories over time may be (see Chapter 4 for this further analysis).

Line 16: Prepaid expenses and other current assets

Line 16 totals up the *accounts receivable* (trade debtors) who have received goods and services but have not yet paid (very small in a retail business, hence not broken out separately as it would be for, say, a B2B company), prepaid expenses and other miscellaneous current assets. *Prepaid expenses* arise when Amazon pays a company to provide a product or service but that company has not yet delivered it. Perhaps it is still being manufactured or perhaps it is a long term contract to provide a service which requires payment in advance. This quantity is evaluated in the same way as inventories.

Line 18

Line 18 totals the current assets.

Line 19: Fixed assets, net

Line 19 totals the tangible assets, such as buildings owned, computers and other equipment. It also includes some intangible assets, such as part of the costs of the computer software developed in-house. Each year, part of the asset value is subtracted from the balance sheet and subtracted in the income statement to reflect the 'using up' or depreciation of the asset. For the computer software, the expected life is two years, so the depreciation is rapid. The word *net* at the end of the label for the line means that the depreciation has already been subtracted. In some accounts the historical values (what was originally paid for them) of the assets are shown separately from the accumulated depreciation (that is, all the depreciation incurred since the assets were bought). Once again these are evaluated and estimated for the future as a percentage of sales.

Line 20: Goodwill, net

Many new economy companies have engaged in a number of acquisitions. When one company buys another company, the assets of the acquired company have to be included at cost in the balance sheet of the acquiring company at the price paid. However, under accounting rules, only the *book value* or historical cost (minus depreciation) of the assets can be directly added to the accounts of the acquiring company. For new-economy companies this book value is usually very small, and the difference between the purchase price of the acquired company and the book value of the assets has to be dealt with in a special way. This amount is termed *goodwill* and is added to the balance sheet assets. Note that between 1999 and 2000 the goodwill has declined a great deal. However, this has been due to a diminution (decrease) in the value of the goodwill, so no cash has been generated. Goodwill is discussed in more detail in Appendix 3.1.

Line 21: Other intangibles, net

These are similar to goodwill (line 20).

Lines 22 and 23: Investments in equity-method investees, and other equity investments

These lines represent the historical value (that is, what was paid for them, minus adjustments) of the investments Amazon made in associated companies (that is, companies in which Amazon has a 20–50% share or some other strong influence, shown on line 22) and in non-associated companies (line 23). There are two questions we need to answer to evaluate these line items' informativeness in our value calculations: will Amazon continue to invest in companies requiring negative cash flows to fund these investments (the answer would seem to be no); and how much are they worth to the company (the book value – already written down – would seem to be a starting point, with a full DCF valuation as the second step)?

Line 24: Other assets

These are assets not falling into any category above. They amount to a modest proportion of revenues, about 2%.

Line 26

Line 26 totals the assets (current and fixed (long term) assets).

Lines 28–53

Lines 28–53 show the liabilities of the business. Although the terminology in the balance sheet suggests that stockholder's equity is separate from liabilities, this is somewhat misleading because both equity and other liabilities (such as debt) constitute 'claims' on the operating assets of the company.

The usual way of modelling liabilities is first of all to study current operating liabilities (that is, liabilities that do not exist primarily for a financing purpose but arise as part of the day-to-day course of doing business) and to evaluate the cash flows they give rise to, perhaps by netting them off against operating assets such as inventory and forecasting the behaviour of the composite quantity. This then gives rise to a figure for net assets (or capital employed). The book equity is then calculated by adding profits after tax or earnings (net of any dividends) to the equity. The debt is then calculated as the balancing item to solve the following equation:

$$\text{net assets} = \text{equity} + \text{debt} \Rightarrow \text{debt} = \text{net assets} - \text{equity}$$

Line 30: Accounts payable

Accounts payable (trade creditors) is the sum of money owed by the company to its suppliers. An increase in accounts payable generates cash, all else being equal. This is usually calculated as a percentage of revenues and compared to competitor ratios. Its behaviour is also tracked over time to identify trends. It should be noted that since retailing is a seasonal business, accounts payable are likely to be higher at the end of the 4th quarter (and therefore at the end of the year) than at the end of other quarters.

Line 31: Accrued expenses and other current liabilities

These are operating liabilities that the company has outstanding, other than monies owed to trade suppliers. These can be items such as rent owed, salaries owed to employees, and any taxes owed (for example sales taxes in Washington state, since there is no income tax yet).

Line 32: Unearned revenue

Unearned revenue is a liability that records the fact that the company has received cash or equity securities but has not yet performed the services associated with that inflow. The cash or securities received are held as assets (that is, revenue should not be booked at that stage), and unearned revenue is present as a liability until such time as the services are provided, at which time the unearned revenue is transferred to the revenue or sales account, and appropriate costs are incurred. Unearned revenue is sometimes called *advances from customers.*

Lines 33 and 34: Interest payable, and current portion of long-term debt and other

Each of these liabilities represents the consequences of financing rather than of operations and are part of the debt of the firm.

Line 36: Total current liabilities

This totals the above lines. However, it is more useful conceptually to think about lines 30–2 as the current operating liabilities. As mentioned above, it may be possible to offset these against the gross operating assets, and to study the composite quantity (net operating assets).

Line 37: Long-term debt

This is one of the main pillars of the capital structure, together with equity. We will discuss the company's debt in detail in Chapter 7, however it may be useful to give a brief introduction here as to why this is not quite 'normal' debt. Amazon's debt mainly consists of *convertible debentures,* a type of debt which can be converted into equity if the share price of the company performs well. The attraction of this to the issuing company is that while a risky company may not be able to issue pure debt (since debt, unless its coupon is enormous, effectively has only downside risk), it may be able to sell convertible debt, which effectively packages debt with an equity-related upside component called a *warrant,* which is a long term call option. The attractions of this security for investors are that it gives access to stock price upside with some downside protection, in that if the company goes into liquidation the convertible bondholders have a prior call (compared to equity) on the assets of the company. However, their claim is 'subordinated' or 'junior' to the claim of *senior creditors.*

To think about how this works, imagine a company going bankrupt. A liquidator or administrator is then employed to sell off the assets. The holders of liabilities 'queue up' to receive a share of the payout from the sale of those assets (let us assume for simplicity that the firm has ceased trading). First in the queue – apart from creditors with special rights, such as the tax authority, the liquidator him- or herself, and secured creditors – are senior creditors such as a bank that has lent the company a normal loan, and trade creditors who are owed payments for services rendered or products shipped to the company. In a 'strict priority' bankruptcy framework such as is generally practised in the UK (especially prior to the introduction of the administration system), they receive *all* the money owed to them before the next group of people in line receives *any*. If there are insufficient proceeds from the sale of the company's assets, these senior creditors receive a proportional share according to the value recovered, and the creditors 'behind' them then receive nothing. That next group of people are the owners of the convertibles. Finally, if there are any remaining funds, these are shared out between equity holders – this is why equity holders are referred to as the *residual claimants*: they get whatever is 'residual', or remaining, however large or small. Therefore, the protection of convertible holders is limited because they will receive funds only if the business has substantial value: that is, enough value to pay all senior creditors with some left over. In a 'meltdown scenario' they will receive nothing. Also, US firms often enter periods of restructuring, negotiations and legal manoeuvring as they encounter financial problems. These negotiations will have some unpredictable effects on the fortunes of *all* creditors, in that they may cause deviations from strict priority, to the possible disadvantage of the convertibles owners. They also have one predictable effect: all creditors have eventually to foot the bill for large costs of the bankruptcy process, which can be as much as 20% of the value of the distressed firm.

Lines 39–49: Book value of shareholders' equity

Lines 39–49 record the investments made in equity of the firm. Line 53 notes the current reserve for money that still needs to be paid to managers as part of acquisition agreements (this is further discussed with regard to income statement line 20). Lines 48–9 record the retained earnings of the firm – in this case negative, because of historical losses. Because the equity holder is the residual claimant, the losses come out of his or her 'pocket', and the accumulated deficit or retained loss in the balance sheet is the accounting representation of this. Line 48 records *other comprehensive losses*, losses which are not shown on the income statement in accordance with GAAP, for example some foreign exchange losses. (These are normally small, they are excluded by convention to avoid complicating the accounts by the use of multiple currencies.)

Line 49 shows accumulated losses that are shown on the income statement (all the losses added together from the inception (start) of the company, not just this year's loss). This is relevant for the calculation of future taxes if and when the company should begin to make profits. In general a company should not begin to pay taxes until its cumulative profits exceed the total losses it made before it became profitable. Amazon's cumulative losses are $2.5bn, as noted in the balance sheet. However, not all of these losses are eligible for favourable tax treatment: some of them are disallowed, such as non-cash costs of goodwill amortization and other non tax-deductible costs. The relevant figure for net operating loss carry-forwards for tax purposes (NOLs) is found on page 74 of the 2001 10K, and is $2.3bn. On reading this section the reader will also notice that the company has valued this tax benefit at close to zero 'because of uncertainty regarding its realization'. This means the company or its auditors are not sufficiently sure that the company will make profits, or at least make them within the 15-year timescale before the NOLs begin to expire under US law (there is no time limit under UK or German tax law). However, this can be seen as in accordance with accounting conservatism and should not be taken as a condemnation of the firm's prospects.

Let us also look in detail at the three-line sections 40–2, and 43–5, which have the same format. These show the 'par value' of each type of share, the number of that type of share 'authorized' and the number *issued and outstanding*. The only important number of these three is the number of shares issued and outstanding: this is the number of shares 'out there' in shareholders' hands, and therefore looking to participate in future earnings. The *par value* is an initial notional value for the stock in the company. It is usually set very low, since issuing shares below this value incurs additional legal costs in changing the par value. The difference between the price actually paid by investors and the par value is noted in line 46, it is called *additional paid-in capital* (*share premium* in the UK). The *authorized shares* has little significance: it represents the maximum number of shares the firm can issue, but can be changed if needed, although this incurs some additional costs.

Line 51

Line 51 totals lines 39–49.

Line 53

Line 53 totals equity and the other liabilities. It should have the same value as line 26.

Cash-flow statement

The last of the three main statements is the *cash-flow statement*, which summarizes cash flows into and out of the business. The cash-flow statement relates the accounting measure of the health of the firm either to the firm's requirement for cash inflow, or its ability to generate cash.

Let us think briefly about what that means. As we discuss below in the section about depreciation, accounting postpones the 'reckoning' of some cash flows, such as large purchases of machines, by spreading their cost out using depreciation. Therefore a firm could be profitable yet not generating cash, because it is investing a lot of cash in fixed assets. The difference would be because fixed asset purchases take a chunk of cash now (so the cash-flow statement looks bad), but only come out of profits gradually (so the income statement does not look so bad). The same is true of inventory purchases: these use up cash now, but are not expensed against profit until the goods are sold. On the other hand, there are possible ways in which the income could look *worse* than the cash flow. For example, a company might be making only a small profit, but freeing up cash by cutting down the amount of inventory it needs to hold.

Let us now look at the Amazon.com cash-flow statement (Figure 3.3).

First of all, let us consider the overall structure of the cash-flow statement. The statement begins with the *opening cash* (cash at the start of the year) on line 7. Lines 9–47 are concerned with calculating how much cash is added or subtracted from cash balances by the business, ending up with the net increase or decrease in cash calculated on line 47. This is added to the opening cash to give us the *ending cash* (cash at the end of the year). Lines 9–47 (the calculation of the cash added) are cut up into three sections. The first section, lines 9–29, is concerned with calculating the amount of cash from the operations, before investments in assets and in acquiring companies. Lines 30–6 calculate the investments in assets or acquired firms. Lines 37–44 show whether cash has come from investors (from a share issue or sale of debt securities), or perhaps has been returned to them (by the payment of interest or dividends).

Going into more detail, the first section of the calculation, that of cash flow from operations, is split up into two parts: lines 9–19 start with net loss, and then adjust it for non-cash items (items which have been subtracted from the earnings, but do not represent cash outflow in this financial year). These are items such as depreciation, which represent the gradual using up (expense) of long-term assets which have been bought (cash flow) previously. The only exception to this is line 16, which is the adding back of a loss on an investment in marketable securities. Since we are going to explicitly count the cash from selling and the cash from buying these securities on lines 31–2, it would be double counting if we did not adjust for the fact that the loss has already been expensed in the income statement. The second subsection of the operating cash flow (lines 20–7) is the adjustment for the changes in assets and liabilities. These are the 'real money' investments in things like inventory. The recognition of these items can be delayed in the income statement presentation (for example, inventory bought for cash is only expensed in the income statement when sold as a finished product, not when bought) but the items still take cash immediately when bought.

The final two sections detail cash flows from investing activities (lines 30–6) and cash flows resulting from the companies financing activities whereby it raises funds and manages its funding needs (lines 37–44). The presentation of

Figure 3.3 Amazon.com: cash-flow statement

1		Amazon.com, Inc.			
2		Consolidated statements of cash flows			
3		(in thousands)			
4		Years ended December 31			
5					
6		**2001**	**2000**	**1999**	**1998**
7	CASH AND CASH EQUIVALENTS, BEGINNING OF PERIOD	$ 822,435	$ 133,309	$ 71,583	$ 110,119
8	OPERATING ACTIVITIES:				
9	Net loss	(567,277)	(1,411,273)	(719,968)	(124,546)
10	Adjustments to reconcile net loss to net cash used in operating activities:				
11	Depreciation of fixed assets and other amortization	84,709	84,460	36,806	9,421
12	Stock-based compensation	4,637	24,797	30,618	2,386
13	Equity in losses of equity-method investees, net	30,327	304,596	76,769	2,905
14	Amortization of goodwill and other intangibles	181,033	321,772	214,694	42,599
15	Non-cash restructuring-related and other	73,293	200,311	8,072	1,561
16	Loss (gain) on sale of marketable securities, net	(1,335)	(280)	8,688	271
17	Other losses (gains), net	2,141	142,639	–	–
18	Non-cash interest expense and other	26,629	24,766	29,171	23,970
19	Cumulative effect of change in accounting principle	10,523	–	–	–
20	Changes in operating assets and liabilities:				
21	Inventories	30,628	46,083	(172,069)	(20,513)
22	Prepaid expenses and other current assets	20,732	(8,585)	(54,927)	(16,758)
23	Accounts payable	(44,438)	22,357	330,166	78,674
24	Accrued expenses and other current liabilities	50,031	93,967	95,839	31,232
25	Unearned revenue	114,738	97,818	6,225	–
26	Amortization of previously unearned revenue	(135,808)	(108,211)	(5,837)	–
27	Interest payable	(345)	34,341	24,878	(167)
28					
29	Net cash used in operating activities	(119,782)	(130,442)	(90,875)	31,035
30	INVESTING ACTIVITIES:				
31	Sales and maturities of marketable securities	370,377	545,724	2,064,101	227,789
32	Purchases of marketable securities	(567,152)	(184,455)	(2,359,398)	(504,435)
33	Purchases of fixed assets including internal use software and web-site development	(50,321)	(134,758)	(287,055)	(28,333)
34	Investments in equity-method investees and other investments	(6,198)	(62,533)	(369,607)	(19,019)
35					

continued

Figure 3.3 *continued*

Amazon.com, Inc.
Consolidated statements of cash flows
(in thousands)
Years ended December 31

		2001	2000	1999	1998
36	Net cash provided by (used in) investing activities	(253,294)	163,978	(951,959)	(323,998)
37	FINANCING ACTIVITIES:				
38	Proceeds from exercise of stock options and other	16,625	44,697	64,469	14,366
39	Proceeds from issuance of common stock, net of issuance costs	99,831	–	–	–
40	Proceeds from long-term debt and other	10,000	681,499	1,263,639	325,987
41	Repayment of long-term debt and other	(19,575)	(16,927)	(188,886)	(78,108)
42	Financing costs	–	(16,122)	(35,151)	(7,783)
43					
44	Net cash provided by financing activities	106,881	693,147	1,104,071	254,462
45	Effect of exchange-rate changes on cash and cash equivalents	(15,958)	(37,557)	489	(35)
46					
47	Net increase (decrease) in cash and cash equivalents	(282,153)	689,126	61,726	(38,536)
48					
49	CASH AND CASH EQUIVALENTS, END OF PERIOD	$ 540,282	$ 822,435	$ 133,309	$ 71,583
50					
51					

this part of the cash-flow statement is a little confusing because there are two lines (lines 31–2: sale and purchase of marketable securities) which are placed in the investing area but which might be more suitably placed in the financing part of the cash flow statement, since this represents the 'shuffling' of the company's portfolio of short term investments, as some of them mature (expire) and the money needs to be invested elsewhere. Lines 33–4 show the company's investments in assets for its business: line 33 in directly purchased fixed assets, line 34 in shares in other companies' businesses.

At this point we know the cash requirements of the business. This tells us how much money has to be raised by the financing activities of the business to keep Amazon 'standing still'. To take the example of 2000:

\$130.4m	cash was used up by operating activities (line 29)
\$134.8m	cash was invested in fixed assets (line 33)
\$62.5m	cash was invested in the associated companies (line 34)
\$37.6m	cash was lost due to exchange rate fluctuations (line 45)
\$365.3m	cash used up by operations (and was therefore required *from* financing activities)

The free cash flow (FCF) of the business was therefore –\$365.3m. Free cash flow is defined here as cash flow from operations minus net investments.

This money was raised by:

\$361.3m	net sales of marketable securities (line 31 plus line 32; line 32 is negative)
\$693.1m	net issuance of securities by the company (line 44)
\$1054.4m	raised

So there was \$689.1m (\$1054.4m minus \$365.3m) 'extra' raised. This is shown in line 47 as the increase in cash for the year, and is then added to line 7 to give line 49, the cash at the end of the year.

Why was extra cash raised? Companies frequently raise cash in one year to invest over an extended period, to minimize the transaction costs that would occur from more frequent capital raisings. A firm may also feel that the market is particularly receptive to its investment ideas and that 'now is the time' to raise cash.

HISTORICAL AND PROJECTED REVENUE

We now look at how we use the accounting data to estimate the future health of the company. We begin by discussing the estimation of revenue.

In the particular case of internet firms and other high-growth companies whose markets are in an early stage of development, the estimation of future revenues is a very difficult task. However, it *is* possible, with the obvious caveat that it is a process of estimation which is likely to yield numbers that are at best an approximation to the future reality.

The tools and evidence at the valuer's disposal are these:

- *Short-term revenue prediction:*
  - company predictions of next year's revenues
  - the company's recent record in growing revenues

- the time series of recent revenues
- online research agencies' prediction of marketplace growth in certain online categories

- *Longer term revenue prediction:*
  - maximum value: performance of 'excellent' growth companies in achieving sustained revenue growth
  - expectation: predictions of growth by research agencies, government bodies and other commentators
  - minimum value: performance of weaker companies or economy-wide growth

- *Very long-term revenue prediction:*
  - In the very long term, revenue cannot grow at faster than the economy-wide growth rate.

In the case of very short term revenue prediction, for the next year of the company's life, management frequently publishes guidance as to what revenues are predicted. These are either published directly in company financial releases or published via analysts' reports. Analysts should expect to hear these numbers at meetings with company management or at conference calls. Increasingly, audio files of these conference calls are being published on the web as part of regulation FD (the US SEC's policy of full disclosure) so that non-professional investors can directly access these forecasts. Especially if the year is part way through, these values can be adopted as the immediate future year's revenues in the projection.

In the case of revenue projections 1–2 years out, the past time series of revenues for firms is a useful source of data. This does not mean that last year's revenue growth will be repeated in the next year. In the very early stages of growth, firms may grow very quickly from a small base. However, this rate of growth tends to decrease over time. For example:

- For Amazon.com, each quarter's annual revenue growth (that is, compared to the same quarter one year ago) showed a pattern of approximately exponential decline, where the quarter's growth was approximately 88% of the previous quarter's growth. This is the *exponential decay revenue growth model.*

- For Yahoo!, for the years to 2000, revenue growth was maintained at extremely high levels of over 100%. There was no clear pattern of decay. This is called the *hypergrowth revenue growth model.* It is limited in timeframe.

- For Microsoft, the company's growth on a five-year moving average basis is 25–30%. However, individual annual growth rates are extremely dependent on whether a major product release (for example Windows 95 or Windows 98) occurs in that year. This is called the *product-release-led revenue growth model.*

- For Time Warner, revenue growth was steady at approximately 10% over the immediate past of the firm. While AOL follows a high growth path (showing some exponential decay), the combined firm of AOL Time Warner would be dominated in the early years by the slower growth revenue streams of Time Warner, for purely mathematical reasons. This is called the *steady state/mature revenue growth model.*

Once a suitable model has been selected and projected forward, *sense checking* should be carried out. There are two different sense checks that can be carried out:

- First of all, forward revenue numbers should be checked against the projected size of the market. Unless the company is very dominant and has some proprietary advantage (Microsoft) or barrier to entry (AOL), it is unlikely to secure more than 30–40% of the available marketplace.
- The second sense check is to realize that very few companies can sustain revenue growth rates of more than 20–25% per annum for extended periods. This is particularly relevant to hypergrowth companies. In the case of Yahoo! the company's period of hypergrowth ended very suddenly due to a market discontinuity (that is, the fall-off in demand for online advertising). Even if such a discontinuity is not looming, one should not assume undecaying hypergrowth for a hypergrowth firm for more than one or two years, depending on the strength of the firm's competitive advantage.

What about our comment that companies cannot grow any faster than the economy in the long term? This may seem rather harsh to some readers, since long-term economy growth rates are typically in the range of 2–4% for Western countries. However, in the indefinite future, any business which grows its revenues faster than the rate of the economy as a whole would expand to take over the whole economy! This understanding is particularly relevant if we are using a formula called the *growing perpetuity formula*, which is a shortcut that adds together an indefinite series of growing cash flows (that is, a formula which converts into today's money the value of a payment which occurs every year, for ever, and grows at some constant annual rate). This formula is often called the *Gordon growth formula*, and we will discuss it (and the problems with it) in more detail in later chapters.

In the *absence* of past financial data, revenue must be projected from:

- the revenues of any similar companies operating in other industries or countries
- the likely market size for the good in the target markets
- offline companies' ability to secure revenues for similar products or services (that is, is there an established market for the service?)
- the likely competitive environment.

For pre-IPO or even pre-VC companies, the management forecasts of revenues will be a key element of the data. We will discuss in Chapter 16 how these should be checked and evaluated. One important element is that the more the research has 'drilled down' into sub-segments and addressed why specific niches will be attracted to pay for the firm's product, the more credible is the management forecast. It is very easy to write that a firm expects to achieve 5% of a large market, but this 'modest' 5% share can be hard to achieve in practice.

It should be noted that only when revenue forecasts are combined with predicted costs can a decision of value be taken. If the cost structure of a firm is too high, then it may not survive despite substantial percentage revenue increases. Firms may also be prone to discontinuities in their markets, or may not reach profitability in time to avoid a *funding crunch*.

VARIABLE AND FIXED COSTS

Future *costs* are usually predicted as a function of future *revenues*. To carry out this prediction we use a simplified economic model of how costs depend on revenues. Clearly, at a broad level it costs more to serve a lot of customers than a few. But how much more? If one is a skilled artisan making handmade jewellery, it takes about twice as long and requires roughly twice as much material to serve two customers as it does one. Since costs depend very much on the volume sold (costs go up in step with sales) we refer to this as a *largely variable cost business*. On the other hand, if one is a professor, it costs no more to teach ten students than it does one. This is a *largely fixed cost business*. With an estimate of what proportion of the costs of the business are fixed and what proportion are available, we are in a good position to predict future costs relative to future revenues.

In other words, what we would really like is an economic classification of costs into what proportion of the costs are fixed and what proportion are variable. *Fixed costs* stay constant with the activity or output (usually measured by revenues) of the company, *variable costs* rise precisely proportionately with the output of the firm. The reason this classification of costs would be useful is that it could help us predict how costs will change in the future, which is our goal.

To illustrate this, consider an idealized example of an internet firm. This internet firm – let's call it Tiber.com (after a large river which was important in ancient times) – sells products on a website to consumers. The firm's costs are of three types.

- There is an initial cost to build the website of $20m. This is a set-up cost which has to be expended once only.
- There is a further cost of $10m to run the website over a year. The website can serve an unlimited number of customers. Because this cost does not change, however many or few customers buy, this is a fixed cost.
- In addition to this, there are costs of buying and supplying orders of product to customers; these costs amount to 80% of revenues. These include buying the products, packing them and shipping them. All of these jobs are done by hourly paid workers who can be hired and fired at will. Because this cost is directly proportional to revenues, it is a pure variable cost.

Tiber.com is a great business, provided it sells more than $50m of product. Once the initial $20m has been spent to build the website, the profit of Tiber.com can be found from the following simple equation:

profit = revenues – (0.8 × revenues) – $10m

If Tiber sells nothing it loses $10m, if it sells $50m it breaks even. If it sells $100m, it makes $10m. If it doubles revenues to $200m, it trebles profits to $30m!

This understanding seems deceptively simple, but the concept, that of *operating leverage*, is at the heart of how internet businesses may or may not make money. A company or business which possesses high operating leverage experiences rapid rises in profits as revenues rise. For example, a B2C e-commerce website is an automated system that replicates many parts of the shopping process, enabling a large number of customers to be served without human interaction. Ideally, the website will replace the browsing process (cutting down on the real estate assets needed), will facilitate customers seeking answers to questions (cutting down on costs of sales assistance), and will facilitate the payment process (eliminating the need for human cashiers). If the website works well it will cause two processes:

- cutting of costs (by eliminating the need to pay rent for shops)
- shifting of costs from variable costs (for example the cost of hiring extra sales assistants and cashiers to respond to extra revenues) to fixed costs (the website needs to be kept running even if there are only a few customers but, once it is up, it can cope with many customers).

The shifting of costs from variable to fixed increases the operating leverage of the firm, meaning that the company's profits will be more sensitive to changes in revenues than would a company with lower operating leverage. If we can determine what proportion of a company's costs are fixed and what proportion are variable, then, given a prediction of future revenues, we can estimate future profits (or losses).

Looking back at the accounting information we have, how useful is it in calculating the values that we require? Recall that accounting distinguishes costs between cost of sales and other costs, where cost of sales is the costs of physical inventory shipped to customers. It turns out that this distinction is not very useful in getting at the underlying economics, because the concept of cost of sales is most relevant for manufacturing companies and for companies which ship physical product. Cost of sales may give us a baseline figure for variable cost, but 'other costs' can include both fixed and variable costs. For example, 'other costs' include a variety of costs, such as selling and marketing costs, and administration costs. While the salary of the CEO and the cost of a brand-building advertising campaign would be purely fixed (that is, would not increase even if a lot of product were sold), such costs as hiring customer service or ordering staff would be variable. Also cost of goods sold can include some fixed costs also, especially if cost of sales is broadly defined, as in the AOL and Razorfish examples.

If we have a number of periods of cost data we can numerically analyse this cost data to help us determine the pattern of fixed versus variable costs. This is done by graphing costs against sales, possibly excluding cost of sales (since these can usually be assumed to be mostly variable). We can then use graphical analysis to analyse how much cost has been added for an increase of $1 of revenue. However, this analysis can be misleading for an early stage firm, because it mixes costs added to serve current customers with costs expended to develop future services. In this case the analysis of the balance between fixed and variable costs must be carried out by estimating the amount of fixed and variable costs in established, more steady-state competitors in similar industries. The analysis of fixed and variable costs may also be assisted by detailed analysis of the cost information given by the financial statements. For example, within the marketing cost category, advertising costs are broken out under US GAAP. These costs may be seen as more fixed than, for example, the costs to employ customer support staff. This is because the cost of an ad-campaign does not increase if more goods are sold, whereas the need to employ customer support staff *may* increase. It should be noted that fixed does not mean 'eternal', just that a change in volume or revenue does not change the cost. For example, both of these costs are determined and can be changed by management decisions: advertising could be cut back or customer support resource economized or automated.

Observation and estimation of how much of a firm's cost is variable and how much is fixed will never be an exact science. Much of a firm's cost is neither fixed nor variable. Think for example of a server to store customer data. Let us suppose the server has the capacity to store 500,000 customer accounts. The cost of storage is obviously related to revenue, but not in any simple way. It remains fixed until 500,000 customers make purchases, but then it steps up to double the cost when one more customer is added. This is called a *step-fixed cost*, because it looks fixed over small ranges of volume, but does vary in steps when volume changes by larger amounts. Similarly, if we think of customer support as a number of persons, that resource needs to be increased when customers are added, so it is variable in big-picture terms. But an extra customer support person gives the company the capacity to handle perhaps another 50 complaints or problems a day, without any rise in the cost (provided that the staff member is salaried). So over this short range, the cost is fixed; but the cost quickly steps up with volume, when we hire another customer support staff member. This is termed a *step-variable cost*, because it looks variable, but is stepped when we consider it in close-up. Finally there are some costs which are *mixed costs*, because they have both a fixed and a variable component. For example, telephone service is usually a mixed cost which has a fixed component (line charge per month) and a variable component (according to the minutes used or the long-distance minutes used).

In the light of these necessary approximations, fixed/variable analysis is still a useful tool. This is because it encourages us to study this key driver of profitability for these firms. It also enables us to make some early judgements on which firms have the most potential to deliver supernormal profits. For example, let us compare and contrast an internet consulting company with a firm like eBay. Although the consulting company may possess tools and methodologies, each project or client added requires the firm to scale up its consulting resources by actually adding more consulting staff. This means that the consulting company's operating leverage is severely limited, because this key resource is a variable cost. A consulting company's key operating assets are its people – and it is somewhat debatable whether such companies should be classed as internet or new-economy companies at all. Contrast this with eBay, where the main operating asset is certainly the website, which can handle a large number of auctions without extra intervention. Of course, eBay does have some variable costs (or more precisely, step-variable costs), such as customer support people to handle disputes between bidders. But the firm's operating leverage is far higher. Because eBay's service does not have to deal with physical inventory, its position is particularly strong.[4] Somewhere in between these two extremes is a firm such as Amazon, which clearly has substantial variable costs since it has to procure physical product, but which has at least the potential to leverage the fixed costs of its website over a large number of users.

THE LIMITATIONS OF OPERATING LEVERAGE

The Tiber.com vignette – especially the assumption that a website can be built and left to run – requires some caveats. In practice, websites have required continuous development to keep up with the (real or perceived) demands of customers for fresh features and enhanced performance, to keep up with feature-based competition from other websites, to eliminate bugs, and to cope with load above design capacity for key equipment. Therefore the website running cost has been *more variable* and *higher* than originally anticipated. Also, customers ordering from a website (or any other remote retailer, such as a catalogue) have to incur extra costs of shipping, and to accept delayed receipt of goods compared with buying the goods in a store. Some customers want instant gratification, and these customers will never order physical products from the internet. (The supply of downloadable content, for example software or MP3 format music, may be a different matter.) These downsides of internet ordering have affected take-up and margins, as internet firms have given discounts to make up for these disadvantages.

In general, operating leverage appears rarer than one might think in the wider world. Running a statistical analysis[5] of US data for firms for the period 1975–98 suggests a relationship of cost = 0.9 × revenues, plus or minus a small constant, *c* (depending on the precise specification, but the constant is never significantly different from zero). Since average pre-tax margins (sales – cost) are about 10–12% over this time period (depending on the year), this means that there is no clear evidence of systematic operating leverage in the population of US firms. As we discuss further in the next chapter, this is not a perfect indicator of operating leverage, because operating leverage is more relevant to a situation in which the business operations of a firm are kept constant while revenues rise. Many of these companies will be growing their operations and anticipating future expansion, and incurring extra costs for that reason. It is also a demonstration of the accepted wisdom that, in the long run, there are few fixed costs. If we shrink the timescale to a 10-year time period, the equation changes to cost = 0.85 × revenues + *c*. However, these experiments are indicative that substantial operating leverage cannot be taken for granted, especially in the long term. It is wisest to assume that most costs will rise with sales, unless we have strong evidence to the contrary.

FUNDING OF ASSETS

As the business grows, it has to fund assets as well as costs. The distinction between assets (expensed slowly via depreciation) and costs is not very important in cash flow valuation, since the cash flow representation does not spread out the representation of the costs either way. However, each type of negative cash flow has to be modelled.

Assets tend to be estimated as a percentage of revenues. This percentage can change over time. A company that is leveraging its assets well, and serving more customers from one facility, is improving its asset efficiency. On the other hand, consumers can sometimes become more and more demanding of firms, which may lead to companies investing in more sophisticated assets which increase their assets as a proportion of sales.

For modelling purposes, let us consider a simple example of a company whose (end of year) assets are 20% of revenues. Let us now assume that revenues in year 1 are 1000, and revenues in year 2 are 2500. Since assets are 20% of revenues, assets would be 200 at the close of year 1, and 500 (20% of 2500) at the close of year 2. This would mean a negative cash flow of $300 (the cash needed to raise the assets from $200 to $500). This can be simply modelled using Excel, which can also allow the simulation of a decay in the relative assets required over time.

CASH INFLOWS FROM INVESTORS

Having discussed the negative cash flows, we discuss the cash received by the firm. Let us consider the relationship between cash paid and cash received:

cash received – cash paid = increase in cash in the balance sheet

The main source of cash for most firms is revenues received from customers. What the relationship above says is that if we receive more cash than we pay out, we will increase our cash balance. However, the normal situation for an early stage company is to expend more cash than is received from customers, as it builds up productive tangible assets and intangible capabilities. In this case, in the absence of large cash balances, cash will also have to be raised from investors (either in the firm's equity or in its debt). Together with any proceeds from the selling of assets or subsidiaries (usually modest in the case of a growing firm), investments inward are the other main source of cash flow for the firm, as we saw in Amazon's cash flow above.

However, investments inwards are not counted in free cash flow for valuation purposes. This is because we are concerned only with the cash flow generated by the operations of the firm, cash flow which is available for distribution to the shareholders and debt holders. To sum this up, we can restate the equality given above, by splitting operations from the funding part of the business:

cash received – cash paid = increase in cash in the balance sheet

Restate as:

cash paid out from operations – cash received from operations = funding required

and:

funding required = equity raised + debt raised + decrease in cash on balance sheet

In other words, if revenues and other cash from operations are less than the costs we pay out plus the costs of assets we buy, we have a shortfall of cash that we need to fund. The funding requirement is secured by raising equity, by raising debt, or by running down our own cash balances that we have from the previous period. Funding required is the reverse of free cash flow. To rephrase, free cash flow occurs when the funding requirement is less than zero, and cash is actually being freed up to debt-holders and equity-holders. In the Amazon historical data, free cash flow is negative because we have to raise money from investors.

EARNINGS AND CASH FLOWS

In the previous chapter we used the terms *cash flow* and *profits* (earnings) in similar senses. We now discuss these in more detail, especially in regard to their role in valuation.

Cash flow, or free cash flow (FCF), is the amount of cash produced by the operating assets of the firm in any one period. As discussed in Chapter 1, this is the cash received from customers as revenue, minus the costs expended and assets bought in the period, minus taxes:

FCF = cash flow from operations – net investment in assets – cash taxes

where cash flow from operations = earnings – increase in working capital + add-back of depreciation and other non-cash items.

This cash is available to pay interest and to pay down debt, to redeem equity, or to pay dividends to equity holders. If management so choose, this free cash can also be reinvested in fresh operating assets to finance projects or lines of business – but we do not anticipate these at the time of projection. The operating assets may be viewed as a standalone business, and the financial assets and liabilities as a separate business whose sole purpose is to finance the operating assets. Both are presided over by management.

Although cash flow could in theory be observed directly by tracking inflows and outflows of cash from and to various departments of the firm (direct method), it is usually measured using the accounting numbers obtained from the company's income statement and profit and loss account and balance sheet (indirect method). This understanding emphasizes the vital nature and importance of accounting data published by the firm.

Earnings is the summary accounting measurement which conveys whether or not the firm is profitable or not. The calculation of earnings rearranges certain cost and revenue items between time periods, postponing some and bringing others forward compared with when the cash associated with the cost or revenue is paid or received. The aim of the accounting system is to match costs with the revenues that cause the costs, so that in any given period the earnings gives a good idea of whether the firm is making money. Cash flow cannot always do this since it views as negative cash flow some cash flows which benefit the business in the future, such as the purchase of raw materials to make products and the purchase of large physical assets from which the company derives benefit over a period of time. Accounting treats these costs differently in the calculation of earnings, respectively postponing the cost of raw materials (until sold) and spreading out the cost of large machinery (over the useful life of the machinery).

In the idealized situation of the KWSN example in Chapter 1, cash flows and earnings were the same. To engineer this situation, we had to made two key assumptions:

- that there were no depreciating assets in KWSN
- that there were no other timing differences creating a difference between earnings and cash flows (for example, buyers paid revenues and suppliers were paid at the same time).

In real life, buyers (especially corporate buyers) may require deferred-payment terms whereby they pay one or more months after the purchase of the goods or services. Suppliers may also allow the business deferred-payment terms. In a business with a large number of fixed assets (long term assets such as factories or plant) depreciation becomes important. Depreciation is a way of spreading the cost of a large purchase over its useful life for accounting purposes.

Table 3.1 gives an example. Suppose HardCompany, Inc. spends \$60m on computer hardware, which is expected to last for three years. In terms of cash flows, \$60m negative cash flow occurs – the first year of business therefore has a negative cash flow (Table 3.1a). However, for the accounting record, specifically the income statement, the cost of the computer equipment would be

TABLE 3.1a HardCompany – format 1: cash flow

	Year 1 ($m)	Year 2 ($m)	Year 3 ($m)
Revenues	100	100	100
Cost of sales	–40	–40	–40
Gross profit	60	60	60
Other costs	–30	–30	–30
Cash on hardware	–60	0	0
Free cash flow	–30	30	30

TABLE 3.1b HardCompany – format 2: depreciation

	Year 1 ($m)	Year 2 ($m)	Year 3 ($m)
Revenues	100	100	100
Cost of sales	(40)	(40)	(40)
Gross profit	60	60	60
Other costs	(30)	(30)	(30)
Depreciation on hardware	(20)	(20)	(20)
Profit	10	10	10

spread over its useful life, and only $20m of cost would be subtracted each year (Table 3.1b). Obviously, for valuation what matters is *when* the cash flow for the hardware occurred – we would use format 1 to value the company. However, for the casual observer, looking at year 1, which type of report is most useful in telling him or her whether HardCompany is a 'good business'? What if he or she were looking at year 2? Remember that in the real world, investors will be looking at one or two years of history in the current annual report, not a tidy plan for the next three or more years.

Note that the use of depreciation is an accounting adjustment intended to give a fairer view of the profitability of the firm – the spreading of cost by depreciation does *not* indicate that there was a hire purchase or lease-to-own arrangement spreading out the *cash payment* for the equipment. It should also be noted that the beneficial effects of depreciation are usually confined to *tangible* assets only, such as computers, desks, buildings and physical plant. Spending on developing a brand image, or on planning a website,[6] must be expensed against profits immediately. This is due to the conservative nature of accounting (accounting tends to produce the representation least likely to overstate asset values and profits). Because these *intangible* assets are harder to separate from the firm and harder to sell, they are treated conservatively and must be 'paid for' at once. One exception is 'goodwill', where *amortization* (a special term given to depreciation of intangible assets) has been allowed. See Appendix 3.1 for a discussion of this important type of intangible asset and 2002–3 changes to its accounting treatment.

It is worth noting that free cash flow, as it needs to be defined for valuation purposes, cannot generally be read off from the cash flow statement. Often cash flow and free cash flow are defined in various, and variously misleading and disingenuous, ways. One of the more common definitions of cash flow is that it is calculated by adding non-cash charges, such as depreciation, to net income after taxes. There is often a summary line in a cash flow statement that shows this number as 'operating cash flow'. (Operating cash flow may also be differently defined, dependent on the company.) While this may be a useful measure for some firms, it is of no use for valuation purposes because it does not factor in purchases of fixed assets that were needed to allow customers to be served. Instead it adds back depreciation (the gradual payment for assets which has already been 'taken off' in the calculation of profit) without any countervailing payment for the assets actually bought. For valuation purposes, free cash flow must be the cash available for distribution to security holders. It must be *after* tax, and *after* the purchase and sale of fixed assets (whether by buying a company (M&A) or by buying assets directly), but *before* any distributions to investors (such as interest and dividends) and *before* any receipts from investors (that is, new investments in company securities).

THE ROLE OF CASH FLOWS AND THE ROLE OF EARNINGS

In this book we use the free cash flow method of valuation. Therefore we project free cash flows forward and discount them to discover their present value. This present value is then compared with the current market value of equity and any debt. We use historical accounting information and other non-accounting data to help us predict what the future cash flows will be.

Current earnings numbers provide a view of current profitability of the firm. While we should be aware of the accounting adjustments made to arrive at earnings, these adjustments are not always sinister, normally being introduced to smooth out discontinuities (for example depreciation) or to impose a sensible conservative slant on the accounting reports (for example immediate expensing of marketing spend). Earnings are extremely informative of the firm's current health and future prospects. For example, except in very 'hot' markets, a firm not making profits under UK or US GAAP has more difficulty in raising funds for further development – making its future prospects poor.

There are alternative valuation models which use earnings or residual earnings (earnings after subtracting the expected return to equity) to form an estimate of value. These are termed *residual income valuation* (*RIV*) models. These are discussed in, for example, Penman (2001). However, the fact that shareholder's equity is often close to zero or negative for internet companies may make these residual value models appear less intuitive for internet companies.

THE ECONOMIC PROFIT MODEL IN BRIEF

The *economic profit model* is the basis for both the DCF methodology used in this book, and for other methodologies such as the RIV model. The economic profit model states that a company can generate shareholder value (that is, be worth more than what the shareholder has put in) by making a return above the cost of the capital (WACC) in the business.

Return on capital employed (*RoCE*) is measured in the following way:

$$\text{RoCE} = \frac{\text{operating profit}}{\text{capital employed}}$$

Economic profitability is defined as spread > 0 or economic profit > 0:

$$\text{spread} = \text{RoCE} - \text{WACC}$$

$$\text{economic profit} = \text{profit} - (\text{capital employed} \times \text{WACC})$$

Capital employed is the book value of the equity and debt instruments issued by the company. This RoCE is then compared to the weighted average cost of capital, which is calculated as per the methods outlined in Chapter 1. If the spread between RoCE and WACC is positive (RoCE > WACC), then the company is making an economic profit. If the spread is unfavourable, then the company is destroying value in the current period. Shares in a company that consistently has a negative spread between RoCE and WACC are worth less than what shareholders paid for them. If the destruction of value continues, the shares will become worthless and the company will go bankrupt.

It is often instructive to break out the RoCE into two elements by a process known as the *Dupont decomposition*, after the company which receives credit for introducing it. This breaks out the contributors to return on capital into *margin performance* (operating margin) and *asset efficiency* (asset turnover):

$$\text{RoCE} = \underbrace{\frac{\text{operating profit}}{\text{revenues}}}_{\text{operating margin}} \times \underbrace{\frac{\text{revenues}}{\text{capital employed}}}_{\text{asset turnover}}$$

For a company which is unprofitable the operating margin should be observed to track its progress into positive territory. Asset efficiency can still be observed. For a company with low or negative capital employed, the value of intangible assets may have to be included to evolve a sensible measure of RoCE. This is further discussed in Chapter 6. The advantage of this decomposition is that it emphasizes the key contributors to improving return on capital.

APPENDIX 3.1: ADVANCED ISSUES

Problems of revenue recognition in internet firms

The comparability of revenues between businesses has been a key concern in the study of internet firms. This is for two reasons: in the (now discredited) comparables viewpoint, revenues were seen as a direct driver of value, therefore comparability of revenues was essential for accurate valuation. In the DCF/value viewpoint that we adopt in this book, comparable revenue figures are also essential because, although we do not value revenue directly, we want to use financial ratios which include revenue to inform our projections of the company's future.

Defining a measure of revenue is not always straightforward. For example, the internet travel website priceline.com records the total price which end-customers pay for airline tickets as revenue. This seems sensible, but normal practice in the travel agency industry is to record commissions and fees as revenue. Total price paid for travel tickets, since the travel agency has no chance of applying more than 10 or 20% of this to its own costs, is noted (if at all) as an informational number. It is interesting that the phone-web travel agency Cheaptickets does not follow the same practice, and nor does eBay, despite being a somewhat similar business in that it brokers sales between two parties. eBay reports the total business transacted through eBay as 'gross merchandise sales', but this figure does not appear in the income statement, which begins with revenues, where 'revenues' is the sum of fees and commissions on the gross merchandise sales. This is the so called 'gross versus net' controversy. eBay's accounting policy (reporting net revenue) is in accordance with both the letter and the spirit of US GAAP, as reinforced by the FASB's EITF abstract 99-19, which guides firms to report revenue as net revenue 'if the company performs as an agent or broker without assuming the risks or rewards of ownership of the goods'. Priceline's 10K statement justifies the inclusion of total transaction value as revenue by stating that it 'purchases and takes title and is the merchant of record' for products sold (Priceline Fiscal 2000 10K form, page 57), suggesting that it does take the risks generally associated with being a merchant. However, on its website's investor relations page (http://travel.priceline.com/PriceLineASPOurCompany/pressroom/whatsnew/html/pressrelease44.htm) it states that 'Priceline.com does not maintain or warehouse inventories in any of its product lines', suggesting that the period of ownership (taking of title) to the goods the firm sells is brief, and the risks of that ownership correspondingly small.

From the point of view of the analyst and/or valuer the distinction is one to be aware of. The method of adjusting for the priceline.com method of revenue reporting (which has come to be termed *reporting gross revenues*) is simply to realize that priceline.com's margins, as a percentage of its gross revenues, will be far smaller that that of a firm which reports more conservative net revenues, taken as a percentage of this firm's (lower) net revenues. So for example, if seeking guidance on possible future margins for priceline.com by looking at travel agency firms using net revenue reporting, adjustment will have to be made for the fact that the other firm will be reporting a margin which is a percentage of the commissions received, whereas priceline's margin will be as a percentage of the (comparatively larger) *gross* revenues. This is in addition to the adjustments which will have to be made for the differences in business model and cost structure.

For example, consider Table 3.2 which compares recent quarterly reports of priceline and the phone-web travel agency Cheaptickets[7]. Cheaptickets reports net revenue (but reports its gross revenues in a note as 'Total gross bookings').

Given the widely varying percentages of gross and net margin reported, it is hard to believe we are comparing like with like, and indeed we are not. If, on the other hand, we calculate priceline's net income as a percentage of its gross profit (which would perhaps be analogous to revenue in a net reporting system), this percentage is 4.7%, quite close to the net margin of Cheaptickets.

Looking at the situation in the UK, accountants have been more conservative. For example, lastminute.com (one of the major travel dot-com brands in the UK) reports net revenues as *turnover* – these net revenues form the top line of the company's consolidated profit and loss account. It also reports gross revenues as 'Total transaction value', this is placed *above* the profit and loss statement, but is not a part of it. Somewhat confusingly, gross margin is reported as a percentage of total transaction value. QXL ricardo plc (the UK-based auction site) also reports net revenues as turnover. PricewaterhouseCoopers (1999)[8] states that this is due to the guidance of IAS 18 (the International Accounting Standards Board guidance): that revenue to an agent or a broker is limited to the commission or margin to which he or she becomes entitled to as part of the transaction.

TABLE 3.2 Cheaptickets: quarterly reports

2nd quarter 2001 ($m)					
	Cheaptickets	% of reported total revenues		priceline	% of reported total revenues
Gross bookings	232.845		Total revenues	364.756	
Total revenues	28.501		Gross profit	60.106	16.5
Gross profit	26.414	92.7	(left blank)		
Net income	1.221	4.3	Net income	2.816	0.8

The other major problem in revenue recognition is the inclusion of barter revenues in reported revenue. *Barter* is the process where two companies exchange goods or services without the use of money. Barter can be an excellent way of doing business, and was used extensively in Eastern Europe at the time of the collapse of Communism – the Eastern European economies required supplies but had little hard currency or borrowing power, so they swapped their products directly for the needed supplies. Both sides of the transaction were trading items of value, and the use of barter was simply a way to get around credit problems and lack of marketing skill. The most common examples of barter between internet firms have been the swapping of advertising on one site for advertising on another site.

The key concept in the valuing of the supplies exchanged is the *carrying value.* If we have to carry the goods or services (if we cannot sell them right now), what are they worth in terms of *realizable value* (that is, what cash are we likely to be able to *realize* if we sell them later)? Suppose we have an item which has zero carrying value – an example of this would be an airline seat the minute after take-off: it cannot be sold or occupied at that point so it is worthless. Now suppose that American Airlines and British Airways (BA) made a deal that they would barter a matched number of unused post-take-off airline seats at a notional price of $500 each (perhaps a BA/American seat cover would be put on the seat for in-flight advertising purposes). Such an arrangement would increase revenues, but would have no effect on earnings (since each $500 seat which BA 'sells' is matched by a $500 seat which it 'buys'). It would be a somewhat ridiculous arrangement, and it would never occur to the airline managers to enter into it, partly because airlines are not valued on revenues and partly because their accountants would be unlikely to permit the treatment.

Advertising pageviews are another example of an *expiring asset*. For the advertising department of the dot-com, the equivalent of aircraft 'take-off' is the moment when the user views a webpage. If the banner exposure on that webpage has not been sold at that point, it expires worthless. Websites customarily advertise a part of their own website or website network, omit the banner, or may give a free banner exposure to a key customer. To give a picture of the scale of the problem, a June 2000 survey by the tracking company Leading Web Advertisers showed that 22% of banner ads on leading web sites were self-advertising banners. For example, 73% of the banners on ESPN.com advertised ESPN or associated sites. Other sample figures were: AOL 45%, Go.Com 30%, altavista.com 10%, Yahoo.com 5%. It should be noted that June 2000 far predated the precipitous drops in demand for online advertising that occurred from first quarter 2001 onwards, so current figures of unsold inventory of banners are likely to be higher.

One alternative to allowing the banner space to expire, or to using it in-house, is to barter it to another website in return for a similar number of banner ads on their website. This is a sensible business decision, but since the decision to barter is frequently made *in extremis* (because no other buyer is available), many companies' practices of reporting substantial revenues (in both income statements!) for these expiring assets are liable to inflate revenues unjustly. In his March 2000 *Fortune* article that alerted many readers to the practice, Jeremy Kahn reports that many start-up companies depend on barter for as much as half of their revenues, and that some established web companies (such as Sportsline and EdgarOnline) may receive more than 18% of their revenues in this way. If matched cash agreements (where barter transactions are hidden by the firms agreeing to exchange equal sums for cash) are included, Kahn reports that Jupiter Online (the market research agency) estimates that as much as 15% of all internet revenues are barter-related.[12]

The US and UK standards bodies have moved to decrease the prevalence of barter revenue reporting. For example, in the USA the FASB issued EITF abstract 99-17, which stated that firms could only report barter revenue if they had received cash revenue for similar transactions during the last six months. The document also forced companies to disclose, in a footnote, the percentage of revenue accounted for by barter.

Other evidence on net/gross and barter revenue is contained in Davis (2000). Professor Davis reports that, in 1999, 38 out of the 52 firms that had the opportunity to use gross revenue reporting did so. Of the 55 firms stating whether barter revenue is included in revenue, 49 said that some barter revenue was included, and 6 said that no barter revenue was included in revenue. (A further 68 firms, which were defined as having the opportunity to report barter revenue, did not explicitly say whether they recognized barter proceeds as revenue or not.)

Goodwill and growth by acquisition

One special intangible asset in the balance sheet is called *goodwill*. Goodwill is created in a company's accounts when the company buys another company at much more than 'book value'. Book value is usually equal to the price the acquired company paid for its tangible assets. For internet companies book value is often very low, so goodwill may be very high. Goodwill may be amortized (the equivalent of depreciation for an intangible asset) or kept on the balance sheet at full value, but subjected to periodic review to make sure that the likely future cash flows are sufficient to justify the value ascribed to it. (This periodic review is termed *impairment review*, because if the goodwill has been impaired it has to be down-valued.) If the goodwill is amortized, this can wipe out an internet company's earnings or, if it is already in loss, cause a big increase in the loss. Many internet companies amortize goodwill over quite short periods, either out of choice or because they have been advised to do so by their accountants. However, they then argue that because the amortization is not reflective of cash flow it should be ignored. One point to note is that amortization is reflective of a past cash flow to purchase the acquired firm. The logic of the accounting treatment is that managers should 'remain accountable'[9] for the investment they have made.

The valuer, of course, is only interested in *future* cash flows. However, he or she should notice that goodwill is being amortized and note that the firm being studied has used acquisition to grow revenues and potential profits in the past. The presence of non-amortized goodwill[10] in the balance sheet should also sound the same warning bell. If further acquisitions will be needed to maintain the rate of growth, the valuer has two choices:

- Assume that the company will continue to make acquisitions in order to grow, and therefore subtract projected cash outflow for acquisitions from free cash flow. The goodwill amortized may be one guideline as to how much cash the firm will spend in future on acquisition. A more reliable guide (since there is some discretion in how quickly the company writes down its goodwill) is the company's track record of spending on acquisitions, as revealed in its historical accounts and in historical news sources. The valuer will also bear in mind changes in the market value of target firms which may make the needed acquisitions cheaper or more expensive.
- Assume that the company will cease to make acquisitions, even if this means retarding its growth rate. The projection will then have to be adjusted to reflect the lower growth rates that will occur if the company grows only by internal growth (internal growth is sometimes termed 'organic growth').

During 2001 there was an increasing tendency for internet firms to write off their goodwill extremely quickly – either by selecting a very short time period over which to amortize the goodwill, or by concluding that the goodwill has become worthless (or at least, worth less than one paid for it) as part of an impairment review, and writing it off against earnings in one chunk. For example, Amazon.com's 10K for FY2000 shows that the company expensed $189m of impairment losses for goodwill and other intangible assets. The company's amortization timescale for goodwill was 2–4 years (page 39), resulting in an amortization expense of $321.8m for financial year 2000. The net result of this (together with come other movements in goodwill) was that balance sheet goodwill for Amazon.com declined from $534.7m at end 1999 to $157.0m at end 2000, a 70% decline.

The advantage of this for Amazon.com in the future is that a lower balance sheet amount of goodwill will lead to lower amortization charges against GAAP earnings in the future. It also means that the company has lower intangible assets which may fall victim to 'impairment'. Although these large charges for year 2000 increased losses, losses were so large anyway that the extra $500m did not attract the ire of shareholders. Some shareholders may also have been persuaded that these costs were not 'real money', thus further decreasing their significance in shareholders' minds.

Recent developments in the standard setting arena in the USA may make the issue of goodwill amortization moot. FASB (the US accounting standard setter) is reaching conclusion on its five-year project to reform M&A accounting. This will have consequences for the issues of goodwill amortization and the pooling-of-interests method of accounting for merged or acquired companies.

The *pooling-of-interests method* is an alternative method of accounting for M&A which allows companies which are of a similar size and which are pooling management, rather than having one set of managers take over the running of both firms, to account for the combination as a 'merger'. Accounting for the transaction as a merger means that the book values (very low in the case of internet firms) are added together (*pooled*) to form the new balance sheet of the firm. Thus the very large dollar or sterling value of the stock that was used to buy the merged firm is not reflected on the combined company's accounts. Also no goodwill can result from the transaction, so the question of amortization of the goodwill (and the negative effect on earnings) does not arise. This method is intended to be used for mergers – where the joining companies are of approximately the same size and where both of the individual firms' managements will join together to run the new firm – but there has been suspicion that the definition of 'merger' has been stretched to get the benefits of the pooling treatment for some acquisitions.

The original intent of the FASB team seems to have been to eliminate the pooling-of-interests method of accounting and to replace it with a system where excess of transaction value over book value would be stated as goodwill and amortized over a period of up to 40 years. However, business interests successfully lobbied for a change in this approach, stating that the requirement to amortize goodwill would deleteriously affect their ability to grow by acquisition. The FASB board reached the decision on 5 July, 2001 to adopt the following policy:

- the pooling-of-interests method will be abolished
- goodwill be recorded in the balance sheet
- the goodwill must be subjected to periodic impairment review, and impairment expensed in the income statement
- goodwill will not be amortized.

This brings the US somewhat into line with the UK practice since FRS10 in 1998, except that the UK rules give managers discretion to amortize goodwill (over a time period up to 20 years) if they so wish.

Understanding pro forma accounting

Amazon.com usually presents both a GAAP income statement (which it is obligated to do under US securities law) and a 'pro forma' income statement. What is pro forma profitability, and is it worth targeting?

Pro forma accounting statements are defined by investorwords.com as 'A hypothetical balance sheet and income statement based on a set of assumptions'. Because companies can use different assumptions for different time periods and for different purposes, pro forma statements are not necessarily consistent across time periods, and there may be more than one pro forma statement in each financial report. Amazon's pro forma statements exclude certain non-cash items and items which the company believes should be classified as non-recurring. Other uses of pro forma include companies which have recently acquired other companies. These firms usually include pro forma historical accounting statements for the merged entity, as well as the GAAP accounting statements. These pro forma statements attempt to estimate how the accounting statements of the company would have looked if the merger had happened, say, a year earlier. This is intended to allow investors an easier basis for comparison between present and past data. Another pro forma statement that companies make is the pro forma statement of income under the assumption that employee stock options are valued in accordance with option models rather than being valued at intrinsic value (usually zero). This is an example of a pro forma statement that companies are *obligated* to make under the US accounting rule SFAS 123 (unless they report the adjusted income as their 'headline' profit, which no companies do).

However, the SFAS 123 disclosure (which we discuss in more detail in the Chapter 7) is something of an exception. Since most pro forma statements are not mandated by the accounting regulators, firms can in theory make any assumptions they wish. However, the US securities regulator SEC recently issued a statement warning firms about pro forma accounting which 'may not convey a true and accurate picture of a company's financial well-being' (Glasner, 2001). No company names were mentioned in the statement.

As an example of pro forma, let us now turn to the way Amazon.com states its GAAP and main pro forma financial results. Let us look at the first quarter 2001 results, which are an interesting example (from the company's 2001Q1 10-Q form).

Commenting on Figure 3.4 we can see sensible rationales for some exclusions but not others. For example, if the company will not make any future acquisitions, it may be sensible to exclude goodwill amortization from income used to predict continuing performance. The exclusion of stock-based compensation which often results from acquisitions can be similarly justified. The exclusion of 'impairment related and other' *seems* sensible since impairment of assets (which have already been paid for) is a non-cash item. However, closer examination of the 10Q reveals that part of this $114m is reorganization costs ($55.5m). See note 6 of the 10Q (Figure 3.5).

Reorganization costs such as these are often excluded from analyst's calculation of headline earnings, but there should clearly be a distinction between the cash and non-cash costs shown here. If the company establishes a pattern of requiring cash restructuring expenses, this will eat up cash that could go to shareholders, and this money therefore needs to be separately reported. (To be fair, criticisms of this sort have been levelled at old-economy companies also).

There is another issue of restructuring costs and pro forma reporting that we should address before concluding this discussion. This is the so-called *'cookie jar' syndrome*, named after bottles of sweet biscuits stored in the pantry for later consumption. The analogy is that although a company will expense the full costs of reorganization at the start of the reorganization process, it does not spend all of the money it expenses in that quarter, and may even carry it over from year to year. In the cookie jar model (note that this model is *not* permitted by accounting rules, but some researchers have suggested that some companies nevertheless do adopt it), a company takes a larger than needed reorganization charge, tells a convincing story to the market as to why this is 'one-off', and analysts 'fall for it' by excluding the restructuring charge from headline earnings. In effect, the restructuring costs are paid for and a large amount of other cost (the cookie jar) has been taken in advance, in the current income statement.

Figure 3.4 Example of a pro forma

Pro forma results of operations

We provide certain pro forma information regarding our results from operations, which excludes stock-based compensation, amortization of goodwill and other intangibles, and impairment-related and other charges. We also provide certain pro forma information regarding our net loss which excludes non-cash gains and losses, net; equity in losses of equity-method investees, net; cumulative effect of change in accounting principle; as well as the amounts excluded from pro forma operating results. This pro forma information is not presented in accordance with accounting principles generally accepted in the United States.

Pro forma results, and certain cash-flow information for the three months ended March 31, 2001 and 2000 *(omitted here for clarity)* were as follows (in thousands, except per share data):

	Three months ended March 31, 2001		
	As Reported	**Pro Forma Adjustments**	**Pro Forma**
Net sales	$ 700,356	$ --	$ 700,356
Cost of sales	517,759	--	517,759
Gross profit	182,597	--	182,597
Operating expenses:			
Fulfillment	98,248	--	98,248
Marketing	36,638	--	36,638
Technology and content	70,284	--	70,284
General and administrative	26,028	--	26,028
Stock-based compensation	2,916	-2,916	--
Amortization of goodwill and other intangibles	50,831	-50,831	--
Impairment-related and other	114,260	-114,260	--
Total operating expenses	399,205	-168,007	231,198
Loss from operations	-216,608	168,007	-48,601
Interest income	9,950	--	9,950
Interest expense	-33,748	--	-33,748
Other expense, net	-3,884	--	-3,884
Non-cash gains and losses, net	33,857	-33,857	--
Net interest expense and other	6,175	-33,857	-27,682
Loss before equity in losses of equity-method investees	-210,433	134,150	-76,283
Equity in losses of equity-method investees, net	-13,175	13,175	--
Net loss before change in accounting principle	-223,608	147,325	-76,283
Cumulative effect of change in accounting principle	-10,523	10,523	--
Net loss	($234,131)	$ 157,848	($76,283)

We are providing pro forma results for informational purposes only. The pro forma results are derived from information recorded in our financial statements.

We expect pro forma operating losses in absolute dollars to be flat to slightly improved for the quarter ended June 30, 2001 in comparison with the quarter ended March 31, 2001. We also expect pro forma operating losses to be between 3 and 6 percent of net sales for the year ended December 31, 2001, with pro forma operating profitability expected in the fourth quarter of 2001. However, any such projections are subject to substantial uncertainty. See the section entitled "Additional factors that may affect future results."

Figure 3.5 From Note 6 of the 10Q report

For the three months ended March 31, 2001, the charges associated with the Company's restructuring were as follows (in thousands):

Asset impairments	$ 58,748
Continuing lease obligations	34,292
Termination benefits	15,088
Broker commissions, professional fees and other miscellaneous restructuring costs	6,132
	$ 114,260

This 'stored cost' can be fed into future earnings as needs be. For example, if earnings are set to fall short of predictions by $10m, the CFO can define $10m of cost as part of the previously incurred restructuring costs: and the $10m then does not appear in the income statement, and the target is achieved. To try and ensure that accounting gives an appropriate measure of the profit for a period, accounting authorities are very wary of allowing companies general-purpose reserves of this type, and auditors should insist that reserves for restructuring costs have a specific purpose and are commensurate with the needs of the restructuring. For example, in EITF 96-9, 'Classification of Inventory Mark-downs and Other Costs Associated with a Restructuring', FASB tightly prescribed what elements can be included in a restructuring cost, for example mandating that inventory writedowns may not be included in restructuring costs but must be taken to cost of goods sold.

How can we tell whether a company is trying to hoard a 'cookie jar'? Well, the notes to the accounts give some information on this, because companies are mandated to show the status of their restructuring reserves, what purpose they will be put to, and how much has yet been spent. Returning to our example of Amazon, we can refer to the company's 2001Q3 10Q report, note 6 (last section only), page 11 (Figure 3.6).

Elsewhere, the company reports that it expensed a total of $109.1m of restructuring costs (*excluding* asset impairments of $67.8m). This means that Amazon still has as much as 65% of that money to offset against future costs: $71.4m – shown as the 'Balance at September 30, 2001'. Is this a 'cookie jar'? We are inclined to think not, informed by the breakdown of the balance into its elements. Much of the balance is continuing lease obligations for premises and machinery no longer needed, which since they fall due in the original schedule of the lease, are naturally deferred.

While we are inclined to judge that the restructuring reserve of Amazon is not an accounting abuse, there are still ways that it may work to increase

Figure 3.6 From Note 6 of the 10Q report

Note 6. Restructuring-Related and Other

At September 30, 2001, the accrued liability associated with the restructuring-related and other charges was $71 million and consisted of the following (in thousands):

	Balance at March 31, 2001	Subsequent Accruals	Non-cash Settlements and Other Adjustments	Payments	Balance at September 30, 2001	Due Within 12 Months	Due After 12 Months
Lease obligations	$34,667	$50,970	-2,693	-18,805	$64,139	$46,437	$17,702
Termination benefits	8,445	599	-2,449	-5,146	1,449	1,449	
Broker commissions, professional fees and other miscellaneous restructuring costs	4,121	2,141	1,559	-1,986	5,835	5,710	125
Total	$47,233	$53,710	-3,583	-25,937	$71,423	$53,596	$17,827

Restructuring-related and other charges recorded during the three and nine months ended September 30, 2000 were primarily associated with asset impairments relating to computer and fulfillment-center equipment to be disposed of, as well as certain acquisition-related expenses, such as bonuses paid to employees of acquired companies and other miscellaneous acquisition-related expenses.

profits in a perfectly allowable way under GAAP. For example, if the company secures a sub-lessor for its unwanted machinery, or concludes that the $7.8m of brokers' and professional fees and miscellaneous costs which has been estimated and expensed was an overestimate, it can take a benefit into earnings. However, once the company has excluded these costs from pro forma on the downside, it will be difficult to reclassify them as in pro forma on the upside.

Summarizing, pro forma accounting statements are frequently scrutinized by investors. Investors want a 'clean' profit measure, that excludes one-off events (sometimes termed 'non-recurring items'), and that ignores non-cash items which investors do not believe will impact returns. However, there are some risks in looking at these statements, since some excluded items are cash (for example restructuring expenses), and, if these do recur they can prevent shareholders gaining a return. Also, the incurring of restructuring expenses can amount to the creation of a 'cookie jar' of future accounting benefits, which firms can use to manage their earnings to reach a declared goal (an example of a declared goal being pro forma profitability). The issue of restructuring expenses is a particularly controversial one. Often firms claim that these are one-off when incurred, but in following years have to take further restructuring expenses (perhaps as a result of fresh problems, or the arrival of new management). Kieso and Weygandt (1998)[11] report two extreme cases: Citicorp, which took six restructuring charges in a row during 1989–94, and Westinghouse, which took a charge in seven out of the ten years 1985–94. Investors should beware of this practice of repeated 'non-recurring' charges.

Although goodwill amortization is non-cash, if a company continues to spend shareholder cash on acquisitions and investments, then the exclusion of amortization of past expense on these items from pro forma looks unconvincing. Even if acquisitions are paid for by shares, the issuance of shares for these acquisitions represents the loss by current shareholders of a piece of the pie.

Finally, the very flexibility which managers have in defining pro forma formats may be the practice's greatest weakness – there is a great temptation for managers to define an expense as 'out of pro forma', even if it may not be. Also, while GAAP profitability, for all the weaknesses it may have, is comparable across companies, pro forma profitability is not.

Assets and operating leases

While pro-forma accounting statements and US or UK GAAP accounting statements are usually clearly visible in the company's reports, there are many interesting and important items which are not emphasized in the accounting statements and are 'relegated' to the *Notes* section. The notes are usually found towards the back of the accounting statements and are headed 'Notes to

Consolidated Financial Statements' or 'Notes to Accounts'. These are items of supplementary information which companies are obliged or choose to *disclose*, but which they are not obliged to *recognize* (recognition is the technical term for including accounting information in the main financial statements of the company).

One example of these notes is the 'Commitments and contingencies' note. We look at an example from Amazon's 2000 10K statement (Figure 3.7).

Figure 3.7 From the 10K statement

Note 9. COMMITMENTS AND CONTINGENCIES

Leases and marketing agreements
The Company currently leases office and fulfillment center facilities and fixed assets under noncancelable operating and capital leases. Rental expense under operating lease agreements for 2000, 1999 and 1998 was $98m, $43m and $8m, respectively.

The Company has also entered into certain marketing agreements that include fixed-fee commitments into the first half of 2002. Total marketing-related commitments amount to $19m; the corresponding costs are recognized according to the terms of the related agreements.

Future minimum commitments are as follows:

	Capital Leases $	Operating Leases $	Marketing Agreements $
Year Ending December 31,			
2001 ...	$13,676	$105,230	$17,495
2002 ...	9,070	88,958	1,016
2003 ...	5,828	55,200	--
2004 ...	41	46,767	--
2005 ...	--	43,936	--
Thereafter ...	--	256,907	--
Total minimum lease payments ...	28,615	596,998	18,511
Less imputed interest ...	(3,778)		
PV of net minimum lease payments ...	24,837		
Less current portion ...	(11,746)		
Long-term capital lease obligation ...	$13,091		

Under UK and US GAAP, capital leases are recognized in the balance sheet, so this disclosure is supplementary. A *capital lease* is a lease in which the lessee (that is, the lease customer, the lease provider being termed the lessor) takes on substantially all the economic risk of owning the asset. An example of this would be a 10-year non-cancellable lease of a piece of equipment with a useful life of 10 years. Recognizing this on the balance sheet means that the company's accountant has to calculate the present value of the lease and place this figure in the balance sheet as both an asset (machinery) and as a balancing liability (included in debt). This process is called *capitalization*. The idea behind this is that there should be no difference in accounting for a machine if it is bought on a capital lease arrangement than if the company first gets a loan from a bank, and then buys the machine (in which case the machine would appear as an asset and the loan as a liability). Since the substance of the transactions is the same, the accounts should look the same.

Operating leases are treated differently. An *operating lease* is normally defined as one in which the non-cancellable lease term is less than 75% of the asset life or the payments over the term are less than 90% of the price of the asset at inception of the lease. These operating leases do not have to be capitalized. The accounting for these leases is through the income statement: lease costs are subtracted within operating costs, and no reflection of the asset or liability is shown on the balance sheet. This can be sensible if the lease is short term, for example. But if a company is using operating leases to provide a large amount of its fixed assets, they can be a way of securing off-balance-sheet financing, which can mean that the balance sheet debt does not fully reflect the borrowings and commitments that the company has.

If the valuer wants to reverse this treatment and actually capitalize the leases as if they were capital leases, the following three-step process can be adopted:

1. determine the present value of the operating lease payments at the cost of capital for the company's debt, perhaps 7–9% for an internet firm
2. place this on the balance sheet as a fixed asset, and also as a debt
3. move the operating lease payments from operating costs to interest payable.

In this case the calculated present value at 9% debt cost (debt for a company such as Amazon would be risky and would attract a high cost of capital, even if secured) is given by the Excel formula NPV(0.09,105230,88958,55200,46767, 43936,256907)=$428.9m. (Figure 3.7 shows that $256,907 of lease payments arise after 2005 ('thereafter') – we approximate by assuming that these payments occur in 2006.) [The equivalent calculation from the 2001 10K is NPV(0.09, 60837,57501,48729,41953,42400,306372).]

Why do this? As one is simply moving cost from one line to another, this makes no difference to the income statement. However, it makes a large difference to the balance sheet, increasing net debt on the balance sheet from about \$1–1.5bn and more than doubling the figure for tangible fixed assets. This higher debt figure would in turn affect solvency ratios that potential lenders and investors look at, such as *gearing* (variously defined as debt/equity or debt/(debt + equity)). It would also depress RoCE at such time as Amazon makes a profit.

If the assets are effectively owned by the company (if Amazon takes substantially all the risks and benefits of ownership) then the assets are better accounted for by capitalization. That operating leases can have risks of ownership is clear – look back at the discussion above of Amazon's pro forma results in 2001Q1 and in particular the restructuring expense. Part of that expense is \$34.3m of continuing lease payments that the company has to pay on the facilities it closed or other leased assets (a further \$51m of continuing lease obligations were expensed in 2001Q2 and 2001Q3). As discussed above, the company has the potential to re-let the space or equipment, perhaps, but it may find that there are few users of heavy distribution centre machinery in McDonough, Georgia, and other closed facilities. Just as if it owned the facilities and equipment, it has been hit with ongoing liabilities from them. The message for valuers is to be aware of the amount of operating leases that a company has, and the potential risks these can carry.

Notes

1 Also, the 1998 data has been restated in the 2000 10K, so do not worry about differences between the 1998 data here and in the case. It is customary to use non-restated data in analysis (such as in the case), although there is no hard and fast rule. (10K and 10K405 are different types of annual report. Specifically the 10K is 'An annual report which provides a comprehensive overview of the company for the past year. The filing is due 90 days after the close of the company's fiscal year, and contains such information as company history, organization, nature of business, equity, holdings, earnings per share, subsidiaries, and other pertinent financial information'. The 10K405 is exactly the same, plus a technicality: 'An annual report which provides a comprehensive overview of the company for the past year. The Regulation S-K Item 405 box on the cover page is checked'.)

2 The concept of 'revenue recognition' – that is, when to recognize revenues and how much to recognize – has been the subject of discussion with regard to some internet firms. We discuss this in Appendix 3.1.

3 Accounting for acquisitions is in a state of some flux, and amortization of goodwill (which is a large part of the cost of an acquired building, corresponding to the purchase price minus historical value of the assets in the balance sheet of the acquired company) may be phased out – we discuss this in Appendix 3.1.

4 However, good operating leverage does not necessarily mean the company's stock is a good deal.

5 Regression adjusting for fixed and random effects using the SAS TSCSREG procedure.

6 UK accounting rules (UITF abstract 29, ASB) allows certain costs *after* the website planning phase to be taken gradually (that is, 'capitalized' – made into an asset – and then depreciated), provided the website is capable of generating revenues directly. Examples of costs which do not have to be expensed immediately are costs of registering a domain name, costs of purchasing software such as an e-commerce engine, and costs of designing and entering content for individual webpages. To allow capitalization, there must be a reasonable expectation that the cash flows from the website will exceed the money spent on developing it. Finally, depreciation timescales are 'likely to be short'.

US accounting rules (FASB EITF 00-2) are more restrictive, and specifically require that the cost of web-enabling existing databases and the inputting of content should be expensed as incurred. In both cases, the planning stage, which includes design, specification, selection of suppliers or scheduling of internal programmers, must be expensed.

7 Cheaptickets was acquired by Cendant in August 2001, subsequent to the period shown.

8 PricewaterhouseCoopers (1999), pp. 3005 section 3.26.

9 UK Accounting Standards Board: summary of FRS 10, published at http://www.asb.org.uk/publications/publication149.html (December 1998).

10 If the goodwill is regarded as having an indefinite life by the company and its auditors, then the company does not have to amortize and take an annual 'hit' against earnings. However, it does have to review the value of the goodwill by carrying out a periodic impairment review.

11 Kieso and Weygandt (1998), p. 158.

12 http://www.fortune.com/indexw.jhtml?channel=artcol.jhtml&doc_id=00001561.

CHAPTER 4

Establishing the Base Case Valuation for Amazon.com

THE STAGES OF THE VALUATION ANALYSIS

Table 4.1 Stages of valuation analysis

1	**CFA**	**Cash flow analysis**	*Chapter 4*
a	CCA	Continuing case analysis	Estimate the net present value of the firm if its current operating parameters persist
b	BCA	Best case analysis	Estimate the net present value of the firm if the operating parameters improve
c	WCA	Worst case analysis	Estimate the net present value of the firm if the operating parameters deteriorate
d	FCA	Funding crunch analysis	Study the cash flow projections to determine whether the firm will be able to raise sufficient funds to execute its plans
e	RoCEL	Return on Capital Limitation *Chapter 6*	Adjust the calculated cashflows to ensure that they do not impound an unreasonably large return on capital
2	**Other tools**		
a	ROA	Real options analysis *Chapter 8*	Determine what value (if any) exists from the optionality of the company's opportunity.
b	SA	Strategic analysis *Chapter 12*	Determine the strength of the company and its market opportunity: the product is a weighting of the three scenarios from CFA (i.e. percentage weightings for CCA, BCA, WCA).
c	DCA	Discontinuity analysis *Chapter 12*	Evaluate the historical accounting data on the firm, together with possible product market developments that may halt or retard growth or margin improvements, or otherwise introduce a discontinuity.

CASH-FLOW ANALYSIS: SETTING UP THE PROBLEM

The initial task, which absorbs most of the time of the valuer, is to construct a detailed cash flow model of the company for valuation purposes. As discussed at the beginning of Chapter 3, this is effectively a summarization and synthesis of the valuer's projections of revenue, costs and assets, informed by study of historical accounting statements. This is usually carried out using a commercially available spreadsheet program – most often Excel, but the leading programs all have a similar format and a similar method of working.

The building of the model is a four-stage process:

1. Tabulate and graph operating and financial data on past performance of the company to be valued and of comparable companies. Identify the key value drivers.
2. Estimate the value drivers for continuing, best, and worst cases.
3. Build a spreadsheet. Drive projections from estimates of the key value driver parameters.
4. Determine the net present value by weighting scenario values (Chapter 6).

Stages 1 and 2 are frequently combined, as it is logical to determine future operating parameters at the same time as studying past values.

We will use Amazon.com as an example.

STAGES 1 AND 2: TABULATION AND GRAPHING OF KEY OPERATING AND FINANCIAL PARAMETERS; ESTIMATION OF VALUE DRIVERS

The key data on operating and financial parameters come from the financial statements. For a company with such a short timescale as Amazon.com, quarterly reports must be used to make the most of the information available. There is one important caveat to using quarterly reports, which is 'seasonality'. *Seasonality* means that a company has seasonal variations in its revenues or profitability. In the case of Amazon the company has a peak period of revenues in the run-up to Christmas; other companies may have a peak at some other point (for example, an ice-cream company might do more business in the summer). If there is seasonality, the quarterly reports have to be processed bearing this in mind. As more information on internet companies becomes available as they mature, annual reports may increasingly be used, eliminating seasonality.[1]

The financial analysis drill is as follows:

1. chart revenue growth
2. chart the breakdown of costs as a percentage of revenues
3. chart the breakdown of assets as a percentage of revenues
4. examine comparable mature companies.

Step 1: Charting revenue growth

The purpose in charting revenue growth is to predict future revenues by devising a prediction *model* for the revenues. As mentioned in Chapter 2, there are five fundamental patterns for historical and future revenues:

1. *hypergrowth:* sustained extremely rapid revenue growth
2. *fast growth with decay:* extremely rapid but declining revenue growth – may decline exponentially or linearly
3. *product-release-led:* rapid revenue growth, especially rapid growth upon release of major products
4. *steady state/mature:* slow revenue growth or no growth or decline
5. *no pattern:* future revenues must be specifically predicted.

Before we start to look at the data, let us consider the general 'roadmap'. In its early years, Amazon.com's revenue growth had followed a clear pattern of fast growth with exponential decay, with seasonality (pattern 2). However, the company's growth has now decayed to low levels, and our forward projections will assume a steady state revenue growth pattern (pattern 4).

Seasonal patterns can be imposed upon any of the five revenue patterns. Therefore, before we distinguish between the patterns, we need to make a choice about the presentation of data. For revenue growth using quarterly financial statements, there are two methods of presentation:

- quarter-on-quarter revenue growth
- compare quarter revenue to year-ago quarter revenue.

The charts for each of these methods are shown below for 1997–2001. As can be seen, the quarter-on-quarter chart (Figure 4.1) shows clear evidence of seasonal variation in revenue growth.

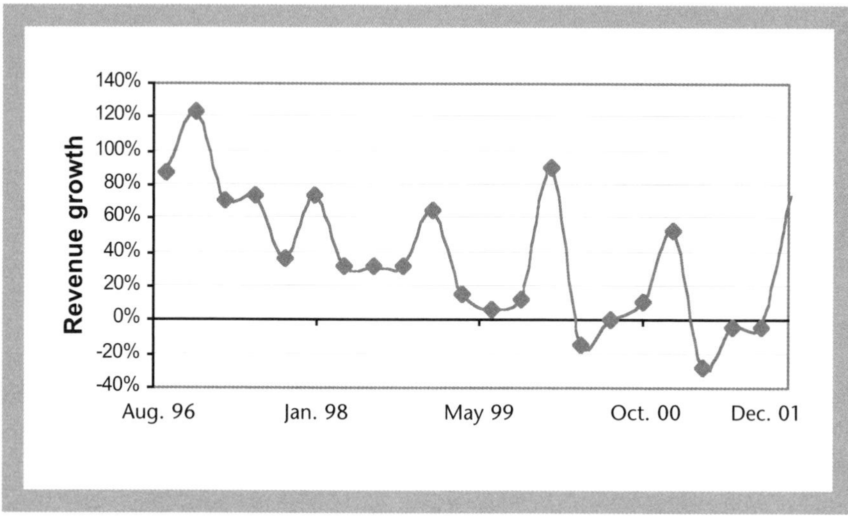

Figure 4.1 Revenue growth (quarter-on-quarter)

For analysis of trends in future revenue growth, it is more sensible to work with Figure 4.2, which mitigates the seasonality by comparing revenue growth this year with growth for the 'same season' last year.

Clearly, both graphs show that the general trend of revenue growth is downwards, and that the suitable pattern of revenue growth is fast but declining – that is, revenue pattern 2. Figure 4.2 data series is smoother but is not a linear series – that is, the revenue growth in Figure 4.2 does not decrease by a fixed amount each quarter. In attempting to analyse revenue growth of rapidly growing companies, the 'exponential decay' model is often useful. This is a subset of revenue pattern 2, fast growth with decay. If revenue growth decays exponentially, the revenue growth this quarter is the revenue growth last quarter *multiplied by* a constant (of less than 1). To illustrate, consider if revenue growth declined *linearly* by $x\%$ per quarter, t:

$$\text{revenue growth}_t = \text{revenue growth}_{t-1} - x\%$$

In this case the graph of revenue growth against time would be a declining straight line.

If revenue growth declines exponentially, the equation for revenue growth in quarter t as a function of revenue growth in quarter t–1 is as follows:

$$\text{revenue growth}_t = \text{revenue growth}_{t-1} \times y\%$$

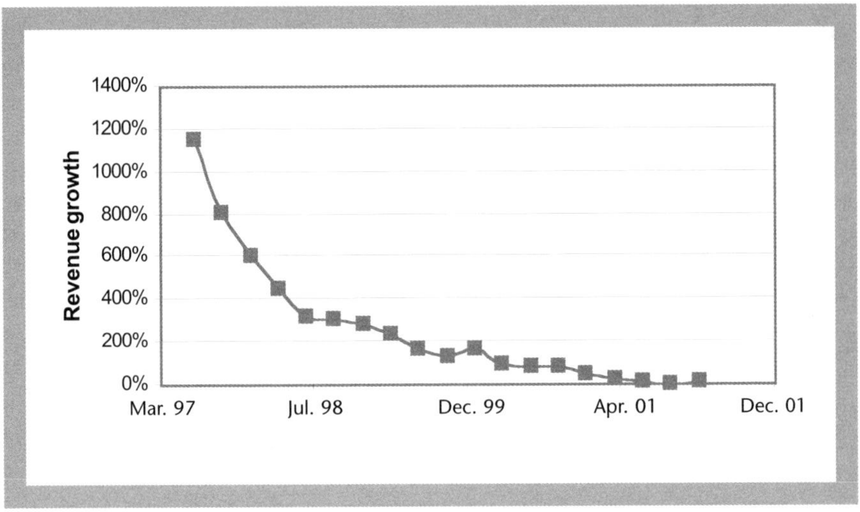

Figure 4.2 Revenue growth (quarter vs. 4 quarters ago)

The resulting graph is an exponential curve, similar to Figure 4.2. Recall that in both cases above, the revenue growth for period t is an annual revenue growth obtained by comparing revenue in quarter t with revenue in quarter t–4 (that is, revenue $\text{growth}_t = (\text{revenue}_t/\text{revenue}_{t-4}) - 1$).

In order to determine whether an exponential model is a suitable fit for the data, the logarithm of the growth figures should be plotted against time. If the exponential decay is a good fit, the log graph will be a declining straight line. We illustrate this with the graph of the log natural (Excel function LN(...)) of Amazon.com's quarterly revenue growth against time between 1997 and June 2001 (Figure 4.3).

A straight line has been superimposed on the chart using the TREND array function in Excel (see below). As can be seen, the exponential model for the decay of revenue growth is only a first approximation. However, the log graph demonstrates clearly the severe slowdown in the company's revenue growth, especially in the third quarter of 2001 (the slowdown in revenue growth in the last quarter of 2000 is partly due to the exceptional nature of Amazon's 1999Q4 growth). Note that what is declining is the *rate of change* of revenue growth (the 'second derivative' of revenue, in mathematical terms). Revenue is still increasing year on year, but the *rate* of increase is getting smaller. Although it is standard to project a constant rate of revenue growth for old-economy companies, we can predict a declining schedule of growth rates for internet companies, a constant rate of growth, or any ad hoc schedule of growth rates in between. For example, in the hypergrowth model an initial high rate of growth

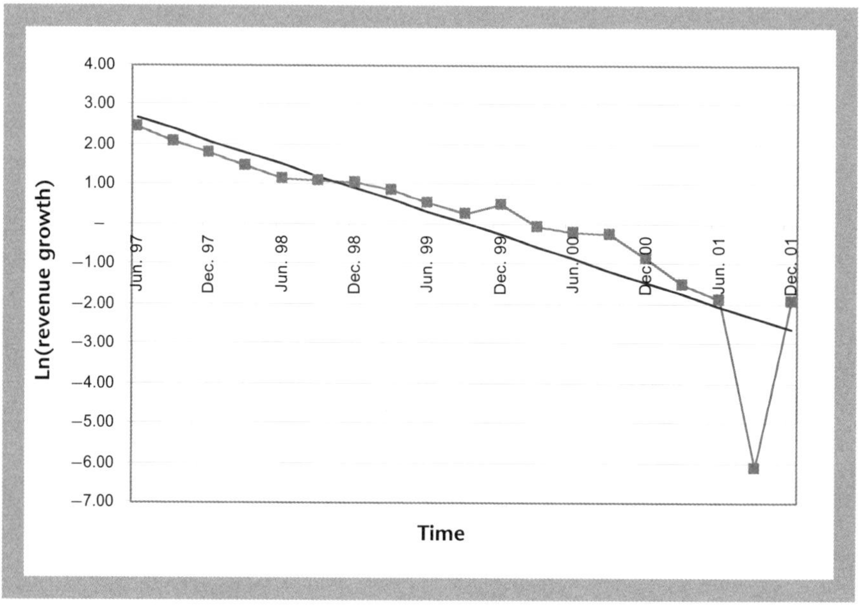

Figure 4.3 Ln(revenue growth) vs. time

can be projected for 1–2 years, then an exponentially decaying growth rate can be introduced. In the case of Amazon, historical revenue growth has followed an exponential decay pattern. The exponential decay pattern in this case has no theoretical or analytical backdrop, and should be viewed as a useful approximation rather than a 'law of nature' for high-growth firms. However, the pattern of declining revenue growth as a firm grows does reflect the frequently observed fact that rapid growth becomes more and more difficult to achieve as a company grows. The simplest illustration of this is that if Amazon.com sold one book on the first day of business, 100% growth was a matter of persuading two purchasers to buy one each the next day. Now 100% growth from annual revenues of $3–4bn is very difficult to achieve, especially if marketing spending is being cut back, and this is reflected in the slowing revenue growth.

If using the exponential decay model for revenue growth, we are required to estimate a rate of revenue decay. In order to dispense with the need to estimate visually a straight-line approximation to the logarithm graph, two Excel functions can be used: LINEST and LOGEST. If desiring to actually fit a line or curve to the data, the array functions TREND (for the (linear) log revenue growth data) or GROWTH (to fit to the raw revenue growth data (exponentially decaying)) are used. LINEST(range) outputs the gradient of a line whose values are stored in range. In this case, if the log graph shown above is processed using LINEST, the function outputs the rate of change in logarithm of growth each quarter (approximately –0.31). The mathematical constant e (approximately 2.718) raised to the power of –0.31 then gives the percentage decline in growth rate per quarter of approximately 27% (that is, each quarter's growth is approximately 73% of the last). The raising of e to the power –0.31 is achieved using the Excel function EXP(…), which can be viewed as the inverse of the natural logarithm. Alternatively, these two processes are combined in the LOGEST function. If LOGEST is applied to the range of growth rates (without taking the logarithm) it fits the best exponential decay line to the growth rate data, giving the 73% figure directly.

TREND and GROWTH are companion functions to LINEST and LOGEST, except that they are entered into a range of cells, and produce a fitted line or curve in those cells, which can then be plotted in the graph. For example, to fit a line which has *x* values (for example, dates) in range1 and *y* values (for example, logarithm of revenue growth) in range2, and to put the fitted values in range3:

1. highlight range3 with the cursor (the 'plus sign' shape in Excel)
2. with range3 highlighted, enter the formula '=TREND(range2,range1)'
3. hold down the CTRL and SHIFT keys, and press Enter.

(Note: range1, range2 and range3 must be the same size.)

The result of the analysis is the 73% quarter-on-quarter revenue growth decay rate. This can be used in two ways. It can be used to estimate quarterly revenues based on seasonal data, or to predict the future path of annual revenue growth. However, the prediction of quarterly data implies a spurious precision in the estimates. In order to use the revenue decay rate estimated from quarterly data for predicting annual revenue growth decay, we have to consider that if revenue growth decays to 0.73 of its previous level in one quarter, it will decay to 0.73×0.73 (0.53) times its previous level in two quarters, and so on. So the implied annual rate of revenue growth decay in this case is 0.73^4 or about 0.29. We can therefore see that the past data suggests that Amazon's revenue growth rate will decay quite quickly. Very inaccurate predictions of current revenues would have been obtained by assuming that a constant rate of revenue growth would persist from early in the company's life to today.

Note that although the use of an annual decay multiplier for revenue growth produces a declining rate of revenue growth, we have not analysed for discontinuities (DCA) as yet – that is, there may be discontinuities which either boost the company's revenues (logarithmic breakout) or cause an acceleration of revenue growth decay. As we can see, such a discontinuity has in fact intervened in Amazon.com's growth in the year 2001. This is the consumer economy slowdown, especially in the third quarter of 2001. Excluding the third quarter data (in which growth was negligible) the decay rate would be 40% per year. Other possible discontinuities include a decision by Amazon to focus only on books, music and videos.[2] This would cause a one-time fall in revenue, and a future path of fairly slow revenue growth. The revenue decay model (exponential) assumes a continuous world, but builds in the fact that growth becomes more difficult as a company gets bigger.

Let us consider how closely the exponential model would have predicted recent revenues compared to a constant revenue growth assumption. For example in 1997 the company achieved revenue of $147.8, representing revenue growth of 838% over 1996. In Table 4.2 we compare the performance of constant revenue growth and decaying revenue growth in predicting true revenues (40% revenue growth decay factor, excluding 2001Q3 data to exclude the effects of the discontinuity (consumer economy slowdown)).

In the first case, revenues grow at 838% per year, and Amazon would have become 'the new Wal-Mart'! But such consistent hypergrowth is impossible. Even successful and flourishing companies (such as Wal-Mart or Microsoft) can achieve consistent growth of no more than 25–30% over several years. The revenue decay model gives a more reasonable estimate which turns out to have been closer to the true outcome for these pre-discontinuity numbers. In line 2, revenue growth in 1998 is $0.4 \times 838\% = 335\%$, and so on. However, the calculation of the revenue decay rate of 40% required all the data from 1997 to second quarter 2001. Let us consider a modeller who knows only the growth for 1996–97 and 1995–96 (1995 revenues ($0.511m) and 1996 revenues ($15.746m) – both of which are pre-IPO – can be obtained from the company's S-1 registration statement or prospectus). The 1995–96 growth rate was 2980% and the 1996–97 growth rate was 838% as discussed, suggesting a decay rate of 28%. This gives the third line of projections. It is less accurate than line 2, but gives the correct order of magnitude for the 2000 revenue of Amazon.com, unlike the constant revenue growth model.

Table 4.2 Amazon.com: comparison of prediction methods

	1997	1998	1999	2000
Constant revenue growth	147,758	1,386,538	13,011,055	122,093,706
Decaying revenue growth	147,758	643,270	1,506,162	2,314,317
Decay (using only 1995–97 data)	147,758	496,108	963,952	1,327,565
Actuals	147,758	609,996	1,639,839	2,761,983

The final element of the data which should be included is analysts' predictions and/or management forecasts of current and near-term revenues. In the news release announcing 4th quarter 2001 results (22 January 2002) Amazon.com's management stated that 'Net sales are expected to grow by 10% or more'. Morgan Stanley (Meeker, 2002) predicted \$3.5bn revenues for 2002 (12% growth). This is in comparison to the full year growth between 2000 and 2001 of 13%.

Going forward, a continuation of the current revenue decay rate would suggest a revenue growth rate falling quickly to close to zero. However, possible scenarios for the future are partly dependent on management action and partly dependent on the progress of the US economy. Management can target growth, or it can target cost cutting, which would mean less spending on marketing and a more stringent pricing policy. A company can always grow quickly by 'selling a dollar for 99¢' (that is, selling the product below cost); selling at 'economic' prices (that is, selling at prices at which the company can make money) will inevitably lead to slower growth, as consumer demand is decreasing in price for normal goods. *Gross margin* (sales minus cost of goods sold, as a percentage of sales) is a high-level indicator of pricing policy. On the other hand, changes in the rate of economic growth, either increases or decreases, can take matters out of management's hands to some extent. These *macroeconomic effects* are overlaid on the firm's strategy.

The revenue history (together with the charts of gross margin that we show below) makes it clear that Amazon.com is currently becoming a mature company, or at the very least is currently in a phase where it looks like a mature company, with relatively modest or even negative growth while it concentrates on achieving profitability.

However, there is one variable which management have control over which we have not yet considered. This is choice of *product lines*. Consider the product line breakdown for 2001 (Table 4.3). Going forward we see three strategic options for Amazon.com, in order of decreasing size of the company

Table 4.3 Amazon.com: product lines

Product line	Sales (%)	Segment margin (%)	Growth 2000–2001 (%)
US books, music, video (BMDV)	54.1	8	–1
Electronics, tools, kitchen (ETK)	17.5	–35	13
Services	7.2	15	13
International sales	21.2	–21	74

Table 4.4 Amazon.com: strategic options

Strategic option	Effect	Future revenue growth
1. Steady as she goes	Continue presence in current markets	5–15% revenue growth
2. Focus on US market	Sell or close international businesses	Initial one-time decline of 20% in revenue, then growth of 0–10%
3. Focus on BMDV	Sell or close international businesses; close all US retail businesses except books, music and DVD/video (BMDV); maintain services product line	Initial one-time decline of 35–40%, then revenue growth of 0–5% (declining)

(Table 4.4). For the moment we will concentrate on option 1, although we feel that options 2 and 3 are likely to be exercising the mind of management. The key decision criteria for management will be the price obtainable for the international businesses (probably somewhere between 0.5× and 1.5× sales revenue), and how much of the cost of the non-BMDV US retail businesses is actually avoidable if these parts of the business are closed down. Although segment profitability of BMDV is healthy at +9%, this does not mean that Amazon could instantly transform itself into a company making profits of $157m[3] by closing its other businesses. First, there would be large one-off costs of closure. Second, the segment profit figures include some allocation of costs which are shared among business areas. Consider the cost of the head office corporate management function. At present the cost of this function is allocated (perhaps in proportion to sales) to the different business areas: however, were international and ETK to be closed, much of this cost would still persist and still go to the bottom line, with the central costs being allocated over a smaller revenue base.

For the product lines of Amazon we project growth in line with growth forecasts of the company and analysts. Revenue growth of 12% is therefore projected as a continuing case (CCA) under the assumption of continuation of current strategy. For a best case (BCA) we look towards the performance of best-practice companies in the same industry. It is for this reason that the accounts of Wal-Mart and Target, two leading US retailers, were included in the case notes. It can be seen that Wal-Mart has the highest sustained sales growth, achieving impressive rates of 15–20% per year. For the worst case analysis (WCA), we use growth forecasts of the company's main marketplaces, as shown in the case study (5–7%) and more pessimistic margin assumptions, using a technique called *return on capital limitation* (*RoCEL*), which models the process of competition by limiting the return on capital employed that the internet firm makes. RoCEL is also used to place an upper limit on the best case, for reasons that will become clear. RoCEL is discussed further in Chapter 6, and also later in this chapter.

Step 2: Charting costs as a percentage of revenues

Continuing the process of financial analysis which forms the first part of CFA (cash-flow analysis), we now analyse the costs that the company incurs over time. We benchmark these initially as a percentage of sales, and then compare them to other best-practice firms to derive BCA (best case analysis) cost values. Just looking at a total cost figure may be interesting in some limited cases (for example, if costs are entirely fixed), but in general it is far more instructive to look at costs as a percentage of sales as a first step in analysis. This gives us the opportunity to compare companies of different sizes in a simple way. Key profitability parameters also come out of this analysis:

- *gross margin* = (sales – cost of goods sold)/sales = gross profit/sales
- *operating margin* = operating profit/sales
- *net margin* = after tax earnings/sales.

Let us look at the chart of Amazon's cost performance over the years since inception (Figure 4.4). This cost breakdown shows that the company's cost parameters have been trending down since end 1999.

Cost of goods sold (COGS) is interesting for two reasons. First of all, it is of interest from the cost perspective. Second, it is interesting from the pricing perspective, as it gives us some insight into whether the business is prioritizing growth-at-all-costs or whether it is prioritizing profitability. See Figure 4.5. Clearly, the company achieved a step change in gross margin between the pre-December 1999 and the post-September 2000 periods, moving from an average of about 21% to an average of about 25%. (The gross margin in the fourth quarter of 1999 was affected by an inventory writedown of $39m (6% of quarterly revenues).) As mentioned above, the gross margin figure for Amazon is not strictly comparable with some other companies' gross margins, because the company does not include fulfilment expenses in its cost of goods sold but states this as a part of SG&A costs.

Let us summarize the Amazon.com cost data for the fiscal year 2001 as a percentage of sales (Table 4.5). If this cost data persists, with costs summing to 101.4%, the company will never make any profits and will have no value.

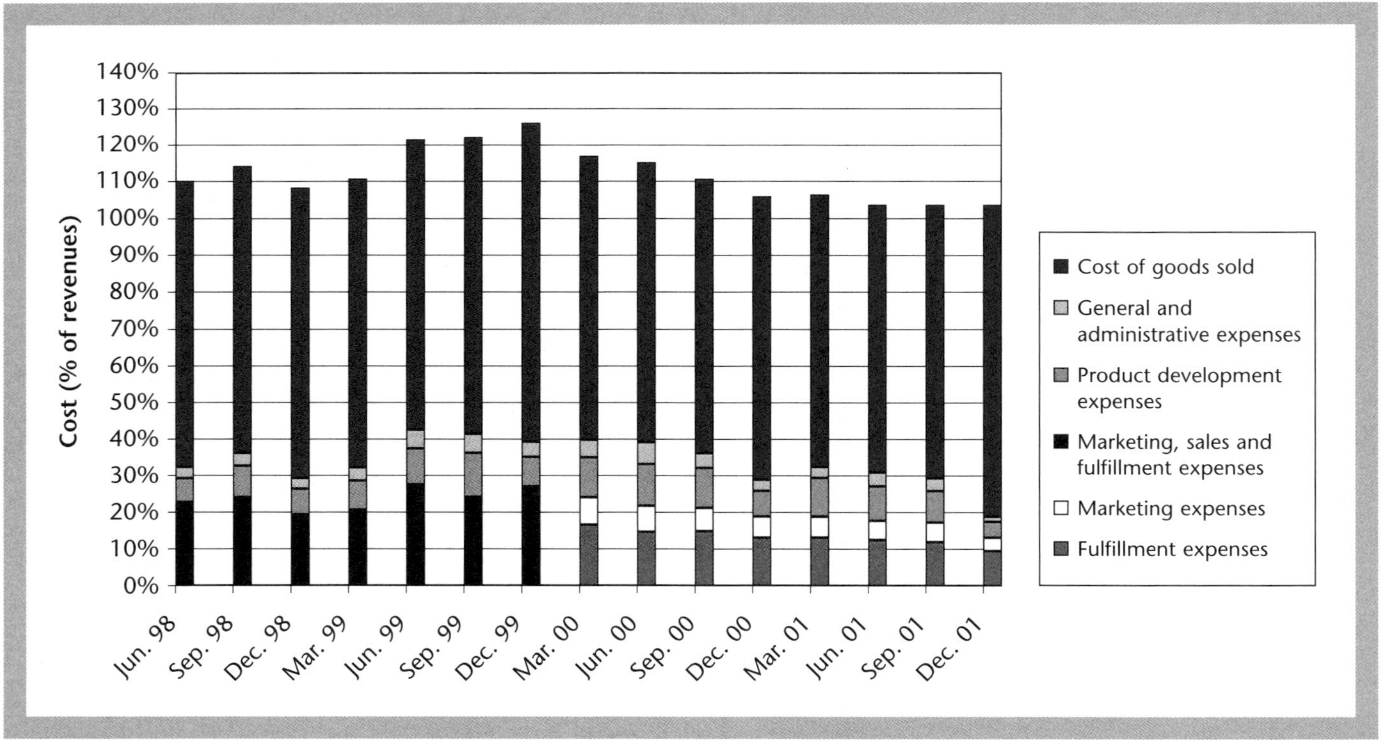

Figure 4.4 Amazon.com: cost breakdown

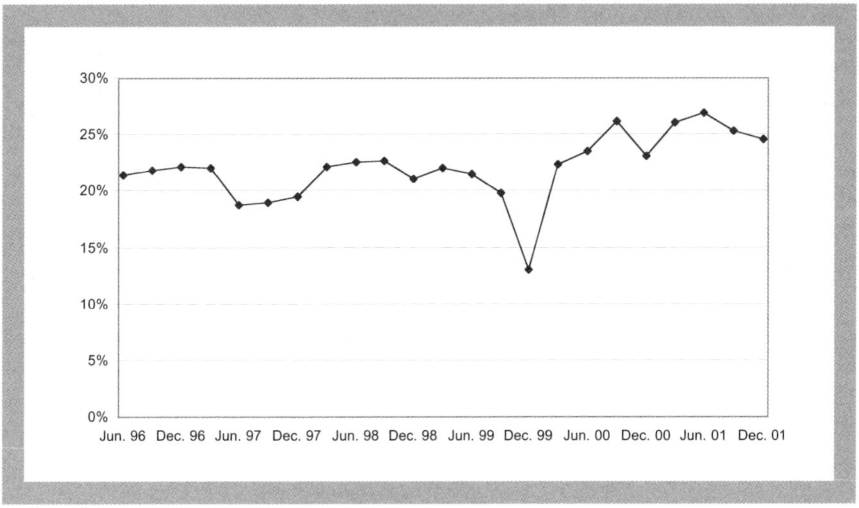

Figure 4.5 Amazon.com: gross margin

However, it is future costs, not past costs, that we are concerned about. Can we project costs forward, and simulate the operating leverage that we discussed in the previous chapter? We are seeking a simple equation that predicts costs as a function of revenues, of this form:

$$\text{costs} = c \times \text{revenues} + F$$

where c = variable proportion of revenues as a percentage of revenues
F = fixed cost.

Simulation of this equation is not a problem: Excel can easily cope with such a formula, but calculating the parameters c and F is more problematic. There are two ways of predicting the values: using past data and using account analysis. We can carry out regression analysis of past data, and this will show us the relationships between fixed and variable cost that are suggested from past data. *Account analysis* is a process of evaluating types of cost and predicting at a headline level how much of each cost is likely to be fixed and how much is likely to be variable.

Moving to the first method, the simplest method of analysis of costs is a chronological plot of costs against revenues (Figure 4.6). This will give us a simple idea of the pattern of costs.

We can see from Figure 4.6 that costs naturally rise with revenues as the process of building the business takes place. If we run a regression analysis (in

Table 4.5 Amazon.com: costs as a percentage of sales

Net sales	100%
Cost of sales	74.4%
Gross profit	25.6%
Fulfilment expenses	12%
Marketing expenses	4.4%
Product development expenses	7.7%
General and administrative expenses	2.9%

Excel, Tools menu: Data Analysis: Regression) of all the available data we get the following suggested relationship:

quarterly costs = 1.04 × revenues + \$19.2m

This means that variable costs are 104% of revenues: in other words, the company has a contribution margin of *negative* 4%. A negative contribution margin of 4% means that for each incremental dollar of revenue, the company loses an extra 4 cents. However, the problem with using past data is that the company was growing for most of this time. As valuers, what we would really like is for the company to freeze its business operations and allow us to observe costs as revenues rise, on the basis of that constant set of business

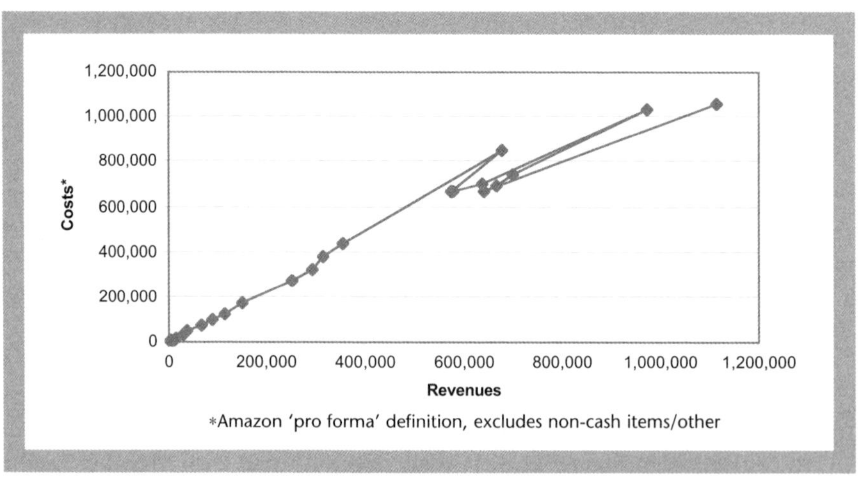

Figure 4.6 Costs vs. revenues

operations. Clearly, no business, in particular no growing business, is likely to operate within such restricted assumptions just for our benefit! Let us look for a period where the firm's activities were fairly static. For example, if we zoom in on the calendar year 2000, we can see that incremental costs and revenues between March 2000 and December 2000[4] have the following relationship:

$$\text{quarterly costs} = 0.9 \times \text{revenues} + \$146\text{m}$$

The situation is complex, because over the period we observe the company has rapidly expanded costs and the reach of the business, and then somewhat decreased the size of the business in 2001. For this reason we should also consider the account analysis method of analysing costs, which classifies costs as fixed, variable, or mixed, depending on the elements of those costs (Table 4.6).

The reasoning behind these judgements (which are unavoidably approximations) is as follows:

- Cost of sales is the cost of the merchandise Amazon.com is selling. These are largely a variable cost, because each sale requires the purchase of goods to fulfil the customer's order (as revenues increase there will be some benefit to the company in terms of more attractive purchase terms).
- Fulfilment expenses will also be mostly variable, because the picking and packing activity is driven by volume.
- Marketing expenses will be partly fixed and partly variable. Promotional spending on near-term advertising can lead to increased revenue, so appears variable. We will assume this to be 50/50 fixed/variable. (Amazon's accounting policy is to net off promotional coupons against sales, rather than to report these as a marketing cost.)

Table 4.6 Cost classification: results of accounts analysis method

	Revenues (%)	Fixed/variable/mixed?
Cost of sales	74.4	Variable
Fulfilment expenses	12	Variable
Marketing expenses	4.4	Mixed
Product development expenses	7.7	Mixed
General and administrative expenses	2.9	Fixed

- The company has cut back on product development expenses in recent periods (as on other costs) but, in particular if the company needs to generate growth, these costs may have to rise to create new storefronts and features. Amazon's ability to open eight new stores in 2001 (see Table 2.1) without increasing technology and content spend suggests that this expense is largely fixed, and that the past spend provides a solid platform. We therefore assume that this cost is 75% fixed, 25% variable.
- General and administrative expenses are largely fixed: this head office and other management activity is a constant need for a company, and a company does not need to increase its management cadre simply because revenues rise.

As mentioned above, these judgements will be approximations. For example, although fulfilment costs are largely variable, there will be an element of fixed cost, because Amazon.com has built a large distribution centre network which can handle larger volumes than the company currently has. There will also be a variable element of cost in general and administrative expenses, as slightly more central management resources are needed to handle a large business.

By the account analysis method we have the following equation:

$$\text{annual costs} = 0.905 \times \text{revenues} + \$339.9\text{m}$$

where $339.9m is the actual spending on general and administrative plus product development (75%) plus marketing (half) for full year 2001.

The account analysis method gives similar results to the regression method over the 2000 period, which was a period in which analysis was made easier by the slow steady growth in that brief period. We therefore feel confident in using this equation for the cost function, because it combines an approximately 90% variable cost rate which is agreed upon by the two methods, and because it used the latest available total spending for the fixed costs elements. Once we have this equation, cost data directly follow from revenue growth data, which we have already postulated above. Therefore cost data can be projected as a function of revenues, at the model-building stage.

Finally, looking at the previous charts, we see that the company has made some progress in reducing costs. Fulfilment cost, according to the case, troughed at 10% of sales. Currently values for this quantity seem to be falling to about that level (part of this projected efficiency gain might come from enhanced gross margin also). Let us assume that level going forward. This adjusts our equation to:

annual costs = 0.875 × revenues + $339.9

For the worst-case scenario, we will assume no improvement in cost structure.

Readers may ask: what is a 'typical' proportion of costs which are variable versus those which are fixed? There is no *typical* value, because operating leverage varies between firms. However, as we discussed in the previous chapter, the average value for variable costs as a percentage of sales is 85–90% (depending on time period), meaning that nearly all costs are variable according to past data. Bearing in mind that the time period examined (1975–98) may be an atypical period, in which companies engaged in profitable growth which skewed the variable percentage of costs, this does give a clear message that the effect of operating leverage should be assumed to be small.

Step 3: Charting asset needs as a percentage of revenues

Concluding the process of financial analysis which forms the first part of CFA (cash-flow analysis), we now analyse the asset requirements for the company. This is important for CFA because, if a company wishes to increase its operating assets from period to period, this will require cash just as surely as if costs increase. So we have to project these asset needs for the future. It is worth noting that in some exceptional (and usually temporary) circumstances, companies can generate cash from their balance sheet simply by increasing sales, if they have a very efficient capital structure. This means that the company has more favourable payment terms with suppliers than it gives to its customers, and therefore generates cash from working capital. It also means that the company does not require a large amount of other operating assets apart from working capital.

Amazon.com has the potential to be in this position, because it receives payment for goods from its customers immediately via their credit cards, but has fairly standard commercial payment terms with suppliers, perhaps 30-day payment terms. Since the company also has quite modest needs for fixed assets such as buildings (in contrast to the company's bricks and mortar competitors), it has the potential to generate cash from its operating assets.

Once again, to ensure that we have a built-in benchmark and basis for comparison across companies, we chart the operating asset needs as a percentage of revenues. Figure 4.7 shows the asset requirements of the business in terms of the two main parts of the asset requirements, which are tangible fixed assets and inventories, and also the minor elements, other current assets (OCA) and other assets (OA). Tangible fixed assets averaged 15% of sales in 2000, but declined to 9–11% of sales in 2001. However, this was partially due to an accounting adjustment as well as to increased revenues.

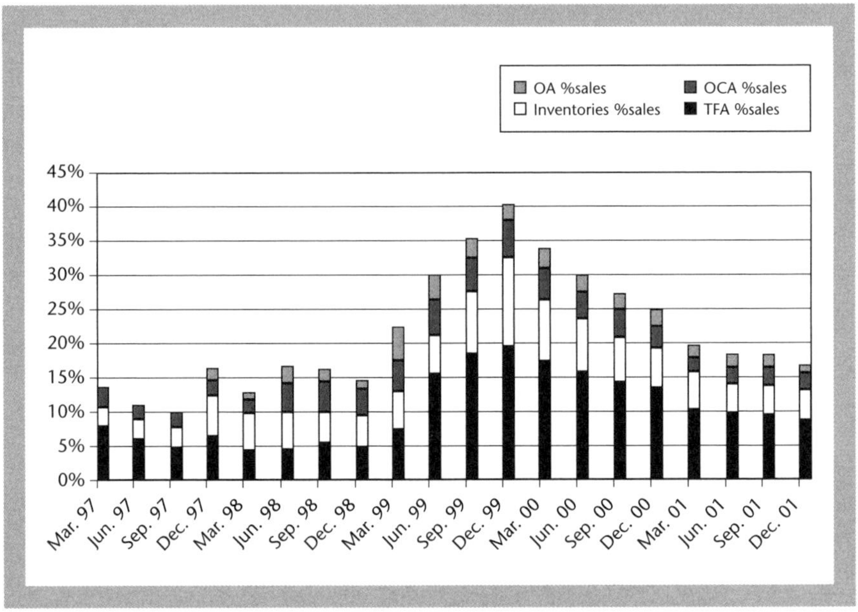

Figure 4.7 Amazon.com: assets as % of revenues

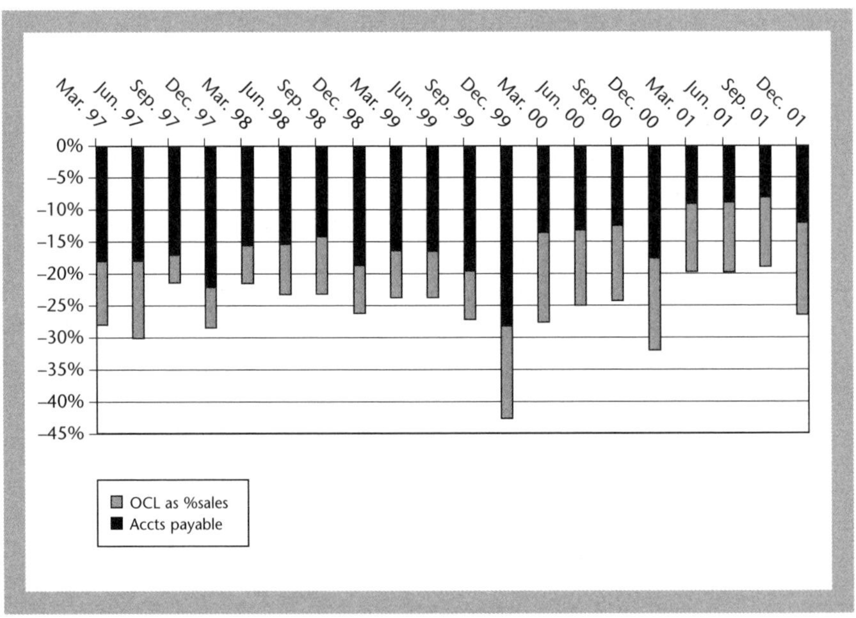

Figure 4.8 Amazon.com: operating liabilities as % of revenues

The company closed one distribution facility and two customer service centres, and curtailed and rationalized other operations. As a result of this balance sheet assets were decreased by $59m (2% of annualized sales) to reflect the permanent decline in asset value at this point.

Figure 4.8 shows the other side of the coin, the non-interest-bearing liabilities that the company takes on in the course of its day-to-day operations. Because these liabilities, such as money owed to suppliers, do not bear interest, they are sometimes described as 'free financing'. It is likely that suppliers do implicitly price in some cost of capital for what is effectively a loan to the buyer, but this method of financing the business has advantages. The graph also shows a declining trend in operating liabilities, but not as steep as for operating assets. The net effect is shown in Figure 4.9, where net assets are close to zero. This is seen as a conservative (low) estimate of net assets, because assets in investee companies and assets in acquired companies are not included in the calculation. Remember that past cash flows invested in other companies are not important: we have to assess whether Amazon can achieve the projected growth *without* future investments of this type. Since the base case is for quite modest growth, this is likely to be a reasonable assumption.

Looking at the above chart, we can see that Amazon had a period, up to December 1998, where it was exhibiting a very attractive operating asset dynamic, a very efficient 'working capital' structure. (*Working capital* is defined as inventory minus accounts payable (plus accounts receivable, which is negli-

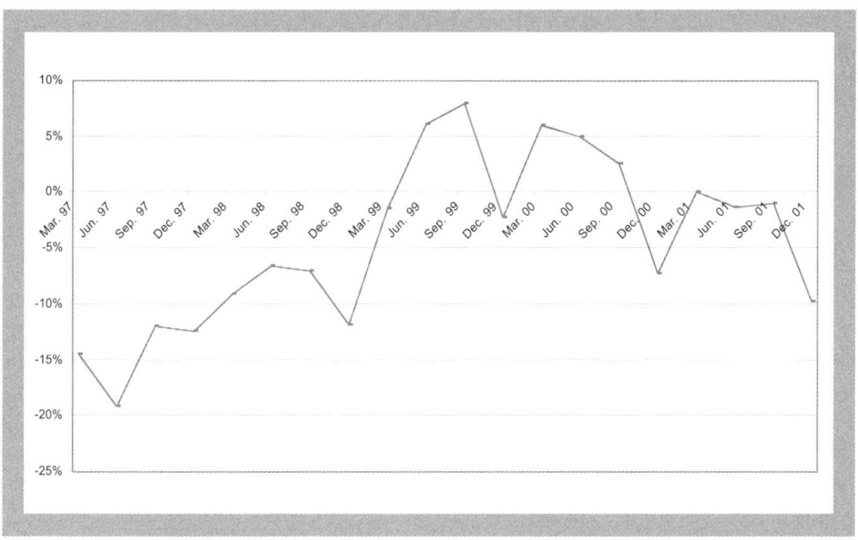

Figure 4.9 Amazon.com: net assets (conservative)

gible in this case).) This was a result of the company's original business model, to act as a cross-docking waystation for goods rather than as a holder of inventory. The company was originally located in Seattle near a large book wholesaler, to optimize the process. However, during 1999 the company altered its business model to hold more inventory and to build a series of distribution centres. These distribution centres were rented (operating lease) rather than owned outright, which means that the land and buildings component of the centres does not appear on the company's balance sheet, but the rental or lease cost is subtracted within the income statement. This coincided with the large increase in tangible assets that can be seen in the accounting statements and in Figure 4.9, presumably partly as a result of non-leased equipment and fittings in the distribution centres and partly because of other expansions. The company has reported (as quoted in the case) that its distribution network will give the company the capacity to ship $10bn of merchandise annually. This is reflected in the fact that the tangible fixed assets have fallen as a percentage of revenues over time.

With this evidence in mind, what is the likely outlook? First of all, let us state that there is nothing mysterious or even particularly interesting about a negative operating assets business. Such businesses have existed for quite some years in the form of traditional retailers and the extreme case of journal publishers. Both of these types of businesses are 'old economy' but have favourable working capital dynamics: they receive money from customers before they have to pay suppliers, and in the interim they can invest that money or use it to fund their businesses. The journal publisher is an extreme case because journal customers generally pay for subscriptions one year in advance, but the publisher only needs to pay for and produce the journals over the course of the whole year. DCF analysis is fully able to estimate the value of businesses like this. Increasing revenues lead to a slow but steady cash-flow benefit to the business, which is generally of modest value but should be included in the DCF.

Whether operating assets as a percentage of sales are positive or negative, the cash flow that results is simply calculated as:

$$\text{asset cash flow} = \text{asset percentage} \times (\text{sales}_{t-1} - \text{sales}_t)$$

In other words, in the more normal case where operating assets as a percentage of sales are positive, an increase in revenues ($\text{sales}_{t-1} - \text{sales}_t < 0$) should lead to a negative cash flow. This follows from the fact that year t–1 assets are asset percentage × sales_{t-1}, whereas year t assets are asset percentage × sales_t. The difference between the two asset figures is what must be funded.

If the company has negative operating assets, a positive cash flow will result from growth. This cash flow can be present-valued over several years by

Table 4.7 Amazon.com: detailed changes in cash 2001 Q1–Q4

Cash flows from changes in	2001 Q1 ($)	2001 Q2 ($)	2001 Q3 ($)	2001 Q4 ($)	Total ($)
Inventories	19,823	25,277	–659	–13,813	30,628
Prepaid expenses and other current assets	27,334	–12,203	2,960	2,641	20,732
Accounts payable	–229,758	–1,632	–22,594	209,546	–44,438
Accrued expenses and other current liabilities	–57,762	52,271	–9,721	65,243	50,031
Cash 'freed up' from balance sheet	–240,363	63,713	–30,014	263,617	56,953
Purchases of fixed assets	–19,437	–10,425	–12,925	–7,534	–50,321
Net cash from operating assets	–259,800	53,288	–42,939	256,083	–6,632

projecting revenue and asset data forward in time. An example of this is shown when we discuss the cashflow.com report in Chapter 9.

For Amazon.com, it seems most sensible to assume that the company will be able to fund operating asset needs from its attractive working capital dynamic. In other words, we project forward operating assets at 0% of revenues. As a sense check let us see how the company has performed in terms of funding its asset needs over the past four quarters, using the quarterly cash-flow statements[5] (Table 4.7).

Note the large negative cash flow in the first quarter of 2001 as the company pays its suppliers for the products sold in its peak Christmas season. This analysis confirms that the company generated only very small cash flows from operating assets in 2001 (about 0.2% of 2001 revenues). This does not mean to say that operating asset cash needs or inflows may not become important in the future, but it means that in the near term the company is likely to stand or fall based on its profitability.

Step 4: Evaluate comparable mature companies

Note also that at this stage the comparable companies should be studied. Comparable retailers' accounts, together with financial analysis of the data such as Dupont decomposition, are included in the case study data. These can be examined to evaluate long-term margins, cost of capital and achievable revenue growth in the longer term.

Table 4.8 Amazon.com: summary of value drivers

	Continuing case (CCA)	Best case (BCA)	Worst case (WCA)
Revenue growth	12%	20%	7%
Variable costs as % of sales	88.5%	88.5%	90.5%
Fixed costs	$340m	$340m	$340m
Operating assets as % of sales	0%	0%	0%
RoCEL [see Chapter 6]	30%	30%	15%

Summarizing the value drivers for CFA

See Table 4.8.

STAGE 3: BUILDING THE SPREADSHEET MODEL

The first part of building the model is planning the overall structure of the spreadsheet. In designing the structure of the spreadsheet, we should have four aims in mind, in order of importance:

1. ease of calculation of value scenarios
2. ease of updating company financial data over time
3. attractive presentation to colleagues and customers
4. exchangeability of data with colleagues.

The first and second aims are best achieved by having a modular structure to the spreadsheet (see Figure 4.10).

The blocks are as follows:

- *Parameters block:* Stores the key value drivers, such as revenue growth, cost of capital, cost as percentage of revenues, and fixed/variable cost mix. The output of value from the model should be stored in the parameters block, since this is the block where the valuer will be editing while running sensitivity analyses, and this juxtaposition aids ease of reference.
- *Past data block:* Stores information on the most recent accounts of the company. These help calculate the initial values for financial items in the

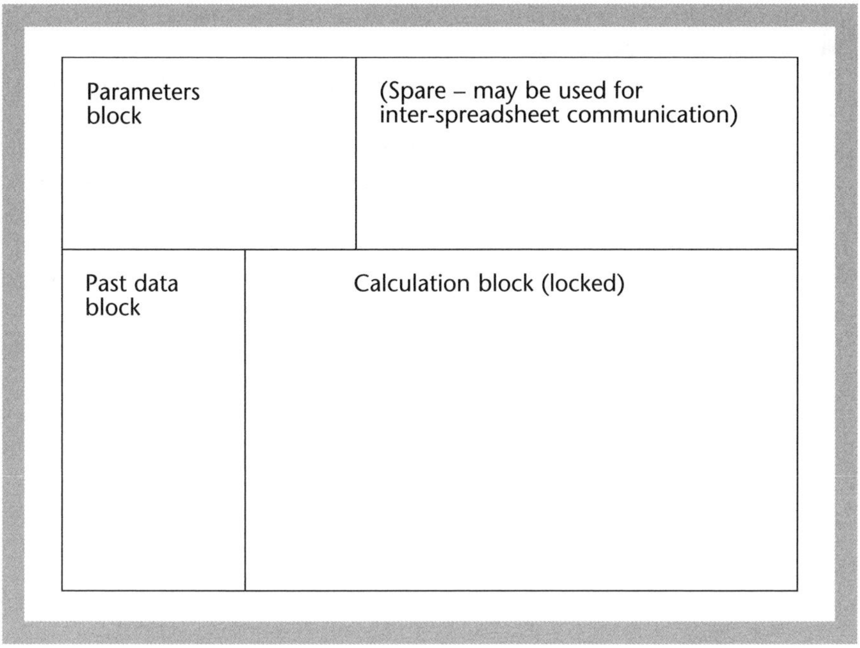

Figure 4.10 The modular structure of the spreadsheet

model, and provide a ready reference for comparing past performance with projected performance.

- *Calculation block:* This block stores the formulae used for calculating the cash flows, which will then be present-valued to estimate value. Often the model also includes formulae to output a projected income statement, a balance sheet and a cash-flow statement.

The calculation block should consist of formulae driven by the parameters in the parameter block (such as the revenue growth rate) and the past data in the past data block (such as the last year's revenue). There should be no need to alter any formulae in the calculation block when running a new estimate of value based on new parameters (although the block will need to be changed if the calculation *method* is changed). In Excel the block can be formally locked by using the sequence: Format menu, Format cells, Protection command. This is a two-stage process, and when the worksheet is finished the Tools, Protection, Protect Sheet command should be used, which activates the protection. Alternatively, if the spreadsheet is to be used only by one person, the user may wish to dispense with the protection process but to have a 'mental protection' in place on the calculation block.

The modular design also assists in quality of presentation. The final issue, of compatibility and communication, is the most complex. This is most relevant in a professional setting, such as an investment bank. If possible, formats should be agreed between professionals in the same firm, so that data can be shared and so that a comprehensive database can be built which can be sold as a benefit for customers and used by the firm's in-house economics and strategy analysts. In the event that agreement cannot be reached (or imposed), the spare block can be used to extract outputs from the Excel Model (such as eps (earnings per share) forecasts, revenue forecasts and so on), and this can then be accessed by a summarizing model held on the server. This method then allows professionals to choose the format of their model, as long as they supply some fixed parameters to the firm's database. Further details of this application are beyond the scope of this book.

We now move to the step-by-step building of the spreadsheet. Please note that, for flexibility and to allow labelling, *row 1 and column A of the spreadsheet are left entirely blank.*

The parameters block

Reserve cells A1:M30 for the parameters block. Lines which are not required can be hidden, but it is desirable to avoid moving or inserting cells, especially if other workbooks are to be linked. Then type in the parameter values, clearly labelled. The parameters section will look something like Figure 4.11.

Lines 5–10 include the parameters from the table summarizing the CFA value drivers. For presentation purposes we have split up our variable costs (88.5%) into cost of sales (74.4% of sales, giving a 25.6% gross margin) and other costs (14.1% of sales, giving a total variable cost of 88.5% as intended). Presentation purposes, and compatibility with past balance sheets, also led us to split up the operating assets into tangible assets (+10% of sales) and working capital (–10%): however the net operating assets remain zero.

There are five groups of parameters that we have not discussed above. The first parameter, the two values for opening and closing cost of capital, is calculated using the CAPM method as discussed in Chapter 1. The initial value is calculated using a β of 1.8 from Bloomberg.com, a risk-free rate of 4%, and a market risk premium of 5%. The final value assumes a decrease in volatility of the firm to just above market levels.[6] We discuss choice of calculation method for cost of capital in Chapter 5.

The second parameter, the coupon rate on debt, enables us to calculate interest on debt outstanding. 6.75% is the coupon on Amazon's highest coupon

Figure 4.11 Parameters block

	B	C
2	Amazon.com Valuation Forecast ($m)	
3		
4	Parameters	
5	Revenue growth	12%
6	COGS	74.4%
7	Other variable costs	14.1%
8	Fixed costs (SGA) ($)	339.9
9	Tangible fixed assets	10%
10	Operating assets/liabilities (net)	-10%
11	Cost of capital (init)	13%
12	Cost of capital (final)	10%
13	Coupon on debt	8.00%
14	Tax rate	35%
15	NOLs (init)	2,300
16	Terminal growth rate	4%
17	Terminal CF multiple	16.67

debt. In order to evaluate the interest payment over the year we would ideally average the beginning and ending debt values (to get the average debt for the year), and multiply by the coupon rate. However, the ending debt in each year is calculated by the model, so it cannot 'feed back' into the early part of the model – this would constitute a *circular reference*. Therefore we adjusted the rate on debt to 8% to give a smooth progression between the historical and projected (historical data for 1999–2001 shows average interest expense of 7.7% of year average debt).

The tax rate is, we hope, self-explanatory. It is the percentage rate of taxation on taxable profits of the company.

The fourth parameter is net operating loss (NOL) carry-forwards. We briefly discussed the issue of NOLs for tax purposes in Chapter 3. These are past losses that protect the company from paying tax until it has accumulated a profit equal to those past losses. This has to be factored into the valuation model. There were $2.3bn of NOLs at end 2001 according to the 2001 10K.

We project forward the first 10 years of the company's future. The rationale for a limited projection is that our ability to judge the reasonableness of the operating parameters going forward decreases the further into the future we go. However, provided the business is still a going concern in 2012 (the extra year is projected to allow the correct calculation of the perpetuity),[7] it will clearly have some ongoing value. The terminal growth rate and the terminal multiplier enable us to calculate that value. The terminal multiplier is the numerical multiplier used to multiply the 2011 cash flow to calculate the value in 2011. Think of this as a 'rule of thumb' estimate of what the business will be worth in 2011. This value is then discounted back to the present day.

The terminal value multiplier is calculated using a formula called the Gordon growth or Williams growth formula (or simply the growing perpetuity formula). This formula gives the value of an infinite series of cash flows C,[8] growing at rate g, with cost of capital r. The formula is as follows:

$$V = \frac{C}{r-g}$$

This formula is calculated in cell C17, using the growth rate in cell C16 and the ending cost of capital (appropriate to 2011) in cell C12 (cell C17: '=1/(C12-C16)'). We discuss this formula and its pitfalls in more detail in Chapter 9. Since this formula assumes an infinite series of cash flows it is important to be conservative in using it. Note that the formula is increasing in C (the cash flow) and in g (the rate of growth). The $g = 4\%$ used is equivalent to accepted values for the long-term growth rate of a mature economy. A value of g higher than this value is inadvisable, because it suggests that the business will grow faster than the economy *forever*, thus dominating the economy. Alternative numerical solutions can explain any value of the multiplier as a combination of fast initial growth and slower perpetual growth. This is discussed in Chapter 9.

The past data block

The next step is to complete the past data block of the spreadsheet. This may consist of one year only (the most recent year), or the valuer may want to have more past data at his or her fingertips in the model. This is presented in the format decided by the valuer, and does not have to follow the format in the company's statements, but should instead be consistent with the format of the model. The most important number in this block is the last year revenue, which is the driver for most of the model; together with other quantities that drive the remainder of the model, such as the opening equity and the opening net debt. The past data section may look like Figure 4.12.

As a convention, all costs and negative cash flows are shown as negative numbers. Payables/OCL is a special case, being a liability. It is shown as

Figure 4.12 The past data block

	B	C	D	E	F	G	H
32				1998	1999	2000	2001
33	INCOME STATEMENT						
34		2000	2001				
35	TOTAL SALES	/sales	/sales	610	1640	2762	3112.433
36	Gross profit	24%	26%	134	291	656	798.875
37	Marketing expense (variable)	-22%	-16%	-133	-413	-594	-512.533
38	Marketing expense (fixed)						
39	Other (variable)	-14%	-11%	-63	-230	-378	-331.027
40	Other (fixed)						
41	Operating profit	-11%	-1%	-62	-352	-317	-44.685
42	Net interest paid			-13	-37	-90	-110.129
43	Profit before tax			-74	-390	-407	-154.814
44	NOLs				845	1650	2300
45	Tax			0	0	0	0
46	NET INCOME			-74	-390	-407	-154.814
47							
48							
49	BALANCE SHEET						
50							
51	FIXED ASSETS	13%	9%	30	318	366	271.751
52	INVESTMENTS	3%	1%	1	371	92	28.359
53	GOODWILL AND INTANS	9%	3%	186	730	255	79.749
54	INVENTORY/OCA	9%	7%	51	300	261	211.335
55	PAYABLES/OCL	-32%	-27%	-161	-694	-889	-837.790
56	OTHER, NET	2%	2%	8	40	60	49.768
57							
58	NET ASSETS			114	1066	145	-196.828
59							
60	Share capital and premium			301	1198	1342	1466.501
61							
62	Reserves:	Opening					
63		Retained					
64		Closing		-162	-932	-2309	-2906.501
65	SHAREHOLDERS' FUNDS			139	266	-967	-1440.000
66							
67			Gearing				
68	LOANS - CASH			-25	799	1113	1243.172
69							
70	CAPITAL EMPLOYED			114	1066	145	-196.828

negative because it is listed in the assets section of the balance sheet and is to be netted off against the operating assets.

Note the use of formulae in columns C and D to show ready-reckoners of the key operating and balance sheet data items as a per cent of revenues. The data were taken directly from Chapter 2 and Chapter 3.

The calculation block

We now reach the most important and main part of the spreadsheet building, the calculation section. We provide a step-by-step guide to building a basic model. Readers will benefit by following this guide in that they will have a better understanding of the model when it is complete, because we step through the construction and explain the rationale of each formula.

Note: The formulae for the calculation block take advantage of the different forms of addressing which Excel has for formulae. This uses the $ sign as a prefix for either row number or column letter to make the addressing for row or column absolute. This can speed up the process of entering formulae, and auto-filling to other years or line items. Readers unfamiliar with this may consult the Excel online help: topic 'Using references', subtopic 'The difference between relative and absolute references'.

Step 1: Fill in the years in row 32

Years 2002–12 should be entered in cells I32 to S32.

Step 2: Calculate the annual revenues

Enter the formula '=H35*(1+$C5)' in cell I35. This addresses cell C5 (revenue growth rate) by column absolute, row relative. So when we auto-fill by dragging the bottom right-hand corner of cell I35 to the right, the column will stay fixed and address cell C5. The formula addresses cell H35 (2001 revenues) by row relative, cell relative. When we auto-fill right this reference will adjust to address the cell one cell to the left of itself – that is, the previous year's revenues. Auto-fill this cell right up to cell S35.

Step 3: Calculate the annual gross margin

Enter the formula '=I35*(1-$C6)' into cell I36. Once again, this uses column absolute, row relative addressing of cell C6 (cost of sales %) to ensure that this addresses the correct cell. Auto-fill the formula right to cell S36.

Skip lines 37–8. (In the section on enhancing the model (below) we discuss how to fill in these details.)

Step 4: Calculate the SG&A cost

The SG&A cost has variable and fixed elements. These can be combined in one line or placed in two lines. For the latter option, enter '= -I35*$C7' in cell I39 and '= -$C8' in cell I40. Auto fill these formulae right, until cells S39:S40. *Note that we have made the SG&A costs negative to maintain compatibility with the historical data and to ensure clarity of what is a cost and what is a benefit in the spreadsheet.* This is the convention throughout the spreadsheet.

Step 5: Calculate the operating profit

This is a simple relative row, relative column formula which adds the gross profits to the costs (negative) to get the operating profit. Enter '=SUM(I36:I40)' in cell I41, and copy across to cell S41.

The spreadsheet now looks like Figure 4.13 (columns C–E omitted to save space). Note that the operating profit follows the Amazon.com pro forma logic. Since our end result is the free cash flow, if we deducted the non-cash items at this point we would have to add them back when we calculate the cash flow. For simplicity, we exclude them for now in both places. Also, although some other income and losses may be cash items, we shall assume these are zero, and exclude them from simulation as well.

We now continue to fill in the formulae below the operating profit.

Step 6: Calculate the interest payable

The interest payable is calculated in row 42 by multiplying the beginning of year net debt by the effective coupon rate, adjusted for the use of the beginning of year debt. Use of the beginning of year debt is needed to ensure that the model flows from left to right, and from the top down, avoiding recursive calculations. The formula used is '= -$C13*H68' in cell I42, where the coupon rate is addressed by column absolute, row relative addressing. H68 is the net debt for the last year of the history. We then auto fill this right to cell S42. All of the cells between J42 and S42 show zero at the moment, because net debt has not been calculated for future years.

Step 7: Calculate the profit before tax

Subtract interest from operating profit by entering '=I41+I42' in cell I43; then auto-fill this right to cell S43.

Step 8: Update the net operating loss carry-forwards

The NOLs represent a stock of losses that we will gradually use, starting when the company becomes profitable. So the formula needs to reflect this. It needs to start from the historical NOLs in cell H44. It needs to be increased if there

Figure 4.13 Projected income statement (after step 5)

	B	F	G	H	I	J	K	L	M	N	O	P	Q	R	S
32		1999	2000	2001	2002	2003	2004	2005	2006	2007	2008	2009	2010	2011	2012
33	INCOME STATEMENT														
34															
35	TOTAL SALES	1640	2762	3112	3486	3904	4373	4897	5485	6143	6881	7706	8631	9667	10827
36	Gross profit	291	656	799	892	999	1119	1254	1404	1573	1761	1973	2210	2475	2772
37	Marketing & fulfilment expense (var)	-413	-594	-513											
38	Marketing & fulfilment expense (fxd)														
39	Other (variable)	-230	-378	-331	-492	-550	-617	-691	-773	-866	-970	-1087	-1217	-1363	-1527
40	Other (fixed)				-340	-340	-340	-340	-340	-340	-340	-340	-340	-340	-340
41	Operating profit	-352	-317	-45	61	109	163	223	291	367	451	546	653	772	905
42	Net Interest paid	-37	-90	-110											
43	Profit before tax	-390	-407	-155											
44	NOLs	845	1650	2300											
45	Tax	0	0	0											
46	NET INCOME	-390	-407	-155											

are further losses in the year. It needs to be decreased if there are profits in the year. However, once it falls to zero, it must stop there (negative NOLs have no meaning). The complex formula '=IF(H44>0,IF(I43<0,H44-I43,MAX(H44-I43,0)),0)' which we enter in cell I44 does this job. Working in from the outside, we start with an IF statement, which is a way of doing one calculation if H44>0 and another if it is not. In the case that H44 is zero, NOLs have been exhausted and the NOLs in following years are also zero (because the model is continuous, we can exclude the possibility of NOLs reappearing after reaching zero). Otherwise the formula 'IF(I43<0,H44-I43,MAX(H44-I43,0))' is evaluated. I43 being the profit before tax in this year, if that is less than zero the NOLs are increased by -I43. If profit before tax is positive, the NOLs are decreased by I43. The expression 'MAX(H44-I43,0)' prevents NOLs from falling below zero; the higher of H44-I43 and zero will be output by the MAX Excel function. *Note:* The output in cell I44 is the NOL at the close of the year.

Step 9: Calculate the tax payable

The tax payable if there is a taxable profit is the taxable profit multiplied by the tax rate. If there is no taxable profit, no tax is payable. However, taxable profit is not the same as profit before tax (line 43). There is only a taxable profit if the NOLs have been exhausted – that is, if I44=0. If I44 (ending NOL for the year) is greater than zero, the taxable profit is zero. If the NOL is exhausted in this actual year, then I43-H44 is the taxable profit. If the NOL has been exhausted in a previous year, then I43-H44 still gives the taxable profit, because H44 is zero. The formula '=IF(I44>0,0,I43-H44)*-$C14' executes precisely that algorithm then multiplies the result by the tax rate, which is stored in cell C14. Enter this formula in cell I45.

Step 10: Calculate the profit after tax (or earnings)

Enter the formula '=I43+I45' into cell I46. Auto-fill right the formulae on lines 44–46.

The income statement is now complete. However, it will not yet calculate properly because the net debt has not been calculated. The income statement will look like Figure 4.14.

The next stage is to construct the balance sheet. Note that the parameters we have suggested, where Amazon.com has zero operating assets, mean that there is little necessity to have a balance sheet. However, it is included so that it can be used in sensitivity analysis should we wish to test the value implications of Amazon improving its asset efficiency or suffering problems with it.

Figure 4.14 Projected income statement (after step 10)

	B	F	G	H	I	J	K	L	M	N	O	P	Q	R	S
32		1999	2000	2001	2002	2003	2004	2005	2006	2007	2008	2009	2010	2011	2012
33	INCOME STATEMENT														
34															
35	TOTAL SALES	1640	2762	3112	3486	3904	4373	4897	5485	6143	6881	7706	8631	9667	10827
36	Gross profit	291	656	799	892	999	1119	1254	1404	1573	1761	1973	2210	2475	2772
37	Marketing & fulfilment expense (var)	-413	-594	-513											
38	Marketing & fulfilment expense (fxd)														
39	Other (variable)	-230	-378	-331	-492	-550	-617	-691	-773	-866	-970	-1087	-1217	-1363	-1527
40	Other (fixed)				-340	-340	-340	-340	-340	-340	-340	-340	-340	-340	-340
41	Operating profit	-352	-317	-45	61	109	163	223	291	367	451	546	653	772	905
42	Net Interest paid	-37	-90	-110	-99	0	0	0	0	0	0	0	0	0	0
43	Profit before tax	-390	-407	-155	-38	109	163	223	291	367	451	546	653	772	905
44	NOLs	845	1650	2300	2239	2229	2066	1843	1552	1188	734	188	0	0	0
45	Tax	0	0	0	0	0	0	0	0	0	0	0	-163	-270	-317
46	NET INCOME	-390	-407	-155	-38	109	163	223	291	367	451	546	490	502	588

The model balance sheet (Figure 4.15) will follow the historical format, although there will not be as much detail. We calculate the fixed assets (TFA), and the other assets and liabilities, and then we update the equity value, which is the record of the value retained by the company as a result of its profit performance. In the case of Amazon the company has made a large retained loss, so equity is negative. Finally, the balancing item is the net debt (debt minus cash). This means that debt is assumed to provide any funding needed to balance the balance sheet between assets and liabilities, and the company is assumed to pay down debt (rather than pay dividends) when it generates cashflow.

Step 11: Calculate the tangible fixed assets in the balance sheet

We use lines 49–50 as title lines for the balance sheet and calculate fixed assets in line 51. The fixed assets are directly derived from the revenues and the percentage of fixed assets, which is stored in cell C6. The appropriate formula for cell I51 is '=I35*$C9': this should be auto-filled right to cell S51. This is equivalent to assuming a fixed asset turnover of 1/C9, in this case 10. Note that this figure does not include fixed assets owned under operating leases. This issue is discussed in Appendix 3.1.

Step 12: Assume that investments and goodwill continue

Copy across the current values for investments (25) and goodwill (111) for cells I52:S53. Changes in these non-cash items introduce unnecessary complexity into the model. (Such a change would not be too difficult: for example decreases/writedowns in these items would simply be balanced by a decrease in equity reserves as a result of lower net profit. Other figures, for example net debt, would be unchanged.)

Step 13: Calculate the other operating assets and liabilities

Since we have assumed in our parameters that other assets and liabilities are equal to 10% of revenues, we are anticipating that liabilities dominate. Since neither inventory nor accounts payable pay any interest coupon or similar, we can net these off in our calculations, therefore we skip lines 54–55. The formula which should be entered in cell I56 is '=I35*$C10.' Then auto-fill right to cell S56.

Step 14: Sum net assets

Sum net assets in line 58 by entering '=SUM(I51:I56)' in cell I58, and copying to the right or auto-filling to S58.

Step 15: Copy across current values of share capital and premium

Set cell I60 equal to '=H60' and auto-fill right. As discussed in Chapter 3, share capital and premium are the record of money received by the company from offers of shares. We assume Amazon will not raise share capital. This is mainly an assumption to simplify the model: it fixes net debt as the balancing item or 'plug'.

Step 16: Calculate the annual value of equity reserves

This step is concerned with the calculation of the retained profit, or in this case 'Accumulated deficit'. The equity reserve for each year is the equity reserve for the previous year plus profit retained or minus retained loss. Retained profit is profit after tax (earnings) minus any dividends paid. We calculate this in three stages. First of all set the opening balance of reserves at the start of the year equal to last year's reserves by typing '=H64' in cell I62. Since Amazon is not projected to pay any dividends – since these are a distribution to security holders, they would not affect enterprise value anyway – the retained profit is equal to the profit after tax or earnings. Therefore we enter '=I46' in cell I63. Then these two values are added together to get the ending equity reserves value (cell I64: '=I62+I63'). This value is then used as the starting point for the same calculation next year, and so on. Once the three formulae in cells I62:I64 have been entered, auto-fill right to row S. Since the previous year's closing reserves are addressed by row relative, column relative, the appropriate figures will be calculated for each year.

Step 17: Calculate total shareholders' funds

These are equal to share capital and premium (row 60) plus closing reserves, so enter '=I60+I64' in cell I65. Equity shareholders' funds for Amazon are currently negative. This means that the historical cost estimate of shareholders' interest in the firm (after deducting all other liabilities) is less than zero. However, this does not stop the company doing business, provided it can meet its financial obligations as and when they fall due, and provided management and auditors can certify that the business is a going concern, which a business is usually assumed to be 'unless liquidation appears imminent'.[9] It also does not mean that the equity is worthless. Although book equity is a good predictor of value in large cross-section studies, individual firms with negative book equity can have positive value if their expected future cash flows are sufficiently large.

Step 18: Balance the balance sheet with net debt

Net debt is the balancing item or 'plug'. Enter the formula '=I58–I65' in cell I68. Gearing (D/D+E) can be calculated in cell I67 if desired, using the formula '=IF(OR(I65<=0,I68<=0),"N.M.",I68/(I68+I65))' – in this case the value returned is "N.M." (not meaningful): gearing is not meaningful if equity is negative.

Step 19: Total the net debt and equity

Total the net debt and equity by entering '=I65+I68' in cell I70. Auto-fill the lines 65–70 formulae across. The figures in line 70 should equal those in line 58.

The balance sheet should now look like Figure 4.15. The interest payable will also have been updated automatically, and will be as Figure 4.16.

The next stage in the model is to calculate the free cash flow (Figure 4.17). In this case free cash flow is precisely equal to operating profit for the early years of the model period (except for year 1, which has a transition between the small amount of negative operating assets to zero operating assets, which causes a small negative cash flow). This is because there are no net assets, and there is no taxable income until 2011 in the current scenario, because the company does not exhaust its NOLs until that year. However, we will calculate the FCF explicitly, to ensure flexibility of the model for firms which have positive or negative operating assets and for scenarios where Amazon has operating assets.

The method of calculating the free cash flow is to take the operating profit, and add back the changes in working capital and the like (other operating assets and liabilities). Ordinarily preparation of the cash-flow statement also includes the adding back of depreciation, but this is not done here for simplicity. The reason we can do this is that an adding back of depreciation to calculate operating cash flow, would necessitate an equal and opposite negative cash flow when we calculate investment in assets.[10]

Step 20: Transfer operating profit to cash flow

After typing headers in line 81, begin the calculation of FCF by transferring operating profit (line 41) to the cash flow. In cell I83 enter '=I41'.

Step 21: Calculate the cash flow

Calculate the cash flow from other assets and liabilities by subtracting last year's value from this year's: that is, in cell I85 enter '=SUM(H54:H56)-SUM(I54:I56)'.

Step 22: Calculate the operating cash flow

Calculate the operating cash flow (ignoring depreciation) by summing these two numbers. In cell I86 enter '=I83+I85'.

Step 23: Calculate the change in operating assets

We now calculate the investing cash flows; beginning by calculating the change in operating assets (net of depreciation). In cell I89 enter '=H51-I51'.

Figure 4.15 Projected balance sheet

	B	D	F	G	H	I	J	K	L	M	N	O	P	Q	R	S
49	BALANCE SHEET		1999	2000	2001	2002	2003	2004	2005	2006	2007	2008	2009	2010	2011	2012
50		2001														
51	FIXED ASSETS	9%	318	366	272	349	390	437	490	549	614	688	771	863	967	1083
52	INVESTMENTS	1%	371	92	28	28	28	28	28	28	28	28	28	28	28	28
53	GOODWILL AND INTANS	3%	730	255	80	80	80	80	80	80	80	80	80	80	80	80
54	INVENTORY/OCA	7%	300	261	211											
55	PAYABLES/OCL	-27%	-694	-889	-838											
56	OTHER, NET	2%	40	60	50	-349	-390	-437	-490	-549	-614	-688	-771	-863	-967	-1082.675
57																
58	**NET ASSETS**		**1066**	**145**	**-197**	**108**	**108**	**108**	**108**	**108**	**108**	**108**	**108**	**108**	**108**	**108**
59																
60	Share capital and premium		1198	1342	1467	1467	1467	1467	1467	1467	1467	1467	1467	1467	1467	1467
61																
62	Reserves:	Opening				-2907	-2945	-2963	-2928	-2830	-2657	-2395	-2026	-1533	-895	-268
63		Retained				-38	-18	35	98	173	263	368	493	639	627	645
64		Closing	-932	-2309	-2907	-2945	-2963	-2928	-2830	-2657	-2395	-2026	-1533	-895	-268	377
65	SHAREHOLDERS' FUNDS		**266**	**-967**	**-1440**	-1478	-1496	-1462	-1364	-1191	-928	-560	-67	572	1198	1844
66																
67		Gearing (D/D+E)	75%	N.M.	N.M.	N.M.	N.M.	N.M.	N.M.	N.M.	N.M.	N.M.	N.M.	N.M.	N.M.	N.M.
68	LOANS - CASH		**799**	**1113**	**1243**	1587	1604	1570	1472	1299	1036	668	175	-464	-1090	-1735
69																
70	CAPITAL EMPLOYED (net)		**1066**	**145**	**-197**	108	108	108	108	108	108	108	108	108	108	108

Figure 4.16 Projected income statement after step 19

	B	F	G	H	I	J	K	L	M	N	O	P	Q	R	S
32		1999	2000	2001	2002	2003	2004	2005	2006	2007	2008	2009	2010	2011	2012
33	INCOME STATEMENT														
34															
35	TOTAL SALES	1640	2762	3112	3486	3904	4373	4897	5485	6143	6881	7706	8631	9667	10827
36	Gross profit	291	656	799	892	999	1119	1254	1404	1573	1761	1973	2210	2475	2772
37	Marketing & fulfilment expense (var)	-413	-594	-513											
38	Marketing & fulfilment expense (fxd)														
39	Other (variable)	-230	-378	-331	-492	-550	-617	-691	-773	-866	-970	-1087	-1217	-1363	-1527
40	Other (fixed)				-340	-340	-340	-340	-340	-340	-340	-340	-340	-340	-340
41	**Operating profit**	**-352**	**-317**	**-45**	**61**	**109**	**163**	**223**	**291**	**367**	**451**	**546**	**653**	**772**	**905**
42	Net Interest paid	-37	-90	-110	-99	-127	-128	-126	-118	-104	-83	-53	-14	37	87
43	Profit before tax	-390	-407	-155	-38	-18	35	98	173	263	368	493	639	809	992
44	NOLs	845	1650	2300	2338	2356	2322	2224	2051	1788	1420	927	288	0	0
45	Tax	0	0	0	0	0	0	0	0	0	0	0	0	-182	-347
46	**Net income**	**-390**	**-407**	**-155**	**-38**	**-18**	**35**	**98**	**173**	**263**	**368**	**493**	**639**	**627**	**645**

Step 24: Calculate the cash flow from acquisitions and investments
Calculate the cash flow invested in acquisitions and equity investments (zero in this case). In cell 190 enter '=(H52+H53)-(152+153)'.

Step 25: Transfer the taxation cost
Transfer the taxation cost from the income statement (line 45) to the cash flow. In cell I92 enter '=I45'. These will be zero for the early years of this scenario as NOLs are being used up.[11]

Step 26: Calculate the free cash flow
Calculate the free cash flow (FCF) by adding the operating cash flow to the investing cash flow. In cell I94 enter '=SUM(I86:I92)'. The FCF is the cash which accrues to security holders, after all cash flows needed to fund the business, free of obligations to the tax authorities. It is *before* interest and dividends. The rationale for this is that value should not depend on whether investors take dividend or interest payments early, late or not at all, since the investors will immediately employ any money received in projects or investments with similar risk and reward to that of the Amazon stock.

Step 27: Transfer the interest and any dividends
Move the interest (and dividends, if applicable) from the income statement to the cash flow. In cell I96 enter '=I42'.

Step 28: Calculate the financing cash flow from equity securities
Calculate the financing cash flow from fresh issuances of equity securities (zero in this case). In cell I98 enter '=I60-H60'.

Step 29: Calculate the change in cash resources
Calculate the increase or decrease in the cash resources of the firm. In cell I100 enter '=I94+I96+I98'.

Step 30: Check that the change in cash matches the balance sheet
Check that the calculated change in cash is the same as that in the balance sheet (recall that cash is minus net debt). In cell I102 enter '=-(I68-H68)-I100'. This cell should have the value of zero. Auto-fill or copy across the formulae to rows J–S, if this has not already been done.

The outline cash-flow statement is complete and should look as Figure 4.17 (columns D–G have been omitted to save space).

Having calculated the free cash-flow values, we are now in a position to present-value these cash flows in accordance with the formulae which we saw

Figure 4.17 Projected cash-flow statement

	B	C	H	I	J	K	L	M	N	O	P	Q	R	S
81	CASH FLOW STATEMENT (outline)			2002	2003	2004	2005	2006	2007	2008	2009	2010	2011	2012
82														
83	Operating profit			61	109	163	223	291	367	451	546	653	772	905
84														
85	Net change in other operating assets/liabilities			-228	42	47	52	59	66	74	83	92	104	116
86	Operating cashflow*			-167	151	210	276	350	432	525	629	745	875	1021
87														
88	Investing activities													
89	Net change in TFAs*			-77	-42	-47	-52	-59	-66	-74	-83	-92	-104	-116
90	Net acquisitions and investments			0	0	0	0	0	0	0	0	0	0	0
91														
92	Taxation			0	0	0	0	0	0	0	0	0	-182	-347
93														
94	**Free cash flow to security holders (FCF)**			**-244**	**109**	**163**	**223**	**291**	**367**	**451**	**546**	**653**	**590**	**558**
95														
96	Interest			-99	-127	-128	-126	-118	-104	-83	-53	-14	37	87
97														
98	Funds raised from equity			0	0	0	0	0	0	0	0	0	0	0
99														
100	Net increase in cash (loans)			-343	-18	35	98	173	263	368	493	639	627	645
101														
102	Checksum			0	0	0	0	0	0	0	0	0	0	0

* Both operating cash flow and net change in TFA exclude equal and opposing depreciation. For further discussion see p. 127 and note 10 at the end of this chapter.

in Chapter 1. As the reader may recall, the formula to convert \$C in the future into its present value in cash today is:

$$\text{present value of } C \text{ in } n \text{ years} = \frac{C}{(1+r)^n}$$

where r is the cost of capital.

In the event that differing costs of capital are being used across time – as in this model, where we have a 13% initial cost of capital and a 10% final cost of capital – the situation is slightly more complex. The calculation can best be understood by considering a simple savings bond case. If a savings bond pays out \$100 in two years, and one expects prevailing interest rates to be 5% and 4% in years 1 and 2 respectively, the calculation of the worth of the investment can simply be split up into two annual calculations, in reverse order. First of all calculate the present value at the end of year 1 by diving \$100 by 1.04, giving a $V_{t=1}$ of \$96.15. Then calculate the present value at time zero by dividing \$96.15 by 1.05 to give $V_{t=0}$ = \$91.58. In other words, we calculate a composite discount factor of:

$$\frac{1}{1.04} \times \frac{1}{1.05}$$

For years 1 to t and discount rates r_1 to r_t, this can be generalized to construct a composite discount factor for years 1 to t as follows:

$$\frac{1}{1+r_1} \times \frac{1}{1+r_2} \times \frac{1}{1+r_3} \times \ldots \times \frac{1}{1+r_t}$$

To do this we must first calculate the values of the cost of capital r_i that pertain to each year of the simulation. To do this we subtract the beginning cost of capital from the ending cost of capital, which gives us the increase (decrease) in cost of capital over the whole period, in this case –3%. Then we divide this by the number of periods minus 1 to get the change in cost of capital per period (because 'for example' for a 10-period model there are 9 increments in cost of capital). Then we begin with the initial cost of capital, and add the increment to each previous year's cost of capital.

Step 31: Calculate the annual costs of capital

To calculate the annual increment, in cell C106, enter '=(C12-C11)/9'. Transfer the initial cost of capital from the parameters block to the lower part of the worksheet by entering the formula '=C11' in cell I107. Do not fill/paste across: both are one-off calculations.

Then, in cell J107, add the increment (column absolute addressed) to the previous year's cost of capital by entering '=I107+\$C106'. Auto-fill right to cell R107. (It is not necessary to carry out this calculation for 2012, as the growing perpetuity is discounted at the 2011 discount factor.)

Step 32: Calculate the discount factor for each year of the model

The first year's discount factor is 1 divided by $1 + r_1$. Therefore in cell I108, enter '=1/(1+I107)'. The discount factor to year 2 (that is, combined year 1 and year 2) is the year 1 discount factor divided by $1 + r_2$ (equivalent to the formula above). In cell J108 enter the formula '=I108/(1+J107)', and auto-fill right to cell R108.

Step 33: Calculate the present value of each individual year's FCF

This is done by multiplying the FCF calculated in row 94 by the discount factor calculated in line 108. In cell I109 enter '=I94*I108' and auto-fill right to cell R109. The contents of cells I109:R109 are the present values of the projected future cash flows. These cells should read as Figure 4.18 (columns D–H omitted).

For ease of reference, we now conduct the final stages of the valuation calculation in the parameters block, so that the user can immediately see the effect of parameter changes on value. The calculation of equity value is a two-stage process. First, enterprise value is calculated by adding the present value of the cash flows in years 2002–11 to the present value of the terminal value (2011 sale price) of the firm. Then equity value is calculated by subtracting the market value of other non-common-equity securities and claims. The stock price may then be calculated by dividing the equity value by the shares outstanding.

Step 34: Calculate the present value

Calculate the present value of the projected flows by adding them together. In cell C22, enter the formula '=SUM(I109:R109)'. Because these cash flows are *already* present-valued, simple addition will suffice to conclude the calculation.

Step 35: Calculate the terminal value

To calculate the terminal value, multiply the after-tax cash flow in the terminal year by the terminal value multiplier, as calculated in cell C17. Since the cash flows in the Amazon model may not be taxed (due to NOLs) for worst case projections, the cash flow must be adjusted to *simulate* it being taxed, as future taxation is likely. (Most of Amazon's NOLs, having been built up in 1999–2000, will expire by 2015.) To achieve this, in cell C23 enter '=((S94-S92)-(S43*C14)) *C17*R108'.

- This formula simply adds back any tax that has been paid (whether at the full rate or if a lesser or zero tax has been paid due to NOLs) by subtracting S92 (which will be negative if tax has been paid) from S94.

Figure 4.18 Calculation of present-value of FCFs

	B	C	I	J	K	L	M	N	O	P	Q	R
105	Calculation of present value of FCFs		2002	2003	2004	2005	2006	2007	2008	2009	2010	2011
106	Cost of capital change per year = -0.33%											
107	Cost of capital in year		13%	12.7%	12.3%	12.0%	11.7%	11.3%	11.0%	10.7%	10.3%	10.0%
108	Discount factor		0.88	0.79	0.70	0.62	0.56	0.50	0.45	0.41	0.37	0.34
109	Discounted FCF		-215.9	85.7	113.9	139.4	162.6	184.1	204.2	223.3	241.8	198.6

- Then we subtract the full taxable liability for the pre-tax profit (S43) by multiplying this by the tax rate (C14). This expression, '(S94-S92)-(S43*C14)', represents the cash flow that would have occurred had there been no NOLs.
- This expression is then multiplied by the terminal multiplier to calculate the future value of the terminal value, and then by the discount factor to discount it to the present day.

Step 36: Find the enterprise value
In cell C24, enter the formula '=SUM(C22:C23)'. This is the value of the equity plus debt in the firm.

Step 37: Find the equity value
Subtract the value of the other securities to get the equity value, the residual claim. Then add the cash the company has, which has dollar for dollar value.

We calculate the value of the convertibles and ESOPs in Chapter 7 as $1895m. Enter this number in cell C25. Enter the cash and marketable securities of $996.585m (as shown in Table 2.6) in C26. Then subtract the debt, and add the cash to the enterprise value to obtain the equity value.

This concludes the equity valuation process. To get the estimated price per share, input the number of shares outstanding from the most recent 10Q, 10K or annual report. Then divide the equity value calculated in cell C27 by the number of shares to get a per share price.

The final valuation section should look like Figure 4.19.

Figure 4.19 Calculation of equity value under CCA

	B	C
21	Calculation of value	
22	PV of cash flows to horizon	1,337.8
23	PV of terminal value	3,131.6
24	Total enterprise value	4,469.4
25	Subtract debt/ESOPs	-1,895
26	Add cash and near cash	996.6
27	Equity value	3,571
28	Shares outstanding	373,218
29	Value per share	$ 9.57

At the time of writing (March 2002), Amazon's share value is approximately $15 per share, with a total equity value of $5.5bn. We discuss the issues of misvaluation and inefficiency in Chapter 10. We would expect the price to trend towards fundamental value over time, although the company may of course manage to improve some operating parameters, to gain extra value. We turn to this possibility – that is, best case analysis (BCA) (we shall, of course, also consider worst case analysis) – in the next section.

COMPLETING CFA: BEST CASE AND WORST CASE ANALYSIS

Having done the hard work of building our model, we can now use it to evaluate rapidly the scenarios which we judged as reasonable from the past historical data of Amazon. Table 4.9 recaps those scenarios.

Ignoring for the moment return on capital limitation (RoCEL), which we will discuss in Chapter 6, we can simply input the new parameters into the parameters block of the model and derive equity values. The parameters block (including the valuation results) for BCA looks like Figure 4.20.

This valuation will be substantially decreased when we run it through the return on capital limitation (RoCEL) algorithm, however. What RoCEL effectively does is to simulate competition by capping return on capital at a specified level. The rationale for this is that if very high returns occur, competitors will enter the market and depress those returns. This addresses a weakness in cash-flow models of this type, that the company becomes extremely profitable at the end of the period because operating leverage really kicks in. For example, look at the profit margins for Amazon in 2011 of the simulation for BCA: operating profit margin is 9.7%. That this is too high for a retailer we can

Table 4.9 Amazon.com: recap of CFA scenarios

	Continuing case (CCA)	Best case (BCA)	Worst case (WCA)
Revenue growth	12%	20%	7%
Variable costs as % of sales	88.5%	88.5%	90.5%
Fixed costs	$340m	$340m	$340m
Operating assets as % of sales	0%	0%	0%
RoCEL [see Chapter 6]	30%	30%	15%
Equity value (model)	$3.6bn		

Figure 4.20 The parameters block under best case (BCA)

	B	C
2	**Amazon.com Valuation Forecast**	($m)
3		
4	Parameters	
5	Revenue growth	20%
6	COGS	74.4%
7	Other variable costs	14.1%
8	Fixed costs (SGA)	$339.90
9	Tangible fixed assets	10%
10	Operating assets/liabilities (net)	-10%
11	Cost of capital (init)	13%
12	Cost of capital (final)	10%
13	Coupon on debt	8.00%
14	Tax rate	35%
15	NOLs (initial)	$2,300
16	Terminal growth rate	4%
17	Terminal CF multiple	16.67
18		
19		
20		
21	**Calculation of value**	
22	PV of cash flow to horizon	2483.9
23	PV of terminal value	7802.4
24	Total enterprise value	10286.3
25	Subtract debt/ESOPs	-1895
26	Add cash and near cash	996.6
27	Equity value	9387.9
28	Shares out (m)	373,218
29	Value per share	$25.15

gather from the comparables in the case. However, RoCEL gives us a somewhat scientific way of checking these excesses.

The valuation for WCA is as in Figure 4.21.

FUNDING CRUNCH ANALYSIS

One of the key and often neglected outputs of the cash-flow model is the financing needs of the business over time.[12] The DCF model of value in

Figure 4.21 The parameters block under worst case (WCA)

	B	C
2	**Amazon.com Valuation Forecast**	($m)
3		
4	Parameters	
5	Revenue growth	7%
6	COGS	74.4%
7	Other variable costs	16.1%
8	Fixed costs (SGA)	$339.90
9	Tangible fixed assets	10%
10	Operating assets/liabilities (net)	-10%
11	Cost of capital (initial)	13%
12	Cost of capital (final)	10%
13	Coupon on debt	8.00%
14	Tax rate	35%
15	NOLs (initial)	$2,300
16	Terminal growth rate	4%
17	Terminal CF multiple	16.67
18		
19		
20		
21	**Calculation of value**	
22	PV of cash flow to horizon	134.3
23	PV of terminal value	1368.7
24	Total enterprise value	1502.9
25	Subtract debt/ESOPs	-1895
26	Add cash and near cash	996.6
27	Equity value	604.5
28	Shares out (m)	373,218
29	Value per share	$1.62

general ignores financing issues. The assumption underlying this is that a positive net present-value project will attract sufficient funding from investors. However, since we are in a non-full-information world where past history and reputation matters, the possibility that funding crunches may prevent a company from executing its business plan is very real. For example, Amazon would have found it very difficult to raise fresh capital from the public markets during 2001, as would most net firms. So we should examine the company's net debt line, to see whether it rises above the current book value of debt of $2.1bn. This would mean that cash at hand had reached zero, and the company would have a potential funding crunch. In the best case scenario, the funding is no problem as the company begins to pay down debt quite early in the simulation. In the continuing case scenario, for which we printed the balance sheet as Figure 4.15, the maximum debt is $1.6bn in 2003. This means that the firm effectively has $500m of spare cash at this point. However, let us look at the worst case scenario (WCA) debt line (Figure 4.22).

As we can see, the company never really manages to begin paying down debt until 2010, and reaches a zero net cash situation in 2006. This indicates that the modest WCA value may be illusory since extra financing would be required.

There is also another large funding crunch awaiting the company in 2009 and 2010. The company's convertible debt may well not be converted into equity. In this case all the convertible debt falls due in two large, lump-sum payments (so-called 'bullet' payments of bond principal) which arise 10 years after initial issuance of the securities. In the best case scenario without competition, the company has enough money to pay these payments, which will amount to a total of about $1.25bn at end January 2009 and a further $615m (at early 2002 euro/$ exchange rates) in February 2010. In scenarios where the company does poorly, its chances of paying these sums without fresh financing are poor. In this case, a renegotiation with the convertible holders would be likely, probably resulting (if an agreement can be concluded) in a debt-for-equity swap, in which the holders of the convertibles would agree to receive common equity in exchange for the convertibles, thus releasing the company from its need to pay coupon payments and to pay back the principal.

If there is a climate of non-availability of public market financing for internet firms, FCA is key. Other sense checks, such as checking margins and end-of-model sales (against the size of the company's market), are also important. In the case of Amazon, the company's potential addressable market is quite large, although affected by potential limitations in take-up and enthusiasm for online shopping. However, there is no hard and fast limit of market size the company is likely to come up against. For most companies, it should

Figure 4.22 WCA debt line

	B	G	H	I	J	K	L	M	N	O	P	Q	R
49	Balance sheet	2000	2001	2002	2003	2004	2005	2006	2007	2008	2009	2010	2011
⋮	⋮	⋮	⋮	⋮	⋮	⋮	⋮	⋮	⋮	⋮	⋮	⋮	⋮
68	Loans – cash	1027	1243	1671	1806	1928	2035	2123	2189	2229	2239	2215	2150

be noted that sales of greater than 30% of the market are quite rare, so projections which produce revenues at the end of the model which are more than 30% of the addressable market should be carefully re-examined.

CAN THIS MODEL BE USED FOR OTHER INTERNET COMPANIES?

We certainly hope so! All internet companies report the data we have studied for Amazon.com, which means one can plot the data on costs, asset needs and so forth, and try to see which way the trends in operating parameters are heading for these firms. With the same type of financial analysis that we have used for Amazon.com, one should be able to estimate operating parameters and build a similar model for a different firm.

The intention in going through the model very comprehensively is to give the reader a sound understanding of the model, so that he or she feels confident enough about how it works to make changes in it when needed. Readers may need to adjust the model to stress different operating parameters which may be important for other firms, or they may want to augment the model in other ways.

AUGMENTING THE MODEL

We are fairly suspicious of complex models. The model we have discussed in this first part of the book certainly is not that complex, but it helps to emphasize the points about what are the key value drivers for the company. However, some possible profitable avenues for augmentation might be:

- breaking out the different types of operating asset and liability and projecting these separately (for example, inventory, accounts payable, and other current liabilities)
- breaking out revenues in the different product lines, and applying a different margin to each product line
- building models that address the strategic alternatives that Amazon has, such as continued presence in all markets, US focus, or BMD focus
- building a simpler model driven by margin predictions rather than variable cost mix.

The problem with predicting a larger number of line items and categories, for example within revenue, is that we inevitably move from predicting a small number of unknowns to predicting a larger number of unknowns. Also, for many of these parameters, such as services revenues, we have extremely short histories indeed, and in general less evidence and knowledge to base our predictions on.

Finally, the revenue modelling for Amazon is fairly straightforward in this case, since constant revenue growth is predicted. The model can be augmented to project growth with exponential decay. In order to do this, set up a separate line for revenue growth, and define a starting value. Then calculate the cells on the revenue growth line as the previous revenue growth (column relative addressing) multiplied by the decay factor (absolute addressing). Calculate each year's revenue in the usual way, but use row relative, column relative addressing to access the relevant year's growth rate.

POINTS OF DEPARTURE

This concludes Part I of the book. After this fairly focused discussion of CFA, readers may wish to refer to the contents for the next area of interest. We continue with Part II, which begins with a discussion of the derivation of the cost of capital, an extremely key parameter which we have so far asked the reader to take on trust. Then we discuss other advanced topics in valuation, including real-option valuation (ROA). Part III is also important. So far we have raw values for the three scenarios. The next step is to adjust them for competition, as we will discuss in Chapter 6. However, at some point we have to weight those values using strategic analysis (SA); this is discussed in Part III. The strategic analysis will also help inform us about potential discontinuities ahead (DCA). Finally, Part IV will be of interest to professionals seeking to value non-quoted equity and to understand the issues in M&A and 'clicks and mortar' valuation.

Notes

1 Arguably, the product-release-led revenue growth model of (for example) Microsoft is an even more severe seasonality, as the company has a product development (negative cash flow) product release (positive cash flow) cycle of 3–4 years.

2 We wish to acknowledge Michael Earl's presentation of Amazon's strategic options (at our London Business School eExperts course) as an influence on this and the following discussion.

3 $157m is the segment operating profit of BMDV obtained from Table 2.9 in the Amazon case.

4 The relationship between incremental costs and revenues using the December 1999–December 2000 incremental costs and revenues is even more favourable, but the

December 1999 quarter had atypically high costs as discussed above, due to inventory writedowns and other factors.

5 There are some problems constructing quarterly cash flows, which often have to be calculated from the information available. For example, there is no separate cash-flow statement for 2000Q4, so this has to be calculated by using 2000 annual cash flows minus the cash flows for the first nine months of 2000, which are shown in the 2000Q3 quarterly report.

6 As mentioned in Chapter 1, the proper calculation of after tax WACC is given by

$$\mathrm{WACC} = r_{\mathrm{Debt}}\,(1 - T_c)\,\frac{D}{V} + r\,\frac{E}{V}$$

We do not use this formula because the company will not be in a taxpaying position for some time and because of the difficulty of evaluating the cost of the convertible capital. To illustrate use of the formula, however, if Amazon's value of convertibles (at market) is 25% of its total capital employed (at market), if we assume a cost of capital for the convertibles of 13% (same as the equity) and the company having to pay taxes immediately, the initial WACC would be 11.86%, which would increase the equity value in CCA by approximately 5%.

7 This is as suggested by Lundholm and O'Keefe (2001).

8 For this formula the first cashflow occurs one year after the present. This is the reason that the 11 years out cashflow is used to calculate the value.

9 Kieso and Weygandt (1998), p. 42.

10 A numerical example may help illustrate (for the purposes of the example we will consider a firm with positive net assets, not the zero net assets we are assuming for Amazon). First of all let us bear in mind that the income statement includes depreciation expenses (it is included in items such as marketing expense, product development expense and so on). Our net asset number is some percentage of sales revenue. Let us suppose that in one year (due to an increase in revenues) assets will increase from $1000 (start of year) to $1200 (end of year). Let us further assume that $50 of depreciation has been included in the income statement as a cost, therefore the book value of start of year assets has declined to $950. We therefore require a cash investment in assets of $250. We can account for that cash investment by adding back $50 to profit to calculate operating cash flow, and then investing $250 ($1200–$950) in tangible fixed assets, or just ignore the depreciation add-back and calculate investment in tangible fixed assets as $200 ($1200–$1000).

11 In practice there may be some timing differences that cause some tax to be paid before NOLs have been used up (for example due to Corporate Alternative Minimum Taxation). The effect of this on value will be modest (but negative), since they amount to a bringing forward in time of some tax liability (rather than new tax liability). However, the reader should be aware of this issue.

12 We are indebted to Chris Higson of London Business School for stressing the funding crunch issue to us.

PART II

Advanced Valuation Topics

CHAPTER 5

The Cost of Capital

WHAT DO WE MEAN BY THE 'COST OF CAPITAL'?

The *cost of capital* is synonymous with the *discount rate*, the *expected return* and the *required return*. The cost of capital is an annual rate of return that is required by investors to compensate them for the risk they take on a risky project, for postponing consumption and for suffering inflationary losses on all projects where they lend or invest money. In low-inflation countries such as the USA and UK in the early twenty-first century, the cost of capital varies from about 2–4% for risk free government bills, and rises to about 10–15% for publicly quoted equities. The cost of capital for a firm as a whole will be a weighted average of the cost of its equity capital and of any debt that it possesses. Due to the fact that most internet firms are all equity- or largely equity-financed, we concentrate in this chapter on the issue of the cost of equity, and particularly on the cost of public market equity. Private equity costs of capital are reported to be far higher than public market levels, at least 20% but sometimes reaching as high as 50–100%. These are discussed in more detail in Chapter 16.

Our topic here is internet company valuation, and some readers may question the need for a chapter on the cost of capital, especially one which goes into sometimes arcane detail. It is true that much of this chapter is relevant not just to internet companies but to the market as a whole. However, internet company valuations have put pressure on received wisdom as regards the cost of capital, and in order to understand how to value these firms, we require a detailed understanding of how much of this pressure may be justified.

TAXONOMY OF METHODS FOR DETERMINING THE COST OF CAPITAL

It is generally agreed that a sensible guide for determining the cost of capital of a project or firm is to look at the returns that investors have demanded on similar projects or for similar companies. There are two ways of carrying out this process, as well as a third method that does not use this paradigm:

1. *model the company's cost of capital against other firms* using stock market data and cost-of-capital formulae such as the CAPM or the Fama and French four-factor model (*formula-based determination*)
2. *build a 'bottom-up' cost of capital by detailed analysis* of the operating assets of the firm and how risky (by measures such as the asset β) projects of this type are (*component-based determination*)
3. *use the capitalization method* to derive the cost of capital which is implied by the market's valuation, given forecast earnings or cash flows, and expected growth in those earnings or cash flows (*reverse-calculation method*).

Methods of type 1 (formula-based methods) can be further classified as to whether they use historical data to form estimates for formula parameters, or other methods, such as adjusting historical data to cater for perceived changes in the market of investor appetite for risk. These methods are the dominant methods of determining expected returns.

Method 2 is difficult unless one possesses a great deal of data about the project. However, some workers who are suspicious of high costs of capital for internet firms have supported this method. Aswath Damodaran (2001) gives some worked examples. Further discussion on this method is contained in Brealey and Myers (2000) and in Foster (1986, Chapter 10).

Method 3 is not appropriate if misvaluation is suspected. As we demonstrate below, firms which are overvalued will generate very low values of expected return, if predicted cash flows are correct. Since there is always a cost of capital which can solve the equation[1] of price = $\Sigma c_r(1+r)^{-t}$, this method will never suggest that stocks are other than correctly valued. However, in a 'hot' market it may cause 'misvaluation contagion', as overvaluations in one stock or group of stocks cause a downward adjustment in cost-of-capital perception in other stocks. (However, there are some workers who suggest that reverse valuation can be useful in investigating the cost of capital of the market as a whole: we discuss this application below.)

THE RECOMMENDED METHOD IS THE CAPM

The first, and dominant, method within the formula-based determination class is the single-factor CAPM. This method models the 'non-specific' risk of companies' equity only. The logic of this is that if the investor holds a diversified portfolio, these company-specific risks will average out. Since it is so easy to avoid the company-specific risks by diversifying, there is no risk premium over the CAPM for taking the risks on. The CAPM looks only at the risk due to the stocks' covariance with the market. Because both individual stocks and diversified portfolios of stocks are highly influenced by the market return, this market risk is one that the investor cannot avoid, and this is the risk that the CAPM 'prices'. The CAPM formula is as follows:

$$E[r] = r_f + \beta(r_m - r_f)$$

where $E[r]$ = the expected rate of return on the stock or share ($E[]$ = expectation operator operating on r)
r = the return
r_f = the risk-free rate or risk-free return
r_m = the market return.

The determination of the cost of capital is perhaps the most difficult single task facing the valuer. The desired rate is not the *previous* return but the 'expected' or 'required' return appropriate for the risk of the project. If the NPV of the project or firm is then positive, the firm's return will have exceeded this required return, will have paid a more than appropriate compensation for the risk, and will therefore be a 'good' investment. However, without entering the mind of the investor at the moment the investment is being considered, it is hard to see how we can determine this precisely. The usual 'shortcut' is to try and use past returns, and parameters which we can observe about companies, to show us what return investors expect from companies which have a given set of parameters.

The single-factor CAPM does this in a very elegant way. The parameters of the firm, as they relate to undiversifiable risk and so to expected return, are summed up in one number, the β of the firm. Under certain assumptions, the β of the firm is related to investors' view of the trade-off between risk and return in a fairly straightforward way. However in finance, as in life, elegance is not everything. The CAPM has been attacked because the theory predicts relationships between β and returns which seem to be testable, and those relationships have not held constant over time. We discuss these challenges to the CAPM, and the alternative theories that have been advanced, later in the chapter.

The principles of the CAPM

The CAPM follows directly from two assumptions about investors' 'utility' (*utility* is an economic term meaning satisfaction or pleasure). Investors' utility is a function of:

- return
- variance of that return (that is, risk).

The latter assumption is really two assumptions in one – that investors don't like risk (fair enough) and that risk can be represented by high variance (more doubtful).

To see how the CAPM follows from the above assumptions, please see Appendix 5.1.

Diversifiable and systematic risk

As mentioned above, the CAPM only prices market risk or systematic risk, the risk of a market-wide fall that shareholders take on by buying a share. These types of risk can be defined as follows:

- *diversifiable risk:* company-specific risk – this can be eliminated entirely by holding the market portfolio, and largely eliminated by holding a basket of stocks
- *systematic risk:* risk that the stock will fall because market falls (measured by β).

Figure 5.1 shows the benefits of diversification. The chart uses the very interesting recent findings of Campbell et al. (2001) which show that diversification benefits have become more difficult to achieve in recent years. The lower line is the relationship between portfolio standard deviation (volatility) and the number of stocks held in the portfolio for 1963–85, and the higher line shows the same relationship for 1986–97. This shows that more recently a larger portfolio was required to achieve a similar level of diversification benefits than in the past. These lines are based on Campbell et al.'s excess standard deviation measures (their figure 6, panel B) added to a market standard deviation of 20% (Campbell et al. report that the market volatility did not show any upward trend during the sample period). It remains to be seen whether the 1985–97 results represent a permanent increase in individual stock volatility, or just a one-off period in which some stocks had a very high individual volatility, and

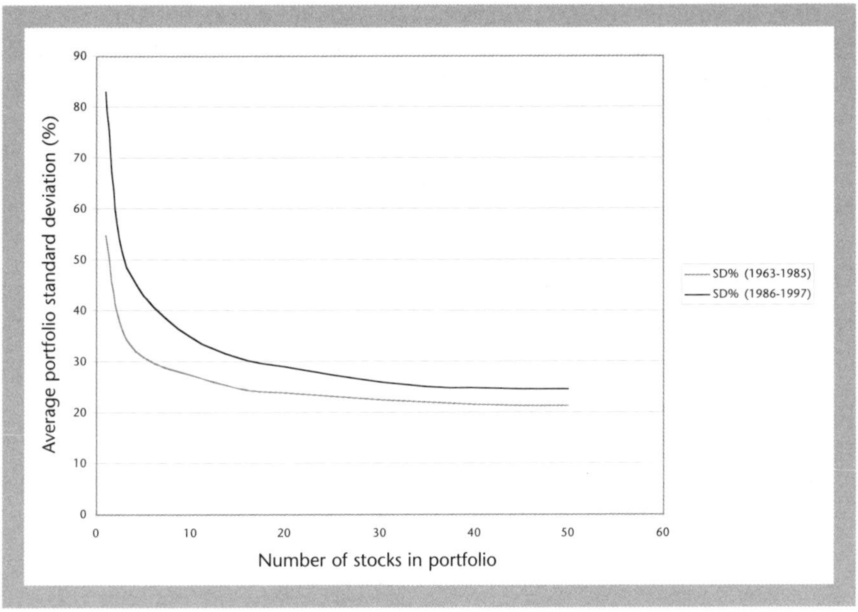

Figure 5.1 Example of the benefits of diversification

made diversification more difficult to achieve. If the results represent a permanent increase, this would make diversification more difficult to achieve and would tend to undermine the CAPM's assumption that all investors hold the market portfolio.

Empirical tests of the CAPM

Since the CAPM is a linear equation:

$$E[r] = r_f + \beta(r_m - r_f)$$

which predicts values of $E[r]$ from values of β (with gradient ($r_m - r_f$ and intercept $(0,r_f)$), the CAPM can be tested by plotting returns against β. In short, we would expect returns to rise with β. Over the longest available time periods (1926–91) there seems to be a linear relationship, albeit not with as steep a gradient as the CAPM predicts. However, over the more recent periods (for example 1963–90 as investigated by Fama and French, 1992) the relationship is unclear, and it seems that returns do not change very much, irrespective of the β.

There have been several defences against these attacks. First, the attacks usually use commonly discussed stock market indices as *proxies* (that is, substitutes or equivalents) for the CAPM's 'market index'. However, the theoretical quantity we are seeking is the index of the whole market of productive assets, including real estate and all human capital (workers' skills) and unquoted firms. Since this quantity is extremely hard to value, and therefore to track, this makes it difficult to test the CAPM. Also, it has been argued that any test of the CAPM is unavoidably a test of market efficiency as well, since we are using market values as the arbiter of expected returns. In such a *joint test*, a failure to show the expected result could be because the CAPM is incorrect *or* because the market is not efficient.

Although these criticisms carry important messages about the difficulty of the problem, they do not satisfy the critics of the CAPM. Also, when researchers have tried to correct for some problems (by, for example, attempting to proxy for the value of intellectual capital assets) the results have not been very appealing. The empirical evidence on the CAPM is ambiguous, suggesting that over the very long-term the theory has good empirical support, but over the recent short-term, β has not been a good predictor of returns.

As supporters of the CAPM, we are nevertheless very aware of its weaknesses. It continues to withstand the attacks not because it is a perfect theory, but because the best alternative theories have weaker analytical support, similar levels of empirical support, and much inferior levels of usability. The CAPM also gives attractive results for internet companies: it suggests that they have high costs of capital which indeed we would expect. Summarizing the CAPM's strengths:

- it is consistent with the data in a broad sense (stocks return more than bonds)
- over long periods r is proportional to β
- it is the best available theory.

In other words, two cheers for the CAPM – which is two more than there are for anything else.

FORMULA-BASED THEORIES

The APT class

The single-factor CAPM is very specific that β is the only relevant parameter for determining risk. The *APT* (*Arbitrage Pricing Theory*) of Stephen Ross suggests that a wider range of risk factors may be relevant, each of which might be related to returns by its own weighting factor, b_i. In an APT world the equation for expected return $E[r]$ might look like this:

$$E[r] = a + b_1(r_{\text{factor 1}}) + b_2(r_{\text{factor 2}}) + b_3(r_{\text{factor 3}}) + \ldots + \text{noise}$$

where a = the rate returned by a stock which has none of the modelled risk factors (a is analogous to the risk-free rate)

b_i = the stock's sensitivity to each factor

r = the risk premium associated with each factor (rewarding investors for taking on this type of risk) – that is, the return of a notional security having only that risk factor, minus the risk-free rate.

However, the APT does not say what the factors are – investors must hypothesize depending on industry or other characteristics, and then test the factor model(s), possibly using regression analysis. Sample risk factors which have been postulated are exchange rates, rise in GDP, certain commodity prices, price/book value of equity ratio, and size of firm.

Fama and French four-factor model

The most popular flavour of APT is the *Fama and French four-factor model* (*FF*). This model emanates from Fama and French's critical evaluation of the CAPM, which we referred to above. As well as casting doubt upon the CAPM, Fama and French observed other patterns in stock price returns. These patterns were principally associated with the size of firms and the firms' price/book ratio (which is calculated by dividing the market capitalization of a company by its book value of shareholders' equity). Small firms appeared to return more than large firms. Also 'value stocks' (low price/book ratio companies) seemed to return more than 'glamour stocks' (high price/book ratio firms). Later research work caused price momentum to be added to the model. This effectively represents the fact that firms which have exhibited good stock returns are likely to continue to outperform (that is, returns are serially autocorrelated, at least over the short-term). To capture risk that is reflected by β, this is also included in the model.

In order to calculate an expected return under the Fama and French model, these four data items (factors) are needed on the firm. They are then inputted into the following formula:

$$E[r] = a + b_1(r_{\text{size}}) + b_2(r_{\text{price/book ratio}}) + b_3(r_{\text{price momentum}}) + \beta(r_m - r_f)$$

Problems with the FF model

There are problems with both the empirical and the conceptual bases of the model. First, while it may seem intuitive that small firms are more risky than large firms (and thus command higher expected returns), it is counterintuitive that high price/book firms (high growth 'glamour' stocks) are *less* risky. To make matters worse (or at any rate to make matters less clear), the small-firm effect seems to have reversed; and during 1998–9, value stocks substantially underperformed glamour stocks, in opposition to what the FF model suggests.

Another explanation for the price/book effect is that the market systematically overvalues glamour stocks (sometimes called *'story stocks'*, because their valuation is often dependent on a story rather than on fundamental analysis of their operational parameters). In this explanation the influence of the price/book ratio on returns is not related to investors' *expected returns*, but to the effect high price/book ratios have in depressing realized returns as the market corrects for the overvaluation.[2] This might seem to be a fairly arcane distinction, but it is crucially important if we are seeking valuation messages. Since investors require or expect returns based on how risky an asset is, short-term misvaluations are not going to make any difference to investors' expected returns. An overvalued dot-com is still a risky firm – it will turn out to have a low realized return, because the penny will drop and investors will correct the overvaluation. However, at all times investors will look at that firm (specifically, at the bundle of operating assets that constitutes the firm's business, which does not change with valuation) and see a risky enterprise, and expect high returns as compensation for that risk.

Use of the FF model and other factor models

The FF model is not widely taught in business schools, perhaps because of habit, or the desire to remain consistent with industry practice. Another criticism raised is that it is seen as being too much driven by data mining and having insufficient theoretical and empirical support to displace the CAPM model (that is, even if it is better, it does not have enough superiority to create change in attitudes). The criticism that the FF model is driven by the data may seem somewhat 'ivory tower', but there is a sound reason for the criticism. If theory underlying a model is correct, it is likely to be more robust over time. On the other hand, a model driven by the data may be correct over the period observed (the past), but may suddenly become invalid because of underlying shifts in the relationships between financial variables. Without a sound theory, practitioner and academic alike are without tools to explain the shifts.

However, the FF model, and other ad hoc factor models, are extensively used in asset management. Hedge funds and investment advice firms are constantly 'crunching the numbers' on past returns compared to firms' characteristics and financial ratios. If these investment managers observe relationships between financial parameters and returns, they will adopt strategies which attempt to capitalize on those relationships if they persist. It remains to be seen how sustained the appeal of these models is, since past relationships between variables may not persist after they have been observed. It seems unlikely that automated analysis of financial data will provide the same returns as careful fundamental analysis of the strategy and performance of firms. Indeed, the increasing ubiquity of automated financial analysis systems will limit the returns available from these systems.

DETERMINING THE PARAMETERS FOR THE CAPM

Leaving aside the competing factor models, we now continue our discussion of the usage of the CAPM. The CAPM is extremely simple to use provided the parameters are known, but there are problems with determining each of the three key parameters, which we will deal with before proceeding.

The CAPM formula is repeated below:

$$E[r] = r_f + \beta(r_m - r_f)$$
$$\Rightarrow E[r] = r_f + \beta(\text{MRP})$$

where $E[r]$ = the expected return or cost of capital (the output)
r_f = the risk free rate
β = the appropriate beta
MRP = the market risk premium $r_m - r_f$.

Determining the risk free rate, r_f

The determination of the risk free rate is the least challenging of these problems. Normally, the shortest-term government treasury bill is utilized, and the appropriate corresponding MRP used. Many textbooks advise valuers to seek longer-term treasury bond rates, given that equity is a long-term security. A more sensible reason is that the long-term bond rate is less volatile. Using the long bond rate can also work well if the MRP is being determined using historical data, as is usually the case. The MRP is then the result of a simple comparison of the returns on equity securities and the returns on government or treasury securities. It will be possible to obtain MRPs for equities compared to both short-term and long-term bonds. The MRP for the difference between equities and the shortest term bills should be used. (This MRP will be slightly larger than that comparing longer-term government bonds to equities, since longer-term government bonds offer a premium yield usually between 0.5–1%.) Dimson and Marsh (2001) list equity market returns and both types of MRP for major markets.

The valuer should make an effort to smooth out perceived temporary changes in the risk free rate, especially if using the short-term risk free rate. We have utilized 4% as the risk-free rate in this book. However, this rate is subject to change, and the reader should review current rates in the financial press.

Determining β

A large number of commercial services provide estimates of β, including Bloomberg (www.bloomberg.com), Marketguide (www.marketguide.com) and, in the UK, the London Business School. For example in our calculation of the cost of capital for Amazon.com in the previous chapter, we obtained a β of 1.8 from www.bloomberg.com. Using $E[r] = r_f + \beta(\text{MRP})$ with an MRP of 5% and a risk free rate of 4%, this gives a expected return of 13%.

Alternatively, β can be determined manually by the reader using the following formula:

$$\beta_i = \text{cov}(R_i, R_m)/\text{var}(R_m)$$

where R_i = the stock's daily return
R_m = the market's daily return.

The β may also be calculated as the slope of the best-fit line of a graph in which stock returns R_i are plotted against index returns R_m.

Be careful of missing data points! Commonly available web data seem to exclude some data points: if these data cover a day when the stock and the market covary widely, they can make a surprising difference to β.

Assuming that βi has a Gaussian sampling distribution (an assumption which is normally adopted), the standard deviation (SD) or standard error is calculated by the following formula:

$$\text{SD}(\beta_i)=\beta_i/(\sqrt{n})$$

where n = the number of non-overlapping data points that have been used.

Daily returns are calculated as follows:

$$R_i = \frac{\text{(price at end of day + dividend payment per share)}}{\text{price at beginning of day}} - 1$$

In figuring R_m, the analogous formula should be used, but an equivalent dividend payment per unit of the index is required. This can be obtained from various online services or from the *Financial Times* or *Wall Street Journal*. In early 2001 this market dividend yield stood at approximately 1.4% of the index per year in the USA, and at about 2.4% of the index per year in the UK, or about 0.5 points per day for the DJIA. Since dividend values tend to be maintained even if stock prices fall, the points per day value should be retained in the event of downward movement in the indices.

Excel has built-in formulae for the variance and covariance for columns of numbers, for example:

- *Variance:* VAR(A2:A61) produces the (sample) variance for three months of returns data in cells A2 to A61 (trading days only, of course)
- *Covariance:* COVAR(A2:A61, B2:B61) produces the covariance between three months of stock return data in column A and three months of index returns in column B, both situated in rows 2–61.

Although we have mentioned daily measurement of returns, the CAPM does not specify whether daily returns should be used, or some other period such as monthly. Bloomberg reported (in a private communication) that they use up to two years of weekly data. Other providers did not respond to enquiries. The calculated value of β is sensitive to the period of calculation and the amount of data, and is changeable over time. Sensitivity analysis should be carried out on various return periods and over time, to track trends in β.

Also, as much returns data as possible should be included in the calculation of β. In principle, all available data should be included (that is, 'outlier' returns should not be excluded). However, there are arguments for excluding IPO day stock returns, since IPO day is not repeated.

It is of some concern to the valuer how accurately β has been determined. This is shown by the standard deviation of the β, which is usually supplied by the commercial services alongside the β. To illustrate this, consider a β of 2 which has been supplied for a company: we are considering how to incorporate this in our valuation model. If there is a standard deviation of the β of 0.6, this means that the standard deviation or, more intuitively, the standard error of the β is 0.6. This means that if the sampling distribution of β is Gaussian, we can be 67% confident that the population β – that is, the 'true' or underlying β that we would find if we had all the stock returns data to infinity – lies within 1.4–2.6. We can be 95% confident that the true β lies within 0.8–3.2. If the standard deviation of the β is very large, there is an argument for sensitivity-testing the valuation model by altering the β and therefore the cost of capital. However, we do not advise this. Instead, we advise that current estimates of β are used, but that (specifically for internet companies) cost of capital is allowed to trend down over the period of the valuation simulation. This allows us to simulate a decrease in β resulting from a gradual lowering in operating leverage over time.

The β which is usually used for the calculation of equity cost of capital is the OLS β. This is synonymous with the regression β and the levered β. Other forms of β are:

- the unlevered or asset β: this is what the β would be if the firm was all equity financed (less than or equal to the levered β)
- the adjusted β: based on the theory that firm βs tend towards the industry β over time, the adjusted β combines the industry and OLS β as a weighted average. This can be based on some arbitrary weight (say, 2/3 OLS β, 1/3 industry β) or weighted based on the statistical reliability of the OLS β relative to the industry β.

The adjusted β method is less suitable for internet companies, since it is not clear with which industry they are comparable in terms of the variability of returns on their operating assets.

Determining the market risk premium

The most challenging parameter to determine is the market risk premium. A generation of MBAs and finance students was brought up to apply an MRP of 8.5%, based on the studies of the difference between equity market returns and risk free rates conducted by Ibbotson Associates. However, more recently, lower estimates for MRP have found favour. Many of these estimates have evolved from reverse calculation of the cost of capital of firms, using financial analysts' forecasts for earnings to calculate cash-flows, and taking current stock price as intrinsic value. Reverse calculation of cost of capital, if β is then measured for each firm from a historical regression in the normal way, will lead to a distribution of estimates for the MRP by firm. These estimates have been far below the historical values suggested by Ibbotson and similar guides. Values of between 1% and 3% for the MRP have been typical of this work.

To illustrate the changing perception of cost of capital, Ivo Welch of the Yale School of Management has carried out instructive survey research of financial economists about their views of the market risk premium. Between October 1997 and end 1998, Welch carried out a survey among 226 academic financial economists, and then held a 'round table' (in June 2000) of a smaller group of financial economists. The survey (which has been published in the *Journal of Business*) shows a mean of around 7% per year (arithmetical). The round table shows the wide range of individual's estimates of the MRP: from 1–2% (from reverse calculation) to 8.1% (from historical estimates). However, when Welch revisited the issue with another survey in summer 2001, he found considerably lower consensus estimates for the MRP, of 3–3.5% (short-term) and 5–5.5% (longer term). In dealing with practitioners and students 'Humility seems a useful starting point', suggests one round-table participant. This is certainly true – there is a lot which we do not know. But valuation is no place for the humble. An estimate of MRP is needed, and we shall seek to justify an estimate of 5% per year.

In arguing for this compromise figure, we shall take as a starting point the 8–9% estimates of Ibbotson and similar work, and discuss the reasons why this has been adjusted downwards, and how much of this adjustment is reasonable. We can see three major drivers for the downward shift in the perception of MRP value:

1. *High observed stock values leading to extremely low implied values for the MRP via reverse calculation.* This line of argument states that investors have gained confidence because of the market's excellent performance, see it as less risky, and therefore do not require as high an MRP. Proponents of this view suggest that underlying changes in the real economy have lowered the risk in equities by making businesses more adaptable and facilitating quicker reactions to opportunities and threats.

2. *Revisionism attacking previous estimates of the historical MRP as too high.* This line of argument holds that the historical MRP may be a satisfactory predictor of what we expect the MRP to be in the future, but that the historical MRP has been wrongly measured.

3. *The inability of recent work in financial economics to explain the observed value of the historical MRP.* If current economic models for asset pricing and investors choices are correct, equity premia in the region of 5–10% imply ridiculously high levels of risk aversion by investors.

Do high observed stock prices suggest that the MRP has fallen?

Although there are many financial economists working to understand the MRP for the most altruistic and ivory-tower reasons, there is no doubt that rises in equity values have provided the main impetus for the interest in the MRP. (Even after the fall in internet stock values, market prices are still at high levels compared to historical benchmarks such as average price/earnings ratios). If analysts predict future earnings (on average) correctly, and the market prices stocks (on average) in line with intrinsic values, the historical β is an appropriate guide for future β, and the CAPM is correct, then the MRP follows directly. If stock prices rise without any apparent change in future earnings or β, then something has to 'give', and that something is the MRP – it must fall because all of the other parameters (analysts' earnings forecasts, market prices, the risk free rate and β) can be directly measured. In such a world, rising stock prices give the observer concrete evidence that the investors' required compensation for equity market risk has fallen. This counterintuitive combination (rising stock market because of a lower expected return) is typical of the tripwires of this field.

Let us take a moment to try to simplify this.

> Let us consider a small country with extremely trustworthy citizens, where nearly all savings are held by a large bank. The bank pays 5% interest per year. This is the expected return on all investments, since all the citizens can be trusted absolutely. I have an agreement with Bob that he will pay me $105 in one year. This 'IOU' is worth $100 today and, if I wish, I can go down to the local coffee house and sell it to another of Bob's friends, just like a share. Now suppose (in a surprise move!) the large bank cuts interest rates to 4%. How much will Bob's IOU now be worth?

The bank's action will decrease expected returns to 4%, since all investments are free of risk. But my agreement with Bob is still in place, and the value of my IOU increases to $105/1.04 = $100.96, were I to sell it today, because if I sold it for less it would pay out more than the prevailing interest rate (now 4%).

The analogy here is that a share in a firm gives us a right to a stream of cashflows from that firm. If the return we expect on the average investment in a firm goes down (because firms are 'looking less risky' these days), the value of the share will go up.

A large sample study published in the *Journal of Finance* by James Claus and Jacob Thomas (2001) is a good example of work in this field. Claus and Thomas examined a large sample of between 1500 and over 3000 US companies between 1985 and 1998. Their methodology is a good example of how successful reverse determination of discount rates and MRPs can be carried out. They obtained share prices from the IBES database and past accounting data from the COMPUSTAT database. They also obtained information on equity analysts' forecasts of earnings for the future from the IBES database. They then used the residual income model (which can be viewed as a mathematical rearrangement of the DCF model) to answer the following question:

Suppose the share price is equal to the sum of future cash flows, what would the cost of capital have to be? In other words, we could set up a DCF equation, but instead of trying to estimate the future earnings (from our financial projections) and the cost of capital (from, say, the CAPM), we could instead assume that market price and estimated future cash flows were correct, and estimate the cost of capital from these.

Imagine tweaking our Amazon model in the last chapter by altering the cost of capital until we got the same valuation as the market. The reader can actually try this with the model we developed and, even better, Excel's Goal Seek function will do most of the work! The steps are as follows:

1. Open the Amazon model in Excel.
2. Enter the parameters for the continuing case.
3. In cell C12 enter the formula '=C11' – this ensures that the cost of capital is the same for the whole model, as Goal Seek can only cope with changing one parameter at a time.
4. Select Goal Seek from the Tools Menu.
5. In the 'Set cell' entry, enter or highlight C29, the current stock price.
6. In the 'To value' entry, enter today's stock price from Amazon.com common (say, $15).
7. In the 'By changing cell' entry, enter or highlight C11, for the cost of capital.
8. When 'OK' is pressed, the system will alter the value of the cost of capital by a sophisticated form of trial and error until the stock price is equal to $15. This takes place instantly.
9. The implied cost of capital (in the case of the $11 price, this is equal to 8.90%) is shown in cell C11.

This means that in order for the projections we have made about Amazon *and* for the market price to be correct, the cost of capital for Amazon has to be 8.90%. If Amazon's β is correct at 1.8, then this implies an MRP of about 2.7%. What Claus and Thomas did was repeat this process over a very large sample of companies and years, using analysts' forecasts of earnings (instead of spreadsheet projections) to 'populate' their valuation models for each firm. How much credence one puts in Claus and Thomas's results depends on one single judgement: how much credence one puts in the market valuations of stocks between 1985 and 1998. Certainly, influential commentators on the market, such as Robert Shiller in his excellent book *Irrational Exuberance*, make a very strong case that the 1985 and 1998 period corresponded to the biggest outbreak of overvaluation we have so far seen in the US stock market. Furthermore, neither the 2.7% we have calculated, nor the 3% that Claus and Thomas headline, seems a very tempting risk premium for the stock market from the point of view of the individual investor.

We stated above that utilizing reverse calculation for cost of capital for individual firms is not advisable if misvaluation is suspected. Since there is very little point in carrying out valuation if misvaluation is *not* suspected, this means we will have infrequent recourse to this technique in individual firm valuation! However, there is more justification in looking at market-wide valuations, especially if we view the valuation of different firms as independent. A wide variety of investors has been, in the past several years, willing to pay more than we would expect for stocks, and there are only two possible reasons for this:

1. The investors have correctly judged that the justified future MRP has fallen to about 3%. This means that risky assets are 'not that risky' any more (perhaps they never were 'that risky'), and a diversified investor investing in a standalone business project of about the same risk as the economy (say a shop or factory) would require a return of about 7% (4% risk free plus 3% MRP), and would be happy with that (without any liquidity premium). In this case stocks' future returns will average about 3% per year over risk-free.
2. The investors have incorrectly judged that the future MRP is 3%, and have bid up shares appropriately, but in fact the MRP is still 8%. In this case risky assets are still very risky, and our hypothetical investor walking in the industrial areas of Oakland or the East End of London will require a return of 12% from a standalone shop or factory. The problem for the stock market investors is very simple. *Firms are just bundles of shops and factories!* If investors can receive returns of 12% in the real economy, that is what they will expect from the markets. Sooner or later, stocks will be substantially down-valued to reflect this.

We should apply a great deal of credence to the view of the whole world of investors, but it would be unwise to accept their view completely at face value. First, individual stock values have not been independently determined – the valuation of the stocks in the market has a lot in common with a *single data point*, in that companies' fortunes are driven largely by economy-wide factors, and investors use those factors to judge the market's value. This means that we should not feel comfortable just because a wide range of shares has been valued to suggest a low MRP: these share prices could just be different manifestations of the same error by the investment community. Second, there is no clear reason why underlying assets should seem less risky now. Third, the rises in stock values were not as a result of a realization among investors that average firm risk had fallen, or had been overstated in the past. In fact, rises in stock values led to the proposal of lower firm risk as an explanation. This is a similar pattern to that in 1929, where talk of a 'new paradigm' in stock investment was just as prevalent as it was in early 2000.

Has the MRP simply been overestimated in the historical returns data?

Dimson, Marsh and Staunton (2001) have suggested that the high estimates of the market risk premium have been partly due to overestimates in the return of the equity markets, due to various types of *selection bias*. Selection bias, in this case, means that the people estimating the equity market return inadvertently overestimated the return by excluding some stocks that did badly. To give an illustrative example, two ways in which this may have been done are by *success bias* and *survivorship bias*. One cause of these biases is judging equity returns using the returns on published stock indices. This seems, at first blush, an eminently sensible way of judging 'typical' stock returns. However, what has often happened is that investigators of share price returns have tried to estimate past returns by using the performance of the index companies back 10 or 20 years. But this will *overestimate* returns. To see why, we need to realize that the kind of companies in an index are companies which have *survived* and, indeed, become *successful*. Let's pretend we are sitting in 1940 using a major stock index to do a 'backfilling' of missing market returns to use for 1920–39. The companies in the index have usually got where they are by 10 or 20 years of high growth and good profit performance, and have probably generated high returns in that time – much more than average (success bias). And that's the problem – we're trying to use them to represent the *average* (that is, the market) return. Also, the companies are survivors: the chance of them having gone broke (–100% return) during 1920–39 is zero (survivorship bias). We know they lasted until now, or they wouldn't be in the index! Thus they are not representative of the average stock.

Dimson et al.'s careful analysis of world stock markets and their performance means that we can, perhaps, have at least some of our cake and eat it. In determining MRP we must be very leery of the recent stock market returns as a guide. Many commentators feel that the returns of 1997–2000 will not be repeated for a long time. Shiller (2000) goes even further and suggests that the whole period 1980–2000 is an exceptional period and should carry a health warning before use in analysis. The study of prospective risk premia by Claus and Thomas which suggested an MRP of 3% was entirely based on data from this period.

Returning to Dimson et al.'s work, the outcome of their attempts to eliminate the various biases have been estimates of the MRP more in tune with the lower values many theoreticians feel are needed, but still based on historical data. Dimson et al. suggest figures of about 5% for the MRP for both the US and the UK.

Why are the observed measures of the MRP so much higher than financial economic theory leads us to expect?[3]

While many old-timers may read the reverse calculation estimates of a 3% MRP with rising anger because it is too low, there is another group of angry, but younger, thinkers who believe it is too high! Financial economics suggests that stocks do not have enough variation in their returns to justify an MRP of more than 1 or 2%.

The logic that these theorists use is to translate into everyday language the level of risk aversion investors would have to show to require an MRP of 8%. Using the Hansen-Jagannathan lower bound on the Sharpe Ratio (which is a fundamental ratio of return over risk, calculated as market excess return/standard deviation of return), the theorists calculate that the postwar excess returns suggest that the representative investor must have a relative risk aversion coefficient of 48. This would imply extreme risk aversion. In order to tempt such a person to gamble 5% of his or her annual salary on a 50:50 bet, one would have to offer odds of 12–1!

This leads the theorists to suggest that the recent high returns since 1950 were not expected by investors, and were not priced into the cost of capital. The investors in this recent period were just lucky. And the lesson from this for future expected returns is that they will not be as high as in recent decades, perhaps only 1 or 2% over risk-free. The divergence between the MRP suggested by theory (1 or 2%) and the stubborn real-world data is referred to as the *equity premium puzzle*.

However, some theories have been suggested that may explain the puzzle:

- The models that economists use for economic behaviour assume that people's aversion to risk is related to their dislike for postponing spending. Some other models which allow for economic agents to be very risk-averse but not much concerned about postponing consumption allow a slightly higher MRP to be explained.
- Habit formation in human behaviour may prevent people from choosing the most attractive investments, leading to underpricing of equities and an increase in the realized MRP.
- The peso problem: economic agents are correctly demanding high-risk premia because of the risk of very large shocks (for example: the collapse of

a currency) which have not occurred in the recent US data. So the volatility data is low because investors have been lucky and have avoided shocks, but they will still demand high returns because the shocks remain possible.

- Various restrictions on trading, such as transactions costs and short sale constraints, prevent appropriate pricing of risk.
- Risks which individual economic agents have are too idiosyncratic and uninsurable to allow predictable behaviour *en masse*. This means that the group of all market participants cannot be modelled as one large 'average' agent, which might mean that the underlying logic of the equity premium puzzle may be faulty.
- Limited participation: only a subset of the population invests. Their consumption and income is much more volatile than the average citizen; so if we measured the volatility of their wealth, the equity premium puzzle might not appear so serious.

None of these theories has been accepted, and the puzzle remains exactly that. But if several of the above tendencies are throwing off the theoretical calculations of the MRP in the same direction, then this could explain the difference between the predicted and the observed values.

PUTTING IT ALL TOGETHER

In summary, then, we have suggested that the CAPM should be used as the main method of determining the cost of capital for publicly quoted internet firms. However, it may be wise to conduct sensitivity analysis based on Fama and French's four-factor model. Unfortunately, data on FF cost of capital is not as easy to obtain as that of CAPM. (FF costs of capital can be obtained from several paid services, including Ibbotson Associates, and academic users can obtain the FF factor returns from the CRSP service.) However, the issue of whether the FF model's lower cost of capital for growth stocks is appropriate is particularly important for internet stocks. If observed low returns on growth stocks are due to the market frequently overvaluing such stocks, we should not assume a low cost of capital for them.

We have also discussed certain concerns with regard to the determination of key parameters of the CAPM model, especially β and the MRP.

The value of β depends on the period over which it is measured. Since the theory gives little guidance on the period, we laid out the method for measuring β, so that valuers can carry out sensitivity analysis by measuring daily returns, weekly returns, monthly returns, and so on.

Finally, we defended an estimate of the MRP of 5%. This is substantially below Ibbotson estimates which have been used in the past, which might be subject to biases as discussed by Dimson et al. It is substantially above estimates of the 'prospective' or 'reverse calculation' MRP of 3% and above the still lower estimate of the MRP from economic theory. The reverse calculation estimates may be unsafe due to the recent period being anomalous. The theoretical estimates are puzzling, but may be due to the model of economic behaviour used in the work being incomplete. Our estimate of 5% is close to the recent work of Dimson et al. who determined the historical MRP for various countries while adjusting for the biases that may have limited the accuracy of previous work.

APPENDIX 5.1: DERIVATION OF CAPM

The CAPM can be fairly simply derived, as demonstrated by Jagganathan and McGrattan (1995), as follows.

Stage 1: Setting up the problem

Suppose a representative (only) investor can choose between 3 assets (0, 1 and 2). He allocates a fraction of his wealth α_0, α_1 and α_2 to each asset or security.

A risk free security (government bond) exists: it is asset 0 (assets 1 and 2 are shares). Note that the risk-free security has zero variance.

The investor's (indirect) utility function, V, is dependent on $E[R]$ (expected return) and $\text{var}(R_m)$ (variance of the return):

$$V = f(E[R_m], \text{var}(R_m))$$

The investor seeks to maximize $V(E[R_m], \text{var}(R_m))$ by adjusting his portfolio α_0, α_1 and α_2.

Stage 2: Equalities and definitions

We know that:

- $\alpha_0 + \alpha_1 + \alpha_2 = 1$ (the investor is fully invested)
- $E[R_m] = \alpha_0 R_0 + \alpha_1 E[R_1] + \alpha_2 E[R_2]$ (that is, the portfolio return is the weighted average of security returns)

- $\text{var}(R) = \alpha_1{}^2\text{var}(R_1) + \alpha_2{}^2\text{var}(R_2) + 2\alpha_1\alpha_2\text{cov}(R_1R_2)$ (statistical identity relating total variance to component variances; 'cov' means 'covariance' – how much the uncertainty of the stocks move together rather than opposite).

Stage 3: We introduce the two key assumptions

- $\alpha V/\delta E[R_m] > 0$ (the utility is increasing with $E[R]$ – that is, the investor likes high returns)
- $\delta V/\delta\text{var}(R_m) < 0$ (the investor's utility is decreasing in the variance of the portfolio return).

Stage 4: Rearrangement

Then we eliminate α_0 by setting it equal to $1 - \alpha_1 - \alpha_2$ (using $\alpha_0 + \alpha_1 + \alpha_2 = 1$):

$$V = V\{(1 - \alpha_1 - \alpha_2)R_0 + \alpha_1 R_1 + \alpha_2 R_2, \alpha_1{}^2\text{var}(R_1) + \alpha_2{}^2\text{var}(R_2) + 2\alpha_1\alpha_2\text{cov}(R_1R_2)\}$$

Differentiating V (taking slope) with respect to α_1 and α_2:

$$(E[R_1] - R_0)V_1 + 2\{\alpha_1\text{var}(R_1) + \alpha_2\text{cov}(R_1,R_2)\}V_2 = 0$$

$$(E[R_2] - R_0)V_1 + 2\{\alpha_2\text{var}(R_2) + \alpha_1\text{cov}(R_1,R_2)\}V_2 = 0$$

where V_i is the partial derivative of V with respect to α_i

Multiply the first equation by α_1 and the second by α_2, and add:

$$\{\alpha_1(E[R_1] - R_0) + \alpha_2(E[R_2] - R_0)\}V_1 \\ + 2\{\alpha_1(\alpha_1\text{var}(R_1) + \alpha_2\text{cov}(R_1,R_2)) + \alpha_2(\alpha_2\text{var}(R_2) + \alpha_1\text{cov}(R_1,R_2)\}V_2 = 0$$

Gathering terms and using definitions of $E[R_m]$ and variance:

$$(E[R_m] - R_0)V_1 + 2\text{var}(R_m)V_2 = 0$$

Express this and the top two lines as functions of (V_2/V_1):

$$E[R_i] - R_0 = \{\text{cov}(R_i,R_m)/\text{var}(R_m)\}(E[R_m] - R_0)$$

Stage 5: Define beta and obtain CAPM formula

Define beta:

$$\beta_i = \mathrm{cov}(R_i, R_\mathrm{m}) / \mathrm{var}(R_\mathrm{m})$$

Substituting:

$$E[R_i] - R_0 = \beta_i \, (E[R_\mathrm{m}] - R_0)$$

$$E[R_i] = R_0 + (E[R_\mathrm{m}] - R_0) \, \beta_i \quad \text{(the CAPM formula)}$$

Note that the investor holds the market portfolio.

In other words, the CAPM can be derived from two simple assumptions: that investors like high returns and that they dislike high variance. It does not just 'come out of the ether'.

Notes

1 There are some exceptions. For example, no positive cost of capital will solve the equation where a positive price is equated with negative future cash flows.

2 This view is supported by Skinner and Sloan (1999), who studied the pattern of stock returns from growth stocks, and found that the low returns from growth stocks are mainly due to large drops in growth stocks' prices around the time of disappointing earnings announcements.

3 This discussion is greatly influenced by Demarzo (1998).

CHAPTER 6

RoCEL: Return on Capital Limitation Technique

COMPETITION LIMITS RETURN ON CAPITAL

How does competition work? Moving forward, from talking about the problems competition causes, how can we actually factor in its effects on our DCF models? Well, first of all, let's look at the facts, and see how competition does directly limit returns on capital and return on assets, and how it ensures that only a tiny fraction of companies do make ultra-high returns. Then we will move on to methods on how to deal with this. Finally, we will pick up the example of our valuation of Amazon.com, to complete the valuation by carrying out the restriction of return on capital that we planned in Chapter 4.

Moving to the data, we can see from the graph in Figure 6.1 that the proportion of firms making returns above 25% is small. An alternative presentation of this data, which shows the cumulative distribution of returns, is shown in Figure 6.2.

Statistically, we can observe the following:

- median: 15%
- inter-quartile range: 9–20%
- <5% of firms exceed 35% RoCE in any firm year.

Also, as demonstrated by Healy, Palepu and Bernard (HPB), few companies make consistently high returns. HPB studied the population of US industrial

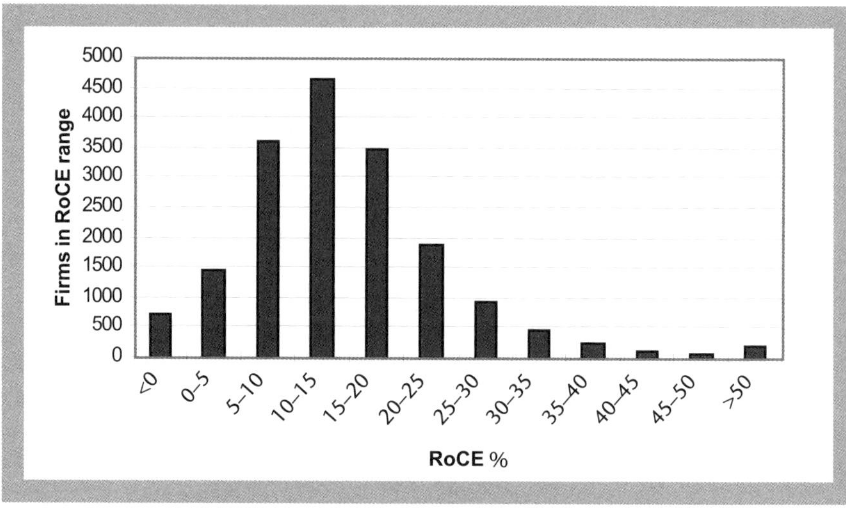

Figure 6.1 Distribution of RoCE (large firms, with revenue > $1m per annum) (1967–1998)

firms, and looked at their *return on assets* (*ROA*) and other parameters by splitting the firms into the highest return quintile (20%) the next highest, and so on. Then they tracked the same firms over time. The highest-return group started off with an average return of 25%, but after 8 years had declined to 12%.

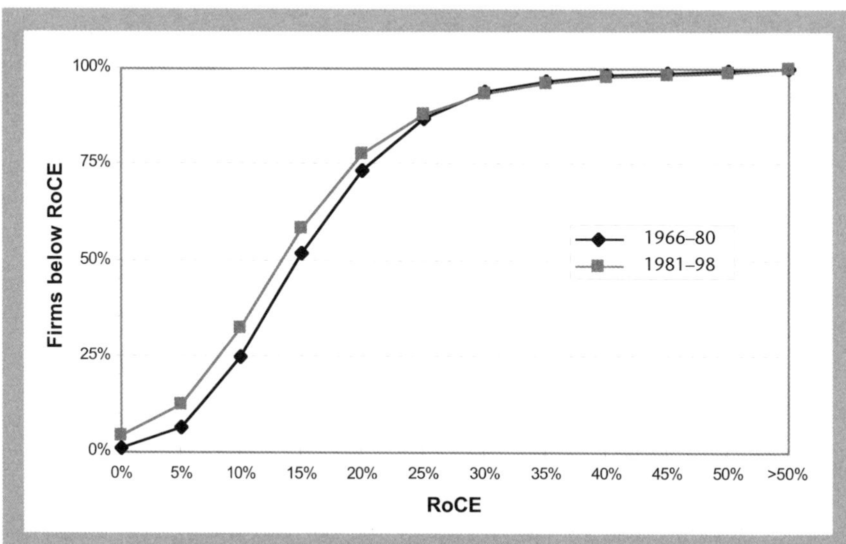

Figure 6.2 Cumulative distribution of RoCE

Table 6.1 Returns on capital (standards)

For a firm in a competitive market	Maximum return on capital = 15%
For a firm with exceptional ability to defend its market position	Maximum return on capital = 30%

So we should expect an average firm to make a return on capital of 15%. Returns above 20% will be rare; and above 35% extremely rare, and likely to be transient. We therefore fix the standards shown in Table 6.1.

A forecast with a high RoA is a bad forecast

In Chapter 3 we discussed the essential *total revenue health check* that should be imposed on a forecast – seemingly modest revenue growth rates (say 20%) can lead to rises in revenues that in later years of the forecast take a firm beyond the total size of its addressable market. For example, many early forecasts of AOL's value had the firm signing up all of the US population as subscribers!

A second essential health check should be on the return on assets that occurs in the later years of the forecast. While the total revenue health check controls for excessive revenue growth assumptions, the *return on assets health check* effectively controls for over-ambitious assumptions of operating leverage, as well as forming a second check on the revenue growth projections.

We can write formulae into the spreadsheet not just to check the return on capital, but to force it to conform with a preset return on capital limit, or even to trend down over time in line with a decay pattern.

PRACTICAL ASPECTS OF ROA CONTROL USING EXCEL

Control of RoA is most elegantly done by macro or by scripting programming. An example of an online scripting application where return on capital is limited can be seen at www.internet-valuation.com/palgrave (login required). However, scripting and programming is beyond the subject matter of this book. Alternatively formulae can be used. In this case it is necessary to limit return on beginning assets employed, to avoid the problem of circularity in the spreadsheet. *RoBOA* (*return on beginning operating assets*) is calculated by taking:

- the operating profit as the numerator

- the start of year operating assets (BOA) as denominator – operating assets are calculated by taking the capital employed (calculated as equity shareholders funds plus debt) and subtracting cash and marketable securities.

The spreadsheet then compares RoBOA with a benchmark maximum (for example, 30%) or a predicted exponential trendline, and if the benchmark is exceeded, operating profit is decreased to force the following equivalence:

operating profit = benchmark RoBOA × BOA

The following spreadsheet coding sequence achieves the desired result:

1. Calculate the beginning operating assets from previous year's data.
2. Calculate the operating profit using sales minus costs.
3. Calculate the RoBOA based on this operating profit.
4. Check the RoBOA against the benchmark maximum.
5. Set the operating profit to IF(RoBOA>Benchmark_RoBOA, Benchmark RoBOA*BOA, Sales-costs).

We now illustrate specific formulae, for the simplest case of a single benchmark return on assets stored in cell C18. Consider our Amazon spreadsheet stored with line items down (rows) and years across (columns), and with column I as the first year in the simulation. See Table 6.2.

Table 6.2 Specific formulae for a spreadsheet

Calculation	Formula
Let operating assets be in line 58, cell I58	
Then beginning operating assets in cell H58	= H58 (previous year)
Let gross profit be in line 36 and costs be in lines 37–40 expressed as negative	
Then initial estimate operating profit can be calculated as	= sum (I36:I40)
RoBOA can be calculated as	= sum (I36:I40)/H58
Let Benchmark_RoBOA be stored in cell C18	
Final estimate operating profit can be calculated in cell I41 as	IF(sum(I36:I40)/H58>C18, C18*H58,sum(I36:I40))

Note the use of absolute addressing for the benchmark maximum return, to ensure that the formula can be used in multiple years without rewriting; and also that we combine steps 3–5 in the single formula in cell I41. This enhances the readability of the simulated income statement. (However, this comes at the expense of the readability of the formulae.) Note also that we have used the accounting net assets as a first-cut estimate of operating assets. This is not appropriate for a company with large intangible assets and we will discuss this in the following pages.

We mentioned that a downward trending RoA can be used (in accordance with the evidence of HPB) to simulate the effect of competition and a gradually maturing market. An example exponential decay pattern would be the following:

$$RoA_{t+1} = \text{Target RoA} + (RoA_t - \text{Target RoA}) * \text{Decay factor}$$

where

- RoA_t and RoA_{t+1} are the returns on assets employed for year t (this year) and t+1 (next year)
- Target RoA would be a typical RoA to which company returns will decline (for example 12%)
- (RoA_t–Target RoA) is, in effect, the excess returns over target, which decays exponentially[1]
- Decay factor is a multiplier which is equal to this year's returns over target as a fraction of last year's: a typical value might be 50–80%, depending on the sustainability of the company's competitive advantage.

WHAT IS THE RIGHT NUMBER FOR OPERATING ASSETS?

So far in this discussion we have used the accepted accounting definition of operating assets:

operating assets = equity + net debt

where 'net debt' is debt net of cash and cash equivalents.

Ignoring quasi-capital quantities such as provisions, operating assets can be equivalently calculated using the asset side of the balance sheet:

operating assets = total assets – cash and cash equivalents

using total assets = equity + debt.

However, many commentators have suggested that accounting does not value intangible assets, such as brand. Marketing spending that might have lasting benefits is immediately expensed (that is, it is subtracted from the revenue in the calculation of profit) whereas spending on a machine is depreciated gradually. The issue of whether intangible assets are valued in the balance sheet is entirely irrelevant to the outcome of a basic DCF valuation, it is the time of cash flow not the time of expensing that matters for DCF. However, it is extremely relevant to the topic of *simulating competition*. Let us outline the reasoning we need to go through to show this, focusing on the issue of marketing spending:

- If accounting treated marketing spending differently, operating assets would change. For example, if marketing spending were treated like spending on building a physical machine (which forms an asset), operating costs would rise.
- Companies considering entry into a market look at the return on the assets needed to enter the market, which may or may not correspond to the return on operating assets as estimated by the accounting numbers.
- Therefore, if we are simulating the effects of competition by limiting returns, we should limit returns based on *all* of the assets needed to enter the market, including any brand equity built up, because to compete effectively competitors would have to replicate this brand equity.

In summary, we should aim to calculate the return on the *full replacement cost of assets*: the total amount of money it would cost for a competitor to build a business in the market in which the subject company is operating. This may include an estimate of intangible assets. The valuer should also consider the issue of whether operating leases should be capitalized (as discussed in Appendix 3.1).

Operating assets and the accounting treatment of marketing spending

Normally, accounting expenses all marketing spending immediately. Suppose we are seeking to build a brand and we spend $200m per annum. The effect on the income statement would be –200 in each year, and the effect on operating assets would be zero.

By contrast, suppose we are spending $200m per year to enhance a factory and adopting a 10-year depreciation timescale. The effect on the income state-

Table 6.3 10-year depreciation: income statement

Year	**1**	**2**	**3**	**4**	**5**	**6**	**7**	**8**	**9**	**10**	**11**	**12**
Total depreciation	–20	–40	–60	–80	–100	–120	–140	–160	–180	–200	–200	–200

Table 6.4 10-year depreciation: balance sheet

Year	**1**	**2**	**3**	**4**	**5**	**6**	**7**	**8**	**9**	**10**	**11**	**12**
New operating assets	+180	+340	+480	+600	+700	+780	+840	+880	+900	+900	+900	+900

ment would be as shown in Table 6.3, and the (cumulative) effect on the balance sheet would be as in Table 6.4.

In other words, the spending on fixed assets does not immediately impact the income statement in the same way as spending on marketing does, because it is 'stored' on the balance sheet as an asset, and gradually depreciated. If we are calculating return on assets, and using it to benchmark returns, we will allow higher profits to the company which has built up higher operating assets under GAAP. However, if the company's efforts to build brand have been successful, and the brand has been effectively built up as a barrier to entry, then that *brand* can be viewed as an asset, and it would need to be replicated by anyone who wished to enter and compete. Alternatively the entrant would have to accept lower, non-premium prices than the incumbent company. Either way, the brand makes it more difficult for them, and would deter them from entering the market.

Note that after the period of 10 years the constant spending on marketing and the constant spending on fixed assets reach an equivalence. The effect on the income statement is exactly the same from year 10 onwards, and the effect on operating assets reaches stasis at 900 greater for the fixed assets than for the possible intangible assets. Also, the accumulated depreciation for years 1–9 summed together is equal to 900, precisely 900 less than the marketing expense over years 1–9. So accounting equivalence is preserved if we imagine the company being liquidated at any period after period 9 – the book value of 900 would be *subtracted* from any liquidation proceeds to calculate the profit over book on liquidation. However, it should be noted that if spending has a positive growth rate, the depreciation treatment (as used for tangible assets under standard (GAAP) accounting) will permanently give a lower expense and a higher profit.

What assets are needed to compete effectively?

Strategic decisions are ultimately driven by investors' search for superior returns. *Everyday* decisions are taken by managers; but, provided that managers are selected for their ability to create shareholder value, and provided that they are appropriately incentivized, managers will seek to enter markets in which they will be able to make returns exceeding the cost of capital. If the market requires that intangible assets be built up to enter, then this is money that must be invested in order to enter the market. In simulating competition using the maximum benchmark RoA, therefore, the assets in the denominator should include an allowance for the intangible assets.

However, the simulation of assets, in particular the simulation of assets built up by marketing spending, is a matter of some controversy. First, assets as we understand them in normal conversation are separable and identifiable. Ideally assets should be saleable, as an ultimate test of value. However, brand assets are frequently 'part of the business': they cannot be sold separately from the business, and can be quickly rendered valueless if the business encounters problems that undermine it (for example a consumer food brand could be very quickly ruined, and its brand value thus erased, by a poisoning scare).

Second, while there is no doubt that some companies, for example Coca Cola, Inc., have built up extremely valuable brand franchises, much marketing spend is addressing short-term needs and objectives. For example, it makes no sense to pretend that offering discounts in response to a competitor's discounting is going to generate long-term brand loyalty. In its early period, Amazon.com classified its fulfilment costs as marketing and sales spending. This classification was criticized, but in general distribution costs are rightly and properly classified as marketing and sales expense (because they are not part of production). However, neither fulfilment nor distribution costs can possibly be seen as anything other than a cost, to be minimized as far as possible while maintaining customer service. In summary, the investment in brand is only a part of the marketing and sales expense reported in the income statement or profit and loss. That investment in brand (a subset of reported marketing and sales) may form an asset, or it may not. It may only have a temporary effect or no effect on consumer perceptions.

As a contrary example to these arguments claiming that marketing spending overstates true investment in brand, let us consider a firm that does not specifically spend on advertising or brand-building, but that generates positive word of mouth and builds up a brand in this way? Using an expense-based model of brand this firm would appear to have no intangible assets, but clearly it does have a worthwhile brand. Another example is Amazon.com and its founder's talent for attracting media attention, which ensures that the firm is frequently in the news. This 'free publicity' does not factor into our model.

The truth is that any accounting model of marketing spending and its effect on brand asset can only be an approximation.

An alternative to an accounting valuation of brand is a valuation of the brand-based benefits it gives to the company possessing it. Some agencies, such as Interbrand and Landor, offer 'objective' brand valuations to companies. These are based on proprietary formulae and procedures. Interbrand issues the following description of its methodology on its website,[2] with regard to its published table of the top 100 global brands which we use below in our discussion of Amazon's brand value:

> Interbrand calculated the brand value in each case using the method it pioneered 13 years ago and has used to value over 2500 brands worldwide. Interbrand's proprietary method has been recognized by auditors, tax authorities and stock exchanges in many countries around the world. Interbrand starts with the economic profit generated by the brand to the underlying business, a similar concept to economic value added (EVA). The valuation process examines three areas: the future economic earnings the branded business is expected to generate, the role of the brand in generating those earnings, and the risk profile of the brand's expected earnings.

We will discuss this further when dealing with the Amazon.com valuation.

The accounting treatment of marketing spending under GAAP (standard accounting) assumes that marketing spending has effect for one year or less. Research that has been carried out on whether marketing spending forms an asset has been inconclusive, with some research suggesting that marketing should be expensed and some suggesting that it does indeed form an asset. The researchers have used various methods, but one illustrative approach is the *value relevance* approach. This forms a regression analysis of market equity values (as a proxy for intrinsic value) and tests whether market equity values are related to marketing and sales spending two or three years ago. If such a relationship is found, this is indicative of marketing and sales spending forming an asset. Some researchers have found a relationship, some have not. Since there is so much random variation in market equity values, and since market values are prone to misvaluation, it is difficult to form a conclusion from these empirical data.

Implementing the simulation of the marketing asset

In order to implement the effects of the need to build up brand in the DCF forecast, we have to estimate what size of asset is built up as a result of the company's marketing spend. Effectively, we set up a 'shadow' accounting representation of the company, whereby marketing is depreciated away instead of being expensed immediately. Then we test whether maximum benchmark return on assets is exceeded, based on our higher estimate of operating assets: operating assets = equity + net debt + marketing asset.

The procedure is as follows:

- Isolate the marketing spend which has the potential to build brand: exclude fulfilment spending, distribution spending, and sales promotion spending (for example coupons or tactical discounting), if identifiable. In the USA a more suitable base figure than marketing and sales may be advertising spending, which must be reported separately in the annual report 10-K filing.
- Determine the depreciation schedule for the marketing asset. This should be between 1 and 3 years, depending on the potential of the firm to build sustainable brand.
- Form a marketing asset. In each year, add marketing spend to the asset; and subtract only notional depreciation in accordance with the depreciation schedule determined above.
- Calculate the beginning operating assets (BOA) to be equity plus net debt plus marketing asset.
- Carry out the procedures for comparing RoBOA with the benchmark maximum RoBOA (as discussed above in the section entitled 'Practical aspects of RoA control using Excel'), using the adjusted BOA figure.

GUIDELINES FOR DEPRECIATION OF INTANGIBLE ASSETS

There is a balance of evidence that *research and development* spending forms an asset. The situation for spending on *marketing* is less clear. Experience suggests that companies' ability to generate long-term benefits from advertising spending may be company-specific. Some companies secure exceptional benefits from advertising, but most advertising leaves the consumer's mind quite quickly and is of short-term benefit. The policy of GAAP appears sensible as a working assumption.

However, valuers may wish to conduct sensitivity analysis based on short timescales for marketing spending of up to 3 years, straight-line.

Research and development spending is prevalent in some internet segments, for example on hardware and software infrastructure. For example, an e-tailer's spending on its e-tail platform may form an asset. Possible timescales suggested by the research are 5–10 years. For relevant companies this can be an interesting area for sensitivity analysis.

Valuers should be aware of some consequences of the process. If a marketing asset is being built up, then increased spending on marketing may actually increase value under competition. (This is not an artefact of the process, but a representation of the fact that an extra $1 of marketing spending creates economic value.) Note that the RoCEL methodology does not say that 'extra assets are good' – it would not be sensible to say that extra dollars spent create value of themselves. Extra spend has the potential to create value only if it creates an asset or a barrier that a competitor would need to emulate or overcome in order to compete.

CONTINUING THE AMAZON EXAMPLE

Let us recall our initial parameters for the estimation of the value of Amazon.com (see Table 6.5).

Now we will use the above techniques to simulate competitive forces by limiting Amazon.com's return on capital. The first thing to note is that the company has a very low projected capital employed, of about $108m. However, in view of the need to include the full replacement cost of assets needed to compete with Amazon, we should factor in the company's intangible assets, and it seems clear that the company has a strong brand, being by far the most well known and most trusted electronic retailer. We should also consider capitalizing the company's operating leases (as discussed in Appendix 3.1) and its e-tail technology platform.

As discussed above, there are two ways to calculate the value of the company's brand. One is the expense/capitalization-based model, which uses the marketing expense as an input, and assumes that this expenditure is forming an asset which depreciates over a limited lifespan. The other is to utilize estimates of brand value which are produced by independent brand-valuation consultancies.

Table 6.5 Amazon.com: initial parameters

	Continuing case (CCA)	Best case (BCA)	Worst case (WCA)
Revenue growth	12%	20%	7%
Variable costs as % of sales	88.5%	88.5%	90.5%
Fixed costs	$340m	$340m	$340m
Operating assets as % of sales	0%	0%	0%
Equity value (unconstrained)	$3.6bn	$9.4bn	$0.6bn
Limit RoCE to	30%	30%	15%

Figure 6.3 Amazon.com: annual marketing spend

	1996	1997	1998	1999	2000	2001
Marketing spend	2.0	12.7	43.2	175.8	180.0	138.3

Using the first methodology first, we need two inputs. First we need the marketing expense that the company incurred. Then we require an estimate of the amortization or depreciation timescale of the marketing assets. In the case of Amazon, in the early years marketing expenditure was not broken out, but was included in marketing and fulfilment. We assume that fulfilment has no branding value, so we break out the marketing costs by assuming that the ratio of marketing to fulfilment in the early years is the same as that in the later years, where we do have data. Figure 6.3 shows the data on marketing spend since 1996.

For construction of the marketing asset, spreadsheet entries are produced using the methods discussed above (Figure 6.4). Depreciation is taken as 3 years straight-line (for example, cell I125=G124/3+H124/3+I124/3) and we calculate the ongoing marketing spend as per our assumptions discussed in Chapter 4, so cell I124 contains '=138.3*0.5+0.022*I35' where cell I35 contains the annual revenues and 0.022 represents the 50% variable element of the cost. Set initial marketing asset (at firm inception) to zero. Then add marketing spend and subtract depreciation to calculate each successive year's marketing asset.

The marketing asset under CCA reaches a value of $274m in 2011. Technology assets are calculated in a similar way (see Figure 6.5 (annual technology spend being calculated as 241.2 * 0.75 + 0.019 × revenues) and would reach $358m in 2011. These rather small intangible assets, together with Amazon's $108m of accounting operating assets, would not seem to represent the value of the full replacement cost of assets that a competitor would need to purchase to compete head-to-head with Amazon. However, if assets under operating leases are capitalized (see Appendix 3.1) the operating assets are increased by a further $381.8m (2000: $428.9m). Why would we take the decision to do this? We would decide to do this if we feel that the operating leases are causing Amazon to take on a substantial portion of the ownership risk, and that they are primarily a source of finance rather than an ownership risk-avoidance tool.

This would lead to the following figure for gross operating assets under CCA in 2011:[3]

Operating assets (base)	$ 108m
Marketing asset (3-year straight-line)	$ 274m
Technology asset (3-year straight-line)	$ 358m
Capitalized value of operating leases	$ 382m
Total operating assets	$1122m

Figure 6.4 Evolution of the marketing asset over time

	B	C	D	E	F	G	H	I	J	K	L	M	N	O	P	Q	R	S
122		1996	1997	1998	1999	2000	2001	2002	2003	2004	2005	2006	2007	2008	2009	2010	2011	2012
123	Beginning marketing asset	0.0	1.3	9.1	33.0	131.6	178.6	152.2	143.3	152.0	161.9	173.0	185.5	199.5	215.1	232.6	252.2	274.2
124	Marketing spend - added to asset	2.0	12.7	43.2	175.8	180.0	138.3	145.8	155.0	165.3	176.9	189.8	204.3	220.5	238.7	259.0	281.8	307.3
125	Amortization	0.7	4.9	19.3	77.2	133.0	164.7	154.7	146.4	155.4	165.8	177.3	190.3	204.9	221.2	239.4	259.8	282.7
126	Ending asset	1.3	9.1	33.0	131.6	178.6	152.2	143.3	152.0	161.9	173.0	185.5	199.5	215.1	232.6	252.2	274.2	298.8

Figure 6.5 Evolution of the technology asset over time

	B	C	D	E	F	G	H	I	J	K	L	M	N	O	P	Q	R	S
129		1996	1997	1998	1999	2000	2001	2002	2003	2004	2005	2006	2007	2008	2009	2010	2011	2012
130	Beginning technology asset	0.0	1.5	9.1	35.1	122.0	232.8	250.6	245.1	252.4	261.0	270.6	281.4	293.4	306.9	322.1	339.0	358.0
131	Technology spend - added to asset	2.3	12.5	46.4	159.7	269.3	241.2	247.1	255.1	264.0	273.9	285.1	297.6	311.6	327.3	344.9	364.5	386.6
132	Amortization	0.8	4.9	20.4	72.9	158.5	223.4	252.5	247.8	255.4	264.3	274.3	285.5	298.1	312.2	327.9	345.6	365.3
133	Ending asset	1.5	9.1	35.1	122.0	232.8	250.6	245.1	252.4	261.0	270.6	281.4	293.4	306.9	322.1	339.0	358.0	379.2

Hint/tip: Clear cells A124, B124, A131 and B131 to ensure your amortization formulae (lines 125 and 132) work properly.

Table 6.6 Amazon.com: Interbrand's valuations

	1999	2000	2001
Interbrand valuation of Amazon.com's brand ($bn)	1.361	4.529	3.130

Now, let us look at the other option for determining the marketing asset, which is independent estimation of brand value. We have some data to help us do this from a leading brand-valuation consultant. The history of Amazon.com's brand valuation (by Interbrand, the leading brand valuer) was obtained (Hof, 2001), and is shown in Table 6.6. Interbrand produces an annual table of the world's leading brands, which it publishes. The precise techniques by which Interbrand carries out its valuation are not released by the company. As discussed above, projected residual income of the firm, how much the brand contributes to that future residual income, and the risk profile of the residual income are key valuation inputs. Comments in the press (Bainbridge, 1999) suggest that the brand is also scored on a scorecard on seven branding attributes, in comparison to a 'notional ideal brand'. The attributes and their weightings are: market (10), stability (15), leadership (25), support (10), trend (10), geography (25) and protection (5). This brand score also contributes to valuation. It would seem that there is some room for subjectivity here, and it is interesting to note that the brand values are stated to the nearest $1m, which suggests a higher degree of accuracy than would intuitively seem to be reasonable.

Since we are projecting the future values of the operating assets, we would ideally like to have predictions for the future brand value, but these are not available. Let us assume that the 2001 figure persists. The estimate of full cost of assets is now:

Operating assets (base)	$108m
Marketing asset (Interbrand valuation)	$3130m
Technology asset (3-year straight-line)	$358m
Capitalized value of operating leases	$382m
Total operating assets	$3978m

For simulation purposes we take the average of the two estimates (the expense capitalization and independent estimate method) of the marketing asset, $1702m, which gives total operating assets as $2550m in 2011. Our justification for this is that the capitalization method of brand valuation underestimates brand valuation in this case, because much of Amazon's publicity and public relations has not been directly paid for (therefore has not appeared in the accounting statements) but has nevertheless added to the company's 'share of mind' among consumers. On the other hand, the assumption that the Interbrand value will persist over the model period is aggressive and may overestimate brand value, since it assumes the company can satisfactorily maintain the brand at its current level (while seeking to spend frugally as it has in recent quarters).

RoCE limitation for Amazon.com: calculations

Now we are ready to implement the RoCEL algorithm for Amazon. In preparation, load the Amazon spreadsheet made in Chapter 4 with the CCA parameters. As stated earlier in the chapter, the RoCEL procedure is:

1. Calculate the beginning operating assets from previous year's data.
2. Calculate the operating profit using sales minus costs.
3. Calculate the RoBOA based on this operating profit.
4. Check the RoBOA against the benchmark maximum.
5. Set the operating profit to IF(RoBOA>Benchmark_RoBOA, Benchmark RoBOA*BOA, Sales-costs).

The calculations and results are shown in Figure 6.6.

Step 1: Calculate beginning operating assets from previous year's data

To carry out the RoCEL calculations, we use free space from cell B130 onwards. In row 139, we use the accounting capital employed from row 70: then we add to this the capitalized value of operating leases ($382m), the marketing asset, which is in row 126, and the technology asset, stored in row 133. For the calculation of marketing asset the average of $3130m (Interbrand) and capitalised value is used. We then add these together to give the operating assets including intangibles, storing this in line 143. Note that in this case accounting capital employed does not change over time because we have assumed zero net operating assets for Amazon. However, it is still important to use formulae to include the calculated accounting operating assets in the simulation. This enables any changes due to increases or decreases in asset efficiency to feed through into the RoCEL algorithm.

Step 2: Calculate operating profit using sales minus costs

In the final calculation of RoCEL, the operating profit calculated in line 41 will have to be overwritten. Therefore we replicate this on line 145. For example in cell I145 enter '=SUM(I36:I40)' and auto-fill right.

Step 3: Calculate RoBOA based on this operating profit

We now divide the operating profit by the previous year's operating assets at replacement. The result is the return on beginning operating assets (no competition). For example in cell I146 enter the formula '=I145/H143'.

Step 4: Check RoBOA against benchmark maximum

The benchmark maximum is stored in cell C18 (parameters section). Enter 30% in this cell.

Step 5: Calculate operating profit to ensure that it does not exceed benchmark maximum RoCE

Overwriting the previous formula for operating profit, enter the following into cell I41 '=IF(ISBLANK($C18),SUM(I36:I40),IF(I146>$C18,$C18*H143,SUM(I36:I40)))'. Auto-fill right to cell S41. The use of the ISBLANK function prevents the algorithm from operating at all if there is no limiting benchmark return.

To check that the algorithm is executing correctly, a check line (line 137) can be added which calculates the RoBOA using the operating profit in line 41 (constrained). The RoCE limitation section (under CCA) should look like Figure 6.6. Note that in 2011 and 2012 the algorithm decreases return on capital (and therefore operating profit and cash flow).

Now load up the optimistic (BCA) parameters into the spreadsheet. Notice how unconstrained return on assets becomes very high at the end of the simulation. Since value is frequently dependent in large part on terminal value, the estimate of late year operating profits is doubly important. If this is done without regard to what returns can realistically be secured in a competitive market, then it is likely to be an overestimate.

Continuing with WCA, change the assumptions to 7% growth (cell C5), 15% other variable cost (C7) and 15% limiting return. The WCA (worst case analysis) remains at $604m ($1.62 per share). Our simulation of competition does not bite here, because the WCA assumptions do not cause a high enough return on capital – in other words, the WCA already assumes a very competitive market.

Final CFA results

The final results of CFA for Amazon are therefore as in Table 6.7.

Figure 6.6 Amazon.com: RoCE limitation section

	B	H	I	J	K	L	M	N	O	P	Q	R	S
138	RoCE limitation section	2001	2002	2003	2004	2005	2006	2007	2008	2009	2010	2011	2012
139	Capital employed (accounting)	(197)	108	108	108	108	108	108	108	108	108	108	108
140	Operating lease: capitalized value	382	382	382	382	382	382	382	382	382	382	382	382
141	Marketing asset: average capitalized & Interbrand	1,641	1,637	1,641	1,646	1,652	1,658	1,665	1,673	1,681	1,691	1,702	1,714
142	Technology platform: capitalized expense method	251	245	252	261	271	281	293	307	322	339	358	379
143	Estimated full replacement cost of required assets	2,077	2,372	2,383	2,397	2,412	2,429	2,448	2,469	2,493	2,520	2,550	2,584
144													
145	Operating profit	(45)	61	109	163	223	291	367	451	546	653	772	905
146	RoBOA (unconstrained)	-2%	3%	5%	7%	9%	12%	15%	18%	22%	26%	31%	35%
147	Check RoBOA	-2%	3%	5%	7%	9%	12%	15%	18%	22%	26%	31%	35%

Table 6.7 Final results of CFA after RoCE limitation

	Continuing case (CCA)	Best case (BCA)	Worst case (WCA)
Revenue growth	12%	20%	7%
Variable costs as % of sales	88.5%	88.5%	90.5%
Fixed costs	$340m	$340m	$340m
Operating assets as % of sales	0%	0%	0%
Equity value (unconstrained)	$3.6bn	$9.4bn	$0.6bn
Limit RoCE to	30%	30%	15%
Equity value (final)	$3.1bn	$3.7bn	$0.6bn

Now it only remains to weight these scenarios, using analysis of the company's strategic position, which we will do at the close of Chapter 12 (these values also exclude any value from real options, which we discuss in Chapter 8).

APPENDIX 6.1: STRAIGHT-LINE AND DECLINING BALANCE DEPRECIATION

When we looked briefly at the depreciation of fixed assets in Chapter 3, to give exposure to the concept of depreciation, we assumed straight-line depreciation. For straight-line depreciation with a 3-year timescale, if an asset is bought at the start of year 1 with price $300, it will appear on the income statement as a depreciation of $100 per year in years 1–3 (see Table 6.8).

Under a declining balance of 50% per year, the depreciation will be 50% of the asset in the balance sheet. In the first year, 50% of the $300 will be depreciated: that is, $150, while $300 – $150 = $150 will remain as an asset. In the next year once again, 50% ($75) will be 'used up'. Table 6.9 gives the schedule for the first few years. (The asset would never be entirely 'used up' under pure declining balance depreciation: write-off or asset resale would be required to extinguish an asset from the balance sheet.) Again, we assume that the asset is bought at the beginning of the year.

For this simple example, straight-line depreciation is more straightforward. But for more complex asset purchase schedules, declining balance depreciation is easier to calculate. This is because under declining balance, depreciation is always calculated as depreciation percentage * beginning operating assets

Under straight-line calculation of depreciation, unless asset purchases are *constant every year* – calculation of depreciation in year t for a timescale of n years requires dividing by n assets purchased in each of the n years $t - n + 1$, $t - n + 2, t - n + 3, \ldots, t - n + (n - 1), t$. For the straight-line method, a formula of the following type is required to calculate depreciation for the year whose data is stored in column X:

```
= X3/$O1+IF($O1>1,W3/$O1,0)+IF($O1>2,V3/$O1,0)+IF($O1>3,U3/$O1,0)
  +IF($O1>4,T3/$O1,0)+IF($O1>5,S3/$O1,0)+IF($O1>6,R3/$O1,0)
  +IF($O1>7,Q3/$O1,0)+IF($O1>8,P3/$O1,0)+IF($O1>9,O3/$O1,0)
```

where

- the depreciation timescale is stored in cell O1
- asset spend data is stored in row 3 (for a 10-year depreciation timescale, cells O3–X3 must be inspected)
- the use of IF($O1>*x*,…) statements is used to allow automatic variation of the depreciation term for up to 10 years – for example, if the timescale is set to 5 years in cell O1, then only cells T3, U3, V3, W3 and X3 need be divided

Table 6.8 Timescale of depreciation (straight-line: 3 years)

Year	1	2	3	4	5	6
Beginning operating assets	300	200	100	0	0	0
Depreciation (straight-line)	100	100	100	0	0	0
Ending operating assets	200	100	0	0	0	0

Table 6.9 Timescale of depreciation (declining balance: 50%)

Year	1	2	3	4	5	6
Beginning operating assets	300	150	75	37.5	18.75	9.375
Depreciation (declining balance)	150	75	37.5	18.75	9.375	4.6875
Ending operating assets	150	75	37.5	18.75	9.375	4.6875

by 5 to calculate total depreciation for year X: the IF statements 'switch off' the calculations in cells O3–S3 (because O1 is not greater than 5, and so on).

In contrast, the equivalent declining balance calculation would be:

=X4*$O2

where X4 = the beginning operating assets for year X

O2 = the % of assets (declining balance) used up in each year.

Frequently, declining balance is more computationally convenient than straight-line depreciation.

Notes

1 Note that Target RoA is never actually reached. This is as expected for an exponential process.
2 Web address: http://63.111.41.5/interbrand/test/html/events/table_1.html.
3 We highlight the required assets in 2011 because these assets help determine the terminal value, which is key to the valuation. 2011 assets are the beginning operating assets for the 2012 RoBOA calculation.

CHAPTER 7

Options I: ESOPs and Convertible Debt

WHAT IS AN 'OPTION'?

An *option* is a type of financial derivative security. *Derivative securities* are derived from what might be termed fundamental securities. *Fundamental securities* are the right to a stream of cash flows (it may be one or many), which are usually based on a company or a government's payments. Fundamental securities are usually some type of debt or equity (shares).

Let us look at an example of a fundamental security and a very simple derivative. Suppose we have a bond that a company has sold to investors for £100 in 1980, paying 11% interest for 30 years, and then paying back our £100 in the year 2010. Given the lower prevailing interest rates early in 2002, this bond would have become very valuable. We could imagine splitting the bond into two derivatives. One of the derivatives would give us a right only to the £100 in 2010; the other would give us the right only to the £11 per bond yearly payments. Why would we want to do that? Well, some investors may want to swap their money today for steady cash flows, to fund regular consumption, but may have no need for a big lump of money in 2010. On the other hand, imagine a nuclear power station looking at a 2010 timetable for decommissioning, and with a lot of current financial assets to invest to fund that. The 'principal only' bond, paying £100 in 2010, would fit in very well with its business plan. Alternatively, the two derivatives might be very attractive to different traders with different views on how quickly interest rates will change. They give traders two new ways to 'bet' on interest rates.

A *stock option* is another type of derivative that is most akin to an 'insurance policy' against rises (or falls) in the price of the fundamental security. Let us suppose now that the fundamental security is the stock of Yahoo! and that Yahoo! is currently priced at $13. The simple options are 'puts' and 'calls'. A $15 April *call* on Yahoo! gives the call buyer the right but not the obligation to *buy* Yahoo! shares at $15 any time until April. The figure at which he or she has the right to buy is termed the *strike price* or *exercise price*. The option is not a good deal now – we would not buy a share of Yahoo! at $15 using our call option when we can buy in the market for $13 – but it may be in the future. For example, if Yahoo! rises to $20 in April, then the option will be worth $5. However, if Yahoo! stays at $13, the option will not be worth anything. But, because we do not have any obligation to buy the Yahoo! shares, we will lose only our initial payment for the option (called the *premium*).

Let us think about the value of the option, and focus on the value at the end of the term of the option – that is, the value in April. Figure 7.1 is called a *payoff diagram*. Clearly, the payoff from the option is very much related to how much the Yahoo! stock sells for in April. The payoff diagram represents this by placing the payoff on the y-axis and the stock price of Yahoo! on the x-axis.

Another diagram readers will often see (or may have already seen) in option textbooks is the *profit diagram*. This is effectively the payoff diagram but minus the *cost* of the option – whatever we pay for it when we buy it today. Let us suppose that the option premium in this case is $2.50: that is, it costs $2.50 to buy the $15 April call (Figure 7.2). We can see that *breakeven* for the call

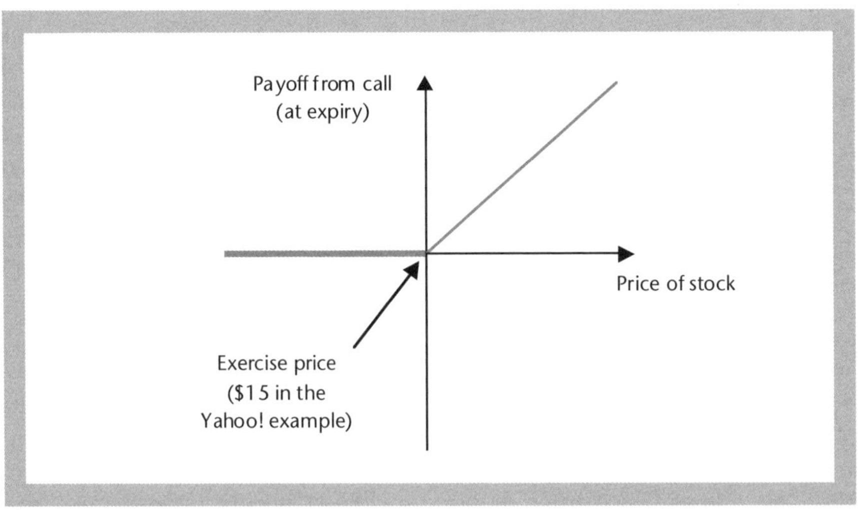

Figure 7.1 Payoff diagram for Yahoo! call options

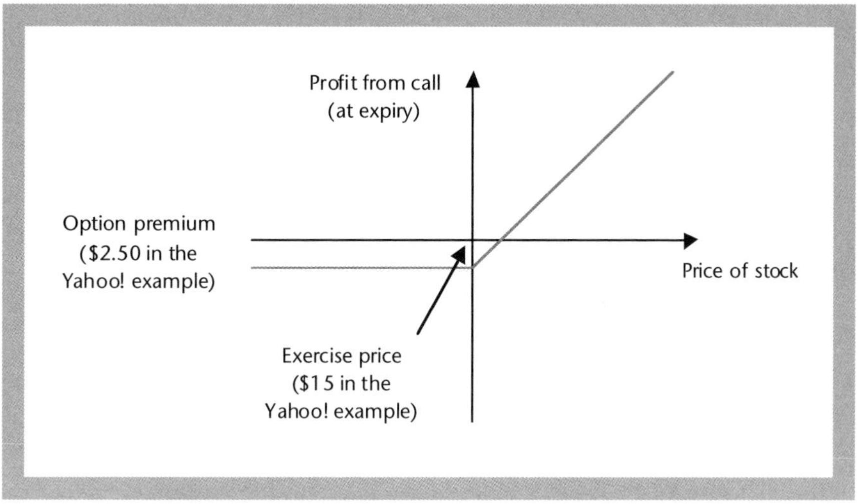

Figure 7.2 Profit diagram for Yahoo! call options

option comes if the price of Yahoo! is $17.50. If Yahoo! is $17.50 in April, the option at *expiry* is worth $2.50, exactly the cost which we paid.

The sibling derivative to the call is the *put*. A put gives the owner of the put the right but not the obligation to *sell* shares at a certain price. For example, an April $10 put on Yahoo! gives the owner the right but not the obligation to sell

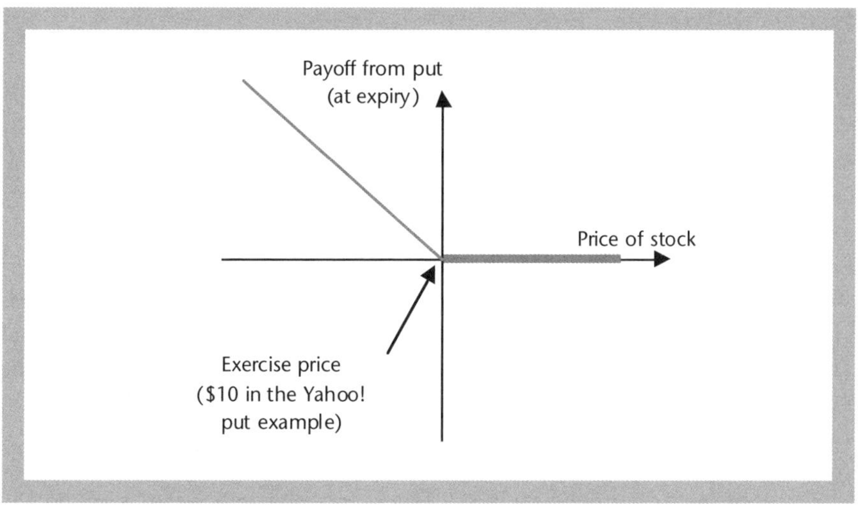

Figure 7.3 Payoff at expiry diagram for Yahoo! put options

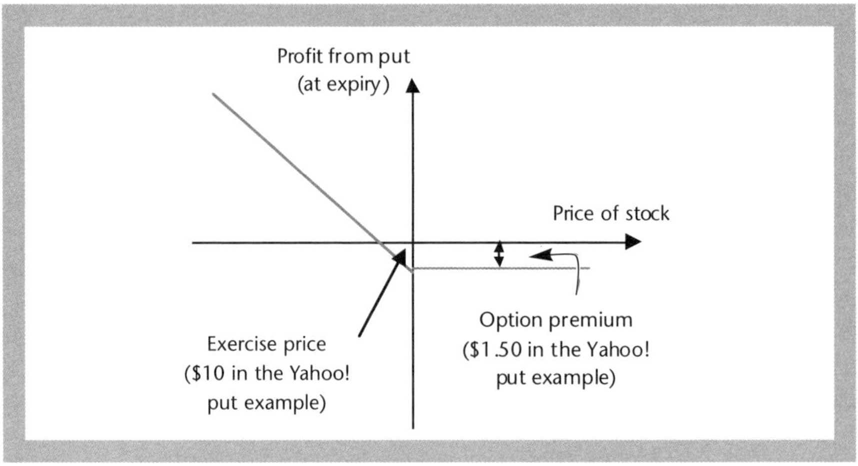

Figure 7.4 Profit at expiry diagram for Yahoo!

a share of Yahoo! for $10 at any time until April. An example of a person who might be interested in buying a Yahoo! put is someone who owns Yahoo! shares and, while bullish on Yahoo!, is also worried that the stock price will collapse – someone who wants 'insurance' against a price decline. In this case his or her maximum loss is $3 plus the option premium, not $13 per share as it would be if he or she only owned the shares. Figure 7.3 shows the payoff at expiry diagram for the April $10 put option and Figure 7.4 shows the profit diagram, assuming an option premium of $1.50. As can be seen from the payoff diagram, the owner of a put makes money if the stock goes *down*.

VALUING FINANCIAL OPTIONS

The financial option is an interesting valuation challenge. In fact, 'interesting' is perhaps an understatement – the people who solved the option valuation challenge won a Nobel Prize, the highest honour in Economics.

To illustrate the problem, imagine the payoff diagram for a *business*, which would be sensitive to economic conditions, but which would look somewhat smoother than the option graph. We would certainly not expect the rapid changes in the slope of the payoff chart that occur at the strike price of the option. Looking at the diagrams, there is a 'kink' in the payoff diagram, and in fact the kink makes options impossible to value using DCF methods because the cost of capital for the option changes rapidly at the kink point.

The solution advanced by Fischer Black and Myron Scholes is called the *Black–Scholes formula*.[1] The formula relates key parameters of the option and the relevant fundamental security to the price of the option. The derivation of the Black–Scholes formula is somewhat complex, and beyond the scope of this book (readers are referred to Rubinstein (1998) for a comprehensive introduction to various option models). Therefore we confine ourselves to outlining the calculation. Also, we can give an outline of the relation between parameters and option value in Table 7.1. First, here is the equation:

call value = [N(d_1) * (share price)] – [N(d_2) * PV(exercise price)]

where d_1 = ln{(share price)/PV(exercise price)} / [(std deviation)* √(time)] + [(std deviation)* √(time)]/2

d_2 = d_1 – [(std deviation)* √(time)]

N(.) = the cumulative normal distribution operator

PV(.) = the present-value operator (using the risk free rate (r_f) as the discount rate).

In other words, first of all calculate d_1 and d_2 using

- share price (S)
- exercise price (K)
- standard deviation (volatility) – this is a measure of how much the share price fluctuates (σ)
- time in years (T).

Then calculate the call value.

- The cumulative normal distribution function is easy to implement in Excel, using the NORMSDIST(.) worksheet function. In other words suppose we have calculated d_1 in spreadsheet cell B2, N(d_1) can be output by typing

  =NORMSDIST(B2)

  into another spreadsheet cell.
- The present value of the exercise price is found using the following equation

  PV_{r_f}(exercise price) = exercise price/$((1 + r_f)^T)$

  where r_f = the risk-free rate

  T = the time to expiry (in years)

Table 7.1 Relationships between parameters and values (Black–Scholes)

Parameters	Effect of an increase on the option value	Intuition
Standard deviation (or volatility), σ	Increase	Volatility benefits option values (unlike DCF values). If the option is 'out-of-the-money' then the 'premium' (option price) is lost. If it is a long way out-of-the-money the loss is still the same, but a high volatility means there is a better chance to be a long way in-the-money as well. So volatility is good for the option holder.
Share price, S	Call: increase Put: decrease	For calls, the lower the exercise price relative to the asset price (the more 'in-the-money' the option is; or, failing that, the less 'out-of-the-money'), the more valuable is the option. For puts the reverse is true.
Exercise price, K	Call: decrease Put: increase	
Time, T	Increase	The higher the risk-free rate and the longer the time (make more money while 'sitting on' the strike price until exercise), the more valuable the option. A longer time also gives volatility a greater time to come 'into the money'.
Risk-free rate, r_f	Increase	

Pricing put options

Put options are normally priced using a relationship called the *put-call parity,* which is an equation that must be satisfied by put and call options; or else risk-free arbitrage profits can be made by purchasing a portfolio of a put, a call and risk-free bonds.

In order to price a put option:

1. Calculate the price of the call option with the same strike price and term as discussed above.
2. Use put-call parity to price the put:

put value = call value + PV(exercise price, K) – stock price, S

Relevance to internet valuation

There are two key areas where option pricing is relevant to the valuation of internet firms:

- Compensation packages and capital structure contain sizeable elements of option-type securities, principally management share or stock options (sometimes called ESOPs), and also convertible debt (convertible debt is a loan certificate which can be converted into a share if the share price rises above a certain price). This effect is discussed in this chapter.

- Some analysts have suggested that internet shares have a similar payoff pattern to options (more option-like than 'normal' shares, which also have some 'optionality') and therefore cannot be valued satisfactorily with DCF but must be valued with option pricing methods. Another way of making this point is to say that internet companies have *real options* – specifically their early entry into internet markets gives them the right but not the obligation to enter follow-on markets, and it will 'exercise' those rights if and only if market conditions become favourable (similar to the holder of the Yahoo! financial call option). This effect is discussed in the next chapter.

WHAT ARE ESOPS OR MANAGEMENT SHARE OPTIONS?

Frequently top managers joining a company negotiate terms which include the payment of some of their compensation by share options or *ESOPs* (*employee stock option plans*). An ESOP usually gives management *very long-term call options* which have a strike price at about the same level as the current price.[2] ESOPs are designed to give managers a big stake in the company's fortunes even if the managers do not have a great deal of money to buy stock, and to get the managers to share in the pain and pleasure of good corporate performance in a way that a normal salary cannot do. If the company's share price goes up a lot, the manager's ESOP call options will be worth a lot of money. If the share price goes down, the share options will be worthless. This means that managers of a company whose stock does not perform well do not gain as much total compensation as those who manage a company whose stock does perform well. However, the managers of the company which does not perform so well will still receive their basic salary.

Advantages and disadvantages of ESOPs

Before we talk about how to value ESOPs, we should briefly mention the advantages and disadvantages of ESOPs. The main advantage of ESOPs is the incentive effect. Having options in a firm means that managers become obsessive about increasing the stock price of their company. Very likely they have been recruited to the company based on a compensation package consisting partly, or in some cases almost entirely, of ESOPs. The most famous example of an ESOP recipient is Michael Eisner of Disney, whose package is extremely weighted towards ESOP compensation. Forbes reported in April 2001 that Eisner received $737m of compensation in the previous five years, yet Eisner's current salary for much of that period was $0.75m per annum, approximately ½% of his total compensation, the remainder being incentive or share-based compensation. At the opposite end of the scale, Warren Buffett does not issue any ESOP options to himself or other executives of his company. However, the tendency towards equity-related compensation is also reflected in Berkshire Hathaway. Buffett only receives $100,000 per annum salary and relies on his large ownership of stock in the firm for most of his wealth.

Do options incentivize managers? The answer to this question is certainly yes. Options give managers a direct stake in the company; managers become focused on increasing stock price; and this aligns their interests with those of shareholders. However, there are three caveats:

- First, the shareholders may be paying too much for the incentive the manager is receiving.
- Second, option-holding managers may engage in some behaviour that does not necessarily help the company.
- Third, ESOPs are a 'blunt instrument', and high ESOP profits often have as much to do with a general rise in the stock market as they have to do with exceptional corporate performance.

The first point has been made by many commentators. It seems hard for many people to believe that Michael Eisner was significantly more incentivized by receiving $737m than he would have been had he received, say, $100m.[3] However, arguably one of the fundamental reasons for adopting ESOP-based compensation is the impossibility of measuring managerial effort – if there was a simple way of measuring effort, ESOPs would not be needed. When managers create large amounts of value, shareholders tend to be fairly sanguine about paying for managers' efforts, even if they may be paying too much.

The second problem is more insidious. Managers who have share options are uncomfortable if share prices go down, but they do not suffer monetary loss in the same way that shareholders do. Look once again at the payoff diagram for the call shown above. Suppose we are the CEO of a company compensated mainly by ESOPs with a strike price of $13. Let the share price also be $13. Someone offers the company an enormous bet on a single coin toss. Heads the stock price will go to $9, tails it will go to $17. If we are focusing only on our own future wealth, we will take the bet. If we win, our options are worth $4. If we lose, our options are worth $0. However, all this transaction has done for shareholders is to increase volatility, since expected value (under risk neutrality) is $13. Now suppose this instead: heads the stock price will go to $1, and tails it will still go to $17. What should we do? We will still take the bet. Our distribution of option profits is exactly the same as before (our call option value at maturity is zero whether the stock price is $1 or $9), but our risk-loving behaviour is damaging to shareholders (because the expected value of the bet, even under risk neutrality, is only $9).

Obviously, this example is simply illustrative – no-one offers businesses big bets on a coin toss. But managers have to decide every day whether to play it safe or to go for risky projects. The ESOP holder may be tempted to go for the risky project, even if this may not benefit the firm. However, in opposition to this tendency there are other factors. If the manager 'loses the bet' he may lose his job. Even if he is close to retirement (and not needing a new job) he may still be concerned to maintain his reputation. (After all, he or she may want to write a best-selling autobiography!) Under these circumstances, where the manager is risk averse, theoretical work by Carpenter (2000)[4] suggests that, in some cases, this risk aversion may counterbalance the apparent incentive of the employee stock options to encourage managers to seek risk. The understanding is dependent on the manager's risk profile, and so our view on how risk averse managers are is relevant to whether we accept Carpenter's thesis.[5] If internet executives are particularly fond of risk-taking (perhaps due to youthful overconfidence and the knowledge they will have plenty of further opportunities to roll the dice), then this risk-seeking behaviour may still be observed and may still 'hurt' firms.

The third problem, that ESOPs often benefit from market-wide rises, has been dealt with by some companies by making share options conditional on the company meeting some *benchmark*. Perhaps, for example, options are only exercisable if the company is in the top quartile of performers in its industry. But these efforts have been confined to a minority of companies. If top management talent is in undersupply, as companies would have us believe, it is very difficult for activist compensation committees to recruit talent on the basis of performance-adjusted ESOPs when other companies are recruiting and providing raw ESOPs. If governments wish to encourage ESOPs to be more closely linked with performance, perhaps changes to the tax system should be considered, to encourage performance-linking.

ACCOUNTING TREATMENT OF SHARE OPTIONS

The accounting treatment of share options is a problem, or a great strength, depending on one's point of view. Some readers may be sufficiently expert as to know already what method of accounting is currently in place in the US and

UK. For other readers, let us pause before considering this, and briefly discuss what might be an *ideal* accounting system, and then see how this compares with real life. The fundamental question is: should the giving of share options to managers be reflected as a cost in the profit and loss or the income statement?

An ideal accounting system would perhaps lie between two extremes:

- *The extreme incentivist school:* Share options incentivize managers to work harder by aligning their interests with those of shareholders, and this hard work increases profits and shareholder value. Therefore, we should not discourage the issuing of share options in any way and should not reflect them as a cost in income statements. Furthermore, since options actually benefit the firm (increasing management effort and making the enterprise value 'pie' larger), their recognition as a cost is illogical.
- *The 'options are (a form of) salary' (OAS) school:* Share options have value, and this is why managers wish to receive them. They are a payment to managers from shareholders, and should be recognized in the income statement in the same way as salary.

Clearly neither of these viewpoints is correct. The extreme incentivist school might advocate infinite dilution by the granting of options, in the cause of increasing incentives. The OAS school completely dismisses the incentive effect of share options, which would also seem to be wrong. The OAS school also creates a further problem: in order to recognize the value of the share options, we have to calculate that value. We have discussed the Black–Scholes formula above, but share options granted to managers have some features which mean that the 'raw' Black–Scholes formula cannot be used to value them. The main problems are that employee share options have a *vesting period*, a period of time for which the employee has to remain with the company giving the options before the employee can get the benefit of the options, and that the employee will usually lose the option entirely if he or she leaves the company before it has been exercised. The options also cannot usually be traded or hedged (without being exercised). out-of-the-money options bought on the open market can usually be sold for a strictly positive value; employee options cannot be traded at all.

Current accounting policies in the UK and USA hold opinion with the extreme incentivist school. Employee options are not recognized as a cost in the income statement, unless they are granted with an exercise price below the current price of the stock. This is seldom done, since it would mean that (if there are no vesting requirements) the option holder could make a profit straight away by exercising the option, and selling the stock. This would not necessarily incentivize him or her to do anything except get straight on the phone to his or her broker: and, for this reason, and possibly also because of the accounting treatment, these 'in-the-money' options are seldom granted. Most options are granted 'at the money' or thereabouts, with the strike price roughly equal to the share price. Therefore these share options are not recognized in any way in the income statement.

One potential defence mechanism against excessive granting is that the granting of a stock option will increase the number of shares in the earnings per share (fully diluted) calculation. *Earnings per share* (*eps*) is an indicator of the amount of value that the company is generating in that year, in return for the capital that it receives from selling one share. Eps growth is seen by many investors as an important indicator of how well a company is doing. Eps is calculated in two ways, basic and fully diluted. Simplifying slightly, here are the equations:

$$\text{eps}_{\text{basic}} = \frac{\text{earnings or profits for the year}}{\text{shares outstanding}}$$

$$\text{eps}_{\text{fully diluted}} = \frac{\text{earnings or profits for the year}}{\text{shares that } \textit{could} \text{ be outstanding}}$$

So, the granting of a large number of share options to a normal, old-economy company will *decrease* the fully diluted eps (fully diluted shares assume that all options are exercised). Since the eps number is watched by many investors, this in itself might represent a check on option-issuing activity. However, this is of course completely irrelevant for companies making no profit. In fact dilution by options would lead to a decrease in loss per share by the above method – which would clearly be absurd. For this reason, fully diluted shares do not include option shares if the options would be anti-dilutive: that is, would increase eps or decrease loss per share. Finally, eps is not a frequently used benchmark for new-economy investors. Therefore the eps 'defence mechanism', as we termed it, is not effective for many internet firms, and there is no reflection in the income statement of any costs of issuing stock options.

Standard-setting bodies in the UK and (especially) the USA have been dragged kicking and screaming to this position. FAS 123 is the major US standard on accounting for employee stock options and was issued in 1995. FASB originally intended FAS 123 to require companies to recognize employee stock options directly in the income statement. Companies would have had to expense an adjusted Black–Scholes value for the options when they were granted. But very vigorous protests[6] on the part of business effectively neutered the standard. After the neutered FAS 123, companies were left with the choice of two standards: the 'old' standard (originally called the APB 25 standard), which allows companies to expense only the 'intrinsic value' (strike price minus stock price, usually zero), or the new 'fair value' (adjusted Black–Scholes) method. Almost without exception (in fact we have not found a single exception), companies adopted the APB 25 method, and continued to show no expense for stock option grants.

Currently, therefore, the situation in both the US and the UK is that option grants are not reflected in the income statement. And now we come to the implications for valuers. If a company is faced with the choice of paying an employee via options (no income statement implication) or by salary (expensed as incurred), it is likely to preferentially pay employees by stock options. This is particularly true of companies which make no profits at the moment. These companies will not even see their option grants reflected in a depressed eps. For this to be true we do not need to assume that the market is concerned *only* with earnings/eps (this is the so called 'mechanistic' view, in which companies are valued 'mechanically' on earnings): we just need to be convinced that some subset of investors cares about earnings. But if employees see these options as in some way interchangeable with cash compensation, we may have a problem for the future. While the market is rising, employees will be happy to accept stock options, but in the 2002 environment in which stock price appreciation is seen as uncertain, employees may demand higher cash compensation. We must factor this into our valuation. So even if accounting does not require a recognition of the cost of stock options, an intelligent valuer must be cognizant of the 'true' salary that the firm will have to pay in the future, which will be based on employees' viewpoints of their own market value, informed by their own transactions in the marketplace with other employers. The other effect is that exercise of the options will increase the number of shares participating in the cash flows of the firm, thus *decreasing* the value per share.

TAXATION TREATMENT OF ESOPS

Taxation treatment of ESOPs has caused some confusing accounting entries which we may briefly consider. The main taxation issue is the taxation impact of the decision by employees to exercise their ESOPs. With a traded stock option the option is bought at one price by the trader, and then sold when the trader decides that market conditions are optimal. The difference between the purchase price and the sale price is the profit or loss. The process of gaining profits from an ESOP is a two-stage one, however. This is because ESOP options cannot be traded – they must be exercised by the original option holder. This involves the employee-holder paying money and receiving stock. Then the stock may be sold, and a profit taken. Alternatively the stock may be held.

US and UK taxation opinion is somewhat harsh in that it imposes tax on the gain *when the option is exercised*. At this point the option holder does not have any profit, because he or she has not sold the stock.

- In the USA, the option holder is charged tax on the difference between the strike price and the current stock price at his or her highest income tax rate (usually 39.6% plus any applicable state taxation).
- In the UK, the employee is charged income tax (usually 40%) and the *company* is charged national insurance contributions (NICs; the UK name for social security) at a special rate of 12.2%. Since July 2000, companies have been permitted to agree with employees that employees will pay the employer's NICs. Employees receive some tax break on the NICs which may decrease their effective tax rate to 47.32%, according to UK Inland Revenue information believed current at mid-2001.
- In the event that the stock is held for a period of time following exercise, capital gains tax is then due on any supplementary profit.
- However, this area is subject to rapid change, and US and UK citizens and/or companies should seek specialist advice on these and related issues.

The accounting effects of these taxation policies are as follows:

- *USA:* When employees pay tax on their option exercise gains, this is recognized as a cost that a stakeholder of the company has paid. Therefore, it decreases the profit (if any) reported and assessable for tax. This line item will decrease or disappear in the event that stock option gains on exercise decrease or disappear.
- *UK:* While companies were forced to pay NICs on option exercise, this led to a substantial cost to some companies. This problem has now been somewhat alleviated because companies are allowed to grant share options that include the requirement that *employees* must pay NICs. Therefore these costs in pre-2000 accounting statements should not be expected to persist at such levels.

IMPACT OF EMPLOYEE STOCK OPTIONS ON ENTERPRISE AND EQUITY VALUATION

As mentioned above, the issuance of ESOPs can affect the valuation process in two ways:

- The existence of ESOP warrants means that, if stock rises, the ESOP warrants will be exercised, and there will be more equity holders to share in the enterprise value. This will decrease the value of equity in issue.
- The fact that ESOPs are received by management as part of their compensation policy may lead to reported compensation numbers being underestimates of true compensation. This is because the issuance of ESOPs is not reflected in the income statement. In the event that ESOPs become less attractive to managers, they may insist on higher cash compensation than they have in the past.

Two adjustments must therefore be attempted. For the former problem, ESOPs may be valued today according to an adjusted option-pricing model. Then this is subtracted from enterprise value, as discussed below. An alternative shortcut root is to assume exercise (dilution) and divide the calculated equity value by the fully diluted number of shares. This is not as accurate, as it assumes path dependency. However, it will be suitable where exercise is almost certain and the number of options is small. Valuers should ensure that one or the other method is used, but not both.

The second factor is more difficult to adjust for, especially since option grants have gone quite deep down the organization in many internet companies, and can be a sizeable amount of money. As a general principle, the adjustment factor should be based on the market salary rate of comparable employees, not on 'making whole' employees who would have received very profitable option grants in the past, and are now concerned that they will miss out. To illustrate why this is, consider the example of Microsoft. Microsoft stock has appreciated by a factor of approximately 250 between its initial issuance (in 1986) and autumn 2001. Many employees of the company have become millionaires as a result of their stock options. It will be impossible for the company to maintain such a pace of appreciation. Should employees applying to Microsoft today therefore demand million-dollar cash compensation payments? No. Of course, they are welcome to try, but they will not receive them. They will negotiate a market rate of compensation for their services, possibly including some option element. This is precisely what their predecessors at the Microsoft of 1986–90 were doing. They did not expect to receive million-dollar option gains, but (at the time) were just concerned to negotiate market rates of compensation. The large ESOP gains they received were a 'surprise' – the result of coming out at the top of a notional 'probability distribution' of companies.

In summary, while top management compensation may be substantially rebalanced by a possible sinking in popularity of ESOPs, this is not normally a major percentage element of cost. For middle level employees, our conjecture (perhaps 'educated guess' would be a better term) is that employees relied on their options for no more than 10–20% of their perceived compensation, so an adjustment of that order, or less, should be considered to compensation, holding job market factors constant. However, since the decline of the attractiveness of stock options has coincided with a decline in job market health (thus depressing arm's-length market salary), this second effect will be somewhat mitigated for the moment, especially at the lower and middle levels of organizations.

Methods of valuing employee stock options

Dismissing the 'intrinsic value' method of calculating stock option value under APB 25 and current UK practice is straightforward. Stock options which have stock price and strike price equal, and which have a (typical ESOP) life of 10 years, are clearly not valueless, as APB 25 would suggest.

The alternative methods in valuing the stock options are Black–Scholes, and some adjusted method. First of all, let us dismiss Black–Scholes. The executive share option compares with the traded option (that is, the option bought at arm's-length on the Chicago Board Options Exchange (CBOE) or the London Stock Exchange (LSE)) in the following ways:

- it does not vest for a long period of time
- it cannot be freely traded prior to exercise
- it is lost if the employee leaves the company.

Most importantly, it has no advantages over the traded option. Therefore it is worth less than the traded option, and the Black–Scholes formula is not suitable to value it.[7] Black–Scholes may be seen as an upper bound on the value of the ESOP (unless the employee has some insider information).

Many workers have been engaged in efforts to value employee stock option. Most of these use Black–Scholes as a starting point. From a practitioner's perspective, Young (1993)[8] suggests that vesting be reflected by taking a base value of the full term (for example, $T = 10$ years) option, and subtracting from that value the value of an identical option which would have a term of the vesting period (perhaps $T = 3$ years). This would then give us the value of an option which is active between years 4–10, the period that the ESOP option would actually be active. However, because of a quirk in the way options work out theoretically, this may underestimate the value of the option. Assuming that the employee is certain to stay with the company, the 10-year option with 3-year vesting period is equivalent to:

- a European call option with $T = 3$

and

- an American call option with $T = 4$ to $T = 10$.

The terms 'European' and 'American' denote when the option can be exercised. European options can be exercised only at the end of the term. American options can be exercised at any time during the term. However (and here is the quirk), in options theory, European call options have the *same value* as American call options. This is because it is never a sensible idea to exercise the American call, because one wastes the time value of the call if one does so. Since the optimal strategy is always to hold the American call to maturity, the European call has the same value. Because ESOPs are non-tradable, employees often exercise them early (because they cannot sell the options), but the vesting period binds them to not exercising. To see precisely why Young's thesis is erroneous, consider an option with vesting 3 years and expiry 3 years and 1 day. The Young concept would suggests that this option has

$$\text{value} = \text{call}_{3\text{ years}+1\text{ day}} - \text{call}_{3\text{ years}}$$

– a tiny value. But in fact the option would have 3 years to get into the money, and would have substantial value, even though the option holder would have only a scant window in which to exercise it.

The approach suggested by FASB in the FAS 123 disclosure is instructive. Recall that the FAS 123 policy was 'neutered' to enable companies to continue not to report stock option costs in the income statement. However, the FASB did insist that companies calculate and report the equivalent stock value in the footnotes (the FAS 123 disclosure), so that interested investors can get an idea how much the stock options may be costing on an adjusted Black–Scholes basis. The FAS 123 method:

1. uses the Black–Scholes value as a base
2. adjusts the time to expiry (T) to reflect the expected life of the option
3. multiplies the resulting value by the percentage of options that are expected to vest.

Adjustment 2 is needed because some employees may be forced to exercise their options, perhaps by retirement, or may decide to cash their option for purposes of personal portfolio rebalancing. Adjustment 3 is needed because some options do not survive long enough to vest (perhaps because a proportion of employees has left the company).

Adjustment 2 is how we adjust the value for the fact that the ESOPs are not tradable – if the employee wants to take profit now, he or she has to exercise early. If the option was a traded option (for example, one bought on the CBOE) the holder could just sell the option, but with an ESOP the conditions of the ESOP agreement are that he or she cannot sell the option, but must first exercise the option, and then sell the stock. (This is an approximate adjustment only: the search for more accurate and precise adjustments is the subject of vigorous research by workers in the field.)

Worked example of valuing ESOPs: Amazon.com

In the exercise on valuing Amazon.com in the earlier part of the book, our main concern was to *value the enterprise*. Intuitively, this means that we value the Amazon.com business in its entirety, by projecting forward its cash flows. However, our fundamental aim in valuing a company for the purposes of this book is to value the equity that is freely traded on the NASDAQ stock market. Not all of the cash flows that come to the Amazon.com business are owned by the equity holders, because Amazon has also issued some convertible debt and some employee stock options. In order to work out the value of the company's equity, we adopt the following approach:

1. Value the enterprise as a whole.
2. Value the debt.
3. Subtract the value of debt from the enterprise value, to obtain the value of equity plus contingent liabilities.
4. Value the contingent liabilities:
   a. warrants (including ESOP warrants)
   b. the warrant element of convertibles.
5. Subtract the value of contingent liabilities from the result of 3.
6. The result is the equity.

For pedagogical reasons we will proceed first to part 4a. First of all we should note that we are limited somewhat in our efforts to value the ESOP

Figure 7.5 Amazon.com: stock option plans

Stock Option Plans

Generally, the Company's Board of Directors grants options at an exercise price of not less than the fair market value of the Company's common stock at the date of grant. Each outstanding option granted prior to December 20, 1996 has a term of five years from the date of vesting. Generally, outstanding options granted on or subsequent to December 20, 1996 have a term of 10 years from the date of grant. Subject to Internal Revenue Service limitations, options granted under the Company's plans prior to April 1999 and granted under certain assumed plans, generally became exercisable immediately but are subject to a restriction on transfer that vests over a period of time. Options granted under the plans since April 1999 generally vest and become exercisable in accordance with the following vesting schedule: 20% after year one, 20% after year two and 5% at the end of each quarter for years three through five. Certain outstanding options that were granted during 2000 and 2001 vest and become exercisable at the rate of 50% after year one and 50% after year two. During the first quarter of 2001, the Company offered a limited non-compulsory exchange of employee stock options to employees meeting certain eligibility criteria. Options granted pursuant to this stock option exchange vest and become exercisable at the rate of 25% after 6 months from the date of grant and 4.166% per month for the succeeding 18 months. Certain options granted in the third quarter of 2001 generally vest and become exercisable as follows: (i) the option vests quarterly in equal installments over a 36, 48 or 60 month period commencing on dates ranging from grant date to October 1, 2003, (ii) the option vests 5% to 12.5% on a date approximately 12 to 16 months from date of grant with the balance vesting quarterly in equal installments over a 48 to 60 month period or (iii) the option vests 4% to 12.5% on dates approximately 6 months and 18 months from the date of grant with the balance vesting quarterly in equal installments over a 24 or 60 month period. Shares issued upon exercise of options that are unvested are restricted and subject to repurchase by the Company at the exercise price upon termination of employment or services and such restrictions lapse over the original vesting schedule. At December 31, 2001, approximately 1.1 million shares of restricted common stock, which includes restricted shares issued in connection with acquisitions, as well as shares issued to certain key employees in 2001, were subject to repurchase or forfeiture.

options by the limited disclosure. For example, Amazon.com's disclosure about stock options in the 10K for the year 2000, although somewhat voluminous, is lacking in some details. Below are selected relevant elements of the disclosure.

The first section, from page 66 of the 2001 10K, shows that Amazon follows usual practice in issuing shares with exercise price equal to stock price (Figure 7.5). Some options have a quicker vesting period that the typical 3 years' period.

The stock option activity table (Figure 7.6) is shown on page 67. This is useful if we want to try and 'back out' the FAS 123 fair-value expenses which are shown later. Note the decline in average exercise price of options outstanding between end 2000 and end 2001 as the company sought to incentivize managers by granting stock options which were closer to current stock prices (that is, giving managers a smaller mountain to climb before the company performance pays off for them).[9]

Figure 7.6 Amazon.com: stock option activity

Stock Option Activity

The following table summarizes the Company's stock option activity:

	Number of shares	Weighted Average Exercise Price
	------------	------------
	(in thousands)	
Balance January 1, 1999...	76,009	$ 6.69
Options granted and assumed...	31,379	63.60
Options canceled...	(11,281)	19.70
Options exercised...	(16,125)	4.00
	------------	------------
Balance December 31, 1999...	80,342	27.76
Options granted and assumed...	20,717	38.13
Options canceled...	(19,502)	37.19
Options exercised...	(11,119)	4.02
	------------	------------
Balance December 31, 2000...	70,438	32.17
Net effect of option exchange:...		
	------------	------------
Options granted...	12,503	13.38
Options exchanged and canceled...	(31,170)	51.94
	------------	------------
Net effect of option exchange...	(18,667)	
	------------	------------
Options granted...	33,706	8.10
Options canceled...	(13,438)	25.29
Options exercised...	(6,089)	2.73
	------------	------------
Balance December 31, 2001...	65,950	10.65
	=======	=======

At December 31, 2001, 63 million shares of common stock were available for future grant under the Plans.

Figure 7.7 Amazon.com: options

The following table summarizes information about options outstanding and exercisable at December 31, 2000:

	Options outstanding			Options exercisable	
Range of Exercise Prices	Number of options	Weighted Average Remaining Life (yrs)	Exercise Price	Number of Options	Weighted Average Exercise Price
	(in thousands)			(in thousands)	
$ 0.03 – $ 1.00	5,000	5.0	$ 0.42	4,222	$ 0.39
1.17 – 5.37	5,095	5.9	4.01	1,943	3.85
5.81 – 7.86	4,838	6.8	7.13	2,360	7.11
7.93 – 7.93	26,071	9.7	7.93	—	7.93
7.95 – 8.55	3,660	8.5	8.51	263	8.23
8.72 – 13.24	1,872	8.2	11.40	471	11.86
13.38 – 13.38	10,712	1.8	13.38	4,227	13.38
13.57 – 19.89	3,602	7.3	16.76	1,575	17.04
20.06 – 104.97	5,100	7.7	35.77	1,903	30.53
0.03 – 104.97	65,950	7.1	10.65	16,964	10.32

Note that from the valuation standpoint, the 63 million shares 'available for future grant' are not relevant until they are granted. This last sentence means that management can grant these 63 million shares without shareholder approval (it having already been granted). However, shareholder approval is usually a formality for most plans (so far!).

The table in Figure 7.7 is the key one, since it gives us the most recent data on the options outstanding. Note that the average option prices we see in some other notes are not very useful to us. Imagine that Amazon, whose shares are trading at about $15 as we write, gave us information that they had 1 million

Figure 7.8 Amazon.com: pro forma disclosure

Pro Forma Disclosure

The Company uses the intrinsic value method in accounting for its stock options. If compensation cost had been recognized based on the fair value at the date of grant for options granted in 2001, 2000 and 1999, under SFAS No. 123. Accounting for Stock-Based Compensation, pro forma amounts of the Company's net loss and net loss per share, which may not necessarily be indicative of effects on reported results for future years, for the years ended December 31, 2001, 2000 and 1999 would have been as follows:

	For the Years Ended December 31,		
	2001	2000	1999
	($thousands, except per share data)		
Net loss -- as reported...	($567,277)	($1,411,273)	($719,968)
Net loss -- SFAS No. 123 pro forma...	(963,085	(1,720,312)	(1,031,925)
Basic and diluted loss per share -- as reported...	($1.56)	($4.02)	($2.20)
Basic and diluted loss per share -- SFAS No. 123 pro forma...	(2.64)	(4.9)	(3.16)

The fair value for each option granted was estimated at the date of grant using a Black-Scholes option-pricing model, assuming no expected dividends and the following weighted average assumptions:

	For the Years Ended December 31,		
	2001	2000	1999
Average risk-free interest rates...	4.1%	6.2%	5.5%
Average expected life (in years)...	3.3	3.0	3.5
Volatility (1)...	98.0%	89.6%	84.9%

options outstanding, at an average price of $50. That could be 1 million options at a strike price of $50 ($5.80 for 3 year life at 98% volatility according to Black–Scholes) or 0.5m options at $5 (worth $12.20) plus 0.5m options at $90 ($4 per option). The same average strike price can therefore be worth an average $5.80 (1m at $50) or $8.10 (0.5m at $5, 0.5m at $95). To make more accurate calculations we need the breakdown, so Figure 7.7 is the main data source we will use.

The table in Figure 7.8, from pages 68–9 of the 2001 10K, shows the FAS 123 disclosure of the notional costs of stock options issued in each year, and then the 'pro forma' profit (loss in this case) which would have occurred had the fair value of the options at grant date been subtracted from the loss. This is a different pro forma to the pro forma profit statement in which companies exclude many costs such as goodwill amortization (discussed in Appendix 3.1). Since 'pro forma' means 'based on a set of assumptions', companies can report as many pro formas as they wish, based on different assumptions.

Note that Figure 7.8 is of little use for valuation. For example, the $300m of options issued in 1999 at an average price of $63.60 (from Figure 7.6) (Amazon traded within $45–$106 during 1999) are worth much less at March 2002, with stock prices at about $15 (because while they were granted 'at the money', they are now 'out of the money' – that is, $K \gg S$).

Although we are shown the main elements of the Black–Scholes calculation (such as volatility, risk-free rate and so on), some elements of the disclosure which we would like to have are missing. We would like to know exactly how the pro forma income was calculated, including what was assumed about what percentage of Amazon.com's share options will or will not vest and the expected life of the options (by strike price, we have average expected life).

Now all that remains to value the options is to apply Black–Scholes and to make some adjustments. We adopt the 13% average turnover published by the Bureau of Labor Statistics in the US (conservative: turnover in internet/IT companies has been reported to be 15–20%). This suggests that $(1 - 0.13) \times (1 - 0.13) \times (1 - 0.13) = (0.87)^3 = 66\%$ of employees are around until their options vest after 3 years. We utilize the average expected life suggested by Amazon.com, and have confirmed that the volatility of the year 2001 is still approximately correct. (We will discuss the estimation of volatility in Appendix 7.1.) We approximate by ignoring the distinction between exercisable and outstanding options (note that 'exercisable' is a subset of outstanding options in Figure 7.7). In fact we could be more accurate and assume a shorter life for the exercisable options, and a longer life for the far-out-of-the-money options. With our approximation, the results shown in Table 7.2 are obtained. (Intermediate results d_1 and d_2 are shown to assist readers trying to reproduce the calculations.)

Table 7.2 Amazon.com: option value calculations

Stock price = $15
Volatility = 98%
Risk free = 4%
Time = 3.3
Will vest = 66%

Range of exercise prices	Number of options (in thousands)	Exercise price (weighted average)	d_1	d_2	*V*(call)	Total ($m)	Vest ($m)
$ 0.03 – $ 1	5000	$ 0.42	2.971	1.191	14.652	73.259	48.241
1.17 – 5.37	5095	4.01	1.704	-0.076	12.749	64.954	42.773
5.81 – 7.86	4838	7.13	1.381	-0.400	11.591	56.078	36.928
7.93 – 7.93	26071	7.93	1.321	-0.459	11.351	295.922	194.866
7.95 – 8.55	3660	8.51	1.281	-0.499	11.266	41.232	27.152
8.72 – 13.24	1872	11.4	1.117	-0.663	10.378	19.427	12.793
13.38 – 13.38	10712	13.38	1.027	-0.753	10.064	107.808	70.992
13.57 – 19.89	3602	16.76	0.901	-0.880	9.404	33.874	22.306
20.06 – 104.97	5100	35.77	0.475	-1.306	7.666	39.099	25.747
0.03 – 104.97	65950	10.65				731.654	481.796

Therefore the total value of the options outstanding at the end of 2000 is $482m. This is a substantial amount of money, about 9% of March 2002 equity market capital.

Amazon's debt and pseudo-debt securities

Continuing our previous drill to calculate the value of equity, we have dealt with item 4a, and now move on to the calculation of the value of debt and convertible debt – that is, items 2 and 4b:

1. Value the enterprise as a whole.
2. Value the debt.
3. Subtract the value of debt from the enterprise value, to obtain the value of equity plus contingent liabilities.
4. Value the contingent liabilities:
   a. warrants (including ESOP warrants)
   b. the warrant element of convertibles.
5. Subtract the value of contingent liabilities from the result of 3.
6. The result is the equity.

Amazon's capital structure is an interesting one. Although it does not have much debt as we normally understand it, it has a large amount of *convertible debt*. This is a special type of loan frequently sold in risky businesses, whereby the person lending the money receives a share in the upside, because the loan element is 'packaged' with a warrant or option element: that is, the loan is 'convertible' into equity. At certain prices, the owner has the option to swap his or her right to any interest payments (debt) for a right to a share in the residual cash flows (equity). Figure 7.9 shows a list of the company's debt outstanding, from the 2001 10K form (page 61).

Of the instruments listed in the table, only the smaller amounts – senior discount notes, capital lease obligations (debt associated with the leasing of a specific building or item of equipment) and other long-term debt – are conventional debt without the option 'packaging'. Let us look in more detail at the two largest elements of the company's long-term debt on lines 1 and 3. How can we value them to see how much of the enterprise value will accrue to the owners of these securities?

The first alternative that the valuer should consider when considering complex securities that are senior to equity is to utilize the market price, if available. Amazon's 2001 10K notes the fair market value of these securities at the close of 2001. At that point the PEACS were valued at $310m (approximately 51% of the debt's book value) and the Convertible Subordinated Notes were valued at $625m (approx. 50% of book value). Clearly investors were not entirely confident that the subordinated debt will be repaid. The Senior Discount Notes were valued at $194m (approx. 83% of book value). At this point it is relevant to mention the 'subordinated' terminology. The PEACS and convertible notes are not just convertible but also *subordinated,* which means that they are junior debt: in some sense between equity and senior debt in a 'pecking order' which will be followed should the company ever go into liquidation. In liquidation, first of all special claimants such as the tax authorities, accountants and secured creditors (provided their security covers their debt) would be paid. Second, holders of unsecured but senior debt would be paid. Then and only then would subordinated debtholders receive any money. If there is any money left over after subordinated debtholders, this would go to equity holders.

Figure 7.9 Amazon.com: long-term debt

Note 8 -- LONG-TERM DEBT

The Company's long-term debt and other long-term liabilities are summarized as follows:

	December 31,	
	2001	2000
	(in thousands)	
6.875% PEACS	$ 608,787	$ 650,463
Euro Currency Swap	33,265	—
4.75% Convertible Subordinated Notes	1,249,807	1,249,807
Senior Discount Notes	231,830	210,278
Capital Lease Obligations	16,415	24,837
Long-term Restructuring	20,640	—
Other Long-term Debt	10,381	8,656
	------------	------------
	2,171,125	2,144,041
Less current portion of long-term debt	(5,070)	(4,831)
Less current portion of capital lease obligations	(9,922)	(11,746)
	------------	------------
	$ 2,156,133	$ 2,127,464
	------------	------------

Table 7.3 Amazon.com: equity value

	($)
Value of enterprise (CCA)	4,469m
Subtract value of debt	260m*
Subtract value of convertibles	1,153m
Subtract value of ESOPs	482
Add value of cash	997
The result is the equity	3,571

* includes $47m of capital lease + other long-term debt

For more recent values than those given in the 10K, readers may refer to the www.convertbond.com website run by Morgan Stanley. This website gave updated values of $62.75 per $100 par for the Convertible Subordinated Notes and $60.75 per $100 par for the Euro-denominated PEACs in March 2002. This would suggest market values of $784m and $369m respectively. Convertbond.com reported at that point that the convertibles factored in a yield to maturity (similar to interest rate) of 18.5% for the US$ notes and 18.7% for the Euro-denominated. No updated information on the discount notes was available; assuming they achieved an uplift of 10% (since they are closer to book value they will not achieve as large an uplift as the convertible) they would now have a market value of $213m.

On the basis of these market values, we are in a position to assemble the data on all of the securities issued by the company, and to calculate the equity value (see Table 7.3).

VALUING CONVERTIBLES WHEN THE MARKET PRICE IS NOT AVAILABLE

Frequently, the market price will not be available (this is particularly likely to be true of convertible securities for smaller or unquoted companies). It is then necessary to value these securities by theoretical means. In order to do this we must zoom in on exactly how convertibles work, and discuss more specifically their part-debt/part-option character.

As an example, let us consider the Amazon.com 4.75% convertible note. The following extract is from the cover of the company's May 13 1999, S-3 filing (to give information for secondary buyers of the notes):

Figure 7.10 sets out most of the details of the bonds.

Figure 7.10 Conditions of Amazon.com Convertible Subordinated Notes

$1,250,000,000

AMAZON.COM, INC.

4 3/4% CONVERTIBLE SUBORDINATED NOTES DUE 2009

Holders of our 4 3/4% Convertible Subordinated Notes due 2009 may offer for sale the notes and the shares of our common stock into which the notes are convertible at various times at market prices prevailing at the time of sale or at privately negotiated prices. The selling holders may sell the notes or the common stock to or through underwriters, broker-dealers or agents, who may receive compensation in the form of discounts, concessions or commissions. Interest is payable in arrears on February 1 and August 1 of each year, beginning on August 1, 1999. The notes will mature on February 1, 2009 unless earlier converted or redeemed. The notes are unsecured and rank below our existing and future indebtedness.

The holders of the notes may convert any portion of a note (in multiples of $1,000) into common stock, at a conversion price of $156.055 per share, subject to adjustment in certain events. Our common stock is quoted on the Nasdaq National Market under the symbol "AMZN." On May 12, 1999, the closing price of the common stock was $142.9375 per share.

We may redeem any portion of the notes at any time prior to February 6, 2002, at a redemption price equal to $1,000 per note plus accrued and unpaid interest to the redemption date if (1) the closing price of our common stock has exceeded 150% of the conversion price for at least 20 trading days in any consecutive 30-day period ending on the trading day prior to the mailing of the notice of redemption and (2) the shelf registration statement covering resales of the notes and the common stock is effective and expected to remain effective and available for use for the 30 days following the redemption dates. If we redeem the notes under these circumstances, we will make an additional "make-whole" payment on the redeemed notes equal to $212.60 per $1,000 note, minus the amount of any interest we actually paid on the note prior to the date the notice was mailed. We must make these "make-whole" payments on all notes called for redemption, including notes converted after the date the notice was mailed.

If an investor wishes to purchase $100 of par value, he or she will receive the following:

If the note is not converted and the firm does not default:

- $2.375 on 1 August 1999, and every 6 months until 1 February 2009
- $100 on 1 February 2009 (in addition to the $2.375 'coupon').

If the note is converted (this is in the option of the note holder):

- up until the date of conversion, the coupon payments of $2.375 every 6 months
- at conversion, 100/156.055, that is 0.6408, of one share of Amazon.com common stock
- after conversion, any dividends or other benefits accruing to the stock owned.

If the note is forcibly redeemed because the stock price has exceeded 1.5 × $156.055 for the time period mentioned above (this is in the option of Amazon.com):

- up until the date of conversion, the coupon payments of $2.375 every 6 months
- at redemption, $121.26 minus the coupon payments already paid.

If the firm defaults:

- up until the date of default, the coupon payments of $2.375 every 6 months
- the company may then be reorganized and the convertible holders' ongoing status will be uncertain
- in the event of liquidation without reorganization, the convertible will rank alongside the PEACS, below senior debt and other senior obligations (for example accounts payable), and above common and any preferred equity.

In order to accurately value the note, all of the scenarios above should be reflected. First of all we must value the coupon which takes place between 0.5 and 10 years after issue, and the final payment in 10 years. These must be valued at the appropriate cost of capital. The main element of the convertible which differs from debt is that the convertible note can be converted to equity at the option of the bondholder. This is equivalent to a call option on Amazon equity at $156.055, because $156.055 of par value can be exchanged for a share. This can be valued using Black–Scholes. However, there is an upside on the maximum value at exercise, because the sensible option holder will exercise his or her option when the stock price exceeds $234.08, to prevent the forced redemption (this redemption option is only applicable until February 2002). When the convertible bonds were issued on 28 January 1999, the Amazon stock was trading at $122.875. At this stage we can view the convertible debt as consisting of:

debt + equity call option component

and can value it by calculating the present value of the debt (using the techniques in Chapter 1) plus the value of the option component (using Black–Scholes). Let us calculate the value of the convertible when issued.

Option components

Buy call at $156.055 until 2009:
Using volatility[10] = 84.9%, $S = \$122.875$, $K = \$156.055$, $T = 10$, $r_f = 5\%$: [11]

Black–Scholes value = $103.45 per option to call one share

Sell call at $234.08 until 2002 (upside is limited):
Using volatility = 84.9%, $S = \$122.875$, $K = \$234.08$, $T = 3$, $r_f = 5\%$:

Black–Scholes value = $51.78 per option to call one share (maximum – see below)

Since one share can be called per $156.055 of stock, these elements are worth $33.11 per $100 of convertible.

Bond component

The calculation of discount rates for debt of this type is extremely uncertain. Using discount rate risk-free + 5% risk premium,[12] we get a cost of capital of 10%, giving a bond value of $68.45 (Table 7.4).

Table 7.4 Convertibles debt element: example calculation

Discount rate			10%						
Years	0	0.5	1	1.5	2	2.5	9	9.5	10
Cash flow	–100	2.375	2.375	2.375	2.375	2.375	2.375	2.375	102.375
PV(cash flow)	–100	2.264	2.159	2.059	1.963	1.871	1.007	0.96	39.47
PV, total		**68.45**	from year 0.5						
NPV	**–31.55**								

This suggests a total value for the convertibles of $101.56 at the time of issue in 1999. Since the convertibles were sold at par the above calculations perhaps reflect the investors' views at the time, or more likely the approximations we have made have cancelled out this time! For example, the option component is more complex than we suggest above, because the bondholder is not writing a straight call to the firm – the stock price has to be above the trigger amount for 20 days; the firm pays the bondholder the make-whole payment if it redeems (a benefit to the bondholder); and the firm may not have the cash resources to redeem the bonds even if redemption is triggerable. For these reasons we are likely to be underestimating the proportion of the value of the bond which investors viewed as option, and overstating the amount of debt value. On the other hand, the underlying assumptions of the Black–Scholes equations are less supportable for stocks such as Amazon because trading may occur in jumps, which is not in accordance with the Black–Scholes model. For further information on this, consult a specialist text.

However, at March 2002, with equity prices at $15, the call option component has declined in value. At March 2002, it is worth approximately $5.26 per $100 (basis 4% risk free, 98% volatility. 7-year life – note that the forced redemption provision expired in February 2002). The bond component is also seen as more risky, because there is more doubt about Amazon's future solvency. Ravi Suria of Lehman Brothers suggested a 1200 basis-point risk premium in June 2000 (albeit with a caveat that this might be insufficient), giving a cost of capital of 16% and a bond component value of $55.31 at March 2002 with 14 coupon payments remaining. This implies a total value (debt + call) of approximately $60.50 at March 2002, compared to the market price of $62.75.

Another way of looking at this is that we view the convertible holders as writing a put for the equity holders. The intuition for this is that the equity holders share in the downside risk of the company only until the total enterprise value dips below the value of debt: that is, when their shares go to zero (obviously, that's not a very comforting picture, but is better than the alternative!). In other words, debt holders sell the equity holders a put option in which:

- the underlying security is the enterprise
- therefore the stock price is the current enterprise value (that is, the market value of the debt or quasi debt plus the market value of the equity) ($7.4bn at March 2002)[13]
- the strike price is the face value of debt (we use book value of debt of $2.17bn from Figure 7.9)

- the volatility is the volatility of the value of the enterprise (since the convertibles closely track equity, we use 98% for this value)
- the time to expiry is the time to the redemption of the debt (at 2002, this is 7 years).

We can value this put using put call parity.

1. First value call using Black–Scholes.
   Using volatility = 98%, S = \$7.44bn, K = \$2.171bn, $T = 7$, $r_f = 4\%$:

   value of call = \$6.79bn

2. Use put call parity to price the put:

   put value = call value + PV(exercise price) – stock price:
   value of put = \$1.03bn

This put is written (sold) by all the subordinated debtholders (although the senior debtholders also write a put to the subordinated debtholders, which we shall ignore for now), so is shared among the \$1.9bn of face value of subordinated debt. For each \$100 of par value it is therefore worth \$49.50. The value of the convertible is then the risk-free present value of the bond element (\$104.78 at 4% future risk-free rate – see Table 7.5) minus the \$54.50 which is the put that the debtholders have written, plus the call 'upside' of \$5.26. This gives a value of \$55.60. Note that when we are taking account of the default risk using a put option, the bond part of the convertible is discounted at the *risk-free* rate, not the *risky* rate – otherwise we would be 'double-counting' the bond's riskiness.

Table 7.5 Convertibles debt element: calculation at risk-free rate

Discount rate = 4%

Date	**Feb-02**	**Aug-02**	**Feb-03**	**Aug-03**	**Feb-04**	**Aug-04**	**Feb-08**	**Aug-08**	**Feb-09**
Years after issue		3.5	4	4.5	5	5.5	9	9.5	10
Cash flow		2.375	2.375	2.375	2.375	2.375	2.375	2.375	102.375
PV* (Feb 2002)		2.070	2.030	1.991	1.952	1.914	1.669	1.636	69.161
PV total* (Feb 2002)	\$104.784								

*values are ex the Feb 2002 coupon payment

Incidentally, the bonds were very popular when issued. Amazon had planned to issue $500m of the bonds, but scaled up its offer to $1.25bn when it saw the high demand. The convertibles fell in the days and weeks after issue to $82, but rose to a peak of $150 in May 1999, troughed at $75 at October 1999, and rose again to $150 in December 1999. They then fell to $35 around January 2001, and have since traded to $60 at March 2002. In general, the value of the convertibles has moved very much in parallel with the stock over the last year, suggesting that their equity/option character is quite pronounced and that they have a high β.

Exploding puts/death spiral convertibles

The most famous example of the exploding puts/death spiral convertibles was pets.com. Companies issue puts on their own stock, or alternatively execute the similar strategy of selling convertibles with strike prices that decline with the stock. Thus as the stock declines, the convertibles 'explode' as the fixed par value of the quasi-debt instrument (the convertible) is convertible into more and more shares. (Equity holders will weep at this; corporate recovery experts, on the other hand, may admire the elegance with which control is transferred to debtholders, without even an administration.)

The writing of puts on own stock by companies is a move which carries substantial danger. Going back to the insurance analogy for options, writing a put is like setting up in business as an insurer, and issuing policies against your own stock going down. Only one thing is guaranteed – if and when the firm is called upon to pay claims, it will already be in a weak position, because the stock will be down. And as the firm pays claims, the equity will fall even further. Hence the term 'death spiral'.

So why do firms adopt this 'crazy' strategy? Well, it's very simple. When a company's stock is highly volatile, traders will pay a lot for options on it. These modest but significant put premia will quietly add to cash flow for perhaps years (admittedly, sometimes before blowing up in the company's face).

APPENDIX 7.1: CALCULATING VOLATILITY

Volatility can often be obtained from online or paper sources. The formula is as follows:

$$\text{volatility} = \text{SD}(\log_e(\text{returns})) \times \sqrt{(\text{number of return periods in one year})}$$

If volatility needs to be calculated, the following method should be used in Excel.

1. Assemble the stock prices in column A, rows 2 onwards.
2. Calculate the return in column B by inserting the formula '=A3/A2-1' in cell B3 and copying down.
3. Calculate the log to base e (natural log) of the return in column C by inserting the formula '=LN(B3)' in cell C3 and copying down. (This converts price variations, which move lognormally according to the Black–Scholes, into returns, which move normally.)
4. Calculate the standard deviation by entering the formula '=STDEV(C3:Cnn)' where nn is the last line of the natural logarithms. This will give the daily volatility.
5. Calculate the annual volatility by multiplying this by $\sqrt{253}$ (trading days) [or $\sqrt{52}$ (if weekly returns are used) or $\sqrt{12}$ (if monthly returns are used)].

Notes

1 Black and Scholes (1973).
2 Joel Stern has suggested that far-out-of-the-money options would be a more suitable incentive, because an option at about the same exercise price as the current share price which lasts for a typical ESOP period of 5–10 years is an almost certain bet and may not help incentivize managers that much. Stephen Ross has even suggested some out-of-the-money put options to optimize incentives for the manager. Warren Buffett, on the other hand, eschews stock options and prefers cash compensation, mainly because the accounting treatment unfairly inflates profitability of option-issuing companies.
3 To put this in perspective, it should be noted that in 2001, a year of disappointing performance for Disney, Eisner received a *total* compensation of $1m. The Disney compensation scheme – unlike many CEO compensation schemes, which can pay high rewards even in poor years – cuts both ways.
4 Carpenter (2000).
5 Carpenter uses an assumption of 'constant relative risk aversion' (CRRA), which assumes that persons have a constant aversion to losing 1% of their wealth as they get richer. This is a realistic assumption for most persons, superior to the assumption made in much economic work of constant absolute risk aversion (CARA), which assumes that a rich man is just as concerned about losing £1 as a poor man.
6 For students of US accounting, the recent rearguard action against the FASB's position on business combinations has been very reminiscent of the FAS 123 struggle (and has ended in the same way).
7 In fact, the Black–Scholes derivation makes such severe assumptions, in particular about tradability and market depth, that it overestimates the value of most *traded* options!
8 Young (1993).
9 It has been a general trend for tech companies which have seen stock price declines to issue lower strike price stock options or in some other way to lower the effective strike

price. Although granting lower stock price options has positive incentivizing effects, some shareholder activists have criticised the trend, saying that option repricing means that managers end up being rewarded even if stock prices go down.

10 1999 volatility from Figure 7.8 (Amazon 2001 10K, page 69).

11 1999 risk-free rate from Figure 1.1.

12 Amazon's convertible securities are rated Caa2 (rating dated 25 January 2002) by Moody's, which is at the top end of the junk bond category. Caa is defined as follows: 'Bonds ... rated Caa are of poor standing. Such issues may be in default or there may be present elements of danger with respect to principal or interest.' As discussed by Altman and Kishore, promised rates of return for this class of bonds were 4.5% above risk-free between 1978 and 1994. However, realized rates were 2.1% above risk-free, due to a large number of defaults especially in 1990–91, mainly associated with LBO-related junk bonds. The assessment of the risk of a bond of this type is not a mechanical activity, however. It is unlikely that Amazon could have issued this amount of pure debt (without an option element).

13 $7.4bn enterprise value at March 2002 calculated as the March 2002 equity market capitalization of $5.5bn plus the market value of the debt ($260m + $1,153m as per Table 7.3) plus the value of the stock options ($482m as per Table 7.3).

CHAPTER 8

Options II: Real Options

This chapter is organized as follows. First of all we discuss the strengths and weaknesses of using real options to value companies, and specifically using them to value internet companies. Then, bearing in mind these caveats, we go on to discuss valuation methods for real options.

THE REAL OPTION ANALOGY

A financial option, for example the April call option on Yahoo! with a strike price of $15 that we discussed at the start of the last chapter, is clearly a very valuable asset, even if Yahoo! is trading at $13. Its character of optional exercise means that option holders can participate in the upside of stock market performance above $15, but will not lose if the price goes down (apart from paying the option premium). For this reason, the option seller or 'writer' will only sell such an option for a high price. The option writer is the *counterparty* who pays out if the option holder gains.

Moving across to real options, there is general agreement that option valuation techniques are of great assistance in valuing pharmaceutical and other similar research and development projects. A patented drug is an asset of potentially enormous value. However, at each stage of the development of the drug, management has the option to abandon the project if the results of trials or certifications are negative. Here, the key thing to note is that the upside is owned by the firm developing the drug. It has no obligation to develop, but the right to any future profits is assigned to the firm. In this case the counterparty is national government on behalf of the national economy, joined by a coalition of international governments. The global economy gives the growth option on patented products to the firms that discover them, because it is considered to be very important to stimulate and reward successful innovation. In this case the option analogy is sensible, the pattern of payoffs looks the same as those of a financial option, and there is a clear counterparty. Figures 8.1 and 8.2 show the similarities between these financial and real options by depicting the profit diagrams of each.

The put option that limited liability gives firm equity holders[1] (to put the firm's assets onto debtholders at a strike price of the face value of debt) is a well known and accepted example of a real option. (We discussed an example of this type of put when considering the Amazon.com subordinated convertible notes in the last chapter.) The counterparty in this case is the debtholder, who gives a put option to the borrowing firm when he or she writes a loan. When valuing precarious industries such as the airline and shipping trades, DCF does not work well. Few would argue with the use of *strategic NPV* (a measure of net present value which includes option upside) for valuing an airline, adding the put options on airline debt onto the 'standard DCF', with *static NPV* as a 'first cut' for this number.[2]

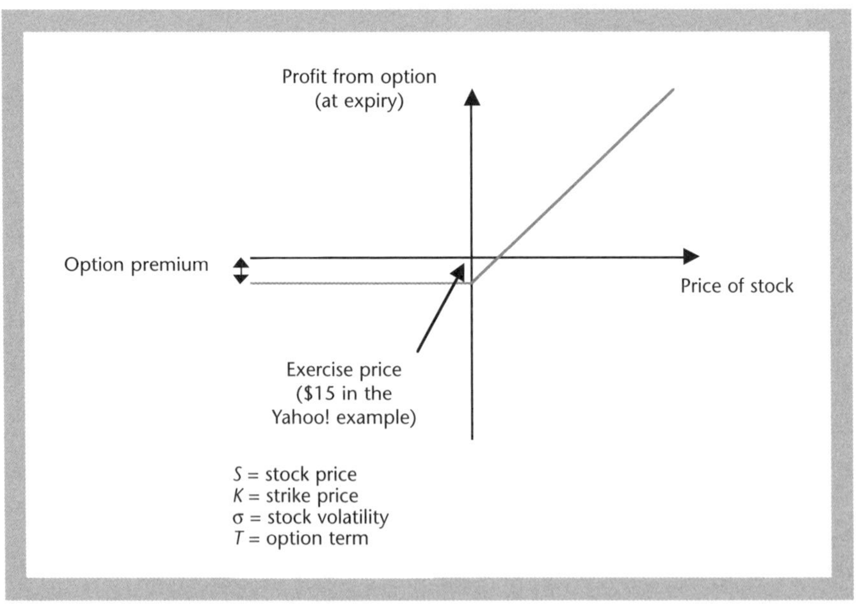

Figure 8.1 Profit diagram for call option

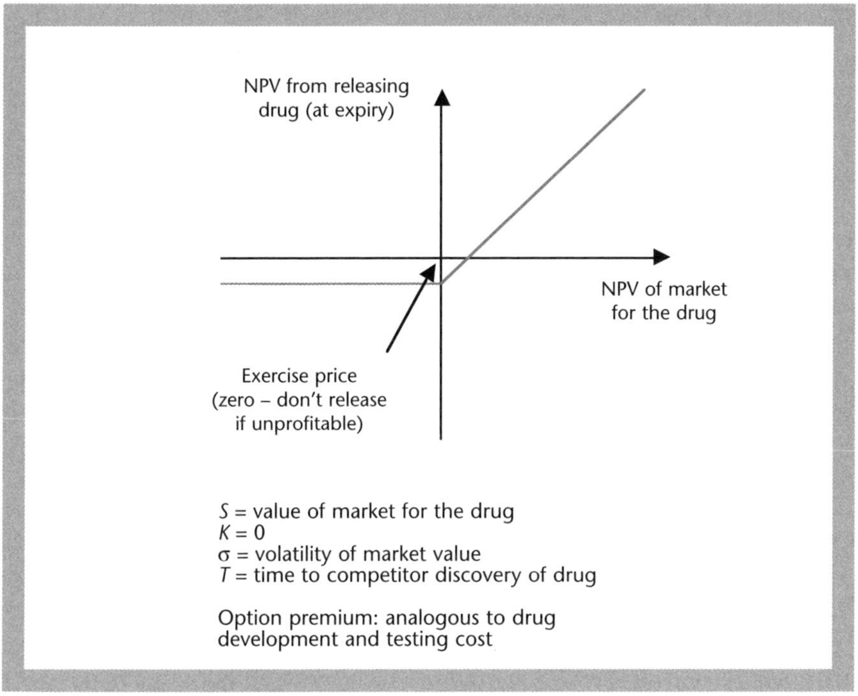

Figure 8.2 Analogous profit diagram for a real option

Similarly, oil and gas reserves have option character. Consider a physical oil well with the particularly attractive properties that it can be emptied at any time and the oil sold immediately, that there are no holding costs while it is dormant, and that the oil does not leak into surrounding oilfields. Such an oil well is identical to a call option on crude oil traded on an exchange. The owner has the upside in accordance with longstanding property rights (that is, he or she owns the well) enshrined in the law of capitalist countries.

More arguably, many real options exponents point to the computer industry as an excellent example of where a real options approach is relevant. An initial loss-making entry into the personal computer industry (pre-standardization) in 1978, for example, may have positioned a company very well to take advantage of growth in the industry, as this growth kicked in during the 1980s. This is an example where there is no counterparty to give the firm the option. However, some option-type upside does exist, due to the possession of strategic assets by the firm which has taken on the initial loss-making project. It has skills, experience, and possibly a useful prototype. However, it is evidently not such a clear-cut and well-defined option as that of a patented product or an oil well that is owned. The upside is shared by competitors, and more competitors will be attracted if market growth is high. Some will have similar strategic assets to our subject firm; some will buy or license these assets; and other new entrants will develop them from scratch. The subject firm has upside, but its option is extensively shared. (In the event, the vast majority of specialist PC makers went into liquidation.)

Pushing the envelope?

Pushing the analogy a step further, we can conceive that there is an option-like character to the potential growth in the Sunday morning street-corner lemonade market in the USA, or the door-to-door car-washing service market in the UK, both of which are dominated by schoolchildren. This market is constantly growing, so in order to calculate the value of a lemonade stand using 'strategic NPV' and to advise our kids on how to spend their Sunday: we should consider not just the 'static NPV' of the profit they can make on this and succeeding Sundays: we should also bear in mind the possibility that our kids may capture the growth in this very large market, and perhaps diversify into the orange juice market. Lemonade stands give the kids growth options they would not otherwise have had, which must be borne in mind when assessing the investment.

However, there are obvious problems with the lemonade market growth option. In the case of our call option on Yahoo!, we had an option because we had bought a security from a counterparty. The counterparty in turn matched our option with a contingent liability on their side. There is no counterparty giving our child the right to take advantage of growth in the lemonade market. All anyone needs to get into the growing lemonade market is some lemons, a squeezer, a jug, a pack of sugar, ice from the family refrigerator, a table and some glasses. In as far as there exists a growth option on the lemonade market, all children share it. For any individual child, it is close to worthless.

Detecting the 'lemonade stand' option

So what about the internet companies' growth opportunities – are they options shared by 'anyone who can buy some lemons', or options whose upside is protected by property rights or guaranteed by a specific counterparty (perhaps under a government-backed patent)? Or are these options somewhere in between those two extremes, having value due to strategic assets that these companies possess?

Clearly, Amazon.com's option to expand into the soap powder market is a 'lemonade stand' option. The company has no strategic assets in this market, in fact quite the reverse. Unilever and Procter & Gamble have a substantial competitive advantage in making and marketing soap powder. Amazon has a nice shop, but is not in a much better position than a thousand other web retailers and a hundred thousand offline retailers.

Yahoo!'s growth options on the banking industry are more attractive, but likely to be extremely time-limited. The company has formed partnerships with leading banks, but many of these banks have developed or are developing their own websites. Strategic assets in the web-banking industry are capital, reputation and transaction-processing expertise. And a website. In that order.

On the other hand, infrastructure internet companies, such as Verisign (which is a company specializing in digital 'certificates',[3] among other products) often have technological lead or even a patented technology. There may be no growth in the market for digital certificates of the type offered by Verisign, but if there is, Verisign will own a large part of that upside. The situation is similar for Baltimore Technologies, the maker of public key technologies[4] quoted in the UK.

However, even if these options do exist and have value, are we double-counting the option value by assuming a very high growth rate in our static DCF? Frequently, modelled DCF values for internet firms impound very high growth rates, especially when they have been based on the 1998–99 data. As Damodaran (2001) has argued, it may be unsafe to take these high growth DCF values, and to postulate that there can be option upside on top of these already optimistic numbers.

Another issue, relevant both to real options analysis and to DCF forecasting, has to do with the issue of optimal exercise. If we believe that real options are commonplace and commonly recognized in many industries, and that we *already* observe the use of management flexibility in many companies, then real options are *already* being exercised on a widespread basis. This means that when we construct a DCF forecast using as benchmark the margin numbers for established firms (firms whose managers are taking advantage of real options by exercising managerial flexibility), we are already impounding some real option benefits by using these *cum real-option* margins in our DCF. If, on the other hand, we believe that real options are 'out there' but seldom exercised by managers, then we still have a problem. Options have to be recognized and have the potential to be exercised to have value. In this world, the role of the real options expert changes from valuing the real options content of a business on a passive basis (because, without intervention to assist managers in using the real options, this real options content has negligible value) to evangelizing within the company about how best to detect and how best to manage real options. To be fair, many real options consultancies see this as *exactly* their role. However, that is not what we are about here. With apologies to Mark Antony, we come to value Caesar, not to change him.

Finally, do the internet companies have enough management resources to take advantage of all the options that are theoretically available to them? We have been picking specific examples of markets on which internet companies can or cannot be said to have an effective option, but surely there is a virtually infinite range of things that can be sold or intermediated via this new mechanism of the internet? This is true, but to 'trial' in each of these markets is clearly beyond the resources of any firm. Furthermore, a lack of strategic assets in many of these markets may well make the growth options on them 'lemonade stand' options, shared by all competitors or even all firms. Strategic choices and prioritizations must be made. This is the process of business.

Table 8.1 When real options are valuable and when they are not

	Valuable	**Less valuable or valueless**
Insights from standard real options theory	Volatile market with high upside (and downside) potential	Predictable 'flat' marketplace
	The PV(exercise price) minus the asset price is large and positive (put option) or large and negative (call)	The PV(exercise price) minus the asset price is small or negative (put option), or small and negative, or positive (call)
	The opportunity to exercise the option will exist for a long time	The opportunity to exercise the option will exist for a short time
Detecting shared, double-counted or impractical options	Clear counterparty 'writing' the option	Option 'from the ether'
	Option upside dependent on limited liability or property rights	No clear legal right to upside
	No competitors or potential entrants	Many competitors or potential competitors
	Patented product	Easily copied product
	Important strategic assets or competencies owned by the firm	Strategic assets owned by others, or easily developed by others
	Growth can be realistically seen as incremental to static NPV	High growth already assumed in DCF calculation (risk of double-counting)
	Close to firm management's experience	In unrelated or distant market sector that management will not have time to explore

Analogy is a useful reasoning tool. By spotting patterns and similarities in objects and phenomena that occur in different places, we can transfer expertise from one field to another. Real options is a good example of analogy in action, and the real options analogy has proved very useful in some very difficult valuation tasks, for example the valuation of oil and natural resources. However, in competitive market places it is less useful – and the markets in which many internet companies operate are very competitive. Many of the options in these markets have low values. Table 8.1 provides a summary.

PROCEDURE FOR DETERMINING REAL OPTION VALUE FOR A COMPANY

1. Detect main real options (3–5 markets per firm).
2. Estimate how many firms will share in the upside.
3. Determine real-option equivalent parameters (whole market).
4. Estimate the market option value – monopoly case (using Black–Scholes risk-neutral method).
5. Estimate the market option value – oligopoly case (using concepts from Grenadier, 2002).

The Black–Scholes method we discussed in the previous chapter. The risk-neutral method we discuss in Appendix 8.1. However, calculating the value of real options once we know the parameters is relatively straightforward – working out whether they exist and in which markets is more problematic.

Note that stage 2 of the procedure is a 'showstopper'. It is at this stage that we detect 'lemonade stand' options. If the product market is competitive, there is no point in continuing with steps 3–5: $T = 0$ (immediate expiry of all real options), and the option value is zero. Basically, if *you* don't exercise the option, someone else will.

In an *oligopoly market* – that is, a market shared by a 'cartel', formal (where legal) or informal – the option value will be lower than in a monopoly and generally the real option value will decline very rapidly as the number of competitors in the product market increases. We use a methodology outlined in Grenadier (2002) to adjust for this. However, since not all of Grenadier's assumptions will hold in the cases we are considering – our fault, not his: we are applying his theory in a different setting – the values we get will not be precise, and should be viewed as rough estimates.

Table 8.2 Effects of competition on option value

Stock option parameters	Real option equivalent	Effect of increased competition
Standard deviation (or volatility), σ	Volatility of the project value, σ	Uncertain
Share price, S	Present value of the market (cash flow not revenues), S	Decreases value of the market
Exercise price, K	Cost to enter the new market, K	Uncertain, may decrease K if a stepping-stone technology decreases in price because more firms are building a platform
Time, T	Time available to learn/resolve uncertainty before exercise, T	Decreases time left to resolve uncertainty before exercise
Risk-free rate, r_f	Risk-free rate, r_f	No effect

Option valuation under competition

Researchers have established methods for calculating option valuation under competition, but these methods usually require knowledge of stochastic calculus, which is outside the scope of this book. There is no debate that competition has the effect of decreasing real option value. Using the Black–Scholes framework, we can see the negative effect on the key parameters (Table 8.2), in particular S and T.

Steven Grenadier has written extensively on the topic of real options and competition, in the real estate industry and other markets.[5] A recent paper[6] derives an expression which compares the real option value of a market with n companies to the real option value with 1 company. The paper uses assumptions standard in the real options literature (for example, constant-elasticity market inverse demand function, and the presence of multiplicative demand shocks which evolve as a geometric Brownian motion). The paper then simulates the firm's decisions, but simulates them while taking into account the other firms' investment strategies. (This is the concept of Nash Equilibrium in economics and game theory – the Nash equilibrium is what people will decide to do (their optimal strategy) if they assume that other players in the game *execute* their optimal strategies.) The result of this is an option value which is declining in the number of firms, n. As Grenadier states, 'Increasing competition leads firms to exercise their options sooner, as

Table 8.3 Real option values: effect of competition

	For option premium = 200% of NPV value		For option premium = 100% of NPV value		For option premium = 50% of NPV value	
Number of firms, *n*	**γ**	**Option premium, OP(*n*) (%)**	**γ**	**Option premium (%)**	**γ**	**Option premium (%)**
1	1.5	200	2	100	3	50
2	1.5	50	2	33	3	20
3	1.5	29	2	20	3	13
4	1.5	20	2	14	3	9
5	1.5	15	2	11	3	7
6	1.5	13	2	9	3	6
7	1.5	11	2	8	3	5
8	1.5	9	2	7	3	4
9	1.5	8	2	6	3	4
10	1.5	7	2	5	3	3

the fear of pre-emption diminishes the value of their options to wait.' This is summarized in the following equation:

$$\mathrm{OP}(n) = \frac{1}{n\gamma - 1}$$

where γ is a parameter within the demand function (a *demand function* is an expression of price as a function of quantity of the good produced, in this case $P(t) = X(t).Q(t)^{\frac{1}{\gamma}}$, but is in this case most simply derived by considering the monopoly option premium derived from the base case analysis (that is, the monopoly case, standard real options analysis). For example, for a monopoly option premium of 200%, OP(1) must be equal to 2. Therefore, γ is equal to 1.5 in this case.[7] Considering option premia of 100% or 200%, which are considered by real options texts to be typical in many cases, we can see the rapid falloff in real option values as more firms enter the market (Table 8.3).

Option value for Amazon.com

Our methodology emphasizes strategic analysis first, numerical analysis second. In order for option value to exist in a market for a company, the real option must satisfy some of the requirements in Table 8.1. For most internet firms, the main options we are concerned with are *growth options*, rather than property rights-backed options such as the option on an oil well which we discussed above. Furthermore, only very rarely will there be patent protection to 'guard' the option while we wait to exercise it. Amazon's liquidation puts written by convertible holders to debtholders are certainly valuable, as we discussed in the last chapter, but the search for upside has generally concentrated on growth options. Growth options are also sometimes termed *platform options*, because they set up a platform for further expansion in a marketplace, perhaps by making a 'toe in the water' small entry into a market. This initial entry may be unprofitable, but by securing technological leads and perhaps brand recognition, the company gains a position from which to participate in future profitable growth in the market. The classic example of this is the platform options in the 1970s PC industry. However, just as occurred there, the options are vulnerable to attack or to a complete shift in the required strategic assets (in that case, many of the early entrants' 'strategic assets' became irrelevant due to standardization around the IBM PC standard).

Step 1: Identify the main real options

Where do Amazon.com's current activities give it the best 'platform'? Given that management time is constrained, the company cannot enter more than a limited number of markets. Presence in the markets, together with optimal or near-optimal exercise of the options, is vital if they are to have value. Our procedure is to use as starting points the markets the company is in now, and then to evaluate where these markets can lead to as 'stepping stones'. We then use the characteristics we have defined which detect valuable real options (as summarized Table 8.1) to evaluate which of these incremental markets have the highest real option values to the company today. Further distilled, as in Table 8.4, these criteria come down to three questions:

- How many competitors are there in the incremental market? Will the subject company have time to resolve uncertainty (essential for real options to have value) before competitors force it to act?
- Does the subject company possess superior strategic assets? Has the company really built a platform for this new market, or is it just starting from scratch, albeit with experience in a related market?

Table 8.4 Identifying the main real options for Amazon.com

Current area	Platform to?	Competitors?	Superior strategic assets gained?	Incremental to current forecasts?
Books	EBooks	Yes	Possibly	Yes
Music	Music digital downloads	Potentially	Uncertain	Yes
Videos	Video digital downloads	Potentially	Uncertain	Yes
International	Extend product lines	Depends	Yes	?/Yes
Auctions	Other auction formats	Yes, dominant	No	No
Services	Other service products	Yes, many	Yes	?/Yes
Home improvement	Wider product range	Yes, many	No	No
Electronics	Wider product range	Many	No	No
Software	ASP (application service provider) or other service provision	Yes, variable strength	No	Yes
Kitchen	Wider homeware range	Yes, many	No	No
Health and beauty	Wider personal products range	Yes, many	No	No
Outdoor	Wider product range	Yes	No	No
Tools	Wider product range	Yes	No	No
Amazon outlet	Wider range of discount products	Yes	Yes/?	Yes
Cellphones/airtime	Other telephone-related sales	Yes, strong	No	Yes
Computers	Wider range of computer products	Yes, strong (e.g. Dell)	No	No/?

- Is the potential growth incremental to current revenue forecasts?

Using Table 8.4 we identify the following markets for further analysis:

- digital downloading – music
- digital downloading – eBooks
- services area
- software/ASP
- outlet.

Step 2: Determine how many firms will share the upside

Steps 2 and 3 of the methodology are concerned with studying the markets where real option value is most likely to reside for Amazon.com. As mentioned above, the reason to start with the issue of competition is that if many firms are likely to share the real option, the value is zero, so we do not need to proceed further. The competitors in the selected markets are shown in Table 8.5. At this stage we can eliminate software/ASP, due to the large number of competitors with superior strategic assets that already exist in this market.

In digital downloads of music the future path of competition is uncertain. Genuine peer-to-peer file-sharing programs such as Gnutella currently under-

Table 8.5 Amazon.com's competitors in identified markets

Industry	Competitors with similar/ commensurate strategic assets	Estimated number
Digital downloading – music	MP3.com, Artistdirect.com, Cdnow.com/Columbia House, Napster, towerrecords.com, virginmega.com, Record Labels(?)	10
Digital downloading – eBooks	Barnesandnoble.com has been aggressive in this area, but otherwise Amazon is in a strong position. Ebook reader producers, publishers may try to compete	1–3
Services area	Yahoo!, AOL, MSN	3
Software/ASP	Many	Many
Outlet	Overstock.com, half.com (eBay), buy.com, ubid.com, others	5

mine paid music download services, which makes music publishers leery about releasing desired music. If and when copyright protection problems are solved, Amazon will be well positioned to leverage its position as the leading seller of recorded music on the internet, but will face competition from Napster (now attempting to find role as a paid music provider) and high street music retailers who will attempt to upgrade their own websites. The real uncertainty in the marketplace is whether music publishers themselves will enter the fray. The temptation to disintermediate much of the recorded-music value chain may prove impossible to resist. The most likely course is that music publishers will stay on the sidelines (with the exception of making licensing agreements and perhaps taking strategic stakes in some service providers) for the first two or three years, and then enter the market with their own websites.

Amazon's recent agreements with Target and AOL are examples of *service* income as it can be most broadly defined. Amazon certainly has expertise in running an online store, and can leverage this by partnering with other businesses that need this expertise. To think of possible competitors in this space, consider a company that wishes to augment or to establish its web commerce presence – to whom would it go? Amazon.com would most likely be the leading choice, combining expertise in commerce and web portal establishment. Other choices would be AOL itself, and the other principal web portals, MSN and Yahoo!

Step 3: Determine real option equivalent parameters (whole market)

The number of firms, n, is as discussed above (1 is added to each number of competitors to calculate the number in the market, as Amazon itself must be included). We assume that Amazon's potential projects are of similar volatility to Amazon's current business and, as convertibles track equity price quite closely, we use the volatility of Amazon equity as an approximation for the volatility of the company's operating assets. However, in the ideal case where a volatility for the relevant project can be obtained, this should be used in the calculation. Since all of the projects we are discussing are e-commerce projects, our approximation is accurate. If we were considering a lower risk project, for example an option on a property project, volatility would have to be adjusted downwards. The value of 98% (from Amazon's 2001 10K) for Amazon equities volatility was used (as per Chapter 7).

The market value, S, is the most difficult to calculate. We sought predictions of market size or incremental market size and then calculated present value by assuming average post-tax margins of 5% before taking a perpetuity at a growth rate of 4%. Since S should represent the current value, not a future rosy projection, revenues closest to the present day are sought. See Table 8.6.

Table 8.6 Market sizes and market values of industries where Amazon may have real options

Industry	Revenues $m (year, source)	Future earnings ($m = 5\%$) ($)	Present value of growing perpetuity of earnings ($r = 13\%$, $g = 4\%$)
Music download	1100 (2003, Forrester)	55m	610
eBooks download	838 (2001, Forrester)	42	470
Services	8,600 × 20% = 1750 (2001, Yankee Group)	87.5	970
Outlet shopping	11,300 × 10% = 1130 (1996, Value Retail News)	56.5	630

In determining the values of the services area and outlet shopping, we viewed the services opportunity as a substantial incremental segment of the online advertising market ($8.6bn revenues) and outlet shopping as a smaller segment of the outlet shopping segment ($11.3bn revenues in the most recent available figures).

We then continue the calculation of real option value in Table 8.7, using the value of each market (from Table 8.6) as the 'stock price' for the option formula.

The strike price (the price of entering the market) tries to compare the difficulty of the market entry and setting up the website to our knowledge that Amazon's spend on its website to date has totalled $680m (to 2001Q3). Therefore ballpark numbers for each website enhancement, of $50m for services and e-books and $100m for music and outlet, have been used. Since these include marketing/launch spend, they are perhaps conservative.

Time reflects the anticipated speed of response of competitors in the marketplace: slower in books and services than in outlet and music downloading.

The basic monopoly value of the call, *V*(call) is then calculated from the Black–Scholes formula (as discussed in Chapter 7), and divided by the strike price to obtain the base premium OP(I), which is in turn used to calculate γ. OP(n) is then calculated (using $OP(n)=1/(n.\gamma\text{-}1)$), and then multiplied by the strike price to obtain the competitive value, *V*(comp).

As shown in Table 8.7, the estimated total value of Amazon.com's real options is $61m.

Table 8.7 Calculation of the value of Amazon's real options

Industry	n	σ	S ($m)	K ($m)	T (X*)	r_f	d_1	d_2	V(Call), monopoly real option value ($m)	Base premium, OP(1)	Implied gamma	Competitive premium, OP(n)	V(comp), competitive real option value ($m)
Music download	11	89%	610	100	1	4%	2.521	1.631	$515.22	515%	1.19	0.082	$8.24
eBooks download	3	89%	470	50	2	4%	2.472	1.213	$425.82	852%	1.12	0.425	$21.26
Services	4	89%	970	50	2	4%	3.048	1.789	$924.36	1849%	1.05	0.311	$15.55
Outlet Shopping	6	89%	630	100	1	4%	2.557	1.667	$535.11	535%	1.19	0.163	$16.34
TOTAL													$61.38

APPENDIX 8.1: RISK-NEUTRAL/BINOMIAL METHOD OF CALCULATING OPTION VALUES – WORKED EXAMPLE[8]

Establishing the platform: platform is negative NPV

This appendix shows a simple example of valuing a growth option when the state of the world changes between two alternatives each year. Specifically, each year, the value of the relevant market goes up by 80% (uptick mulitplier, u=1.8) or the market decreases in value by 40% (downtick multiplier, d=0.6). This is a binomial model, since there are two possible outcomes per year and, since there are two further outcomes from each outcome, the number of outcomes in year n is 2^n. For example in year 2 there are four outcomes or nodes.

First of all, we see the situation without flexibility, as shown in Figure 8.3. Each branching occurs in one year, we assume an initial market value of \$100m, a cost of capital of 20%, and that the subjective or 'real world' probability of branching either way is one half. With no optionality we can quickly calculate the NPV, using weighted probabilities. Bear in mind that we use the u and d values to derive market value in year 2, and then work backwards to determine NPV. Thus if the market develops well for two years its value is \$100m$\times u^2$=\$324m. Working backwards, value after one year is either V^+=\$180m or V^-=\$60m. Value at the start is confirmed as the discounted value

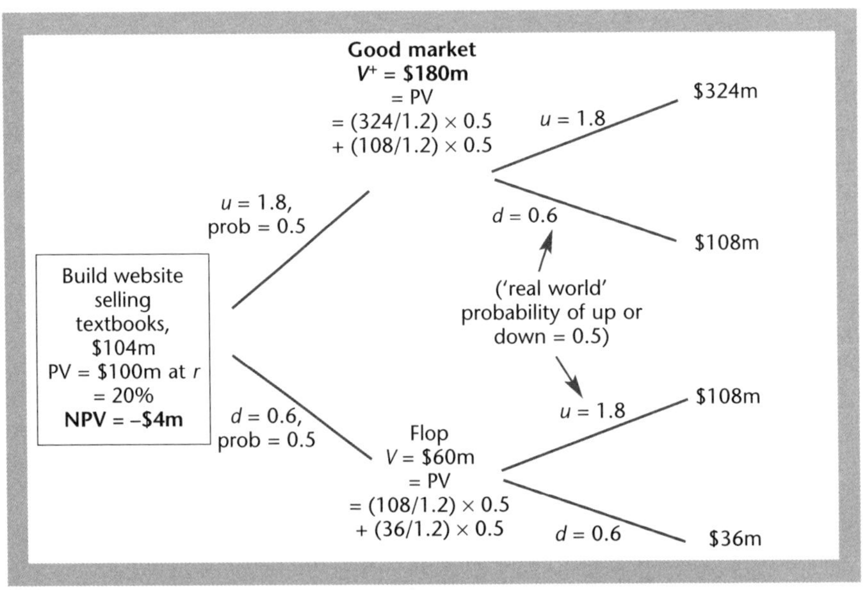

Figure 8.3 Platform NPV calculation: binomial world

of V^+($180m/1.2=$150m) multiplied by probability 0.5, plus the discounted value of V^-($60m/1.2=$50m) times 0.5: a total of $100m. Since we assume cost of $104m, the project has negative NPV of –$4m. Next we introduce a growth option and see how this, and the resolution of uncertainty, can affect value.

Growth option: description

Now we assume that we have the option to invest $80m after one year on advertising and making new webpages to sell novels (on top of our $104m). Suppose this will double the scale of our business in year 2. An important thing to note is that during year 1 (before we have to decide whether to increase scale) uncertainty is resolved: we see whether the market is in an up state (V^+) or a down state (V^-).

Next we incorporate the cost of expansion ($80m) and the effect of expansion (doubling value) in a decision rule. At any point we can accept market value, V, or expand and gain $2V$ minus the cost of expansion, $80m: so the decision rule is that we will always choose max(V, $2V$– 80). So we now calculate this expression in the up state V^+ (where V=180) and in the down state V^- (where V=60):

- up state: $V^+ = \max(V, 2V - 80) = \max(180,280) = 280$
- down: $V^- = \max(V, 2V - 80) = \max(60,40) = 60$

Note that the max expression rule has delivered different decisions for each outcome. To obtain the $280m value in the up state we must expand, but to deliver the $60m value in the down state we *do not expand* at the end of year 1 (the project would only be worth $40m if we expanded). All the outcomes

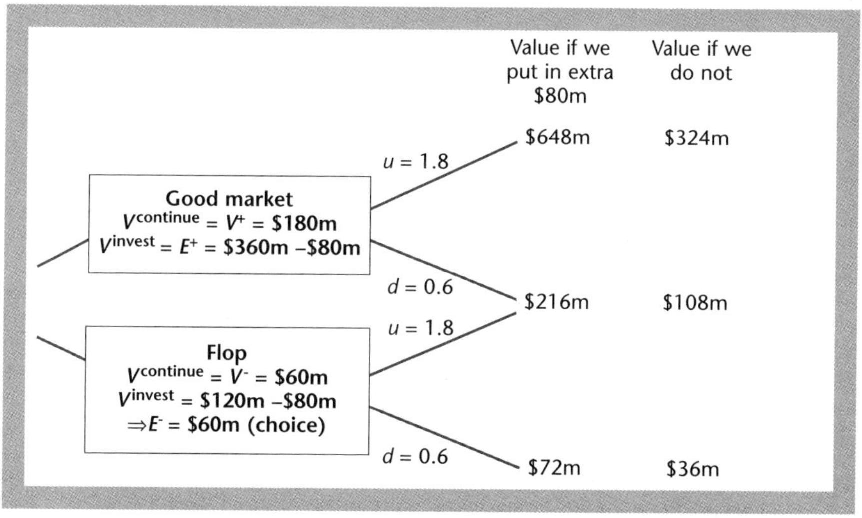

Figure 8.4 Growth option 'tree' diagram and calculations

under each decision are shown in Figure 8.4 (which only depicts the world from year 1 onwards. Year 0 value (strategic NPV) is off to the left of the diagram).

Growth option: calculation

In order to deal with the optionality, we calculate the value using risk-neutral probabilities. Let the risk-free rate be 5%. We then calculate the risk-neutral probability, p. This is the implied probability which would give the observed prices for known outcomes, in a world where people are indifferent to whether they get risky or risk free-cash flows:

$$p = ((1 + r_f) - d)/(u - d) = (1.05 - 0.6)/(1.8 - 0.6) = 0.375$$

Then we calculate the 'Strategic NPV':

$$\begin{aligned}\text{strategic NPV} &= [(pE^{+} + (1 - p)E^{-})/(1 + r_f)^{t}] - I_0 \\ &= [(0.375 \times 280 + 0.625 \times 60)/1.05] - 104 = \$31.7\text{m}\end{aligned}$$

$$\text{option value} = \text{strategic NPV} - \text{static NPV} = \$31.7 - (-4) = \$34.7\text{m}$$

Thus a project that would have been rejected (NPV = –$4m) is accepted once the option value is borne in mind.

Clearly, there are some caveats to be considered. The binomial world is not a realistic picture, and the u and d factors were arbitrarily chosen. However, these problems can be overcome by simulating very short periods in the binomial 'tree' and deriving u and d values from interest rates. What is more difficult to justify is that we assumed that substantial benefits from growth would be captured without competitors getting in the way. This binomial illustration assumes no competition, which makes it less realistic. Competition will decrease option value in general. Trigeorgis (1996), Chapter 9, discusses modelling of competition.

Notes

1 Equity can be viewed as ownership of firm assets plus ownership of a put at the face value of debt *or* ownership of a call on assets at the face value of debt.
2 The strategic NPV and static NPV terminology is due to Trigeorgis (1996).
3 Digital certificates are electronic files that are used to uniquely identify people and resources over networks such as the internet. This definition is from Robinson (2001), which also gives a brief introduction to related concepts.
4 Public key technology is a method of encrypting data frequently used in digital certificates and other internet security applications.
5 See, for example, Grenadier (2000).
6 Review of *Financial Studies*, forthcoming.
7 OP(1) = 200% = 2. Since the equation for OP(n) = $1/(n\gamma - 1)$, for $n = 1$ and OP(1) = 2 ⇒ $2 = 1/((1)\gamma - 1) \Rightarrow 2 = 1/(\gamma - 1) \Rightarrow 2(\gamma - 1) = 1 \Rightarrow 2\gamma - 2 = 1 \Rightarrow \gamma = 1.5$.
8 Based on Trigeorgis (1996), p. 153.

CHAPTER 9

Assessing Current Practice in Valuation

THE VALUATION CHALLENGES OF 1995–99

The field of internet valuation can be traced back to the IPO of Netscape, Inc., in August 1995. At the time of the Netscape IPO there was a convention that companies should be profitable before seeking a listing on the public markets. However, Netscape reached a market capitalization of $2.2bn at the close of its first day as a listed company, despite having recorded losses of $14m in the previous year. Clearly, *price/earnings (PE) ratios* were of no use in valuing Netscape!

In the years following Netscape, the increasing number of internet companies quoted and the variety of technological frameworks that needed to be mastered created a need for stock analysts and fund managers who were concentrating on the internet field. As the rapid stock price appreciation of internet stocks played out in 1998–99, investment managers demanded innovative analysis to assist them in their decision making.

Facing great valuation challenges, internet analysts sought to meet these needs. While PE ratios cannot be used for companies with no current earnings, the DCF methodology which we mentioned in Chapter 1 is sufficiently robust to provide valuation insights under these conditions. Many analysts initially used this as their basic valuation toolbox.

DCF was used sensibly and innovatively to attempt to make sense of internet stock values. One good example is 'Cashflow.com', a Credit Suisse First Boston research paper on internet valuation (Mauboussin, 1998). This paper sought to explain internet valuations by pointing out the low asset needs of internet businesses, and the positive cash flows which would accrue and create value. The paper attempted to stretch the envelope of cash-flow valuation in the internet space, and to draw internet investors' attention to the positive effects of asset efficiency, a well-known effect in other businesses (for example, supermarkets and periodical publishing). However, one weakness is that little attempt was made to quantify the positive effect in NPV terms. We discuss the strengths and weaknesses of this paper later in the chapter.

As internet stock values progressed rapidly upwards, increasing use was made of other methods of valuation. A small number of analysts discussed the advances in real-option theory, and posited that some of the value of internet stocks was due to the great potential profits of these firms being contrasted with much smaller potential losses if the internet stocks were unsuccessful. Future returns to internet companies were thought to possess 'asymmetry': relatively small and limited potential losses (the current equity value) but the *potential* for enormous value generation, essentially unlimited in the view of the analysts, if the internet companies 'took off'. Since these posited payoffs were similar in pattern to call options on a stock, call option valuation techniques such as the Black–Scholes formula were proposed as potential valuation paradigms. As practised at that time this approach had severe weaknesses, both in concept and in execution. The issue of the importance of competition was almost entirely neglected – competitive markets do not have unlimited upside, since positive economic profit will attract other firms into their markets. Analysts also erred in execution by failing to attempt to quantify potential option value. Under reasonable assumptions of timescale and potential value (even assuming ideal Black–Scholes conditions hold), real-option value is modest for many firms, as demonstrated in the example shown in Chapter 8.

THE RISE OF COMPARABLES

Analysts looking at internet companies had the same 'time famine' as equity analysts studying other industries. Unlike academics, equity analysts cannot spend years writing books and doing detailed research: each analyst has between ten and twenty firms to cover, and they are expected to produce opinions for investors on a daily basis. Therefore, just as in other industries, there was a desire for rules of thumb and simpler valuation metrics. This demand was increased by the fact that DCF-based analysis did not produce the 'right answers' – internet stock values continued to increase throughout 1999, despite the fact that DCF projections suggested that the stocks were overvalued throughout that year.

The rules of thumb adopted were a group of ratios which we term *comparables*. The underlying logic is an extension of the logic underlying the PE ratio, which we discuss below. The PE ratio tells us the multiple of earnings which investors are prepared to pay in return for a stream of future earnings or cash flows. This concept was extended to the multiple of revenue investors were prepared to pay for a firm, and then to multiples of more esoteric parameters such as users, *page views* (the 'serving' of a single web page to an individual user's PC), and subscribers. These multiples would then be compared between internet firms (hence 'comparables') and judgements would be made about which firms were 'expensive' (high value of the comparable ratio) and which were 'cheap' (low value of the comparable). However, while a large volume of accounting rules and regulations seek to ensure that $1 of earnings corresponds to a genuine cash flow or future cash-flow benefit to equity holders, there can be no similar assurance that a number of users or page views will ever generate cash for the equity owner. Even without this basic problem, different firm sizes, stages of evolution and differences in business model meant that the companies being compared were seldom sufficiently similar for the use of 'comparables' to convey any clear valuation message. In fact, these rules of thumb, although seductive:

- gave incorrect relative valuation messages, and
- distracted investors from performing fundamental valuations – valuations might have alerted investors to increasing divergences between market value and the range of possible fundamental values.

Examples of comparables

See Table 9.1.

P/E RATIO: THE FIRST COMPARABLE

The PE or price/earnings ratio is a commonly accepted yardstick for old-economy firms. The PE ratio is simply the current price divided by the most recent earnings figure (historic PE ratio), the total earnings for the most recent reported 12 months (*TTM – trailing twelve months –* PE ratio) or the nearest future predicted earnings figure (prospective PE ratio). PE ratio can be calculated on a per-share basis or on a whole-company basis:

$$\text{PE ratio} = \frac{\text{price per share}}{\text{earnings per share}}$$

Table 9.1 Examples of comparables[1]

Comparable	Relevant to
Market capitalization/users*	General
Market cap./page views*	General, particularly ad-supported companies
Market cap./ad views*	
Revenue multiple (or market cap./revenue)	This is the comparable that was primarily used, since earnings were not positive
Revenue per subscriber	ISPs, subscription-based websites
Market cap./POP*	For comparing ISPs that have points of presence
Market cap. to industry potential market share	General (basically means market cap./projected revenues)
Market cap/total internet users*	Firm value relative to maximum potential reach
Revenue/direct e-marketing	Shows yield of marketing spend
Market cap./Websteader*	Useful for valuing community of free home page providers
Revenue/Websteader*	Measures yield on community sites, how effective Websteads generate revenue for community firms
Price/discounted earnings	Project earnings and discount back to current stock price
Sales/employee	How efficient is the use of staff
Revenue/bandwidth*	Useful in determining how effectively management deploys its bandwidth to generate sales

* Internet specific

Also, since market capitalization is equal to earnings per share multiplied by the number of shares, and firm annual earnings are equal to earnings per share multiplied by the number of shares:

$$\text{PE ratio} = \frac{\text{market capitalization of equity}}{\text{firm annual earnings}}$$

The PE ratio tells us how much investors are prepared to pay for a dollar of earnings (profit after tax). Investment professionals are comfortable with and used to dealing with PE ratios. High-growth firms customarily have high PE ratios; low-growth firms have low PE ratios. This is because if a firm is growing quickly, future earnings will be larger (for a given amount of current earnings) than for a slow-growth firm. There are other possible reasons for differences in PE ratios between firms (different cost of capital, earnings temporarily depressed by transient problems or temporarily boosted by an exceptional item), but holding these constant, the growth rate is the most important parameter.

Also we can derive growth rate from the PE ratio. This will become very relevant to studying *price/revenue* multiples (*P/R ratio*) also, because we can back out PE ratio from P/R ratio, and then execute the same algorithm to determine implied growth.

How to convert PE (and P/R) ratios into growth rates

It is possible to convert a PE ratio into a perpetual growth rate using the Gordon growth formula which we discussed in Chapter 4. However, we discuss below why this is unwise, because perpetual growth rates above the economy growth rate are not sensible. Instead we set up a simulation where we have a terminal value at end of year 10 of the terminal value based on the economy-wide growth rate ($1/(r - 4\%)$), and solve for PE as the net present value of a simulation where the earnings grow at $g\%$ per year.

Formally, we make the following assumptions.

1. Value is composed of a series of cash flows in the near future (up to year T), plus a 'terminal value' representing the cash flows after year T.
2. The near-term cash flows grow at a constant rate of $g\%$ per year.
3. The terminal value is the final year's cash flow multiplied by ($1/(r - 4\%)$).
4. For a firm with modest assets, earnings are approximately equal to post-tax cash flow.
5. The cost of capital or discount rate is constant over time at $r\%$.

We can then 'flex' the spreadsheet by altering g to solve for the desired PE ratio, or this can be done automatically by the Goal Seek Function. This occurs when the value given by the DCF divided by the year 1 earnings is equal to the PE ratio. A sample spreadsheet would look like that in Figure 9.1. Formulae are:

- B7 = 1/(B5–0.04)
- B8 = NPV(B5,C12:L12)+M12/((1+B5)^10)
- B12 = 1

Figure 9.1 Converting PE into growth rate

	A	B	C	D	E	F	G	H	I	J	K	L	M
5	r =	10%	Enter cost of capital										
6	PERa =	98	Enter the PER to be converted to g										
7	PER10 =	16.67	(Old economy PER 10 years out: calculated)										
8	Value =	$98.00	(Used by goal seek macro: calculated)										
9	ga =	27.6%	Output: implied growth rate in earnings										
10													
11	Year	0	1	2	3	4	5	6	7	8	9	10	TV
12	Earnings	1	1.28	1.63	2.08	2.65	3.38	4.31	5.50	7.01	8.94	11.41	190.16

- C12 = B12*(1+$B9) (auto-fill to L12)
- M12 = L12*B7

The user can now invoke the Goal Seek command on the Tools menu (enter 'B8' for 'Set Cell', enter the values in B6 ('98') for 'To value', and enter 'B9' for 'By changing cell'). Alternatively, a simple macro can automate the process of goal-seeking, such as:

```
Sub TVcalc()
   Range('B8').GoalSeek Goal:=Range('B6'), ChangingCell:=Range('B9')
End Sub
```

In order to back out the growth rate implied by P/R ratio, first convert it into a PE ratio by dividing by the projected margin. We assumed average economy-wide post-tax margins of 5% (source: Compustat).

PRICE/REVENUE RATIOS

PE ratios have limited usefulness for internet firms. Very few internet firms are profitable. A PE ratio containing a negative '*E*' is meaningless. Therefore analysts have focused on the price/revenue ratio as a comparable which can still be used. P/R ratio is calculated similarly to the PE ratio:

$$\text{P/R ratio} = \frac{\text{firm market capitalization}}{\text{firm revenues}}$$

or, equivalently

$$\text{P/R ratio} = \frac{\text{price per share}}{\text{revenue per share}}$$

The relationship between P/R ratio and PE ratio is a simple mathematical one if we make one important assumption. Define post-tax margin, m, as:

$$m = \frac{\text{earnings}}{\text{revenues}} \Rightarrow \text{revenues} = \frac{\text{earnings}}{m}$$

$$\Rightarrow \frac{\text{price}}{\text{revenue}} = \frac{\text{price}}{(\text{earnings}/m)} \Rightarrow \text{P/R ratio} = \text{PE ratio} \times \text{margin}$$

Given that this ratio appears so closely related to PE ratio, analysts and investors felt secure in describing firms with a low P/R ratio as comparatively cheap, compared with similar firms with high P/R ratios. However, this use of P/R ratios was and is inappropriate. It is unsurprising that, faced with the uncertain outlook of the 1997–99 period, internet analysts sought to seek guidance in the P/R ratio and other analytical methods. However, it is a matter of some concern and astonishment that its use persists.

The use of P/R ratios is inappropriate for three reasons. First of all, the P/R ratios can imply very high growth rates. Second, valuation using P/R ratios, even as a relative valuation indicator, can lead to poor investment performance. Third, valuation using P/R ratios sets up the wrong incentives for managers. We discuss and illustrate these factors below.

P/R ratios imply high growth rates

The problem of high P/R ratios is compounded by the difficulty in interpretation of P/R ratios. This gave rise to P/R ratio values in the marketplace which were, and in some cases still are, far too high. Difficulty of interpretation can be partially overcome by using the relationship in the previous section between P/R and PE ratio:

$$\text{P/R ratio} = \text{PE ratio} \times \text{margin} \Rightarrow \text{PE ratio} = \frac{\text{P/R ratio}}{\text{margin}}$$

The post-tax margin is calculated by dividing earnings by sales revenue. As can be seen from the histogram in Figure 9.2, common values of post-tax margin are between zero and 15%, with an average of about 5% (that is, 0.05 of sales). Some companies exhibit high values of margin, such as some consumer products companies, and companies with patent or copyright protection.

Thus dividing P/R ratio by 0.05 gives us an equivalent ballpark PE ratio, assuming that the company achieves average profitability. This allows us to do two things. First, we can see immediately that modest price/revenue ratios correspond to very high PE ratios. Common values of the PE ratio are between 10 and 25. Second, we can make a simulation of how much growth in revenues the company will require to satisfy this simulated PE ratio, using the method shown above.

In Table 9.2 we look at some of the peak values for P/R ratios at November 1999, and derive the PE and implied growth rates using the methods above.

A purported 'relative valuation' indicator such as P/R ratio is of no use as a guide to valuation if all firms in the sample are overvalued, as was the case here. It is worth noting that this simulation assumes an immediate and

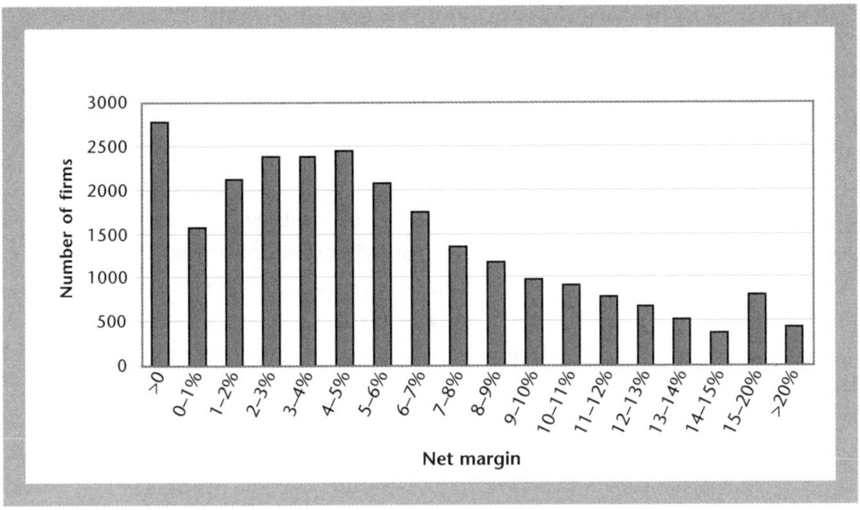

Figure 9.2 Distribution of net margin: large firms (revenues > $1m) (1967–2000)

sustained transition by these internet firms to average rates of profitability, so true required growth rates would have been even higher. For some firms, even after big falls in value, current values of the P/R ratio correspond to rates of revenue growth which are extremely unlikely.

Table 9.2 Price/revenue table (November 1999)

	P/R	Implied PE, $m = 5\%$	Implied g (PE = 16.7 year 10, $r = 10\%$) (%)
eToys	165.5	3310	84.2
Drugstore.com	144.9	2898	81.7
eBay	97.1	1942	74.4
Priceline	21.3	426	49.1
Amazon.com	13.4	268	42.1
Bn.com	12.5	250	41.0
Beyond.com	4.9	98	27.6
Cdnow	2.7	54	19.4

P/R ratios give the wrong relative investment signals

The final problem is that P/R ratios, as used in the key period of the internet bubble, did not 'work'. As we have said, the basic idea of comparables valuation is to compare multiples, such as the P/R ratio, *between* internet firms: firms with a high P/R are viewed as expensive (sell), and firms with a low P/R are viewed as cheap (buy). Ideally, the comparables 'expert' will seek to confine the valuation exercise to groups of firms that are similar (comparable), but examples exist of analysts comparing companies across national boundaries and across segments of the internet industry.

In order to test the investment performance of comparables,[2] we selected the most universal comparable ratio, the P/R ratio, and the widest accepted sample, the Internet Stock List (from INT Media: www.internet.com). Then we tested the investment performance of portfolios of quintiles of shares ranked by their P/R ratio, rebalancing quarterly. In other words, we first of all ranked stocks in the internet stock list by price divided by revenue[3] each quarter (when their quarterly revenues were announced). Then we divided up the stocks into fifths (quintiles) counting down from the top of the ranked list. For example, if there were 20 stocks reporting in a quarter, there would be four stocks in each quintile, with the four highest P/R stocks in quintile 5 and the four lowest P/R ratio stocks in quintile 1. Then in each quarter, we calculated the average performance of the stocks in each quintile. Then we compounded[4] the performance of the different quintile 5s (high P/R stocks) and compared it to the compounded performance of the other quintiles.

If comparables valuation works, we would expect to see a higher stock performance of the low quintile stocks ('cheap' P/R ratios), and a more disappointing performance from the high quintile stocks. If comparables valuation

Table 9.3 Return of P/R ratio quintile portfolios

Portfolio	Low P/R	2	3	4	High P/R
Total annualized return	–20%	–9%	16%	47%	50%
Individual yearly quintile portfolio returns*	%	%	%	%	%
94–95	–10	113	82	65	–5
95–96	–17	–4	–5	–44	28
96–97	22	29	21	14	54
97–98	–31	–42	–14	59	113
98–99	–6	89	160	300	680
99–00	–82	–60	–26	–15	4

*August to August. Database limitations prevent the inclusion of the most recent data

does not work, we would not expect to see any pattern in the performance of the quintiles. In fact, the high quintile firms outperformed the low quintile by a large margin. The performances are shown in Table 9.3.

It can be seen that the outperformance of the high P/R ratio portfolio (and therefore the underperformance of the comparables model) is concentrated in the years 1997–2000, exactly the time period when P/R ratios were being popularized by commentators. We suggest in the next section that the promotion of P/R ratio and other comparable valuations may have distorted management objectives, leading to valuation irregularities. It should also be noted that the years 1997–2000 were a period of poor performance for value-based investment strategies. Value-based investment strategies are characterized by investment in low PE ratio or low PB (market capitalization divided by book equity) firms. The comparables strategy, although it purported to be a new investment strategy, is most similar to a value investment strategy (specifically, a value strategy executed within a universe of high-growth firms), and this may partly have accounted for its extremely poor performance. It is also possible that investors correctly surmised that the high P/R ('expensive') stocks had superior business models, and paid a premium price for these stocks, in an environment where the whole universe of similar stocks was overvalued (and therefore the high P/R stocks were 'less overvalued'). Finally, investors may have invested in the premium P/R ratio internet stocks preferentially to the low P/R internet stocks for irrational reasons. Perhaps they herded on high P/R stocks because more speculative pressure had built up on these stocks (the bubble was most strong in these stocks). Whatever the reasons for the relative outperformance of high P/R ratio stocks, it is clear that an investor using a simple comparables model would have performed poorly.

The incentives problem

The third and fundamental problem is one of incentives for the managers of internet companies.

The P/R ratio values today's sales revenue. The only way in which this can be sensible is if sales revenue today directly translates into *earnings* or cash flows tomorrow. However, this may not be the case. Value-maximizing firms do not compete for revenues in the same way that they voraciously and determinedly compete for *profitable revenues*. If all firms are value-maximizing, revenues may function as a leading indicator of earnings. However, as soon as investors are guided by the P/R ratio and value *today's revenues*, the need for the firm to ensure that the business they do is profitable or potentially profitable disappears. Firms seeking to maximize their revenues are not value maximizers in any conventional way. Investors using P/R ratios as a decision rule will be 'paying for revenue', which firms can simply increase by making unprofitable sales. (There are also more complex schemes for increasing and/or inflating revenues, of which barter advertising (see Chapter 3) is the most well known.)

This would not be a problem if a couple of 'wounded steers' at the edge of the herd were using the P/R ratio as a supplementary valuation technology. But when the whole herd, or even a sizeable proportion, is using the P/R ratio, then the incentive to firm managers is to increase revenues, not to increase future profits.

Similar misaligned incentives arise if investors judge firms on other non-earnings-related comparables. Users can easily be attracted by one-time special offers. But in order for these offers to be profitable the users must be retained, and must be prepared to buy product at economic prices. *Clicks* or *page views* can be created easily by a large number of methods, as discussed below in 'Gaming the comparables'.

Contrast this with an industry or a scenario in which firms are valued on the basis of an earnings multiple. This is not a perfect situation because (as many commentators have noted) earnings, and accounting data in general, is backward-looking. But it is a far superior valuation paradigm to any non-earnings comparable, because it gives managers incentives to take on profitable projects and customers. Introduce some weighting for future expected earnings in the mental model of investors, and present-value maximization is closely approximated.

LYIN' EYEBALLS:[5] GAMING THE COMPARABLES

Quite apart from the incentive problems that cause managers to seek to increase sales or user counts without regard to the future profitability of the projects under consideration, there are other ways of affecting these statistics that have been noted by commentators:

- increase unique users by paying another website to generate a hidden (background) pop-up of your site (example: About.com until late 2000)
- increase visitors by routing from lotto or gaming sites where users have to click through to bet (examples: Dealtime, coolsavings)
- increase reach by seeking to attract visitors or users more likely to be in a panel observed by an internet market survey (for example, the Mediametrix panel is thought to contain a higher proportion of older web surfers than the average web user population).

These methods may artificially inflate comparable valuation parameters. Analysts seeking to use comparable valuation should be aware of the potential for affecting these statistics in ways designed to undermine their already feeble linkage with value. These practices certainly persist, as shown by the appearance of X10.com (seller of the xCam2 web camera) as the top e-commerce site in June 2001 (Jupiter MediaMetrix survey): in June 2001 X10.com achieved twice the unique visitors of Amazon.com, but did this almost entirely by non-user initiated webpage pop-up advertisements.

MAKING THE BEST OF COMPARABLES

There might be very limited situations where companies are very similar and comparables might be a sensible valuation metric. Firms would have to possess similar scale, similar margins, and be at similar stages of their evolution. In practice, these situations are unlikely to arise. Finally, comparables are of no use in fundamental valuation if the whole sector is over- or under-valued.

Making the best of comparables is like cooking a soufflé with feta – hard to do and, when you're done, not very tasty. When there are no alternatives to using comparables, the sensible analyst will try to make sense of comparables using DCF logic. For example, why is eBay's value per user greater than that of Amazon.com? This must mean that the market expects the present value of cash flows from each current eBay user to be greater than that of each Amazon user. Thinking back to how we would construct a DCF model for these firms (as briefly discussed in Chapter 4), this in turn means:

- eBay's future margins are expected to be greater than Amazon's
- and/or Amazon is expected to suffer more competition (suppressing its margins and/or growth) than eBay
- and/or eBay is expected to grow revenues faster than Amazon by gaining more customers or cross-selling more products to existing consumers
- and/or eBay is expected to require fewer operating assets than Amazon in order to serve its customers
- etcetera.

The 'etcetera' is necessary because any occurrence or operating parameter which affects cash flow can affect the value of a firm and thus the correctness of a valuation or relative valuation. However, the main influences on any valuation are:

- margins
- growth

- asset efficiency.

Using this logic we can talk about *direction* (that is, if expected margins, asset utilization and growth for Amazon all looked better than for eBay we would have a sound basis for stating that the comparables were favouring the wrong firm) but not *magnitude*. Except under very restricted circumstances, there are no rules of thumb which guide us as to what the ratio of value per user should be for given assumptions. We would need to construct a full cash-flow model to inform our discussion of this.

Note how we always discuss *expected* operating parameters ('expected margins', 'expected growth'). Once again, this is due to the forward-looking nature of investors' valuations. It is not a case of 'what have you done for me lately', but a case of what returns a firm will offer in the future. However, the main evidence that a financial analyst has available with regard to future performance is current and recent historical performance.

In the case of start-up companies, the amount of financial history is negligible, and the analyst has to seek clues elsewhere, as we will discuss in Chapter 16. But in the case of firms like Amazon and eBay, there is more than sufficient financial information to form the main basis of a prediction of the future, as illustrated in Chapter 4.

PROJECTED PE RATIOS

Some analysts have used predicted earnings numbers, together with predicted PE ratios (that is, future price/earnings multiples, the analysts' expectation of what investors will pay for $1 of earnings in the future) to carry out valuations of internet firms. This is a sensible approach in principle. Projecting earnings forward is identical to projecting cash flows forward for the special case of a company with no operating assets. Even for companies with large amounts of operating assets, earnings are identical to after-tax cash flow once the company has reached a steady state where capital expenditure equals depreciation. Earnings will be close to cash flows for companies with few operating assets, as in the case of many internet companies.

Residual problems have occurred in this work for two reasons. First, analysts have been over-optimistic in some projections of future margins and revenue growth, leading to larger than warranted future earnings numbers. This over-optimism can, we believe, be dealt with by more methodical study of past financial data of internet firms. The process of projecting earnings is closely akin to that of projecting cash flows, a process we have discussed in Part I.

The second, more serious, problem is the use of forward PE multiples which are far too high. In traditional financial modelling, as exemplified by Copeland et al. (2000), detailed modelling of financial data is projected into the future until the firm reaches a steady state. From that point on, low or no growth is expected. Assuming economy-average growth rates of approximately 4%, the highest multiplier that can be justified for earnings at the end of that modelled period is about 17 for $r = 10\%$. However, some analysts have been utilizing terminal value multipliers as large as 250. We now discuss the Gordon growth model, whose use and misuse has given rise to these numbers.

THE GORDON GROWTH FORMULA: USE AND ABUSE

A common valuation formula known to most professionals is the *Gordon growth formula* (sometimes called the *Williams growth formula*), which gives the present value of a growing perpetuity. The formula is as follows:

$$V = \frac{C}{r - g}$$

This states that the value of an annual cash flow of $\$C$ starting at the end of year 1, which grows at g per year, discounted at a discount rate of r, is $\$V$.

As the rate of growth g approaches r, $1/(r - g)$ 'explodes', becoming undefined when $r = g$. This reflects the fact that a perpetual project growing cash flow at greater than its cost of capital would have infinite value: such a project clearly cannot exist. How sensitive the formula becomes to r is clear from Table 9.4.

As Table 9.4 shows, the situation would appear to be clear. Secure a project or firm with growth rates close to its cost of capital and ensure that it will last for ever! Sadly this is easier said than done, and the high multipliers that the Gordon growth model ascribes to such projects exist because such businesses are seldom found. The Gordon growth model is not in error in the above examples: it is simply being applied inappropriately. The growth rates of 15–20% mentioned above seem laughably low in some internet circles, but analysts should be aware that *perpetual* growth in earnings at such an apparently modest level is an impossibility. Indeed, any firm growing earnings or cash flows at an above-average (that is, more than 4%) rate *for ever* would eventually overwhelm all other companies! The third row illustrates growth rates implied by such multiples, assuming more accurate assumptions about how long supernormal growth can persist. To calculate these values we used the algorithm discussed in the section on 'How to convert PE (and P/R) ratios into growth rates'.

One solution is to project forward internet financials until a steady state can be reached and then use the appropriate terminal multiplier for economy-wide average growth rates of $1/(r - 0.04)$, where r is the cost of capital. This may require the projection of financial data as far as 20 years into the future. One

Table 9.4 Earnings multipliers for perpetual growth (Gordon model) and years 1 to 10 growth

Growth rate, g ($r = 20\%$)	**15%**	**16%**	**17%**	**18%**	**19%**
Gordon multiplier $\left(\frac{1}{r-g}\right)$	20	25	33	50	100
10-year growth required for this multiplier, if terminal PE is 16.7 at 10 years	15.8%	19.1%	23.1%	29.1%	39.5%

alternative workaround is three-stage DCF. This involves specifically predicting 10 years of cash flows, and using a current market average PE ratio as a multiplier for the final year's earnings. The market PE is sense-checked by simulating the growth rate in earnings required for years 10–20, if the PE ratio at year 20 is fixed at 16.7 (1/(0.10 – 0.04) for $r = 10\%$, the approximate expected market return). This assumes, in effect, that the firm will become a firm with 'average growth prospects' after 10 years, rather than a firm with growth prospects approximately equal to inflation.

Certainly, forward post-tax earnings multipliers of greater than 30 should not be used. If seeking to calculate a terminal value based on 'operating cash flow' as it is variously defined, or any other pre-tax metric (such as operating profit), *lower* multipliers should be used, of not greater than 20. Ideally, multiples in the region of 15 and 10 should be used. If analysts believe these multiples do not adequately reflect the growth prospects of the company from the terminal value period onwards, the specifically projected period of cash flows should be extended, allowing sense-checking of revenue numbers (and other operating parameters) at the terminal year against predicted market size.

As the specific forecast period is extended 10–20 years in the future, it becomes steadily more difficult to have confidence in the specific predictions for later years. However, this is preferable to 'hiding growth' in an above-market terminal PE ratio. Also, this is a case in which the DCF method, by forcing analysts to project far into the future, undermines confidence in the DCF result in a way that is highly appropriate. DCF addresses our minds to the key issues of whether growth is sustainable over those long periods, and whether the internet firm can gain such large revenues and market share. Value dependent on cash flows in the far future makes us worry about whether we can depend on that value, as well we should. Comparables valuation does not raise such questions, and that is a great weakness of that method.

Table 9.5 From DLJ analysts' reports on Amazon.com (Von der Porten, 2000)

	February 1999		June 2000	
Revenue	$ 180.00		$ 133.00	
Gross margin	$ 45.00	*25.0%*	$ 30.59	*23.0%*
Marketing allocation (fulfilment)	$ 11.70	*6.5%*	$ 18.39	*13.8%*
G&A/R&D allocation	$ 3.60	*2.0%*	$ 2.49	*1.9%*
Customer CM per year	$ 29.70	*16.5%*	$ 9.71	*7.3%*
Cost of capital	13.3%		12.9%	
Growth rate	11.8%		12.5%	
Capitalization rate	1.5%		0.4%	
Multiple	67		250	
Estimated customer value	$ 1,980		$ 2,428	

Example of use of Gordon growth model

Table 9.5 shows an example of the use of the Gordon growth model which demonstrates the potential problems of 'pushing' the formula. The analyst recommended Amazon as a buy both in February 1999 and in June 2000. However the operating parameters had deteriorated in the interim, and *contribution margin* (usually defined as revenues minus variable costs, but here defined as revenues minus cost of sales, fulfilment, G&A and R&D) per customer had deteriorated from almost $30 to less than $10 per annum. However, the situation could very rapidly be made much more attractive by a small increase in perpetual growth, and a small decline in cost of capital! The numbers work, but the underlying concepts are faulty (see Table 9.5).

If we use the conversion spreadsheet for PE to growth rate which we discussed earlier in the chapter, in effect assuming that growth is concentrated in the first 10 years, the difference between multiples becomes clear. A multiple of 67 requires growth of 30.3% in years 1–10 (at 13.3% cost of capital). A multiple of 250 requires growth of 49.5% at 12.9% cost of capital. Not 0.7% of incremental growth, but 20%.

HIGH ASSET EFFICIENCY AND ITS POTENTIAL EFFECT ON VALUE: 'CASHFLOW.COM'

Within the value-based or DCF framework, there are many ways in which companies can be 'exceptionally' valuable. High monopoly profit margins, for

Figure 9.3 Balance sheet

Assets		Liabilities	
Fixed assets	0	Creditors	100
Inventory	0	Capital employed	(87)
Cash	13		

example. Rapid, profitable growth. One characteristic which was envisaged for internet companies is the low proportion of operating assets which they may require. For example, electronic retailers do not have need of expensive high street shopping premises, and online content providers do not require costly printing equipment.

Credit Suisse published 'Cashflow.com' in 1998, as an effort to lay out the potential effects of this perceived advantage. This was an equity research document and not a historical document, but we discuss it here because it is an example of how expert analysts thought within the DCF framework to further understand internet stock values. However, we seek to critique and extend its analysis.

Consider a firm which receives cash from customers after 7 days, but only has to pay suppliers after 60 days. If it has low inventory and no or few fixed assets, this firm will have a very strange balance sheet (Figure 9.3)

The firm will have negative capital employed, and will not require cash from investors to fund future growth. As the firm grows, since it requires no inventory and has the free use of capital for 1.75 months, the firm can pay out cash to investors even if it breaks even on the sales that it makes. This sounds like an infinite money machine, and indeed if the hypothetical firm can continue growing, the cash payments can last indefinitely. However, we know how to present value such streams of everlasting payments using perpetuity formulae. Their value is limited.

Valuing the efficient use of capital

Cashflow.com observed this possible difference between new economy and old economy firms. The authors suggested that 'cash earnings for a New Economy company ... can dramatically understate the company's total free cash flow'. Therefore valuation by conventional methods was likely to underestimate new economy firm value. However, it was the second step, of putting a cash value on the efficient use of operating capital, that the authors of Cashflow.com failed to carry out rigorously. Although some traditional methodologies (such as PE ratio-based valuation) may be unable to carry out such a valuation correctly, the DCF framework is robust enough to do so.

Let us consider the example of Amazon.com. Even making some generous assumptions about Amazon.com, we can see that the value of efficient use of capital could not account for the peak values of the Amazon.com. In Table 9.6 we project forward the revenue growth from the financial data known about Amazon in 1999 (using past revenue declines to that point to derive the revenue decay rate), with the aim of isolating only the cash flow due to efficient use of working capital. We assume that the firm receives two full months' use of its cash receipts before having to pay suppliers, and discount the resulting cash flows at a discount rate of 15%. This yields a value of $0.9bn, assuming that the efficient use of capital persisted indefinitely. The story demonstrates two things about the irrational optimism that was a major factor in 1998–99. First, the value of this efficient use of capital, even under the generous assumption that we have made here of the extra efficiency persisting for ever, could only account for a small portion of Amazon's value at that time. Second, in order for the efficient use of working capital to have an effect along the lines that the author envisaged, it would have to last for at least several years. In fact, it did not even last one more year. Financial data on Amazon since 1999 shows that the efficient use of capital did not persist, and this source of value was therefore very limited.

The transient nature of the Cashflow.com model

When the Cashflow.com paper was published, Amazon.com's most recent balance sheet was its 1998 balance sheet, which showed net assets (net assets = fixed assets + net working capital) equal to approximately minus 10% of revenues (excluding assets held under operating leases). This asset-efficient capital structure was based on Jeff Bezos' original business strategy of fulfilling orders by obtaining inventory from book wholesalers, with that inventory only staying on Amazon's 'books' for a matter of days or even hours. However, after 1998 Amazon's business strategy shifted. The company sought to gain more control over customers' experience by ensuring on-time delivery. This necessitated holding more products in inventory rather than relying on wholesalers' supply chains. The company also decided to speed its diversification into other markets using growth by acquisition. Finally, Amazon's use of operating leases accounted for a further tranche of assets for which the company took on some ownership risk.

1998 net assets = –10% × revenues
1999 net assets = 20% base

Table 9.6 Amazon.com: projected revenue growth, based on 1999 data

Growth decay: 44%
Mid-term growth: 7%
Cost of capital: 15%

	1998	1999	2000	2001	2002	2003	2004	2005	2006	2007	2008	2009	perpetuity
Growth (%)		169	74	33	14	7	7	7	7	7	7	7	multiple
Revenue	610	1640	2858	3793	4338	4642	4967	5315	5687	6085	6511	6967	20
Cash flow*			203	156	91	51	54	58	62	66	71	76	1519

NPV = $895m

* 2 months free credit for increase in sales year on year

+ acquired assets: 40% of revenues
+ leased assets: 16% of revenues

Therefore the pattern of negative net assets reversed almost as soon as it was observed, and the true value of the efficient use of capital for Amazon was not infinite, or even $1b, but close to zero. Amazon's change in business strategy was not a unique one in retailing and consumer merchandising. Many firms which initially adopt a policy of holding minimal inventory discover that they need to alter this policy to cement a good reputation with customers. However efficient a supplier's infrastructure may be, the supplier never has the same incentive to serve the end-customer as the customer-facing business. They do not face the complaints and, more importantly, they know that they do not have any guaranteed share of the future value of the customer, irrespective of how good a service they provide.

LOOKING AT DCF

DCF has been the dominant valuation methodology for some time. However, as internet companies reached high values in the late 1990s, DCF projections showed wide divergence from market values. While it is possible to justify any value with a DCF projection by making the assumptions sufficiently aggressive, internet stock values were outside the range of any believable assumptions for such key variables as revenue growth, projected margins and cost of capital. As internet stock values have declined, DCF and market values have gained a closer relationship, but the debate is not yet over. Some investors still hope for a return to the 'glory days' of early 2000. And clearly, if DCF is a valid method of projecting value for internet firms, these glory days are going to be slow in returning.

We strongly believe that DCF is the correct method for valuing internet firms. However, we should not dismiss the key points and questions raised against its use, but rather try to answer them convincingly. These points are fourfold:

- DCF is not relevant to the new economy
- DCF discount rates are 'too high'
- DCF cannot capture the value of flexibility
- DCF needs 'too many assumptions': we cannot 'accurately' project growth and margins, so there is no point in trying.

We will seek to answer these points in turn.

DCF remains relevant to the new economy

While investors are buying shares to make money, and not for entertainment, DCF is the appropriate valuation paradigm.

It is possible to conceive of changes in investor attitudes that would make DCF obsolete. For example, investors might become less interested in the cash they obtain from investments, preferring to own stocks in companies they identify with, or seeking to own investments because these investments mark them out as a certain kind of person, or even because the investment certificates are beautiful. In other words, DCF would not be relevant if investors began to view investments in firms in the same way as they view paintings or sculptures.

However, shares are very much unsuited to being prized in this way. Items which have 'collectability', such as paintings and sculptures, possess aesthetic appeal and limited supply. Shares in a company have no aesthetic appeal, and any rarity value a stock may seem to have is very fleeting. Firms can issue unlimited stock in their businesses if investors so demand.

Another form of entertainment is gambling. Shiller (2000)[6] has suggested that one contributory factor in the large rise in US stock prices during 1982–2000 is a rise in gambling opportunities changing investors' attitudes to risk. A basic tenet of DCF valuation (as normally practised) is that investors shy away from risk unless they are rewarded for that risk by a high return. Clearly, if all investors are buying shares just for the enjoyment of seeing whether they go up or down the next day, as a 'more upscale form (of gambling)', then DCF will be (at least temporarily) irrelevant.

However, the entertainment in owning shares is closely tied in with the making of money from them. Some people are trapped in gambling, and need the excitement of risking money on the card table at a basic level. But for most gamblers, a trip to Las Vegas can be enjoyed and talked about even if modest losses occur – in fact, the casinos go to every effort to take the 'customer's' mind off the loss with a variety of entertainments! There is no similar fun to be experienced from losing money on stocks. While there may be some subconscious gambling impulse in buying a stock, the conscious thoughts of most investors are that stock ownership is different from gambling, in that it offers a stake in real businesses and that it has a long-term record of providing excellent returns to investors. In this context DCF is the appropriate valuation metric.

Incidentally, these two characteristics (lack of fun while losing, and link with the real economy) make stocks a poor source of entertainment for the gambler. The latter characteristic, in particular, makes stock speculation a heartbreaking form of gambling in a bear market. Everyone but the most addicted gambler is easily able to walk away from a game of roulette that they know is stacked against them. By contrast, stock speculators sitting on losses can make all sorts of arguments for continuing to hold their investment, usually based, directly or indirectly, on the previous (high) price being a price agreed upon by the 'efficient market'. However, as we shall discuss in Chapter 10, market efficiency is not about the market being right, but about the market not being predictably wrong. In summary, just as stock investments are a poor choice for collectors, they are also a poor choice as a source of gambling pleasure. Therefore, if such usages 'break out', they are likely to be short-lived.

DCF: the empirical evidence

In the above paragraphs we have briefly rehearsed the arguments for treating internet firms similarly to other firms. It is worthwhile to briefly touch upon the evidence why 'other firms' should be valued by DCF. The economic profit model on which DCF is based is supported by a large number of studies. Examples of this evidence are provided by Copeland et al. (1998),[7] who plot DCF values based on value line forecasts and find a 94% correlation with stock values. Kaplan and Ruback (1995) studied the valuations of private transactions such as management buyouts and leveraged recapitalization, and found that DCF produced mean value valuation errors of 8% or less, whereas comparable company valuation methods can produce valuation errors of more than 16.6%. Some workers (for example Penman, 1998; Feltham and Ohlson, 1995) have pointed out similarities between the residual income valuation model, the dividend discount model, and both the DCF and accounting earnings-based model (while favouring the residual income model). In this context, papers such as Bernard (1995) can be seen as support for the class of economic profit-based models (of which DCF is a member), since they point out the very high correlation between equity market values and the two key accounting parameters, earnings and book values.

The study of Core et al. (2001) is particularly persuasive in that it compares the effectiveness of the income and book value valuation model (a member of the economic-profit class of models) over time, both before and during the new-economy period. They find that although the explanatory power of an accounting-based model (as represented by earnings, book value and other accounting items which may proxy for expected growth in profitability) has declined for new-economy firms, the structure of the implied valuation model has not changed, suggesting variation around the accounting model, but with greater potential error due to the uncertainty in determining future operating parameters. Also, the decline in the explanatory power of the earnings model is not out of the ordinary, similar declines having been seen in the mid- to late 1970s.

Are DCF discount rates too high?

DCF methodology does not impose any specific choice of discount rate. Criticism has been focused on the generally accepted method of determining discount rates: the single factor capital asset pricing method (CAPM). However, even if the CAPM is not supported, this does not validate DCF.

As analysts began to study internet stocks, it became obvious that their β values were astonishingly high. Normal values of β are between 0.6 and 1.5. Internet firms had βs as high as 2 or 3. This led in turn to discount rates of 15–20%. Such high discount rates led in their turn to low projected values for the internet companies from DCF valuations. DCF-based analysts were, once again, accused of not 'getting it'.

In our chapter on cost of capital we discussed some of these problems. Different timescales of the calculation of β can be examined. Calculation of β using daily return often produces lower values of β and is not contrary to CAPM – there is no stipulation of correct timescale for calculation of returns and β. Also lower values of MRP which can be justified, such as 5%, can mitigate the perceived problem of high cost of capital.

However, perhaps there is really no problem, and perhaps the high costs of capital were appropriate. Another tag that was often applied to internet companies in 1997–99 was that they were 'public venture capital', meaning that they were companies quoted on the public markets and available to be bought and sold by the public investor, but that their businesses had the look and feel (and financials) of firms that would normally be pre-IPO, still supported by venture capital. However, to a company's cost of capital, and the underlying riskiness of its operating assets, *where* (or whether) *it is quoted* is irrelevant.[8] What matters is the β of its assets, which we can best calculate from the returns expected on similar firms, in this case venture-backed firms where expected returns start at 20% and up. If publicly traded internet companies had many characteristics of venture-capital firms, then we would expect them to have high costs of capital. One interesting issue is how these costs of capital have changed and generally decreased. This is a process we predicted, and we built the option of using declining costs of capital over time into the models discussed with students. This was demonstrated in Chapter 4.

Does DCF capture the value of managerial flexibility?

Much has been said on the application of real-option valuation to internet companies. DCF fails, in the view of some analysts, for two reasons. First, DCF assumes that firms blindly continue a project once it is started, but in reality firms scale up good projects and abandon bad projects (the managerial flexibility argument). Second, DCF ignores the 'option type' payoff profile: that there is limited downside (100% of equity value) but enormous upside due to network economies, Moore's Law and other positive effects of the new economy (the growth option argument).

This common perception of real-option valuation is that there is a tree of golden apples (growth options) outside every company headquarters entrance, waiting to be eaten (exercised)! However, as discussed in Chapter 8, this 'growth option argument' picture of the world is perhaps flawed. First, in a competitive market, growth opportunities attract competitors. The facile mental model of a real option being equivalent to a stock or commodity call option (where the option owner has an exclusive right to his or her upside) is therefore flawed. Second, the approach of assuming that real-option value can be added as upside to current equity values (effectively assuming that current equity values are 'DCF only') is incorrect. The market has long experience of valuing real options, the airline industry (where the liquidation put is often a key element of value) and the natural resources industry being examples of industries where real options are especially important. Therefore it is safe to assume that if real options have value for a firm, some or all of that value is already impounded in current equity market values.

Surely DCF has too many assumptions?

A complex DCF model may have a hundred or more line items of financial data, driven by a large number of assumptions. Complexity, in this regard, is not always a good idea. Our models for the firms studied are fairly simple, and the parameters to drive them are less than a dozen. However, the parameters can be boiled down even further:

- pattern of future revenues
- pattern of future margins
- pattern of future asset needs
- pattern of future cost of capital
- terminal value assumptions.

Five assumptions for firms about which we know next to nothing seems like a lot, but there are two reasons why this is not true. First, for many US internet firms and for a smaller but still significant number of European and Far Eastern firms, a significant amount of financial data has now been built up, enabling us to learn from past performance. Second, there is no way around making these assumptions. Consider the process by which we unpacked the P/R ratios earlier in the chapter. This was a way of showing that assumptions of cost of capital, revenue growth, margins and the like are 'hiding' within even the simplest ratio. If we have no data except sales and market price, we still cannot be guided by the P/R ratio. P/R ratios embed 'market' perceptions of margins, asset growth and revenue growth for companies which the market sees as similar. But these companies may *not* be similar. And the companies or the whole sector may be overvalued, impounding growth or margins which are beyond the possible. Without carrying out DCF analysis we cannot tell.

In the case of a company for which we have very little data, this might require assessing the company by seeing what similar companies in other industries had as margins and revenue growth, to test what is feasible. When we studied Pacific Century Cyberworks with Hong Kong executives in 2000, we saw a company that did not even have any significant revenues, but by comparing media companies who were 'farther down the track', and by perusing the business track record of the management team (for example, their ability to attract audience when at 'Star TV'), it was possible to get a long way towards identifying the firm's potential. Tougher than just picking a single ratio? Sure. But this process has two important advantages. First, it gives us a more accurate valuation message than comparables. Second, it alerts us to the key parameters that affect valuation, in a way that a single ratio-based valuation never can.

OTHER POTENTIAL ISSUES IN EQUITY VALUE

During the peak periods of the stock market between mid-1999 and March 2000, theories attempting to explain high stock market values extended beyond sensible value-based logic. Many market-inefficiency-based theories were widely discussed. We discuss and comment on some of these theories in this section.

Influences on equity value of support levels and resistance level

Technical analysts often discuss how a stock 'makes repeated attempts' to go below a certain level ('support') or above a certain level ('resistance'), but appears to find a barrier which prevents it from exiting its 'trading range' between these two points. They believe that these support and resistance levels, once observed, can help provide guidance to stocks' future movements. Specifically, an investor has only limited risk in buying stock close to a support level, because there is little chance of downside. Stockholders should consider selling or shorting as stocks reach their resistance levels, because if the resistance level holds, the stocks will not go any higher. This concept is contrary to weak-form market efficiency. It is also contrary to common sense. Stocks are not 'attempting' to go anywhere; the stock price time series is a result of the interaction between buyers and sellers in the market. Patterns of support and resistance levels are almost entirely the result of chance, perhaps slightly augmented by the trading behaviour of the small number of people following technical trading schemes and programs. Far more damaging for technical traders, technical schemes can appear to work for months at a time (sufficient time to build up an apparently impressive performance record to attract new users) and then fall apart catastrophically as a result of market-wide rises or falls. Claims of good performance for technical trading schemes may also be as a result of omitting losing investments, failure to adjust for bid-offer spreads and transaction costs, good market-wide performance, or good luck. A stock-trading strategy which can be replicated by purchasing a $20 per month email bulletin or a cheap software package is too easily replicable to provide consistent returns.

Break out above or below moving averages

Technical analysts plot moving averages for stock prices to give them guidance as to future stock values, and to help fix values for support and resistance levels (see above). Stocks 'breaking out' from the range of these moving averages are thought to be particularly attractive (or unattractive, if they are breaking below the moving average). We do not believe that moving averages are a reliable guide to future stock values, because the success of such a method would be contrary to weak-form market efficiency. Again, it would be too easy to replicate and is likely to fail as a strategy during wide market swings.

The Monday effect, the January effect, and other seasonal patterns of stock price performance

Stocks appear to perform anomalously well on Mondays. In fact Wang et al. (1997) indicate that stocks perform well specifically on the last or last two Mondays of each month. This effect is well known but is unlikely to be supporting of a profitable trading strategy, or it would have been arbitraged away. In another example, from 1979 to 1994 the Russell 2000 index consistently posted bigger gains in January than in November and December.

However, this effect may have already ceased. In 1995–2000 average returns on this index in January have been negative (Stires, 2000).

The baby boomer effect, and the wall of money from mutual funds

Some commentators had observed that the large number of baby boomers (those born during the demographic bulge between 1946–66) planning for retirement has created a large amount of money which needs to be invested in equities. Many boomers have channelled this money into mutual funds, and some commentators have suggested that this 'wall of money' will be able to keep stocks above fundamental values for some time. Shiller (2000) persuasively argues that the baby boomer effect is mythical or that, at least, its main effect on stock prices has been to inspire confidence rather than to affect fundamental supply and demand. He points out that if a large number of citizens of the USA and the Western world were competing to save for retirement, this would increase the value of all *assets*, not just stocks, but stocks and other investment vehicles (for example, real estate and property) have been quite uncorrelated. Also, savings rates are quite low in the USA currently, approaching zero according to some estimates. This is hardly consistent with 'wall of money' saving activity.

Lock-up effect

When companies undergo their *IPO* (*initial public offer*, called a *float* or *flotation* in the UK) key investors and managers are forced to enter a 'lock-up' agreement. They undertake not to sell their stock in the company for a prespecified period (the 'lock-up period'). The reason for a lock-up period is to try and minimize the effects of information asymmetry on public market investors. Insiders (who are aware of some or all of internal company documents and reports) have far more information on the companies' prospects than do outsiders (who only have the prospectus and any other private research they have been able to carry out). Allowing insiders to sell soon after the IPO would enable them to take advantage of this private information. Insisting on a lock-up period ensures a more level playing field, because some public information will have been revealed in between IPO and the expiry of the lock-up.[9] However, some commentators have suggested that this should result in a predictable negative return around the time of the end of the lock-up agreement. This is because releasing a restriction on a seller, if there is a strictly positive probability that that seller will wish to sell, will increase the selling pressure and put downward influence on price. Arguments have also been made suggesting that at the close of lock-up investors will be keen to realize their gains, either because they lack confidence in the valuations of the firms or because they require the money to meet other expenses or to fund new investments.

There are two potential problems with this picture. First, if a lock-up agreement is expected to end on day T with a predictable negative return, the price fall would not occur on date T but would be anticipated by the market. The predictable negative return can be anticipated on day $T-1$ and indeed, by induction, would be expected to be impounded immediately after IPO. Second, we can imagine a game-theoretic picture in which selling pressure may cause a decrease in price on day T, but this would partially be offset by strategic buyers who had been waiting for this buying opportunity. This debate can be provisionally settled by recent empirical evidence in a paper by Brav and Gompers (2000) which suggests that there is a small negative return on days T (end day of lock-up) and $T-1$, confined to companies which are venture capital-backed, and of magnitude 1.2% to 2.5% (that is, commensurate with transaction costs). Even if this effect persists, we can assume that it provides little or no arbitrage potential.

Low float effect

It is a well-known characteristic that internet firms customarily issue few shares when they initially come to the public market (that is, they have a 'low float' of shares). It is thought that this low float was responsible for high stock prices, because a large number of investors wished to buy the shares in internet companies and there were, initially, very few companies available. It is worth noting that internet stock floats 'turned over' at unheard-of speeds during times of high valuation.

However, the low float concept is not consistent with the way the internet stock boom played out. The highest internet stock values were seen at the close of the first quarter 2000. At this point several hundred internet companies had been floated, and higher values would have been expected earlier in the cycle of these companies when there were genuinely few internet companies available to buy. Finally, empirical evidence (Hand, 2000) suggests that the effect of low floats on stock value was modest and confined to B2B stocks. One could conceive that this could be due to their short history and the lack of financial data to form an alternative valuation paradigm.

PULLING IT ALL TOGETHER

The DCF valuation method has a firm theoretical basis (discussed both here and in Chapter 1), and we can be confident that if our assumptions are correct, it will yield sensible estimates of value. That is, of course, a big if. But, as we have seen, competing valuation methods can be misleading, even with apparently sensible assumptions. The other main advantage of the DCF methodology is that it places emphasis on the key operating parameters that a business needs to prioritize to generate value for shareholders. It is this emphasis that was often absent in the valuation at the height of the internet stock bubble, but it is vital in going forward, in the internet as in other businesses.

Notes

1 Based on Harmon (1998).
2 Briginshaw (2002).
3 Revenue was calculated on a trailing 12-month basis, as is standard. This means that for a firm which has just reported its June 2002 results, the relevant trailing 12-month revenue is that between 1 July 2001 and 30 June 2002.
4 Using the holding period return technique, as standard. To combine returns using HPR, use the following formula HPR = $\Pi(1+ret_i)$ (that is: add each return, ret_i, to 1 and compound the $(1+ret_i)$ multiplicatively. That is:

$$HPR = \prod_{i=1}^{T}(1 + ret_i)$$

5 See Forbes' entertaining discussion entitled 'Lyin' Eyeballs' for more details on some of the examples discussed (Forbes, 2000).
6 Shiller (2000), p. 43.
7 Copeland, Koller and Murrin (1998), p. 84.
8 The only exception to this is that venture capital firms may attract a premium to reward them for the lack of liquidity of their investments.
9 Insiders are allowed to sell stock as part of the IPO, provided that this is clearly disclosed – outside investors can then factor this evidence into their valuations.

CHAPTER 10

Market Efficiency and Internet Stocks

HOW IT HAPPENED

Figure 10.1 tells an astonishing story of stock market volatility. However amusing it might be to characterize it as 'a story of greed' or foolishness, neither description is correct. Certainly, both greed and foolishness have

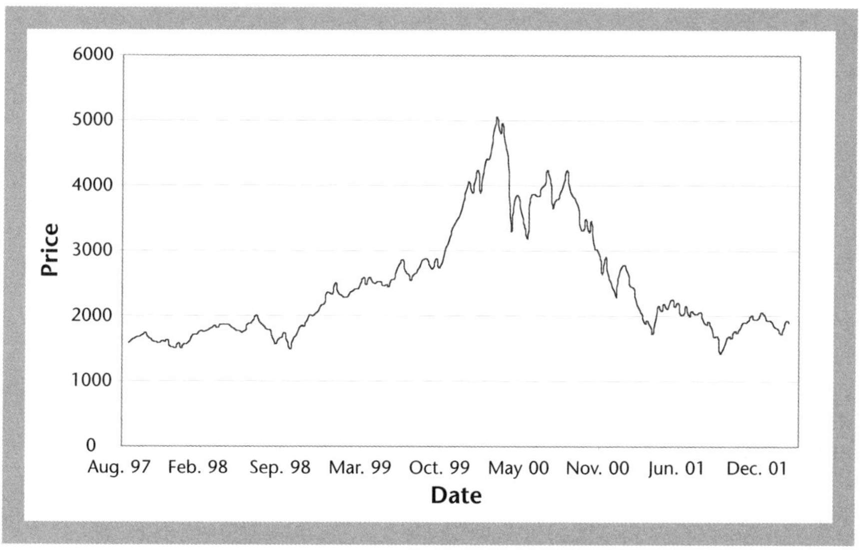

Figure 10.1 NASDAQ composite

played their part in causing volatility in internet stock values, but the underlying reason for that volatility is the difficulty of estimating value for early stage businesses. Add to that a dose of mania ('investor overconfidence', if one leans towards less hyperbolic terminology), leave to simmer, and we have a recipe for a wild ride.

Hypergrowth or bubble?

There are three possible explanations for the high valuations that internet companies commanded and, in some cases, still command. These are:

1. *The market had identified new sources of value within internet firms, sources of value not associated with earnings or cash flows, and therefore missed by traditional valuation paradigms.* Because internet firms work within the 'new economy', where network effects and co-operation are of vital importance, earnings and future cash flows do not fully capture the value these firms have.
2. *The market was correctly anticipating 'hypergrowth' in company earnings under 'new-economy paradigms'.* Because internet firms have are faster moving and more efficient than 'old-economy' firms, they can grow far more quickly and profitably (after an initial period of losses necessary to build up their businesses to a critical mass). In this view of the world, earnings and cash flows are still important, but they are anticipated to grow at unheard-of speed.
3. *The market was overvaluing these stocks due to a 'speculative bubble'.* Investors systematically overvalued internet stocks. However, this overvaluation persisted because observed high returns from holding internet stocks attracted fresh investors into the market. This third explanation sees internet stock valuation as an example of a Ponzi or pyramid scheme.

We reject explanation 1. Network effects, in as far as they exist, can be represented as lower ongoing marketing costs for a firm, and can therefore feed into cash flows. Other 'non-traditional' ways of generating value, such as ultra-efficient control of inventory and exploitation of intellectual capital, are easily incorporated into the cash flow framework. Finally, value from real options, which we discussed in Chapter 8, is limited, and is still essentially dependent on firms' abilities to generate profits in some possible future states of the world.

The only way to test between the remaining explanations is to conduct *fundamental valuation analysis* of internet firms, as discussed in Part 1 of this book. Even then, we can only form a viewpoint of which explanation is correct *on the balance of probabilities*. Clearly, since we now know that the high values of

March 2000 did not persist to the present day, it seems likely that these values were not supported by fundamental analysis. Carrying out fundamental analysis using data existing at the peak of the bubble (which we did in a co-authored paper, Higson and Briginshaw, 2000) further confirms that fundamental analysis could not explain the bubble values. By a process of elimination, explanation 3 is selected as the likely cause of the stock market's high values in early 2000.

We discuss further evidence for market irrationality in the section below. However, first of all we introduce the concept of market efficiency and discuss why even valuation errors that are clear to everyone are not evidence of market inefficiency. That is, market inefficiency and market irrationality are distinct concepts.

HOW EFFICIENT IS THE MARKET?

Discussion of how closely market and intrinsic values track each other leads us to the issue of market efficiency. One commonly used definition of *market efficiency* focuses on speed and certainty of order execution. In an efficient market:

- an investor should be able to buy or sell quickly
- large orders should not cause wide fluctuations in prices (depth)
- new information should be quickly digested into market prices.

Empirical studies of market efficiency concentrate mainly on the speed of reaction to information. Studies of reaction to earnings information for individual companies, and of reaction to changes in interest rates (affecting the market as a whole), show that major stock markets (such as those of the US and the UK) react in minutes to announcements. Although there is some quasi-predictable drift after certain types of announcements which can persist for several months, the bulk of reaction to an announcement occurs in the first 15 minutes after the announcement occurs.

Other empirical studies have addressed the issue of whether there is residual value in knowing information about a company, which can be used to trade profitably after this initial response has occurred. Studies such as those of the post-earnings announcement drift (predictable positive returns in the months after an earnings announcement that beats market expectations) and of the PE anomaly (higher than expected returns from companies that have low PE ratios) are examples of this strand of research. These studies cut to the heart of the academic debate about market efficiency. Is the new information digested not just quickly but completely? A strong-form efficient market would be the most efficient market in terms of complete digestion of information. This is defined most simply as one where all information (public and even private information) is impounded into stock prices. In such a market, there would be no need for fundamental analysis, because prices would already reflect the result of painstaking analysis of accounting data. Even insider trading would lose its sting, because the highly efficient market would instantly impound the insider data from the signal of the order attempting to take advantage of that data. Clearly we are not living in such an ideal world.

However, there are less restrictive levels of market efficiency. The most basic statement of market efficiency is more difficult to disagree with. This is the '*no risk-free arbitrage*' axiom, usually abbreviated to *no-arbitrage* or *NA*. (*Arbitrage* is the practice of buying and simultaneously selling similar securities to profit from relative mispricings.) Under NA there are no strategies a trader can execute which will give him or her a risk-free profit after transaction costs. For example, a trader cannot buy US dollars for UK pounds in London, and simultaneously sell the US dollars in New York at a higher rate. Rapid communications technology and trading counterparties' use of bid-offer spreads prevent this from occurring. Clearly, if such an opportunity did arise, the demand for it would be infinite, and the counterparties would have to adjust their prices quickly to avoid ruin. Note that NA does not preclude the trader from buying dollars in London, and waiting to obtain a profit from currency fluctuations before selling in New York. However, this is not a risk-free profit because the market might move against the trader instead of in his or her favour (and the element of 'arbitrage', since the securities in London and New York are identical, is arguably illusory).

Other levels of market efficiency have been posited. This list goes from the least restrictive definition of efficiency to the most restrictive:

1. *no arbitrage:* no risk-free profit opportunities exist in the market
2. *weak-form market efficiency:* current market prices impound all information from the time-series of previous prices
3. *semi-strong form:* prices impound all information from analysis of publicly available financial information (as well as from the time series of previous prices)
4. *strong form:* prices impound all information from a painstaking analysis of all public and private information, including previous prices
5. *'perfect foresight' market efficiency (PFME):* the current market price is equal to the discounted future value of the stock.

GOOD NEWS AND BAD NEWS ABOUT MARKET EFFICIENCY

Current research supports market efficiency perhaps reaching level 2, but there is a great deal of disagreement. Some market participants believe the market is not at all efficient.

For example, risk-free profit opportunities (contravening level 1) have been claimed to exist in some markets for short periods of time. Specialist firms attempt to exploit these opportunities, by dealing in larger volumes and at lower costs than the average market participant, and by developing expertise in specific transactions and strategies which are generally kept secret to avoid emulation by other players. One part of Long-Term Capital Management's (LTCM) business was to exploit tiny differences in yield between 30-year ('on-the-run') treasury bonds and treasury bonds of slightly shorter duration (for example 29 years) by trading in massive volumes. These differences seemed to offer a risk-free arbitrage opportunity, by selling the on-the-run bond (which exhibited a slightly lower yield) and buying the less liquid, but otherwise virtually identical, shorter duration bond. However, this example shows the difficulty of finding an executable risk-free arbitrage. During a period of high volatility in world markets the attractions of liquidity (which is greater for the on-the-run bond) caused the differences in yield to widen in defiance of LTCM's predictions, causing LTCM's highly leveraged position to deteriorate. This contributed to the crisis which required that the company's portfolio be refinanced.

There are a large number of unbelievers in level 2. Chartists and technical analysts believe that 'support levels' on the downside and 'resistance levels' on the upside provide important information to guide stock traders. However, it is difficult to believe that an easily executed technical strategy can offer lasting returns (as market participants will anticipate its effect and influence prices accordingly). Many academic researchers have documented *market anomalies* which offer abnormal returns (returns higher than would be expected for the risk) for traders following a trading strategy suggested by the anomaly.

One of the most well-known anomalies is the so-called *post earnings announcement drift (PEAD)*, as mentioned above. This is a phenomenon documented by several researchers whereby stocks which have positive earnings surprises (earnings greater than analysts' predictions or greater than predicted by projections based on past earnings growth) reliably outperform those which have negative earnings surprises. What is not surprising is that this happens over the period of the earnings announcement (the market reacts to the good or bad news when it is announced). What *is* extremely surprising is that an apparently reliable abnormal (risk-adjusted) return can be obtained by buying the 'good news' firms even a day after the news is announced, and at the same time selling short (this term is explained in the next section) the 'bad news' firms. This implies that the market does not react *enough* to the good and bad news at the time of the earnings announcement. This has long seemed to be a puzzling anomaly. It suggests that surefire returns can be obtained from fairly straightforward analysis of accounting data, casting doubt on level 2 market efficiency.

However, the highly mixed experience of hedge fund managers trying to make money out of these anomalies suggests that very few of these strategies are profitable when actually executed (rather than modelled). This may be due to short-sale constraints, wide bid-offer spreads or low market depth in the small minority of transactions that frequently account for the bulk of returns, to errors in modelling by the experimenters, or to the transient nature of some of the anomalies.

Level 3 is the highest level of market efficiency which attracts any support. We strongly doubt that market prices are semi-strong form efficient; and, of itself, the fact that investors and analysts dedicate such a large amount of time to analysing companies' published financial information provides some evidence that this activity is seen as value-additive.

There is no support for levels 4 and 5 of market efficiency. The profitable activities of insiders such as Ivan Boesky and the continued efforts of the SEC to prevent insider dealing are strong items of evidence against a contention that insider information is impounded into stock prices.

It is hoped that no readers felt that the market exhibits level 5 efficiency: the PFME terminology is meant as a joke. Sometimes, articles in the popular press seem to indicate that the market, with Joel Stern's 'lead steers' at the head, can show an effortless prescience as to companies' future prospects. It is important to understand that this is not the case. Neither individual market traders *nor the market as a whole* have a reliable picture of the future. Equities would not be risky securities if the market had perfect foresight. As the performance of internet stocks in 2000–01 shows, equities remain extremely risky.

MISVALUATION AND MARKET EFFICIENCY

In our discussion of market efficiency we keep talking about *profit* – arbitrage profits, insider profits, and so on. The test of a market inefficiency is whether one can make money out of it. If the market is inefficient, there should be 'surefire winners' out there. As we discussed above, it is often difficult to make money out of apparent anomalies, even if they have been observed by several researchers and look strong in the past data. The well-known comment of Roll (1994) (UCLA professor and fund manager) is worth reproducing here:

> Many of these effects are surprisingly strong in the reported empirical work (that is, in the research), but I have yet to find one that worked in practice, in the sense that it returned more after cost than a buy and hold strategy. Note that I am in a relatively

> advantageous position … (reading) working papers long before the findings are published in a journal.

So the test of whether the stock price bubble was a market inefficiency is simple. Could we make money out of it? Well, with the benefit of 20/20 hindsight, of course! We just sell at the top of the graph in March 2000, and buy back now. But the situation at the time was less clear.

The main way that the 'lead steers' can 'vote' against stock values that are too high is by 'going short'. *Going short* means that traders borrow stock from a large holder of the shares, and then sell it in the marketplace, to buy it back at a profit later. If this is unfamiliar, think of a concrete, very simple example. Suppose a trader who feels that Beanie Babies are too expensive borrows a beanie doll from his or her young niece (who keeps them in the cupboard anyway and only takes them out on her birthday, October 31st), and then sells it to another collector for $500 on November 10th. By next April, the price of the Beanie doll has fallen to $200. The trader, who sold the beanie for $500, buys an identical doll for $200 from another collector, returns the new doll to his or her niece's cupboard, and pockets the $300 (perhaps buying an ice cream for the niece out of the proceeds). It is exactly the same with shares. Borrow from one's broker, and sell short. When the shares are bought back they are returned to the original owner. The original shareholder is even less likely to notice than the niece, since shares are only a claim on colourless, odourless cash. And if the original owner wishes to sell in the meantime, the broker can notionally borrow the stock from another owner instead. This process is generally unseen by both owners (who are borrowed from) and shorters. The broker does, however, require *margin payments* if the position is going against the shorter. To use our Beanie Baby example again – imagine that, during December, the price of the borrowed Beanie doll had gone up to $1000: perhaps the trader's sister would then have demanded a $500 surety, to make sure she would be able to buy another Beanie for her daughter should the trader run off to the Bahamas. This surety is akin to the margin payments brokers demand on short sales.

The point, of course, is the profit not the process. The upshot is that shorting gives one the opportunity to have a negative position in a share. Shorting 100 shares on Amazon.com is exactly like owning minus 100 shares of the stock, except that we may have to pay some margin interest (ice cream) to the broker, and perhaps some margin payments if the position goes against us (surety). Now, we have established the ease of making profits with the benefit of hindsight, and short selling allows us to execute the hindsight strategy. However, the most difficult thing to get right in any trading strategy is *timing*. Consider the plight of an investor who got the short sale wrong by even six months, and sold an internet stock such as Yahoo! in September 1999, when Yahoo! was trading between $80 and $90 per share. A nice investment, since Yahoo! was trading at about $9 in October 2001, but our intrepid shorter might have been wiped out by margin payments in early January 2000, when Yahoo! rose to a heady $237.50 per share.

This difficulty of making money out of bubbles is nothing new. Shiller (1989) notes that:

> some people seem to think that there is a theoretical argument [against bubbles ... But] such fashions or fads may not create spectacular profit opportunities if the future paths of the fashions or fads are not very predictable ... Consider those who, in the late 1950s and the early 1960s in the United States, thought that the bull market had gone on too long and that stocks were overpriced. Even if they knew that the market would eventually fall, there was no way for them to get rich quick from this knowledge. They had to wait years to be vindicated; they could not predict when the bull market would end.

From the theoretical standpoint, recent work by Abreu and Brunnemeier (2001) suggests that even if a proportion of 'lead steer' risk-neutral arbitrageurs have certain knowledge of overvaluation, they cannot 'burst the bubble'. This is particularly true if there is wide uncertainty about what the precise value should be, if there are a large number of 'me too' momentum traders in the market, and if the arbitrageurs are capital-constrained and concerned about their reputation (that is, they do not want to miss out on the 'run-up' to the top of the bubble).

MARKET EFFICIENCY: WHY SHOULD WE CARE?

The reason for discussion of market efficiency is to bolster the case for fundamental analysis. However, to state that the market is not accurate in determining intrinsic value is a double-edged sword: an argument both for and against fundamental analysis.

Clearly, if the market was perfectly *efficient*, or even efficient to the level 3 'semi-strong' form, fundamental analysis of company financial information would have no utility, since the output of such analysis would already be impounded in the market price. If, on the other hand, the market was completely *inefficient*, led purely by sentiment or other non-'value-related' factors, fundamental analysis would be a waste of time. A market where prices are not related to fundamentals would never 'recognize' fundamental value. In a market led by sentiment, the best way to determine whether prices will rise or fall before the end of the day would be to survey market participants at the start of the day. Like a pre-election poll, such a survey would not be reliable (experience shows that it would be especially unable to detect the precise timing of stock market reverses), but it would be the best available method.

In a way, fundamental analysts are walking a 'market-efficiency tightrope' between these extremes. To paraphrase Saint Augustine, we want the market to be efficient, but not yet. We want the market to be prone to misvaluations sufficiently wide that we can detect them with fundamental analysis techniques. However, we want the underlying relationship between value and price to be firm. Like the spouse in a solid marriage, price may stray, but eventually it will come back to the bosom of value. Such a worldview is perfectly consistent with past experience of technological market cycles. The internet cycle seems to have followed this pattern.

THE TROUBLE WITH VALUE

The limitations of value-based investing are also clear from the tightrope analogy. Even the best tightrope-walkers cannot balance indefinitely. During the market's divergences from value, increasing numbers of sages and not-so-sages are 'taken in'. This is not 'group hypnosis', but rational economic behaviour on the part of analysts and commentators. Consider an analyst who believes that the market overvalues a stock, while all the other analysts (the 'herd') rate the stock a buy. There are two possible outcomes in this situation. The (non-herd) analyst may be wrong in his or her conjecture, in which case he or she is alone in having read the stock's value incorrectly. Such an analyst is likely to be dismissed. On the other hand he or she may be correct, in which case the analyst looks very wise but his or her colleagues and competitors, while wrong, made an understandable mistake shared by many! They do not *look* that dumb, so the non-herding analyst does not gain much advantage. It's a case of tails you lose a lot, heads you win a little: a bad bet.

Now suppose further that the analysts are rated annually by a body seeking to gauge the accuracy and helpfulness of their advice. The suspicious analyst is faced with a further disincentive to deviate from the market consensus. Not only does he or she have to be right, but the market has to converge to fundamental value within the year, to avoid damage to his or her career. It is not difficult to see that there will be scenarios in which analysts will 'herd' on doubtful information rather than 'deviate' from the herd viewpoint to state what they believe to be the truth, and risk their livelihoods.

The final problem with value-based investing is that the market, rather than being 'wrong but efficient', may be right. This should always be the assumption unless the evidence is very strongly against it.

SUMMARY: THE EFFICIENCY OF THE MARKET

The market is 'efficient enough' for our purposes. Traders are constantly watching for the opportunity to make risk-free profits or, failing that, for the opportunity to make 'abnormal returns' (returns which are higher that one would expect for the risk taken in the investment). This is the first firm bulwark. There are no risk-free arbitrage opportunities. Traders should not expect to make surefire profits by buying or selling any traded stock or bond.

If we hold a stock to infinity, the future cash flows and the stock's price will converge. Fundamental value will equal price in the long term. This is the second firm bulwark.

But the market lacks perfect foresight. In fact even to suggest it has perfect foresight is a ridiculous contention. Annual, even monthly, fluctuations in price for stocks cannot correspond to variations in any sensible foretelling of value. However, *the market does not diverge from fundamental value in any predictable or unambiguously detectable way*. Such a clear divergence would constitute an arbitrage opportunity. The rises in internet stocks to March 2000 fit into this paradigm. It seemed clear to many of us that internet stocks were overvalued in March 2000, but unambiguity or certainty was impossible. Also, even assuming certainty that the market was overvalued, investors could not be confident when the deviation from fundamentals (bubble) would end.

In this worldview, there is a role for investors conducting fundamental analysis for valuation purposes. However, it must be accepted that for technology firms, the process will be more imprecise and liable to error than it is for old-economy companies, for which there is more history and more experience of valuation (and the process of valuation even for old-economy companies is not *precise*). It must also be borne in mind that fundamental analysis is only suitable for the investor investing for the medium to long term.

As Benjamin Graham wrote, the output of fundamental analysis may not be precise, may not give a 'dependable value'. A range of maximum and minimum values will be the likely output of fundamental analysis of a stock in a firm which faces great uncertainty in the future. If the stock price is below the minimum, the stock is a buy. If the price is above the maximum, the stock should be sold short. However, the stock may be between the fundamental minimum and maximum, in which case (after all that work!) the analysis will suggest we take no action.

In closing, it has been suggested that fundamental analysis is of no use for a stock which is an investment in an uncertain technology – such a stock should simply be viewed as a 'bet on the technology'. We beg to differ. Fundamental analysis is still needed to ensure that it is a *fair* bet. So often, it is not.

PART III

Addressing the Strategic Issues

CHAPTER 11

The Profitability Imperative and Competitive Advantage

INTERNET BUSINESS MUST BE A BUSINESS, NOT AN 'ENTERPRISE'

One central assumption of this book is that internet businesses must 'obey' the rules that normal businesses obey. However, this is not as bad as it sounds! Normal businesses may incur substantial start-up costs, and may record start-up losses in the early period of operation. But there must always be the expectation that these losses will transition into profits in a clearly defined way. There should not be any need for a separate concept of *path to profitability* (*P2P*), since it is understood that any undertaking which is a 'business' should have a route map to profitability embedded in its plans. For example, biotech companies are extremely high-risk investments, but if successful they have a clear path to profitability because they can take advantage of patent protection of drugs produced by their research, and license or produce these drugs to sell to customers at high margins. Many internet companies also have clear potential paths to profitability. Internet-based retailers will aim to sell products to consumers and make sufficient margins to cover their costs. Internet-based consultants will aim to employ consultants, and then to clump consultant teams together to be sold at daily rates which provide a large enough margin to pay down overhead and make profits. Neither of these models is necessarily profitable, but both are recognizably 'businesses' with a finite probability of success.

This is in contrast to internet ideas with no clear way of generating profit. Let us make clear here we are not talking about firms that adopt recognizable business models, or variants of recognizable business models, but then fail to generate profits due to operational problems, shortfalls in demand or the inability to control costs. We are talking about firms that have *enterprise models* which do not resemble recognizable *business models* and do not have any intuitive way of generating profit. Neither type of firm will survive, but the latter type has no *ex ante* chance of surviving at all (unless a new enterprise model is 'bolted on') and is better classified as a hobby or non-profit organization. Such an enterprise model *may* find a place in an existing profitable business as a service to customers or the community, or as a brand-building method for the existing profitable business. However, this limited objective should be reflected in valuation, and in a lean cost structure.

One example of an enterprise model with a questionable potential for profitability is the sending of electronic greetings cards, a service which has been offered free by several providers. An example of this enterprise model, Bluemountain.com, was initially set up by Stephen Schutz as a cheap way to promote his (physical) greeting cards business, and because he was interested in the internet. The business was sold to Excite@home for $350m in cash and $430m in Excite stock in October 1999, plus possible bonus payments of up to $270m in stock. The founders (Stephen Schutz and Susan Polis Schutz) planned to spend this money 'to support world health, hunger relief, and peace'. At the time, Excite highlighted that 'this acquisition brings reach, (and) a chance to monetize significant new page views – each with an event-focus' (source: http://corp.excite.com/news/pr_991025_01.html). Perhaps Excite were also attracted by the fact that Bluemountain.com features love poetry by Leonard Nimoy. Looking back, the motivations of the Schutzes seem to have better stood the test of time.

In September 2001, the business was reported to have been resold to American Greetings for a cash consideration of $35m.[1] This existing, profitable greetings card company may be able to use the Bluemountain site as a brand-building method: specifically, American Greetings has experienced success in issuing money-off coupons for physical greetings cards from its existing website, and therefore in generating greetings cards sales. Excite@home, of course, has no physical greetings card business, and was attempting to use the Bluemountain.com site to generate interest in its broadband ISP service, as well as attempting to sell banner advertising and focused e-commerce links on the pages viewed by Bluemountain.com users. Shortly following the Bluemountain sale, Excite@Home filed for Chapter 11 Bankruptcy protection.

Another interesting enterprise or business model is that of epinions.com, a website that began by paying its members one per cent every time one of their consumer reviews of products and experiences was viewed. The concept was that users who submitted excellent reviews would receive a large number of page views and therefore significant payment. However, people are not usually paid to express views, and the human drive to communicate normally leads to free expression without payment, as can be seen on the letters pages of newspapers and on the review pages of e-tail websites such as Amazon.com. Epinions plans to make money through selling advertising on the epinions website, selling the epinions content, and licensing epinions technology.[2] This could be a new business model in the making. On the other hand, it could simply be a transfer of wealth from the equity investors to the users and employees of the website, as the 'Get Paid to Surf' website AllAdvantage.com turned out to be. Alternatively, epinions may change its business model and cut costs, including by decreasing, restricting or optimizing payments to writers. In November 2001 it moved towards this, by ceasing 'base eRoyalties' (which were dependent only on page views) and moving to an 'income share' programme, where reviewers receive a part of the 'income share pool (which) is a portion of Epinions' income'.

MOST EARLY STAGE BUSINESSES ARE PRIVATELY HELD

Many firms go through a stage of operation when they are losing money. However, ordinarily this is before they reach the IPO or flotation stage. It is quite unusual for quoted companies to seek equity funding; in fact it is surprisingly rare that quoted firms seek any outside funding. For example, over the period 1983–91, US firms relied on internally generated funds (that is, retained earnings or retained profit) for 82% of their investments, raising some debt, and actually paying back equity via share buybacks (Cantillo, 1997). There are some exceptions in the normal course of business. For example, firms may be expected to go to the market for large capital projects or to fund cash acquisitions, especially during 'hot' markets, where investor demand for IPOs is high, such as during the late 1990s. However, the presence of a large number of pre-earnings companies on the public markets was a feature confined to the 1989–91 biotechnology sector boom and the 1998–2000 internet sector boom.

STRICT CASH DIET FOR PUBLIC INTERNET COMPANIES

Whether or not pre-earnings companies may find a ready audience in future public markets, the investment climate in 2002 is that internet firms are unable to raise fresh funding from public investors. This means that the concept of Funding Crunch Analysis becomes especially important. Firms which are unable to reach profitability before exhausting their current cash will have to find alternative sources of funding than the public markets. Example of alternative sources are:

- sales of assets or subsidiaries (for example, the sale of Bluemountain.com by Excite@Home – see above)

- financing rounds by existing investors (many examples)
- financing rounds by 'strategic' investors (for example, Amazon.com raised $100m funding from AOL in July 2001, as part of a partnering arrangement to enhance AOL's e-commerce[3])
- use of cash flow from profitable subsidiaries (for example, eBay's purchase of old-economy auction house Butterfield could be used for this purpose, but so far eBay has remained profitable)
- negotiate acquisition by a profitable firm and use this firm's cash flow to continue development (for example, interactive investor international plc's (iii.co.uk) acquisition by the Australian insurance company and financial conglomerate, AMP).[4]

THE NEED FOR SHIFTS IN BUSINESS MODELS

This shift in attitude by public market investors has generated the need for fundamental changes in the business models of firms. Companies with enterprise models rather than business models have attempted to transition from the former to the latter. Companies with business models which are failing to generate profits have begun to address these. Business model failure can occur for several reasons, for example:

1. *operational problems*: the company has a realistic business model but has been unable to execute against it (due to management incompetence or some error in translating the business model into operational strategy and tactics, selection of the wrong niche, or similar)
2. *shortfalls in revenues*: the company's business model required a certain amount of volume/revenue to reach profitability, and this has not been achieved (the projected volumes *may* have been unrealistic, or the market may have changed due to competitor entry or changes in consumer taste)
3. *inability to control costs (related to 2)*: the company has been successful in attracting paying customers, but has a bloated cost structure.

In the market environment of 1999–early 2000, there was the potential to postpone considerations of profitability because valuations were (at best) revenue-based or (at worst) 'story'-based. If valuations are based on revenue, firms which generate revenues are seen as valuable even though they may have uncertain prospects for generating profits. If valuations are story-based, firms which can spin an attractive tale about their potential are seen as valuable, even if revenues are low or negligible! If firms can secure high market valuations based on revenues or their perceived potential, then they can issue fresh equity to finance their operations (and, having no earnings, raising external funds is indeed their only option).

We spoke in Chapter 3 about the vital importance of *operating leverage*. Operating leverage is the potential of a business with large fixed costs to reach very high profitability as revenues increase. There is a problem with large fixed costs, however. If revenues are modest, large fixed costs translate into large losses and rapid burn of the firm's cash. Internet firms have responded to this threat in two ways. First (and not surprisingly), by cutting costs. Second, by transitioning to business models characterized by *lower* operating leverage. The case of the *business-to-business (B2B) exchanges* provides an illustrative example of this trend, as well as introducing some other important concepts, including that of *competitive advantage*.

THE CASE OF B2B EXCHANGES

One example of companies with what appeared to be a sound business model were the B2B exchanges. *B2B exchanges* were firms which would provide web interfaces to allow businesses to sell product to other businesses. Since business-to-business volumes are larger in currency terms than business-to-consumer volumes, this type of business was predicted to have great potential in early 2000. Examples of these businesses were Ventro/Chemdex and VerticalNet in the USA and Just2Clicks in the UK.

The initial business model of the B2B exchanges was to encourage businesses to access the B2B exchanges' portals free of charge, in the expectation that, as the number of firms using the exchanges reached a critical mass, firms would be encouraged to transact large volumes of business using the exchanges. However, although some B2B exchanges reported encouraging interest in the service in terms of number of registrations, this did not translate into revenues or profits.

Unfortunately, the assumptions underlying the B2B exchange business plans were too optimistic, in some cases obviously so. At the core of many B2B exchange business plans was the provision of a *commodity service* (that is, the very simple action of matching a buyer to a seller and facilitating price discovery) at a *value-added price* (commission rates of as much as 2% or even above 5% of transaction value were projected in by some firms). By contrast, the commission rates for established markets which perform similar very basic price discovery functions (such as the Chicago Board of Trade, LIFFE or stock markets) are small fractions of 1%.

Less obvious was the failure of customers to transition to the new ways of doing business as rapidly as predicted. In this regard the B2B exchanges had underestimated the benefits to business purchasers of customization of supplies and of relationships between buyer and supplier. They had also underestimated the inertia of buyers and suppliers in sticking to existing methods of transacting business, and in some cases had not made their user interfaces sufficiently user-friendly to encourage the transition. Only when B2B exchanges realized that they would have to carry out extensive 'hand-holding' for firms to encourage them to use the exchanges did revenues start to rise. However, this provision of a value-added service was fatal for the B2B exchange's business models, which were predicated on *scalability* – that is, the ability to use the same system and staff to handle very high volumes as is needed to handle low volumes. B2B exchanges found that, to earn commissions, they had to provide not just a website, but a human-resource-intensive, high-cost service. Clearly, business models had to change in order for the companies to survive.

Table 11.1 illustrates how business models did change, tending to transition from model 1 to model 3 or 4. (Note: in addition to transaction and subscription revenues, B2B exchanges also earned advertising revenues). Initially B2B exchanges 'sold' the concept of their exchange to customer firms and secured their registrations by offering free memberships. However, as investors became more revenue-focused and less story-focused, the B2B exchanges transitioned to a subscription model, where there was at least some revenue 'reward' for incurring the cost of signing up businesses. Although imposing a fee decreased the absolute number of clients, many of the firms registering for the free service had taken no further interest in it after registering!

Finally, with the change in sentiment in the public market, B2B exchanges needed to conserve cash and attempt to transition quickly to profitability. To do this they largely abandoned exchange-based models and changed to more established business models of software sales or supply-chain management consultancy. In other words there was a shift from maximizing *potential* equity value by highlighting the explosive operating leverage of the transaction-fee

Table 11.1 Changing business models

Model		Logic	Examples
1	Share of transaction revenue	Small share of enormous market	Chemdex to end 2000
2	Subscription revenue (with transaction revenue)	Need to show some revenue became paramount	Various
3	Software sales revenue	Still high operating leverage, but strong competition	Chemdex in 2001
4	Service provision revenue	Low operating leverage – consultancy model	Freemarkets in 2001

model (albeit a model which was based on optimistic commission rates) to safeguarding at least *some* equity value for investors and employee option holders.

Competitive advantage and the B2B exchanges

In illustrating the inappropriate business model of the B2B exchanges we used the same means as we used for many of our judgements on the Amazon.com modelling exercise – that of comparing the revenue assumptions to existing comparable firms in the old economy. We highlighted that, while B2B exchanges predicted transaction fees of up to 5%, similar organizations in the old economy secured transaction fees of less than 1%.

However, there is another approach to understanding why the B2B exchange's business models did not work, and that is by considering whether they possessed a sustainable competitive advantage. *Competitive advantage* is any advantage that a firm has over competitors. In practice this generally means performing an activity better or more cheaply than the competition:

1. If customers gain more value from company A's product or service (perhaps it dovetails into their production process more smoothly than does company B's offering), then they will be prepared to pay more to buy from company A than from company B. If costs are the same, company A will then be able to gain a higher unit profit.
2. If company A can produce the product or service cheaper than company B, then, for a constant selling price, company A will have higher unit profit.

Competitive advantage is perhaps most intuitively understandable in the business-to-consumer (B2C) world, where we are accustomed to think of 'branding' as a key competitive advantage. *Brand* is a very important competitive advantage in the B2C world, and it can be seen as representing a package of benefits in the consumer's mind (that is, it is a competitive advantage of type 1 above), such as quality, reliability, freshness, fashionableness. The benefits of brand can persist even when competitors may have caught up with many of the tangible features of the leader's product. Brand can allow brand holders to obtain premium prices over long periods. Therefore, brand (although difficult to build) can potentially be a *sustainable* competitive advantage.

In the consumer world, families can gain direct psychological benefits from consuming branded products over non-branded. They have more confidence in the product and may feel that it enhances their image and lifestyle to consume the branded product over the non-branded. In the business world, however, branding is not enough. Since procurement executives are actually *paid* to get the best deal for their companies, ethereal concepts of branding will be insufficient to persuade their superiors that they should pay premium prices to deal with a specific portal or partner. Another way of thinking about this is that, in a B2C business, consumers generally have low power to influence events – they are disparate and have other matters to think about than getting the best deal. Buyers (and indeed suppliers) of a B2B commerce company tend to be professionals, and will invariably control a larger budget than that of a household. Stuck between the rock of large commercial *suppliers*, and the hard place of powerful *buyers*, B2B exchanges were not in a good position.

Unable to rely on any concept of brand, B2B exchanges would have had to deliver some genuine performance advantages to the procurement executive. Since the B2B portals were initially aimed as commodity products, just giving access to a list of products available for sale, and facilitating price discovery by displaying the price or allowing an auction process, this would prove difficult. Although construction of the B2B exchange website, and connection of the website front end to the underlying database of available product is not simple, it is something that many potential players in the market could carry out. In other words, there was a real and realized *threat from new entrants* into the markets of the B2B exchanges.

Therefore in the absence of competitive advantage from features, and because the presence of competitors prevented any single exchange from rapidly building critical mass, B2B exchanges were forced into price competition. In the absence of collusion, price competition is extremely fierce in an industry where fixed costs are high and where excess capacity exists. Prices for the product or service will be forced down to closer to the marginal cost of servicing the extra customer or user. Since this marginal or variable cost of adding another listing to a B2B website (once the system is in place) is close to zero, transaction fees for B2B exchanges were forced down to levels which were also close to zero. In this environment of strong *rivalry*, fixed costs of running the website could not be recovered, and the sunk costs of initial website development were lost.

Another problem for the B2B exchanges was that they were competing not just with each other, but with 'traditional' methods of doing business as well. These traditional methods were effective and attractive *substitutes* for the product the B2B exchanges were selling. The web-based interface was perfectly suitable for standardized products, such as plain white paper or standard industrial components. However, in the event that any customization or non-ordinary requirements for parts or supplies came into play, the web interface was *less* suitable. B2B exchanges in specific industries moved to enhance their interfaces to allow more complex specifications to be communicated, but procurement executives showed reluctance to leave traditional channels. Their actions seem quite sensible in the light of a 2000 Harvard

Business School study. Professor Das Narayandas studied five purchases intermediated by Freemarkets, one of the leading B2B marketplace/procurement consultancy firms, and found that four of the buyers later returned to their original suppliers.[5] It seems that the buyers initially underestimated the importance of having habitual suppliers who precisely met their needs, in ways that they apparently could not specify in an RFQ (request for quote).

Increasingly, the remaining B2B exchanges are concentrated on ancillary supplies for businesses, such as paper, stationery and other overhead items. These are more standardized, and therefore more suitable for selling over the web interface. They are also less salient to the business processes of the customer firm, so the potential benefits of customization are likely to be less important. Even in this case, however, the strategic environment for a pure B2B exchange could not be more negative, and profitability is likely to be limited. However, returns to buyers and suppliers using web-based procurement may be attractive, and buyers and suppliers themselves may find it necessary to set up intermediaries to carry out that function (for example, the big three automakers' setting up of Covisint). Some former B2B exchanges have changed their business models to assist firms in this. Other B2B exchanges are targeting the small business/SME sector, where buyer power is less strong, and offering the exchange-based procurement service as part of a package of services.

SUMMARY: THE PROFITABILITY IMPERATIVE

In the 2002 market environment, fresh capital is hard to secure for internet businesses. Therefore, firms have been placed on a 'strict cash diet': required to achieve profitability, or at least required to be cash-positive, and likely to be required to sustain growth mainly by calling upon internally generated resources in the future. Internet enterprises with no clear business model have been forced to re-aim their enterprises to pursue profitability. Internet businesses have been forced to address operational, revenue-generation, and cost-control problems which an easy supply of public market capital might have allowed them to postpone addressing. Faced with these challenges, many internet firms have failed, finding the challenges of re-aiming their businesses too severe, or being confronted with the fact that their underlying enterprise model or business model was unworkable, however adjusted. Other firms are likely to succeed; others still may become 'nice little businesses' – that is, they will continue to exist, but within modest niches (within which they can exert competitive advantage) and attracting modest valuations.

In this environment, sound strategic analysis is key in informing valuation. We discussed in some detail the case of B2B exchanges. While commentators focused on the huge growth potential in B2B exchanges (projected B2B e-commerce revenues of $3trillion in 2003, according to Forrester), what was more important was to examine the business's unattractive strategic environment. We presented an intuitive discussion of the strategic positioning of the B2B exchanges, in which we highlighted the fact that they faced powerful suppliers and buyers, strong threats from new entrants and substitutes, and fierce rivalry. These five factors have been highlighted in the work of Michael Porter, as the five forces which can help us make a judgement on the attractiveness of an industry or industry segment. We discuss formally this important element of strategic analysis, as it applies to internet firms, in the next chapter.

Notes

1 http://www.corporate-ir.net/ireye/ir_site.zhtml?ticker=ATHM&script=411&layout=0&item_id=206435.
2 http://www.epinions.com/about/show_~faq_understanding#007.
3 SEC form 424B2 and news reports.
4 iii website and news reports.
5 *The Economist* 9 May 2000.

CHAPTER 12

Applying Standard Strategic Models to Internet Businesses

'TRADITIONAL' STRATEGIC INSIGHTS ARE RELEVANT TO INTERNET FIRMS

Is the firm profitable? Does it or, at least, will it produce higher returns than its cost of capital? Does it have a competitive advantage over other firms which attracts customers and allows it to secure supernormal profits? Is the firm's competitive advantage sustainable and defensible? Can the firm erect barriers to other companies coming in and trying to take its market?

These are key insights for old economy firms. They are absolutely vital questions for internet firms. Far from providing a benign environment where the holy waters of network effects flow to each company, creating unlimited value for venture capitalists and public market investors alike, the internet has proved to be a viciously competitive place. This should not have proved unexpected.

THE INTERNET IS A HARSH MISTRESS

The very reach and ease of access of the internet is the reason for the tough competitive environment that exists on it. The technical characteristics of the internet (packet switching, multiple pathways for data transport, and so on) are arcane, and to some extent unimportant to the end user. Their effect, however, is very simple. They provide cheap and reliable connection in a universal format, revolutionizing communications. A company wishing to connect to the internet does not have to concern itself with local requirements for data formats or connection machinery. It may utilize standard connection and equipment by a variety of suppliers, who work to published standards. This process has become even simpler, as a wide range of *web hosting* providers have opened up to take care of all of the technical processes, so that businesses merely have to make decisions about their business needs.

A presence on the internet is simple to obtain, giving merchants and sellers of products access to the vast number of internet users as a potential market. If the product being sold is machine-readable, such as software or MP3 music files, the internet can also serve as the delivery medium. Otherwise, logistics companies such as FedEx or UPS or, in the UK, Consignia (formerly the Royal Mail), can handle the delivery of physical products nationwide and worldwide. Payment can be transacted through a wide range of services, some of which have fee structures competitive with merchant accounts taken up by existing high street stores. It is easy to set up to do business on the internet, and one gains access to hundreds of millions of consumers.

However, the trouble with the ease of setting up a business on the internet is that it is also easy for everyone *else* to set up a business on the internet. To illustrate, in the early years of the internet we saw two possible futures for internet commerce:

- the *land grab* view:
  - internet firms can build brand
  - firms with a strong brand can gain supernormal margins

- the *competitive wasteland* view:
  - the internet is great news for consumers
  - but shopping bots and competitors 'only a mouse click away' will kill margins!

In our first talk on this topic in late 1998, we estimated that the competitive wasteland view was 65% likely to be the outcome for internet firms. We were influenced by the ease of comparison shopping by mouse, facilitated by 'shopping bot' price-comparison websites such as mysimon.com, ecompare and pricescan.com. To many commentators at that point, and more so during 1999–2000, this assessment seemed hopelessly pessimistic. However, as it turned out, quite the opposite was true. Both commerce companies and content companies were beset with competitors. Only in a limited number of areas (for example, B2C commerce) was brand-building even worth attempting, and within these areas only a handful of companies made it work. Even firms with strong brands, facing competition from lavishly funded competitors who were attempting to buy market share to secure the perennial next round of funding, were unable to charge premium prices.

Although, obviously, the threat of lavishly funded 'pure play'[1] web-based competitors has receded, the effects of competition are unlikely to do so. In fact, quite the reverse. Offline retailers are finally starting to get their act together. B2B exchanges have been virtually eliminated in their original form, as commercial marketers find that they can utilize out of the box e-commerce systems to at least dip a toe in the internet market. In software and services, old economy giant IBM claims to be the biggest internet company. 'Born on the web' consultancies are dying, on the web. Content-based companies, having had a brief lease of life due to the temporary boom in internet advertising (a boom which was largely led by the internet firms themselves), are changing their business models to subscription or more complex models in an attempt to stay afloat. For content companies the accessibility and standardization of the internet was arguably their downfall. It was easy to build a presence on the internet for pure-play content companies like salon.com, but it was also easy for nytimes.com and dailytelegraph.co.uk to build a web presence. And the latter firms had an enormous advantage in their access to the underlying inventory of the content process. They already had machinery (human and mechanical) in place to produce hundreds of thousands of words per day, already 'paid for' by existing users and subscribers.

THE SEARCH IS ON FOR SUSTAINABLE COMPETITIVE ADVANTAGE

The reason why many internet businesses have failed is that they could not gain a competitive advantage. Or at least, if they possessed an advantage (perhaps a lead over competitors) it proved to be a fleeting one rather than a *sustainable* competitive advantage. These firms could not defend their positions against competitors, they had nothing to tie users in to their product, and they could not stop other competitors from entering their marketplace and competing much of their profitability away.

What we do in this chapter is discuss some tools by which we can evaluate *strategies* of firms which we are attempting to value. Our aim will be to see whether the firm is in the right marketplace or niche to exert competitive pressure and to defend itself against the pressure of others. We will look at how to evaluate firm strategy and organizational assets. We will also study the product life cycle and see how to gauge whether buyers are likely to make a quick decision or not to buy and use ('adopt') a company's product. This helps us to decide how long to 'give' a company to become successful.

These are strategic insights, but without them, attempting to value a company is meaningless. Companies which do not develop competitive advantage are worthless. Companies which develop a competitive advantage but not a sustainable one are not worth much. These firms are destined to be 'strivers', with management oscillating between a menu of strategies and tactics to attack profitable niches and segments – but facing competitive pressure on profits at every turn. Businesses like this are destined to provide low returns to shareholders, because they will never be able to provide super-normal returns for extended periods of time. Of course, there is a degree of adaptation in any successful business, but successful strategies will be based on core competencies, strategic assets and intellectual property that together constitute a sustainable competitive advantage.

At all points during the strategic analysis, potential discontinuities and changes should be noted (to feed into DCA).

How to gain competitive advantage

There are two elements in gaining competitive advantage. Once we see these, we will be able to detect whether businesses we are studying or considering are likely to achieve this vital aim. Put very simply, these elements are:

- being in the right place (industry, niche)
- doing the right things (strategy, tactics).

ARE WE IN THE RIGHT PLACE? DETERMINING INDUSTRY ATTRACTIVENESS

The fundamental tool for determining whether a company is in the right place is called the *five forces*. This is a strategic framework developed by Michael Porter (1980) which is designed to tell one how attractive an industry or industry sector is to do business in; how defensible a position is likely to be against competitors and potential competitors; and how much bargaining power is possessed by the firm, and how much by its customers and suppliers. The five forces are not an exhaustive list of every strategic factor that should come into play in judging the likely returns in an industry, but they are a good starting point to analysis.

The five forces are as follows:

- power of buyers
- power of suppliers
- rivalry

} nature of competitive environment

- threat of substitutes
- threat of new entrants

} effects of extended competition

The stronger the forces are in an industry, the more 'uncomfortable' a place that industry is. The weaker the forces are, the more bargaining power the firm has, and the more opportunity to make supernormal profits. Ideally, a firm wants to operate in an industry where suppliers and customers are weak, where there are few or weak competitors, where there is little threat of new entrants into the market, and where there is little chance of a substitute (different product) being adopted by existing users. By contrast, we saw an example in the last chapter of the B2B exchange business model, which was an internet business model where the five forces were all strong. The five forces always operate in opposition to the business, so this environment (where the forces are strong) is an unattractive one for a business. It is a measure of the intuitiveness of the five forces framework that, while students of strategy will have recognized the five forces as old friends in the previous chapter's narrative, for other readers they may have blended into the discussion. It is for this reason that they were italicized.

It should be noted that the use of the five forces in analysing internet commerce is not entirely uncontroversial. For example, the September 2001 edition of the new economy magazine *Business 2.0* ('Reinventing Business', according to its homepage) reports that Porter has been 'criticized in some quarters for his belief that the internet hasn't fundamentally changed the rules of business'. However, it remains to be seen how long *Business 2.0* remains in print to continue to publicize this criticism.

The five forces are extensively discussed in Porter (1980, 1998), and the ideas in this chapter are heavily influenced by those discussions.

Using the five forces: example of online book retailing

Let us examine the example of online book retailing (for example Amazon.com) to see how the five forces are applied. We will estimate whether the power of each force is low, medium or high. To help our focus, we will also assign a numerical estimate out of 10 to the severity of each force (0 being the minimum, 10 the maximum, with 5 representing an average industry). We should also consider the strength of the five forces when Jeff Bezos embarked on the adventure of setting up Amazon in 1995, and how the five forces changed or are changing over time (partly in reaction to this new entrant). This latter point emphasizes the ability of the five forces to guide us as the situation changes, as any good strategic framework should.

As a reminder, the five forces are:

- power of buyers
- power of suppliers
- rivalry
- threat of substitutes
- threat of new entrants.

First of all, let us consider the first two forces. The key challenge is to determine who is the buyer and supplier immediately adjacent to the business we are looking at in the supply chain. Considering the example of book retailing, the supply chain or value chain looks like Figure 12.1.

Thus, if we were considering the business of book distribution, we would be interested in who sells the books to distributors (that is, the publishing companies) and who are the immediate buyers (that is, book retailers). It is interesting to note that, although physically books may be sent directly from printers to distributors, the printers are most aptly seen as a supplier service to the publishers. Moving from the physical to the intellectual property, authors themselves might be considered as another supplier to the publishers. Also, if we were studying a smaller bookseller than Amazon.com, there might be an intermediate part of the value chain between distributor and retailer, perhaps a regional wholesaler of books.

For Amazon, then, the main suppliers are the distributors. We can conceive of other suppliers – such as the employees as suppliers of labour, and the suppliers of utilities, and so on – but we will not consider these suppliers in detail. The customers are the end users of books: private individuals who buy

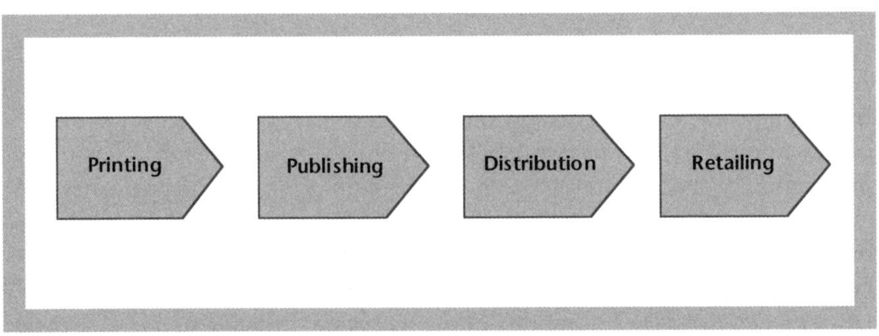

Figure 12.1 The supply chain or value chain

for their own personal and professional reasons, as well as companies and other institutions who need to purchase books. Broadly, consumer books represent 70% of the book market.

The power of suppliers

In order to analyse the power of suppliers we can look at certain contributory factors. Porter suggests that supplier power will be high if:

1. relative concentration of the supplier industry is high
2. there are not many substitutes for the raw material supplied
3. the supplier group has many other industries to sell to
4. the raw material supplied is very important
5. the raw material is very differentiated
6. there are costs to switching between suppliers
7. the supplier group can threaten the industry being studied by *forward integrating* – that is, getting into its customers' business directly.

For example, in the case of book retailing, distributors have quite high concentration relative to booksellers (many of whom are small single stores): that is, booksellers are smaller than distributors and distributors have many client bookstores, rather than the other way round. For Amazon, because of its relatively large size, catering for approximately 5% of the US market, the situation is better. Amazon had total revenues of $2.76bn in the year 2000 ($3.12bn in year 2001), of which approximately $1.7bn was US book, music and video sales. Amazon also has two large competitors who predate it, Borders ($3bn revenues year ending January 2001) and Barnes & Noble ($4.4bn revenues year ending January 2001). By comparison, the largest book distributor, Ingram Books, recorded revenues of $1.8bn in 1999. An industry dominated by one or two companies will tend to exert high power – this is not the case in book distribution which is somewhat 'middle of the road' in concentration (especially relative to book retail).

Continuing down the list, we consider the issue of whether there are substitutes for what the book distributors are supplying (2). Since Amazon's books division is focused on books, there are no substitutes for books as a 'raw material'. However, conversely, book distributors generally tend to be focused on selling books, so they do not have any other industries to sell to –

they have large sunk cost investments in distribution centres that can only be used for books (unless extensively modified). Continuing on to the issue of importance and differentiation, the distributors' raw material is vital to Amazon, but it is *not* differentiated. While individual books are, of course, very different from each other, it is at the publisher level that exclusivity occurs (for books which are in copyright). For Amazon, it makes no difference if it sources the latest Danielle Steele or Tom Clancy from Ingram or from Baker and Taylor. Costs to switching exist but are low. Finally, the book distribution industry would experience high costs if it tried to market directly to consumers (bypassing retailers), although Amazon itself shows that this *could* be done. For example, Baker and Taylor's website possesses ordering functionality, but is restricted to retailers or libraries. When Amazon.com was set up, the threat of forward integration was remote. Now, the threat of forward integration is medium, and may grow.

In summary, *power of suppliers* is *low to medium* (score 4 out of 10).

The power of buyers

Moving onto the power of buyers, Porter advises that this will be high if:

1. the buyers are concentrated relative to the industry
2. the product represents a large fraction of the buyers' spending or costs
3. the products are standard or undifferentiated
4. buyers face few switching costs to change suppliers
5. the buyer has full information.

There are two other considerations that can cause high buyer power, which are most relevant if the buyer is a business:

6. if the buyer earns low profits (and therefore needs to constantly shave costs and to exert pressure on suppliers)
7. if the buyer can threaten the industry by *backward integration* (that is, if it can get into the business of the industry).

As we heard, most buyers of books are consumers, or individual buyers buying for a corporation (that is, they are buying for a corporation but often not taking advantage of the corporation's buying power). So buyer concentration is very low. For concern 2, the book product is almost invariably only a small part of the buyer's personal or corporate budget. For concern 3, the books are obviously very different, but the same book can be bought from several bookstores. There is potential for differentiation in service standards and (in the case of physical bookstores) ambience. Concern 4 for buyer power suggests high power, because switching costs are low.

Issue 5, full information, is an interesting one. Full information means that the buyer knows competing market prices and has an accurate picture of the supplier's costs, giving him or her valuable knowledge in any negotiation. Clearly, the end consumer for books usually does not have full information. However, for the online book buyer, full information on market prices can be gained at 'shopping bots' or comparison engines such as mysimon.com and dealtime.com. At these websites the user can type in the name of a book and the website will 'shop' the price databases of the available online bookstores, and the user can then rank the results by price of the book, by availability, or even by total price (including shipping and handling charge, since the shopping bots can either access or emulate the bookseller websites' rules for shipping and handling). Not all buyers bother to arm themselves with this information, but the number doing so may well increase. This information was not available when Amazon was considering setting up its business.

Items 6 and 7 are, as we mentioned, most relevant if the buyer is a business or business group. The equivalent of the former for consumers as buyers would be that consumers who are poor would exert pricing pressure. We see this in discount food retailing which is selling to poorer clients. For book retailing, which generally comes out of disposable income, this consideration is weak. The equivalent of the item 7 (backward integration) would be if consumers could buy directly from distributors, which at present they cannot (although this may change).

Due mainly to the very low concentration of buyers, we estimate that *buyer power* is *low* (score 1 out of 10). Buyer power may rise if buyers increase their use of the available price comparison tools.

Intensity of industry rivalry

Intensity of rivalry speaks to the way competitive interactions between industry players occur. Porter mentions common terms to describe intense rivalry: competition is 'warlike', 'bitter' or 'cutthroat'. Such rivalry is not generally associated with book retailing, although there is no doubt that the entry of Amazon and other online retailers has made rivalry more intense. In the UK, the ending in 1995 of the 'Net Book Agreement' (which was a price maintenance agreement between publishers and retailers) led to a marked increase in price competition, and increased share for supermarkets.

Price sensitivity is the normal state of any business customer or supplier. While consumers may be prepared to pay premium prices and (when they are occasionally in the role of seller, for example of used cars) accept low sale prices, businesses cannot usually afford to do so. Consumers have aims other than profit, businesses do not. Exceptions to the tendency of businesses to be price sensitive do exist. For example, when a business is buying supplies which form only a small part by value of its purchases, it may not wish to expend a lot of time on negotiation. Conversely, any element of its supplies which is very salient to the ultimate performance of the business's products may be bought on quality before price. Considering consumer behaviour, consumers will be more price sensitive as the cost of an item rises as a proportion of their purchases, and also if the product is not very differentiated. In consumers' main sale transactions, in which they sell their own labour, they are sensitive to price. The general rules for businesses and consumers are the same (except when we think of the psychological benefits consumers gain from brand – and these are ascribed a limited price) but we will tend to observe less price sensitivity in consumers as they tend to be smaller players in the individual product markets than business buyers or sellers.

Let us survey the full list of factors proposed by Porter that lead to a high value of industry rivalry, and proceed to examine how they affect the book retailing industry. Rivalry is strong if:

1. there are numerous or equally balanced competitors
2. there is slow industry growth
3. there are high fixed costs or high storage costs
4. there is a lack of differentiation
5. these are low switching costs for customers
6. capacity must be added in large 'chunks'
7. competitors have diverse strategies and goals
8. there are high 'strategic stakes' – a firm may have announced an intention to succeed in a marketplace or may have resolved internally (without publicity) to do so for strategic reasons
9. there are high exit barriers – it is expensive to get out of the business, or difficult for other reasons, perhaps assets have little or no salvage value or because there are cash costs of exiting the business.

With regard to book retailing, rivalry has undergone change. At the point when the Amazon project was being considered, the spacious bookstore model was being rolled out in the United States by Barnes & Noble and by Borders. In an industry used to fairly 'gentlemanly' competition between small booksellers who specialized in books which their clientele wanted, this was an increase in competition for a number of reasons. The book industry had been plagued with high inventory storage costs (item 3); (somewhat mitigated by standard contracts that allow retailers to receive refunds for unsold books). Now some players entered with higher fixed costs (item 3) due to the higher start-up and ongoing costs of the large bookstores, and therefore an extra incentive to increase sales. Switching costs were decreased (item 5): given the large selection in the spacious bookstores, customers had less incentive to stick with their existing booksellers. However, competition was still mainly on features rather than price. The large bookstores would offer some discounted loss-leader books, but many books would not be discounted. Growth remained fairly slow at 4% per year (item 2).

The expansion of Amazon.com, and the followship of 'me-too' book retailers such as bn.com (started by Barnes & Noble, Inc.) and borders.com in the USA, and by whsmith.co.uk in the UK, led to further increases in rivalry. Competitors became far more numerous (item 1), fixed costs of web-based retailers were enormously in excess of any high street store (item 3), and the diversity of strategies underwent an upward step change (item 7). Finally, with regard to item 8 (strategic stakes), at least one competitor (Amazon) entered with the ultimate strategic stake: life, and the next round of financing, depended on making bookselling work. Over 1995–98, rivalry went from low to medium/high. Rivalry is only now starting to ease off as some competitors drop out or partner (for example, Waterstone's September 2001 partnership with Amazon in the UK) and as discounting becomes slightly less fierce.

Currently we would estimate *rivalry* as *medium to high* (score 6 out of 10). There are two countervailing influences that will determine the future path of rivalry. First, the trends for a decrease in price competition for existing players as – in the clear absence of 'cheap' capital – the players concentrate on rebuilding (or, in the case of Amazon, building) profitability. There will also be the exit of some marginal online competitors. The second influence is that of the internet's potential to allow cheap shopping models. It is possible that small independent booksellers will recreate themselves on the internet, without expensive premises, and taking advantage of the potential of cheap payment methods by companies such as paypal.com and billpoint.com.

The threat of substitutes

What is a substitute? A *substitute* is a product that fulfils a similar function to the product being considered, in this case books. Consistent with Porter's concept of 'extended competition', substitute products can cause customers to buy fewer books, and therefore to compete away industry revenues, and therefore profits. What kind of product may substitute for books? Clearly, e-books can substitute for physical books (*e-books* are electronically downloadable files that can be read on special electronic readers). On a wider scale, if we view books as entertainment, movies/cinema, live and recorded music, videos/DVDs and magazines can be potential substitutes. Considering textbooks and commercial titles, online teaching or live consultants respectively can be seen as substitutes. One defence against substitutes is to sell them as well! For example, if paperback books were the only product sold by Amazon.com (and by book retailers in general), hardback books would be substitute products. This threat is mitigated by the fact that book retailers generally sell both hardback and paperback books. Amazon.com is also the largest online seller of video tapes, DVDs and recorded music CDs, and it owns one of the major movie information websites, imdb.com, which may eventually position it to gain some revenues from movie theatres.

The emphasis in addressing the threat of substitutes on an existing product, such as books, should be not on the existence of substitutes, but on changes in the attributes of the substitutes that make them more appealing, perhaps (as Porter notes) by improving their price/performance trade-off. For example, the existence of movies as a competitor for the entertainment time of potential book buyers is a problem, but it is one that is factored into current consumption of books. Only if we feel that movies are likely to become more attractive to book buyers should we prioritize them as a highly threatening potential substitute.

In general, the book retailing industry suffers from a *low* threat of *substitutes* (score 2 out of 10).

The substitute for books that is most likely to experience change in its price/performance trade-off is e-books. Currently, e-books are available for several mutually incompatible reader devices. The devices are increasing in user-friendliness, but take-up has been limited to tech-addicts. In somewhat of a chicken and egg situation, the number of books available is very limited. Publishers do not want to issue many e-books until there is a large potential user base; but there will not be much take-up of the units until a lot of e-books are available. Also the publishers' pricing structure seems unwise. It would seem that the way to initiate interest in e-books is to give away the reader devices (or, at least, to sell them very cheaply) and to attempt to make money by issuing the media or data. This is the model which has worked for zip disks, and for cellular telephones. Currently the e-book readers represent a sizeable investment of more than $100. Inexplicably, the e-book files for download are priced similarly to printed books. In these circumstances, it is not surprising that take-up has been poor – in fact, it is surprising that there has been take-up at all, in the absence of any economic incentive. Thank goodness for gadget freaks!

It is normal for companies in an industry to be wedded to the existing way of doing business. Publishers have also professed concern about the potential for copying of e-book files, a concern which seems reasonable in the light of the analogous problems faced by the music industry. However, e-books may provide substantial opportunities for eliminating cost from the book production business – costs of printing, costs of book raw materials, costs of shipping, other costs of the supply chain including distribution, and costs of returns (publishers usually allow retailers to return unsold books for credit – e-books would make returns a thing of the past). It is not hyperbole to say that e-books could revolutionize the book industry, if they achieved high adoption rates among readers. For this reason publishers will eventually adopt a more sensible strategy for promoting them. At this point the publishers who get this right early will reap supernormal profits, for a time. However, after a short period, competitive actions by other publishers are likely to drive prices down, and the benefits of the technology will then go to consumers, in the form of cheaper reading material, and a wider selection of it. It is a normal result of the competitive process that consumers reap the rewards of advances, unless there are some barriers to companies competing in the field of a new advance. This brings us neatly on to the final one of the five forces.

The threat of new entrants

The search for profit opportunities is at the core of capitalist existence. This means that there are great opportunities for firms and individuals: but at the same time, once you are making profits, someone else is coming after you! Think of a firm like Coca-Cola. Its supernormal profits in selling Coke are constantly under threat. Supermarkets try to market own-brand cola; and its powerful competitor, Pepsi, fights it in virtually every market. And Coca-Cola's success in defending its position is very much the exception. Partly by accident, partly by design, Coca-Cola's profits have been effectively defended from new entrants by Coca-Cola, Inc.'s ability to erect barriers to entry, and by its fierce and tenacious activity when other firms do challenge it (as well as by its competitors' missteps – but that's another book).

Entry means that a firm that previously did not make a product, and therefore was not in the market, enters the market by commencing production of the product. Barriers to entry are any means that an existing player in a market uses to deter or prevent entry by firms or individuals who may be looking at setting up a business to compete with it. Remember, if it 'looks easy' to enter a market, if there are profits in making something and if it is simple to make and sell, then firms will do it. Extensive numbers of entrants will kill profitability by increasing the supply of a good. Over the long term, the ability of companies to enter a market drives returns down to what is called the *marginal cost of capital*, which is the return that exactly pays the investor back for the risk he or she is taking (in other words, good but not great – Chapter 5 contains further discussion on the cost of capital). In the short term, returns may even fall below zero if entrants price aggressively and so eliminate profits in the industry as a whole.

For an industry where profits exist, there will be a real and immediate threat of new entrants unless barriers to entry exist. We talked about barriers to entry being a means of either preventing or deterring entry. A barrier which *prevents* entry is the best type of barrier, but it is rare. Examples of barriers which prevent entry are having a unique product (one which cannot be replicated, either now or ever), or making a product which other firms are not permitted to make or provide by law. There are few examples of a unique product that cannot be replicated. For example, the large telecom providers of the US and UK had a unique position in possessing telecom cables in the 1960s and 70s, but that product was replicable, and now there are many providers of backbone data mobility, and some providers (such as cable television companies) who have even offered direct competition in traditional telecom's last redoubt, the 'last mile' connection from switching devices to homes and households. An example of a unique product would be live appearances by a singer or entertainer – no other person or firm can replicate that (although cloning specialists are no doubt working on it). The marketing of recorded performances by singers falls into the second category – competitors to the licensed provider of recording are not allowed by law. If firms obey the law, entry should be prevented. Another classic example of a barrier to entry which prevents entry is to have a patented product. An example of this is a patented drug or medicine. These patents provide extremely effective barriers to entry, and given the high demand for life-saving or enhancing medicines, drug companies produce very high, sustained profits. Another example of a barrier to entry is to have a piece of software or hardware on which a firm has *copyright* or *patent* protection. This may prevent entry; although in the example of Intel's microprocessors, AMD was able to compete by emulating the functions of the Intel microprocessors (functions like adding, branching and binary shifting could not be patented), but using different underlying circuitry to Intel's patented circuitry.

Far more common are barriers which make entry *difficult*. They deter entry but do not prevent it, making it a less certain or certainly less profitable proposition. In the example of Coca-Cola, these barriers to entry are things like the taste of Coca-Cola, the brand of Coca-Cola, the scale of operation required to make Coca-Cola concentrate, and the relationships with bottlers, retailers and other business partners. Because potential competitors would have to emulate the formulation that provides the taste of the soft drink, and do that on a scale that would make it profitable, entry into this marketplace is much more difficult. It is harder to be sure that one will make a profit, and sure that the profit would not be as big as it would be if there were no barriers to entry.

Let's look at the more general principles, and then let's drill back down to the example we are concerned with, that of Amazon.com and specifically the online book-retailing business.

As a starting point, Porter identifies six generic types of barrier to entry that exist:

1. economies of scale (including economies of scope)
2. cost advantages other than due to scale (for example lower costs due to learning)
3. product differentiation (for example, branding and product features)
4. capital requirements
5. switching costs
6. government policy.

Finally, if there is a credible threat of retaliation, this may also deter entrants.

Unfortunately for book retailers, few of these entry barriers exist in book retailing, and the ability to erect entry barriers has diminished due to the internet. Economies of scale and the related issue of capital requirements are somewhat important. Amazon.com has invested large sums in its distribution warehouses and customer service infrastructure. This is seen by some as an example of a *first-mover advantage*: that once Amazon had built its distribution warehouses and network, it would not be worthwhile for other firms to do so – and the 'first mover' would reign unchallenged. It may well be true that if another firm wanted to 'create an Amazon.com', this might be difficult to do. But entry into book retailing on a small scale, and especially into online book retailing, remains easy. Small firms may not be able to obtain the same prices as Amazon.com from suppliers, however. Possibly a bigger problem is that there are many other firms which do not need to build a distribution network, because they already have one! Examples include, UPS, FedEx, Wal-

Mart in the USA, and Tesco, Sainsbury, and Asda (a supermarket chain owned by Wal-Mart) in the UK.

To move on to item 5, there are no switching costs for users switching between online book stores, except for the fairly small task of setting up a new account, and typing in delivery and billing information. In fact, it would seem that the tough hurdle is to get users to make their very first order on the internet: from then on they become relatively more 'promiscuous' in their choice of partner. Switching between high street bookstores costs only the shoe leather needed to walk from one to another. Government policy does not extensively regulate bookstores; in fact they are generally seen as 'desirable' enterprises to which to give planning permission. One can imagine a council or city baulking at having too many liquor stores or off-licences in a town, but few would protest about an extra bookstore. This is bad news if one is already in the business!

Cost advantages independent of scale are not particularly important for internet-based book retailing. Amazon has attempted to patent some of its e-commerce engine technology, with limited success. The issue of cost advantage by learning cuts both ways. While Amazon has gained experience and has been a trail-blazer, how much of this experience has given the firm a sustainable competitive advantage? Many of the expensive lessons Amazon has learned are now incorporated in off-the-shelf e-commerce packages that can be bought by firms for relatively small sums.

The main barrier that can be built up in book retailing is brand and differentiation. This can be a powerful barrier to entry, but it is very difficult to build. Think about Coke, McDonalds and Marlboro. Then try to think of other examples of brands that are so strong. Barnes and Noble and Borders in the USA have now both rolled out large numbers of large, roomy bookstores, ideal for browsing and most likely having a coffee shop in store. However, if we were to blindfold an observer and place him or her in the middle of one of these bookstores, he or she would find it very difficult to determine which of the two he or she was in! Worse still, there is nothing to stop another firm that has existing distribution relationships rolling out another similar chain. Starbucks and Peets Coffee in the Bay Area, or Starbucks and Costa Coffee in London provide similar examples of closely comparable competitors. In travel literature, Lonely Planet has been effectively competed against by recent entry Rough Guide, despite a long history and notable expertise.

Given the difficulty of building brand and differentiating the experience, Amazon.com has done a good job. They are featured in every article or book on the internet, a source of substantial free publicity. (Incidentally, in this we are happy to be one of the crowd: most readers will have a base of knowledge about Amazon which helps leaven the discussion and form a grounding for the points we seek to make.) Also, Amazon's website has an attractive layout, is personalized to each user by detecting *cookies*[2] and provides user reviews of most books and videotapes. In this last regard, Amazon can leverage its large user base by having more reviews of each product. But there is nothing to stop the price sensitive shopper from having one window open to Amazon.com to look up book reviews, and another open to www.mysimon.com to compare book prices. Finally, and most importantly, Amazon has built up an impressive reputation for reliable fulfilment and delivery. This has proved difficult for many competitors to emulate. The key element of this is timely information. This has given rise to a well-known vignette that illustrates Amazon's ability to react to customer comment. Many emails from customers were requests for information on when their requested products were going to be dispatched. Obviously, checking on this and preparing email responses to these requests was causing a direct drag on financial performance, as well as leaving customers concerned in the interim. Amazon responded by putting a 'Where's my stuff?' link and a 'Your Account' button on most pages, which route users to a log-in page from which their account can be accessed and recent order status inspected.

The threat from new entrants is diminished by Amazon's ability to gain this good reputation, but it is not eliminated. The appearance of off-the-shelf packages which allow stores to build an online shop, has made entry to various retailing categories easier. Integration of these packages with back-end systems will enable small stores to emulate many of the Amazon.com features. For example, if a small online book retailer uses UPS to fulfil its book orders, then, provided its electronic shop application can serve the UPS tracking number to the customer when he or she logs in, the customer can then use the extensive tracking capability of the www.ups.com website to track his or her package once it has been dispatched. As discussed above, the book distributors, if they altered their business model, could enter the business of marketing books to consumers.

In summary, we would evaluate the *threat from new entrants* to Amazon as *high* (score 8 out of 10).

Industry attractiveness: bringing it all together

To gain an approximate understanding of the attractiveness of an industry, the points for each force can be added together (in this case, we would score 21 out of 50, compared to an average industry which would score 25). However, analysts should watch out for a 'showstopper' force. Think of an example niche where suppliers are weak, buyers are weak, there are no substitutes for the product, and rivalry is not intense. Very attractive; but if there was a threat of new entry, it would not remain so for long. Equally, an industry that was otherwise attractive could be 'held to ransom' by a monopoly seller of raw materials or a monopsony buyer of the product output. It would be unattractive simply because of that governing force.

In the same way, the threat of entry to book retailing (8/10) is the presiding force here, which makes the book retailing industry somewhat unattractive. However, if barriers to entry can be erected, the remaining forces are comparatively weak. Amazon's efforts to erect barriers having been somewhat successful, we have a reasonably attractive niche, but that there will be no long-run superb returns because of the residual threat of entry. Amazon's profitability will be dependent on tactical efforts and its ability to quickly change strategy and emphasis in response to market opportunities which present themselves. We are probably not looking at 'the next Microsoft'.

Other lessons from the five forces

To consider the scorecard from the five forces is interesting, indeed essential to valuation. However, to consider only this end result is to throw much away. Two key issues can also be informed by the five forces analysis:

- how industry attractiveness is likely to change
- how industry players should aim their strategies.

Change in industry attractiveness

We mentioned the issue of change in a couple of places: it is time to bring them together and to consider their effect in future strategy and therefore valuation. The two main areas in which the strategic position is likely to undergo major change are in rivalry and in the threat of substitutes. There is also a possibility of change (deterioration) in the area of power of suppliers. It is interesting to note that the threat of new entrants determines the future path of rivalry, together with the propensity of existing players to exit, and that is indeed the case here. With the likelihood that the threat of entry into book retailing will continue, rivalry will remain intense. The short-term path of rivalry will be downward, however, as venture- and angel-funded online competitors go bankrupt and exit the marketplace.

The main issue in the threat to substitutes is the possible improvement in e-book technology. This is extremely unpredictable. The path of technology is the most predictable element; e-book readers will become lighter, better and cheaper. The key imponderable is whether users will adopt them. Certainly, the effect on the threat of substitutes of these developments will be to increase the force against players, by what quantum remains to be seen.

The effect of discontinuities was hinted at by the 1998 proposal by Barnes and Noble to take over the largest book distributor, Ingram Books. This proposal (abandoned in 1999, after pressure from small independent booksellers who were arguably even more vulnerable to such a move than Amazon) had the potential to put Amazon's supply chain under some threat, or at the very least to complicate matters. This illustrates that the book distribution industry, being somewhat concentrated, may provide a more intense threat in the future.

Using the five forces to help aim strategy

Once the five forces have been evaluated, the underlying analysis can be a useful guide in helping the firm position itself. We should consider not just the fact that strong rivalry and threat of entry are the key problems in book retailing, but also the underlying issues that cause these forces to be strong. Can we mitigate these forces? Can we lay plans that will defend us in case they deteriorate further?

In the case of rivalry, Amazon's sensible strategy has been to eliminate rivals by partnering with them, helping them out of the market while enabling them to save face, save some margins, and meanwhile channel some piece of the pie Amazon's way. This has been the case in the partnership with Waterstone's in the UK and, outside books, in the partnership with ToysRUs in the USA toy-retailing industry.

In the case of the threat of new entrants, the prevention of the threat will come from erecting barriers to entry, primarily brand and reputation. These barriers, although difficult to build and not always very strong (especially when ranged against offline players who may already have existing brand-names) are 'the only game in town' for many B2C businesses. Amazon will also try to attract businesses considering entry or expanding their current businesses, to follow the Waterstone's 'partnering' model. Finally, while the company's current healthy cash balance persists, this will help to deter large-scale pure-play internet entrants. However, these latter potential entrants do not seem to be the main problem right now.

In order to mitigate potential threats from substitutes, Amazon is attempting to be the source of choice for e-book files and e-book readers. This is an excellent strategy, which largely negates the threat from e-books, or at least ensures that Amazon will be one of the less damaged competitors, should the e-book 'revolution' come to pass. In order to mitigate against threats from suppliers exerting negotiating power over Amazon and the book retailing business as a whole,

Amazon is cultivating relationships with a wide range of distributors, as well as maintaining contacts with publishers. The company's corporate accounts feature (introduced in summer 2001) addresses the needs of its more powerful buyers.

KEY ELEMENTS OF THE INTERNAL STRUCTURE OF THE CORPORATION

Given the level of industry attractiveness, what parts of the corporation are the most important? Michael Porter has also proposed another framework, the *value chain*, for structuring the study of company functions and for studying how individual companies in an industry fit together and where value is created. This model is introduced and extensively discussed by Michael Porter (1985, 1998).

We saw an example of an industry-level value chain earlier in the chapter. We will return to the industry-level value chain analysis in the following section. The format for firm-level value chain analysis is that firm operations are split into five primary activities, whereby product is received, handled, shipped, sold and serviced; and four 'support' activities, which provide the firm with the base of technology and other infrastructure that it needs to perform its primary activities. These are listed below in Table 12.1.

Firm-level value-chain analysis is instructive for internet companies, especially companies such as Amazon.com which handle physical product and so have clearly recognizable *inbound logistics* (receiving) and *outbound logistics* (picking, packing and dispatch) functions.

The usefulness of the value chain is to focus study of the company's resources (human physical and intangible) on key areas. The model gives a checklist of the main areas in any company's business. Some of these will be more important than others in any business. In particular, in an internet business, which is characterized by higher fixed costs and operating leverage, the support functions are likely to be more important than they are for a 'traditional' firm. By studying Amazon's value chain, we will understand not only this company, but also other e-commerce companies which share features with it.

Table 12.1 Value chain analysis

Primary activities	Support activities
Inbound logistics	Firm infrastructure
Operations	HR management
Outbound logistics	Technology development
Marketing and sales service	Procurement

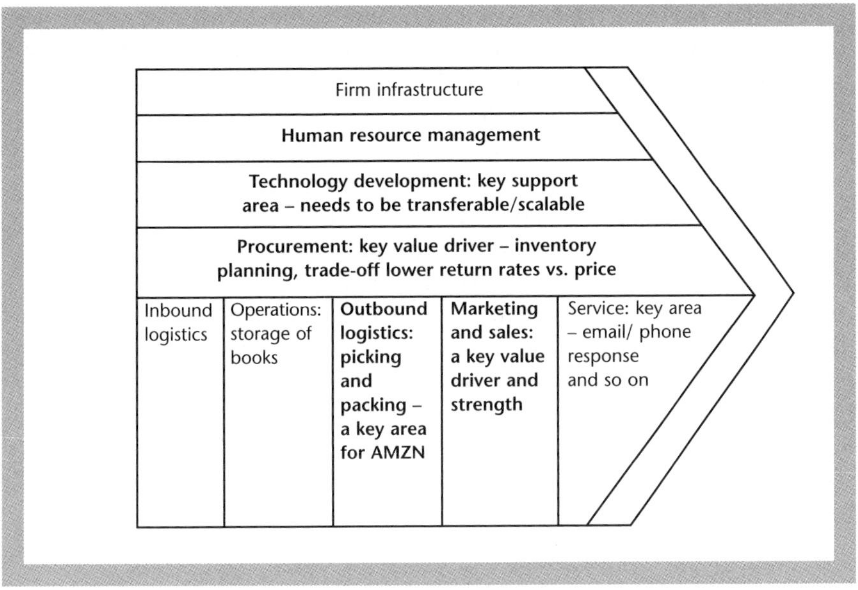

Figure 12.2 Amazon.com's value chain

Source: (Diagram format) Reprinted by permission of Free Press (Simon & Schuster) from *Competitive Advantage: Creating and Sustaining Superior Performance*, by Michael E. Porter. New York, 1985, p. 37. Copyright © 1985 by the Free Press, all rights reserved.

In Figure 12.2 we show a value chain for Amazon.com, highlighting the more important areas of the value chain. As for a traditional retailer, the *procurement* function is key. As discussed in Chapter 4, Amazon's original model was to minimize inventory or stockholdings, so that it would have little or no returns (unsold books returned for credit to the publisher). This should translate into lower purchasing costs – in this model, once books are sold to Amazon, they 'stay sold', because a customer order already exists. For low-demand books, Amazon still executes this model and procurement policies must elicit savings to reflect this in purchase price.

For many books Amazon has had to adopt the traditional model of stocking these books in its own inventory. For this model, the company has something of an advantage, because it needs to ship returns only from one central location back to the publisher. It should be noted that the problems of inventory control are considerably more severe in some other areas of Amazon's business. The company has to take irrevocable title to many toys and other products which it may stock. Because of disappointing demand for certain goods, the company had to take a writedown of $39m against inventory in the fourth quarter of 2000.

The other problem which inventory planning must deal with, apart from too *much* inventory, is too *little* inventory – that is, the problem of stocking out. As an example, Amazon's reported 350,020 advance orders for Harry Potter Book 4 (*The Goblet of Fire*) were the largest advance orders ever recorded. The procurement function had to build relationships with publishers to ensure supplies of this large quantity of a book that was in great demand.

Of the other support functions, technology development is the most important. 'Technology and content' costs accounted for 10% of Amazon's sales in 1999 and 2000. Technology development is intimately tied in with human resources. At the time when Amazon was building its e-commerce platform, demand exceeded supply for programmers of the calibre required to 'trail-blaze' in building the software. Technology development remains important because Amazon is continuing to enhance its website, and is also leveraging its technology expertise by forming partnerships with AOL, ToysRUs and Waterstone's. In these partnerships, technology expertise, to some extent, is directly being sold. Technology needs to be scalable (with increasing volume) and transferable (across product lines and marketing models, as well as across national boundaries).

Now we move on to the primary functions, such as inbound logistics, operations, sales, and service. Since the process of order-taking, order-tracking and payment is largely automated, operations is a small part of the picture – operations procedures are performed by the system that has been created under the technology development function. This is somewhat typical of a retail organization. Outbound logistics, which the *customer* takes care of in a traditional retail store (!), is a far more important part of the value chain for Amazon. In total, 'fulfilment' costs have accounted for 10–15% of sales for Amazon – cost control and performance in this part of the business is key. Fulfilment is described as 'those costs incurred in operating and staffing our fulfillment and customer service centers, including costs attributable to receiving, inspecting and warehousing inventories; picking, packaging and preparing customers' orders for shipment; credit card fees; and responding to inquiries from customers'. This is quite a broad list of activities, some of which might be included in cost of sales for many retail businesses, but which are included in selling, general and administrative cost by Amazon.

The other important primary activities are service and marketing. The marketing operation is concerned with gauging demand for products and promoting them. The company must plan its offerings of free shipping and the like, and must expand its advertising and partnering when demand slackens. Amazon, unlike many dot-com companies, has stuck mainly to using online methods for paid promotion. It has relied upon free publicity, for example interviews with Jeff Bezos, and the fixation of authors like ourselves, to gain most of its media coverage. It did air a somewhat zany TV commercial before Christmas 2000. In terms of online promotion, the company currently has an associates program whereby even small websites can earn 15% of sales if they refer customers directly to a book which the customer then buys, and 5% of any other sales that customer makes in that session. It seems likely that this program will be made less generous at some point, since this eats away much of the margin on these purchases, and many potential customers have been introduced to the company at this point. The firm also makes extensive use of banner ads. Since Amazon is a direct sales channel, its main concern is click-through rates and sales per clickthrough. Clickthroughs for banner ads have declined, as we will discuss in Chapter 14, which decreases the effectiveness of Amazon's strategy. However, banner ad prices have also fallen, and will continue to fall, providing a countervailing effect.

Service is a key differentiating factor for Amazon.com. There are two issues for the company, shared by most other e-commerce firms:

- respond to customer issues
- if the issue is a common one, automate it.

With some small exceptions, Amazon has adopted a 'The customer is always right' policy, with generous returns terms and responsive customer service. This could become a cripplingly expensive policy if not automated. Amazon automates order status enquiries, and aggressively draws users' attention to the relevant links, to head off customer queries before they take up expensive human resources. The company's proactive emails confirming when orders are received and dispatched are a further example. What about returns? Automation of returns, which the Amazon website allows, has at least two results. First, there can be little doubt that it increases the percentage of returned products compared to sales. Given the choice, people who are returning a product would rather not contend with making excuses to a human as to why the product is no longer wanted. However, the other result is that the process of receiving returns, being automated until the unavoidable physical activity of actually receiving the returned product, is far cheaper for the firm.

There are other results of a liberal exchange policy, which are not so easily calculated but are potentially of great benefit. One benefit is the increase in confidence of the shopper. This may in turn lead to more revenues from specific shoppers, and also reinforcement of the company's reputation by positive word-of-mouth. *Positive word-of-mouth* is one of the most powerful marketing communications.

Bringing it all together from this discussion of Amazon.com's value chain is not as straightforward as summarizing our discussion of the five forces in the previous section. The value chain gives us a framework to discuss Amazon's organization, to draw out lessons from the company's experience, and to prioritize areas for change. However, in the absence of companies with very similar business models (especially ones with positions in the same number of markets as Amazon), it is not easy to quantify how much better the company is than other companies.

The value chain of an industry

As discussed above, Figure 12.1 shows the value chain of the book publishing industry, from publisher to user (reader). This type of industry-level value chain can be very helpful, because for a product with healthy demand from the end user, there are almost invariably profit opportunities, unless the product is a commodity or can be made into one. This is not the case for books, so it is likely that at some point in the value chain there are profit opportunities. The way to proceed in analysing where those profit opportunities are is to carry out five forces analysis on each of the niches – that is, to commence a five forces analysis for printers, then move to one for publishers, and so on. The key issue is where value is being extracted, and this is likely to be in the part of the value chain that has the most benign environment in terms of the five forces.

One shortcut which may be useful in some industries is to ask oneself who has the proprietary assets or, if there are no proprietary assets, the scarce resources. In this case the answer is clear. If we want to buy the latest John Grisham, we can go to whichever bookstore we prefer. The bookstore can order it from a choice of distributors. But the distributors have to order it from one publisher (who can get it printed wherever he or she likes). Once an agreement to acquire the publishing rights has been obtained, the publisher possesses those rights exclusively in the territory and over the time specified. The benefit of extra demand not anticipated in the rights agreement (net of the royalty payment) will go to the publisher.

This is a shortcut, so let us briefly check the five forces for publishing.

■ Power of buyers	Distributors – medium (4), decreasing (threat of disintermediation)
■ Power of suppliers	Authors, printers – weak (2), author power increasing
■ Rivalry	Gentlemanly (2), increasing
■ Threat of substitutes	Low (1)
■ Threat of new entrants	Medium (5)

These are quite weak. It is worth noting at this point that our omission of the authors as suppliers to the publishers may make our analysis somewhat incomplete, especially in the current environment. Typically authors have been a disparate group of individuals, without the ability to exert power against publishers. However, some leading agents, for example Martin Amis's agent Andrew Wylie, have begun to exert that power on authors' behalf. This increased return to the creative talent or star performer is similar to changes in patterns of value extraction in the movie and sports businesses led by, respectively, Michael Ovitz's Creative Artists Agency and Mark McCormack's IMG.

At this point the reader may be saying: 'All very interesting, but I thought this was a book about internet valuation?' The reason for the slight digression is to make this point: look for industries or niches in which the firm being evaluated can exert power by holding a proprietary or scarce asset. It is no accident that many of the most attractive internet-related business models still achieving high valuations are ones which are developing patented hardware or copyrightable software. These proprietary assets can create *choke points* in an industry – buyers have to use your system to fulfil their role in their own value chain. However, we must be realistic. B2B exchanges thought they could act as choke points for vast quantities of B2B sales and purchases. But they forgot one thing. They forgot about the other B2B exchanges.

THE PRODUCT LIFE CYCLE

The *product life cycle* is a stylized picture of the evolution of the market for a good or service. Intuitively, we understand that products go through phases in which pricing, volume and profitability are different. Initially, the product is in development, and little or no money may be made out of it at that stage. Then the product is initially released to the marketplace. At this stage there are only likely to be small quantities available, and prices are likely to be high. The next stage is the mass market release, where the market is mature and large quantities of the product are released at prices 'normal people' can afford. Finally maturity and decline of the market occurs: the product is commonplace and is probably a utility item, and is priced appropriately. This generic product life cycle is illustrated in Figure 12.3.

We can see from the diagram that early losses in an industry can be a normal part of the evolution of a market. However, the key issue in analysing internet firms is detecting when the market for the good has left the introductory stage (where we expect losses) and reached the later part of the rapid growth stage (where we expect profits). If a product is still in the introductory phase, more funding or development may help it to be profitable. However, if

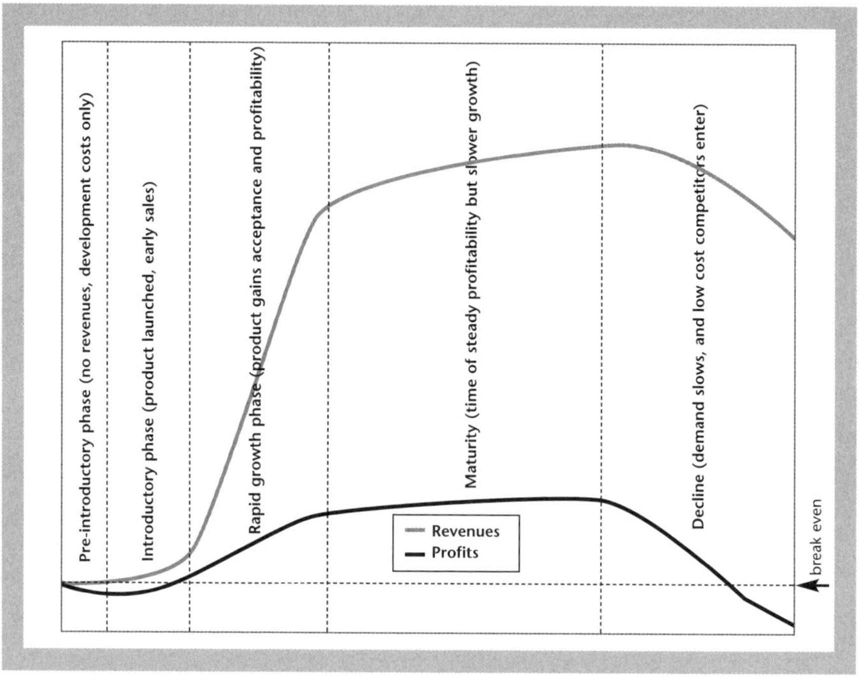

Figure 12.3 The generic product life cycle

a product is still unprofitable when it has entered the rapid growth phase, it may never be profitable. Therefore a key piece of information we can use in assessing internet business models is any guideline on how long the introductory stage of a product will last.

Characteristics of long and short introductory phase products

The length of the introductory period and the ultimate profitability of the business are different issues. For example, the microwave oven took two decades to gain acceptance (a very long introductory period) but is now a profitable product. A computer game disk has little or no problem gaining initial acceptance and trial but, if unattractive to gamers, may nevertheless be unprofitable in the long run.

The following guidelines to detect products with a short introductory phase are by McCarty and Perrault (1997):

- a greater comparative advantage of the product over those available (also influences total value)

Table 12.2 Products with a short introductory phase: a comparison

Parameter	**Internet stock trading**		**PC/web calendar applications**	
Comparative advantage	High	8	Uncertain	5
Ease of use	Moderate	3	Low/medium	4
Can communicate benefits	High	8	High	8
Ease of trial	High	8	Low	2
Fit with consumer values	High	9	Low/medium	4

- the product is easy to use
- benefits are easy to communicate
- a low or limited cost trial is available
- the product fits with consumer values and experiences.

Let us consider a couple of examples to see how these concepts work. The first example is internet stock trading (compared to phone-based trading) and the second is PC-based web calendars for executives (compared to keeping a diary). See Table 12.2.

Note how important it is to encourage *trial*. Trying out the service is how demand is generated, and how positive word-of-mouth eventually gets started. It is hard to trial PC-based calendar applications because there is no point having 'half a calendar': when the switch from paper to PC is made, the user's entire calendar has to be entered into the system. On the other hand, internet stock traders can try a couple of trades without having to enter data on their whole portfolio. Also, they can browse through the research data on the stock trading system without making a trade, and this easily available data is one of the best features of the online stock trading systems. Finally, the issue of consumer values should not be neglected. Many of the advantages of web/intranet calendaring services is that other company employees (for example, the boss) can have access to employees' diaries, and can enter and inspect appointments. While this may be a comparative advantage for the *employer*, it may not fit in with the *executive's* values and his or her desire for control. By contrast, the extra data availability on internet stock trading systems, and the ability on most systems to watch the market before individually placing trades in real time, is very appealing to stock traders. It appeals to their desire for control and to their self-confidence that if they can time their trades and base them on their own painstaking analysis, then they will do well. This therefore fits well with their values – even though, as Barber and Odean (2000) suggest, their self-confidence is often illusory – and is another reason why the introductory or adoption period of internet stock trading services was extremely short.

It is interesting to note that, during 2001–2002 many internet stock trading firms, having been through a period of profitability, have encountered financial difficulties. This is because a downturn in stock trading, caused by the downturn in the market, has limited demand for their services. A short period to maturity is not a guarantee of profitability. In fact, a quickly maturing market at a time of oversupply of capital such as 1999–early 2000 was a red rag to a bull, and caused the establishment of perhaps too many players in online stock trading. The point is that, in the case of online stock trading or any similar quick-maturing business, if the business has not demonstrated profitability in about a year, further investment is likely to be 'throwing good money after bad'. In the event that there are convincing reasons that the product might be expected to have a longer introductory period, then even if there is not yet profitability, further investment should be considered. But the long-term comparative advantage needs to be evaluated carefully, to ensure that there is a reasonable chance of consumers adopting the technology. There also needs to be an estimate of what the best revenue model is, and how much users are willing to pay for the functionality. In the case of the web calendaring service, it seems that consumers' need for the service is low, so their willingness to *pay* should be low (this may be slightly different for users with portable devices). An intranet-based service for firms (with the concomitant need for greater security and varying levels of permissioning) is likely to be the most attractive model, and bundling with workflow products as a software licence or sale seems to be the desired route to buy the service.

STRATEGY: BEYOND PORTER ANALYSIS

The frameworks we have discussed are useful and enduring, but they hold some danger because of the confidence they give us. Our friend, the London Business School's Ken Simmonds, an accomplished strategist in his own right, has a favourite saying that 'Strategy isn't Porter' and of course he is right. From our point of view as analysts, a Porter analysis may be a good starting point, but we will expect company management not just to conduct analysis, but to fight a war on many fronts, eliminating adversaries (when the law allows), capturing customers, growing their territory (niches) and anticipating and defending itself against competitors' moves. Evaluating top management as warriors, and evaluating what type of warrior is needed for this stage of what now seems like a long conflict, are important tasks. For example, in 1997–98 an evangelist like Jeff Bezos was the right leader: a believer, someone who would not be put off by the pooh-poohing of sceptics. During 2001–2002, for example, with the recruitment of Terry Semel to lead Yahoo! in May 2001, we see an emphasis on cost control and profitability. Also, returning to the issue of strategic frameworks, it should be noted that in a rapidly changing environment, any strategic analysis needs to be frequently revisited, and changes in the marketplace incorporated into it.

VALUING AMAZON: WEIGHTING THE SCENARIOS

We now return to complete the valuation of Amazon using the strategic analysis (SA) from this chapter.

In weighting between the land grab (BCA) and wasteland (WCA) scenarios, we consider the strength of the five forces, and whether these give Amazon a specific advantage that will enable the company to protect a high return on capital such as 30%. Particularly important are:

- barriers to entry
- strength of brand
- technological advantages
- competitors in the marketplace.

In looking at the overall weighting of the scenarios, we have to consider both books and the other markets Amazon is in, and how competitive these markets are. Amazon is dominant online in books and music, but these cate-

Table 12.3 Amazon.com: final valuation

	Continuing case (CCA)	Best case (BCA)	Worst case (WCA)
Revenue growth	12%	20%	7%
Variable costs as % of sales	88.5%	88.5%	90.5%
Fixed costs	$340m	$340m	$340m
Operating assets as % of sales	0%	0%	0%
Equity value (unconstrained)	$3.6bn	$9.4bn	$0.6bn
Limit RoCE to	30%	30%	15%
Equity value (final)	$3.1bn	$3.7bn	$0.6bn
Weighting	**60%**	**10%**	**30%**
Weighted equity value	**$2.4bn**		

gories have slow growth. The company's other categories (auctions, consumer electronics, toys) have a number of competitive players. In view of the uncertain prospects for the economy, but combined with Amazon's good performance in cost cutting in recent periods and the increase in profitable services revenues, we view the slow-growth-continuing case as most likely at 60% (Table 12.3). The worst case, where growth continues to be slow but cost structure stays the same as current or slightly deteriorates, we rate as 30% probable. The best case is least likely at 10%, because the high revenue growth is unlikely to be supported by the company's recent low marketing spend. The final valuation of Amazon is, therefore, $2.4bn (plus $61m of real option value as discussed in Chapter 8 under Step 3).

DISCONTINUITY ANALYSIS (DCA)

Detailed analysis of potential discontinuities should be conducted. Since discontinuities are by their nature unexpected and uncertain, precise valuation implications may not be determinable. However, indications of where potential discontinuities may lie are still of interest to potential investors. *Analysis of discontinuities should be integrated into the wider SA (strategic analysis) process.*

In the case of Amazon, potential discontinuities include:

- economic slowdown
- security scares in online purchasing
- change in Amazon's strategy (e.g. if Amazon concentrates only on books)
- acquisition of key suppliers.

Notes

1 Pure play firms are companies which do business only on the internet.

2 Cookies are 'client-side persistent state files' which record basic user identification information on the user's machine. They are managed by the browser (usually Netscape Navigator, Internet Explorer, AOL or Opera) which allows a website access to the 'cookies' it created, so the website can tell who is logging on. They are so-called because they are small files, and one can imagine them being stored in an electronic cookie jar or biscuit jar. Many commentators feel that there are potential privacy problems with cookies: for example, if you log into Amazon.com from a colleague's machine, the website will serve you up recommendations tailored to him or her (which could conceivably be embarrassing). However, sensible websites will not give you access to his or her credit card (which could be costly!).

CHAPTER 13

Assessing the New-Economy Models

IS THE NEW NEW STUFF OLD HAT?

There cannot be many students of internet valuation who haven't heard of *network effects* and perhaps of *Metcalfe's Law* which describes them: 'The value of a network rises in the square of the number of users'. This 'law' was proposed as a reason for many high valuations of internet companies. If one couldn't see the value, never mind. The network effects would be along soon, and this mysterious source of value would justify the stock prices. We call it the 'Field of Dreams' approach to valuation.

However, Metcalfe's Law is simply a way of saying that the greater the number of people who communicate by some method or network, the more useful that method is to them. The key words there are 'to them'. As we said in the last chapter, the process of competitive advantage usually results in most or all of the benefit from advances going to the *consumer*. Rather than being in a benign Metcalfian world where building a 'network' is all that's necessary to capture substantial value, we're in the same old world, where we still have to get people to pay for our product, and we still have to be aware that if we do not price it competitively, then someone else will. Is there a network effect? Of course ... but it cannot be relied upon to deliver value to firms, unless their competitive strategy is sound enough to capture it.

While few 'laws' were misinterpreted as badly as Metcalfe's Law, many new-economy terms are now reaching their 'sell by' date. Who remembers valuation on the basis of $ per 'websteader'? Or the tendency of strategy writers to coin a new strategic metric by prefixing a word with an 'e'? Here we survey some of the strategic frameworks which have been most commonly discussed, and assess whether they can help us to explain and understand the road ahead. Here is the list of issues we will discuss:

- the tendency towards disaggregation of product and data
- the decrease in the importance of the richness versus reach trade-off
- changing from a value chain to a value web
- customer-time economics
- frameworks for consumer propensity to buy
- eliminating the value-subtracting intermediary
- the network effect: when it works and when it does not
- the auction economy
- chameleonization.

DISAGGREGATION OF PRODUCT AND DATA

In their 2000 book, *Blown to Bits*, Evans and Wurster have a very interesting discussion of the way in which universal connectivity via the internet enables businesses to deliver their products in new ways. In the old economy, we are used to receiving bundles of information and physical product ('things') from businesses. Think about the car salesman, who gives us data on the specification of the car, as well as arranging physical delivery of it. A newspaper is a similar proposition, where information (words) is combined with a physical carrier (paper).

What the internet allows is for the *information* to flow from business to consumer in the cheapest possible way, and for an *entirely separate delivery mechanism* to be set up for the physical good, independent of the need to convey information. For example, car salesrooms are expensive, attractive buildings which are designed with twin, somewhat incompatible aims: to present and convey information about the product, and to store and convey the product. In a new-economy model, company websites can convey all of the information the consumer may need about the car, but storage and delivery can take place by the cheapest means, or by the consumer picking the car up from a nearby depot. It appeared that, as Evans and Wurster put it, 'Car dealers are sitting ducks'.

It should be noted that this increasing disaggregation is not a trend entirely dependent on the internet, but it has been speeded up by the internet. For example, car magazines and consumer guides have for a long time been an ancillary source of data for the car buyer, a source not associated with the physical source of the good. Another issue is that the 'poster child' business model for this strategic trend, that of B2C car retailing, has not yet proved to be successful. Some of the well-funded firms executing the model in the USA have exited the business. For example, iMotors (the name has been relaunched by Next Phase media), which received a reported $139m in venture funding, closed in April 2001; and greenlight.com, which counted Amazon.com as one of its funding backers, was bought by CarsDirect.com in February 2001 (which planned, according to Associated Press, in effect to close it down). Just as in the case of B2B exchanges, the 'invisible' benefits of the old way still exerted a strong pull on consumers. Also a test drive is still an important source of data for car buyers, and one cannot do that on the web. At any rate, the 'ducks' are still sitting there, for now at least.

The situation has been a little better for B2C car retailers in the UK. This is because car manufacturers have extracted premiums from British car buyers for some time, a practice which is only now starting to be eroded. Internet car retailers, by obtaining cars on the mainland of Europe, can offer a price benefit to buyers, while there is no parallel advantage for online car retailers in the USA.

While shakeout in the car retailing business may be a long-term process (Evans and Wurster note that the commitment of manufacturers to the dealers may significantly delay their demise), some current examples of using the internet as a competitive weapon can be seen. Certainly, car firms and car retailers see the web as a way of helping to lock in consumers. For example, Ford sees its internet strategy as important in gaining a greater share of the after-market parts, maintenance and resale market. Many car company main dealers offer website services where car owners can keep a record of their car's mileage, and maintenance and other data. This benefits the consumer as he or she can gather data more easily when the time comes to sell the car. The benefit for the company is that the website can then send the driver reminders of periodic service appointments. The service appointment is a major selling opportunity for the dealer, enabling him or her not only to sell non-routine maintenance and enhancements, but also to get the consumer near to the new and used car stock once every three months. However, this trend is not particularly associated with disaggregation of data and things. It is illustrative of how old-economy firms have been using the internet for marketing purposes.

DECREASE IN IMPORTANCE OF THE RICHNESS VERSUS REACH TRADE-OFF

Evans and Wurster also identify a trade-off which is important in the old economy, but less so with the presence of universal connectivity. In the old economy, it is expensive, in terms of marginal cost, to offer the customer a 'rich' customer experience. A *rich* experience requires human interaction to tailor the experience to the consumer, and to respond to his or her needs and requests. To look at an example, consider stock trading before the advent of the internet. Large-volume traders could access a personal broker, who would give them whatever information or advice they required, and 'hold their hand' during trades. However, this was an expensive service, and only available to a few traders whose commissions could support the cost. For the majority of traders, the most cost-effective way of trading was through a discount, execution-only broker. This is a non-rich experience, but one which is available to a large volume of users – a large reach. This trade-off can be seen in Figure 13.1.

In the old economy, businesses could only move along the frontier shown as a line in the diagram. If you want reach, richness must fall: a richer interface can only be offered to a smaller reach of consumers. However, if we use a web interface it becomes far cheaper (in marginal cost terms) to supply the user with extra information. Because of this, the internet changes the economics of stock trading. For the same or a lower marginal cost as the execution-only broker, the internet-based stock broker can offer a rich, customized interface. This includes updates on how his or her portfolio is performing, and access to

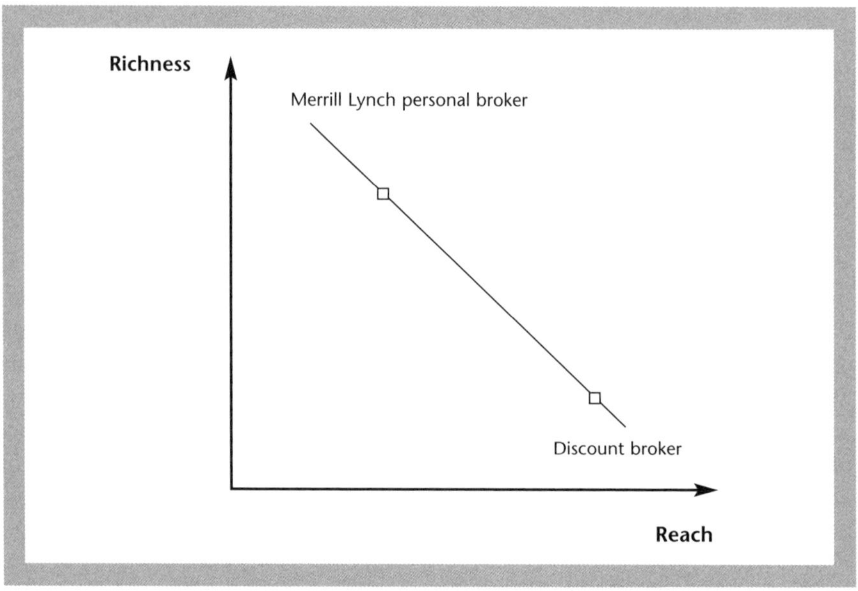

Figure 13.1 Richness vs. reach trade-off

Source: (Adapted) Reprinted by permission of Harvard Business School Press from *Blown to Bits* by Philip Evans and Thomas Wurster. Bostson, MA 2000, p. 76. Copyright © 2000 by the Harvard Business School Publishing Corporation, all rights reserved

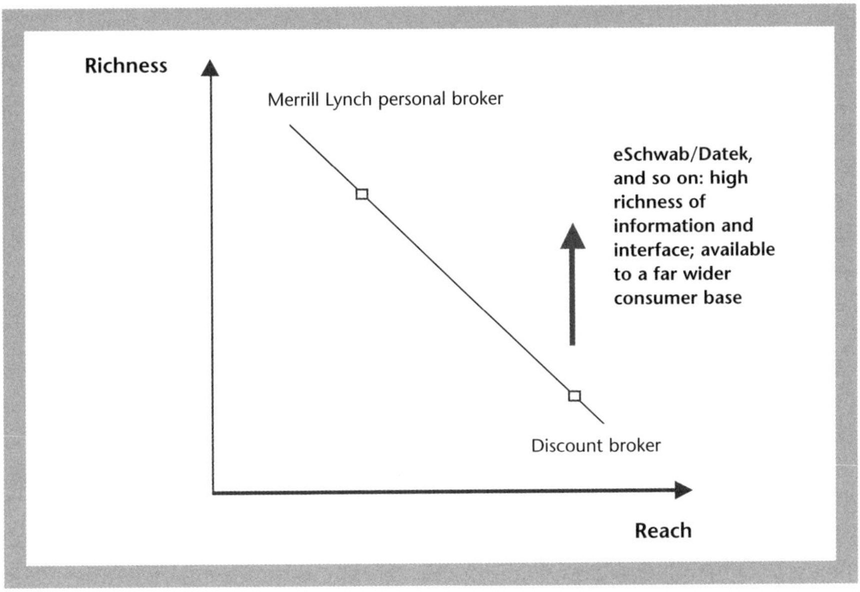

Figure 13.2 Richness vs. reach: use of internet interfaces

Source: (Adapted) Reprinted by permission of Harvard Business School Press from *Blown to Bits* by Philip Evans and Thomas Wurster. Bostson, MA 2000, p. 76. Copyright © 2000 by the Harvard Business School Publishing Corporation, all rights reserved

research and other financial data. Figure 13.2 illustrates how this transforms the competitive environment.

The breakdown of this traditional trade-off will lead to opportunities for new and existing businesses, and to an enhanced customer experience.

THE VALUE CHAIN AND THE VALUE WEB

The traditional *value chain* is a straightforward linear set of relationships. Communications between parties generally flow through the chain, either in the same direction as the product or in the opposite direction. These communications are often facilitated by intermediaries. Figure 13.3 illustrates such communications for the metals industry.

However, with enhanced ease of communication, and especially with the ability to automate communication between databases of various market players, the picture gets more complex. We can envisage a *value web* in which information flows, not via the chain, but to wherever it is needed. Ideally, there should be less need for *intermediaries*. Figure 13.4 illustrates this, with arrows representing the flow of information.

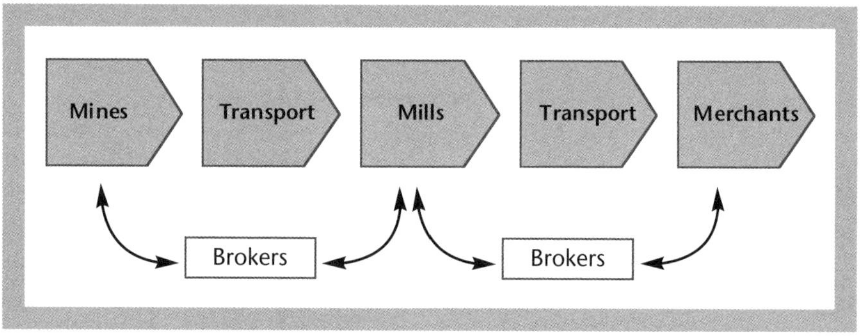

Figure 13.3 Communications within the metals industry via the value chain

In this framework, if the customers' needs are for a certain type of steel reinforcement bar, perhaps of a non-standard length or thickness, this information can be communicated directly to the mill. Similarly, if merchants see a slowdown in demand, this can be communicated not only to the merchant's neighbour in the value chain, but also to the mine, if such a slowdown is expected to continue for such time. It should be noted that, in the old economy, there was

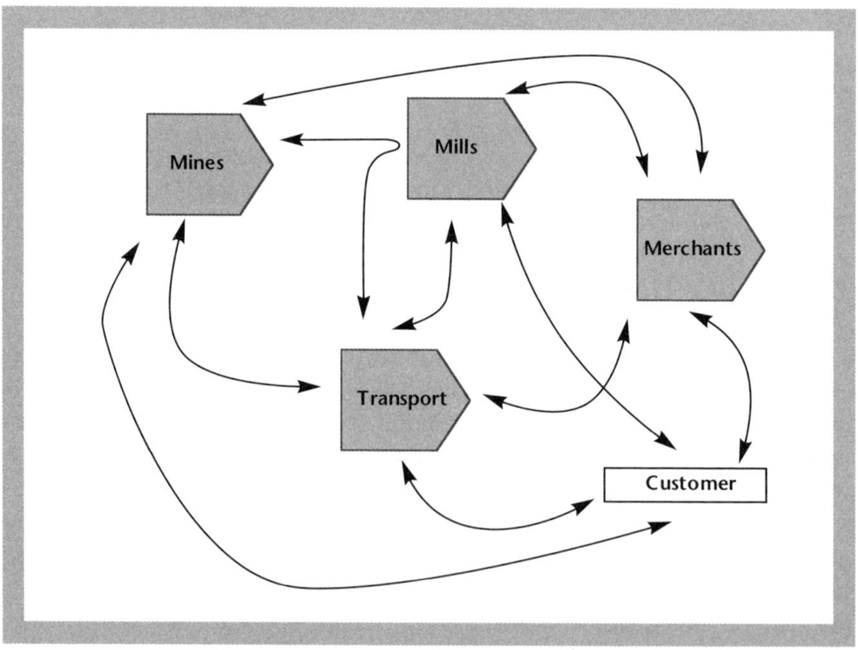

Figure 13.4 Communications within the metals industry via the value web

nothing to stop people from 'picking up the phone', but the internet makes it easier to get systems talking to each other, and to automate communications. For example, purchase orders from customers can not only feed into orders at the merchant, but can also set off an *information cascade* so that aggregated demand data is communicated instantly to mills and mines. This facilitates *real-time supply-chain management* (*SCM*), which we will discuss further in Chapter 20.

Note that in Figure 13.4 we have eliminated brokers from the diagram. Arguably the merchant is also an intermediary, but has been retained in the diagram because the merchant's ability to hold inventory close to customers and to carry a variety of products *adds value*, especially for smaller customers. In general, intermediaries who simply act as conduits for customer orders are threatened by *universal connectivity*, which makes the job of communicating easier and simpler to automate. Added-value intermediaries, who not only act as a postbox but actually add significant expertise and value over and above their costs to customers, will still be able to find a role. All brokers in industries are possessed of expertise, but the market knowledge and industry experience they bring to bear has to outweigh the commission they charge, once customers have the opportunity to trade direct, via a B2B exchange, or at the online site of the metal supplier.

The value web also has implications for the organization of corporations. According to the insights of Coase and Williamson,[1] corporations exist to minimize transaction or interaction costs. One aspect of this is that related tasks are best and most cheaply done 'under one roof'. However, with much cheaper and more flexible connectivity, companies no longer need to locate related functions together. Examples of this are offshore remote processing by banks and financial institutions. Credit-card email and telephone enquiries can be forwarded seamlessly to countries such as India, where low cost of living is combined with a large base of educated workers. This movement is not confined to financial institutions, with airlines and other firms transferring administrative functions to offshore locations. British Airways is reported to save at least £1.25m per year by moving its frequent-flier processing to Mumbai (£12,500 per employee). Clearly there is an opportunity both for corporates and for professional service firms which can assist corporates with the transition to a distributed organization.

CUSTOMER-TIME ECONOMICS: EXAMPLE OF FOOD RETAIL

Customer-time economics is a simple way of communicating the concept that some businesses are predicated on saving the customer time, and getting him or her to pay for that privilege. In its purest form this has been a disastrous model. Several internet 'concierge' services were set up, to help people by carrying out tasks (booking theatre tickets, cleaning shirts, and the like) that their busy schedule did not allow them to do, and very few of these are still in existence. Busy customers often did not want to pay to evade the problem. Customers who were *very* busy did not have time to find the webpage!

However, time saved is also relevant to electronic commerce (B2C and B2B). E-commerce companies attempt to generate trials by offering discounts, but they are also offering added convenience and time saved. Often (apart from the unavoidable delivery time delay) internet commerce businesses are selling the proposition of 'easier, faster, more convenient', or they are selling nothing. However, even if they achieve this, it's not certain that they can make money. Is *enough* time saved to cover costs? Are there competitors who can do it better/cheaper?

One example of customer-time economics is shown in D. Aldrich's book, *Mastering the Digital Marketplace* 1999. Aldrich shows the diagram in Figure 13.5, which contrasts the physical shopping process with online shopping. This is a good example of how time *can* be saved by e-commerce. However, we have to ask the economic questions that we mentioned above.

First, is *enough* time saved to cover costs? The problem with time is that it is hard to put a value on it. The people we need to talk to about valuing time are consumers – and we now know how much they are prepared to pay for this service. Zero, or perhaps up to $5 or £5 in some areas. Then let us address the costs:

- picking and packing costs (which the consumer does him- or herself in the traditional model)
- delivery costs (again, the consumer usually does this)
- the cost of infrastructure (if a pure play).

These high costs spelt a deathknell for pure-play online grocer Webvan. Also, we have not discussed the *attraction* of the existing way of doing business, which caused great problems for B2B exchanges. It is rumoured that some consumers *enjoy* grocery shopping – or at least do not dislike it so much that they want to pay to avoid it.

The next question is: are there competitors who can do it better or cheaper? In assessing the attractiveness of a standalone online grocery store, it is hard to ignore existing grocery players, especially in the UK. Existing grocery players already have an extremely efficient delivery and supply-chain system which efficiently gets produce onto the shelves. During the last two decades, UK supermarkets have decreased inventory from 20 days of revenues to about 5 days. A pure-play entrant would be unlikely to be able to achieve that level of

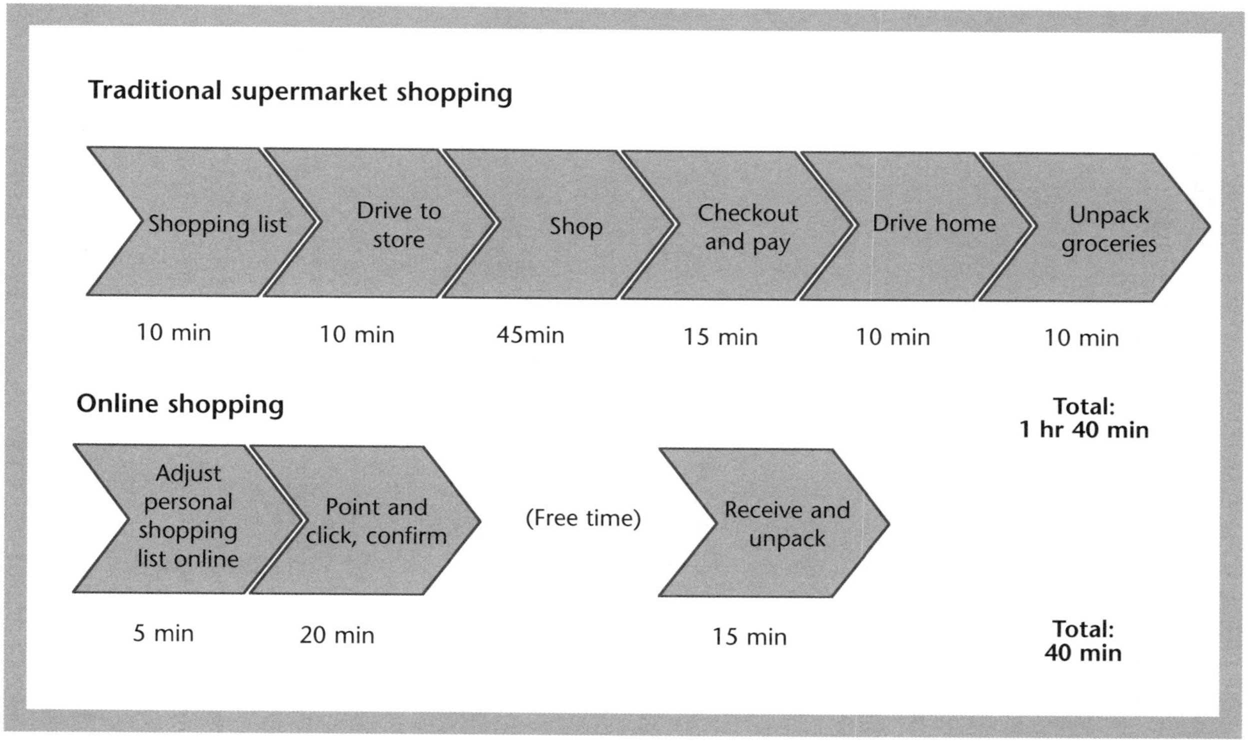

Figure 13.5 Traditional vs. online shopping

Source: Mastering the Digital Marketplace, Douglas F. Adrich, copyright © 1999. This material is used by permission of John Wiley & Sons Inc.

skill. Existing grocery players also have the potential to use time when their stores and staff are not busy (mornings and mid-afternoon weekdays) to pick and pack grocery orders. This will tend to minimize the incremental costs.

Let us look at an example, using estimated figures for Tesco Ltd,[2] a pre-eminent British supermarket. We can try to evaluate profitability at the full-cost and incremental-costs levels. Some facts about Tesco:

- largest online grocery store in the world
- 370,000 customers in 2000 (13,500 in 1999)
- lower margins for online ordering (approximately negative 3% vs. offline 5%)
- average order: £85
- cost of delivery: approximately £7.

In order to evaluate expected margins on Tesco's orders of groceries, let us study the underlying economics of the firm, as given by the company's accounting data.

The basic metrics for the year 2000 are these: revenues (£18,796m) and operating profit (£1,030m), which show a full cost margin of 5.5%. However, let us think back to our discussion of fixed and variable costs in Chapter 3. If we have some fixed costs, then we may be able to get benefit from extra revenues, provided these give us a contribution to fixed costs – that is, provided that the variable or incremental costs (the extra costs of filling this order compared with the cost if we did not) are less than the revenues. Also, the new order must not 'cannibalize' our existing orders – we will talk about this later.

For now let us consider Tesco's fixed costs and semi-fixed costs:

- fixed costs:
  - £401m administration costs
  - £428m depreciation on tangibles

  ⇒ contribution margin = 9.8%
- semi-fixed costs:
  - £1,865m staff costs

  ⇒ 'liberal CM' = 14.8%

Now let's use these margin numbers to evaluate the profitability of the £85 average order.

If we fully cost it, we expect 85 × 5.5% = £4.67 operating profit from an £85 order. Clearly a £7 delivery cost means that this is unprofitable on a full cost basis. However, if we are just looking at contribution to fixed costs, an £85 order will on average create 85 × 9.8% = £8.33 of contribution margin (store-bought). Allowing for the incremental cost of £7 for delivery, a small contribution margin of £1.33 is created even for the online order. (The economics of online ordering for Tesco has subsequently been further improved by the company's introduction of a £3.50 to £6.50 service charge for deliveries.)

The reason for discussing the staff costs as semi-fixed is that if we imagine the ideal situation in which staff are picking and packing groceries when they would otherwise be idle, the contribution margin would be even greater. However, this is not realistic. Tesco has reportedly had to increase staff to cope with the online demand. This bodes well for the performance of the online business, but suggests that staff costs cannot be treated as fixed. Also, staff are a fairly adaptable resource for a supermarket, and are seldom idle. They are used to stack shelves and to move products. In the event that staff are remaining idle, supermarkets can easily cut down the shifts of temporary staff.

We said we would return to the issue of 'cannibalization', because it is instructive to discuss it in the context of online grocery shopping. Cannibals engage in eating their own species; *cannibalization* in business usually means that a firm is offering new customers (at least, it hopes they are new) a good deal to encourage them to trade or shop with that firm, but in fact the new deal may just be eating away existing revenues. In the case of online shopping (before introduction of delivery charges), the good deal Tesco offered was not a directly discounted price, but it might as well have been, because Tesco was absorbing the cost of delivery, estimated at £7. Suppose all of Tesco's existing customers, who already shop at the Tesco supermarkets, had switched to delivery service. This would have been total cannibalization of Tesco's existing profitable business by its online business. The company's profitability would have disappeared overnight: on average, each £85 of revenue would get an extra £7 of cost added to it (8.2%); and the company as a whole would go from profits of £1,030m (5.5% of revenue) to losses of £518m (2.8% of revenues (rounding)).

Note that when we calculated a contribution margin of £1.33 above, we assumed no cannibalization – that is, that every online order is a *new* order, and that no existing shoppers are deserting the supermarket to go online. This is clearly not a sensible assumption, although without detailed survey data it is hard to evaluate *how* wrong it is.

Given the threat of cannibalization, UK supermarkets were expected to adjust their existing business models. Delivery charges will continue to be introduced, especially for peak delivery periods such as Friday and Saturday. Also, supermarkets will be making efforts to decrease costs by eliminating deliveries to remote areas, and by 'clumping' together other deliveries. One example of a business model where deliveries are clumped together is the Waitrose@work business model in the UK, where deliveries are made not to the customer's home but to his or her workplace, where several customers are likely to be co-located. This decreases the per-customer delivery cost and allows Waitrose to accept lower minimum orders. However, consumers may object to carrying groceries home if they have a long commute on public transport (as is customary in parts of the UK, especially London and the South East), which may limit the take-up of this type of service. Finally, supermarkets are already attempting to use their closer relationship with online customers (who supply matched data on address and grocery needs that are harder to obtain for shop customers) to sell other products, such as insurance and banking.

CUSTOMER PROPENSITY TO BUY

The issue of whether customers will buy online is important both to pure-play B2C businesses and to High Street/Main Street stores entering the world of e-commerce. Will the internet gain a similar share of commerce to that of catalogues (of the order of 10%)? Or will it be much bigger? Our view is that ultimately the online volume will be commensurate with that of catalogue-based shopping. However, the key is in focusing on the parts of commerce which most suit themselves to online shopping. Clearly, intangible products such as banking and insurance lend themselves well to online shopping, especially if credibly backed by established brands that the customer trusts. The more difficult problem is establishing which physical products lend themselves to online shopping. There are three simple, fundamental rules that determine customer propensity to buy physical products on the internet:

1. The internet cannot deliver goods which are needed immediately.
2. Customers will tend to buy goods remotely if the benefits of feasible, physical trial are outweighed by the costs of *performing* the physical trial.
3. Within the subset of remote shopping, online shopping will be emphasized if the web interface can provide an acceptable substitute for physical trial.

Figure 13.6 summarizes the framework with sample physical products.

A 2000 survey of 1999 e-commerce revenues confirms that some of the most successful sectors are sectors where the product is intangible. However, some physical products did achieve large volumes. The largest sectors were:

- computer software/hardware: $7.5bn
- travel: $7bn
- stock brokerages: $5.8bn

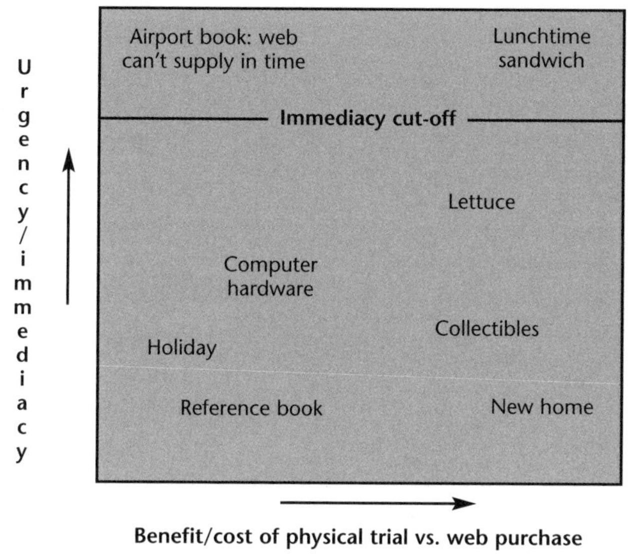

Note: Bottom left corner is not attractive for net commerce.

Figure 13.6 Purchase of physical products

- collectibles: $5.3bn
- music, books, gifts: $1.5bn each

Computer software and hardware seem to stand out as something of an exception to the dominance of intangibles. The figures are from 1999, when direct download of software was not popular due to slow connections, so both computer hardware and software required physical shipment. One explanation for the high revenues in this sector is that computer users were natural early adopters for online shopping. Also the influential leadership of Dell Computer increased the rate of increase of hardware revenues. But the key issue is not the physicality of the product but the *benefits of physical trial* of the good. If a consumer will not gain benefits from physical trial, then she or he will be more disposed to buy remotely. The case of computer hardware is a good for which benefits of physical trial are small. Computers are bought on the basis mainly of specification and brand. A Pentium III computer with 256MB of RAM from one leading supplier will have approximately the same performance as one from another leading supplier: performance differences are much better researched by looking at magazines such as *Computer Shopper* which carry out benchmark tests between large numbers of machines. Physical trial can still give some benefits, however – potential buyers can check form factor, sturdiness, and so on.

We have discussed the advantages and perceived advantages of online stock trading in the previous chapter. We will discuss the issue of travel below, but at this point we should note that the physical purchase for travel is confined to a small ticket or even an *e-ticket* (that is, an electronic reservation where the customer identifies him or herself by a code number, by his or her photo ID, or by printing out the computer receipt from the travel firm's website). Also, although there might be extensive benefits from physical trial of that villa in Tuscany where one is considering spending a week or two, the costs of such a trial would be prohibitively high.

The high volume of the other non-tangible categories is certainly partly due to category-leading marketing from eBay in the case of collectibles and Amazon.com in the case of books. While the benefits of physical trial from books are relatively low (and mitigated by the generous return policies of leading online booksellers), benefits of looking at and handling a collectible item would appear to be high, and the large quantity of collectibles traded remains anomalous in our framework. However, it should be noted that the internet is particularly suitable for the marketing of collectibles, especially through the medium of the eBay interface. For the ultimate collectible, there will only be one example, and there will be one consumer who will gain more pleasure from that artefact than any other consumer. The eBay interface provides a greater opportunity for uniting the two than traditional dealers of collectibles, who generally have a tight geographical area of activity. Also, if a highly desired collectible is situated many hundreds of miles away, costs of physical trial (or, more accurately in this case, inspection) of the collectible become prohibitive, outweighing benefits.

One area which has gained attention, for which the physical benefits of trial are high, and the purchase is also very salient to individuals and families (implying a desire to trial by all available means), is the purchase of homes and real estate or property. In the UK the online model has not made much headway, due to the quite low levels of agency commission (typically 2–3%) and the relatively small geographical distances involved. However, in the USA, where real estate broker commissions tend to be 5% of property price or more, the business has attracted several entrants. Since many Americans consider moves over long distances (for example, to take up attractive offers of employment), the online model allows them to 'window shop' from a distance. Most of the online real estate brokers do offer the house viewing as part of their service, and consumers are not expected to buy a house online by clicking and giving their credit card number. We would see this model as a use of the internet as an advertising and browsing medium rather than a new business model.

THE VALUE-SUBTRACTING INTERMEDIARY

Disintermediation is an expected result of the increasing influence of the internet. The first victims of internet disintermediation seem to be the travel agencies and stockbrokers. Although it is difficult to separate the effects of the internet from the 2001 economic downturn, and the terrible events of 11 September 2001, the high revenues gained by leading online travel sites such as priceline.com and expedia.com have put pressure on traditional travel intermediaries. The rise of internet travel agencies is not surprising since travel agency, and in particular the booking of airfares, was becoming a largely electronic process in the years leading up to the increase in internet-based travel. The SABRE system created by American Airlines was providing the data input for many travel agencies booking airfares, and internet travel agency is largely a process of putting an attractive 'front end' on this database (and on its competitor databases) so that it can be used by the end consumer. If a travel agent is simply acting as a front end to the SABRE system, then no value is being added. Frequently, skilled travel agents can optimize routings and fares to assist travellers in obtaining itineraries which may not arise as the default options from SABRE. However, many fares and itineraries can be simply booked using the computer system, and for these fares the travel agent simply performs a function of typing the data into the SABRE system, and conveying the results to the consumer. In this subset of the tickets booked, the agent incurs costs (agency commission) for the user without adding any value, and can therefore be termed a *value-subtracting intermediary*.

Whenever a human intermediary is employed simply to enter data, the potential for value-subtraction exists. The key is that the web-based consumer is performing a task (entering data into the web form) that the company would otherwise have to pay an employee to do. The value-subtraction potential is maximized if there is a need to gather a great deal of data, for which an example is auto insurance. Auto insurance quotations require large amounts of data, such as vehicle identification numbers, driving licence IDs, date of qualification. A telephone-based insurance company will employ a staff-member to enter the data from the potential insured, and that staff-member's time could be wasted while the potential client obtains required information from the car or auto (for example, the vehicle ID, the precise model number, or vehicle options). If the potential client is using a web interface, he or she can simply walk away, get the information, and continue the data-entry process. Banking, travel, insurance, and shopping (compared to catalogue-based telephone shopping) are other examples.

There are also downsides, especially in insurance. Insurance companies compete partly on estimating the risk differences between different groups of drivers, different types of car or automobile, and different residences (for theft risk). If the insurance company has a website where customers can experiment with coverage, it runs the risk that competitors may be able to access that website and explore the company's risk model. This does not have to mean 'hacking in' to the system. Scripts can be written that emulate user input so that various coverage and vehicle scenarios can be automatically gathered by the inquiring firm. The website is fooled (*'spoofed'*) that a user is requesting the scenarios. This can be made more difficult for the spoofing program by making the server reject repeated requests from a given *IP address* (a computer; or a group of computers, if IP addresses are being dynamically assigned). Another tactic is to present the user with a graphic of disguised characters or numbers (blended with other backgrounds or shapes), which the user has to type into a box simply as a security measure. A human can easily read and reproduce the characters or numbers 'hidden' in the graphic, but a spoofing program cannot easily interpret them.

There are two factors which will slow down the replacement of human intermediaries by internet-based interfaces. The first factor is that some intermediaries do add value. Travel agencies which specialize in certain types of routing (for example, round-the-world travel), or which serve certain ethnic communities, can add value by their specialist knowledge. Purchasing executives in firms were initially seen as likely 'roadkill' for B2B exchanges, but recent research suggests that they do add value in specifying their companies' needs precisely. The second factor is inertia. We have spoken about the potential problems of insurance companies falling victim to competitive intelligence by putting quoting engines on the internet. But the internet remains an ideal channel for much insurance business, and there is no doubt that inertia is the main factor holding back the switch. New players have no such 'ties to the past', of course. To take the example of the airline industry, recent European entrants easyJet and Ryanair secure respectively 90% and 75% of their bookings from their websites.[3] This compares to figures of below 25% for most established airlines.

THE NETWORK EFFECT: WHEN IT WORKS AND WHEN IT DOES NOT

Is your industry vulnerable to the network effect? Are you selling communication or interaction with others? Or are you just selling widgets? The network effect can be important, but is only relevant for a limited number of industries, and even then does not always work in a company's favour. Also, the network effect is not new. Old-fashioned networks such as telephone, mail and even railways became more useful the more people or places they were connected with.

Metcalfe's Law (Bob Metcalfe was involved in the invention of the Ethernet) attempts to quantify the increasing value of networks when participants are added: 'The value of a network rises in the square of the number of users'. Shapiro and Varian (1999) suggest not only that Metcalfe's Law is not a law, but that it was not originated by Metcalfe (although he is 'willing to take credit for it'). Shapiro and Varian report the derivation of the law (which they suggest would be more appropriately termed a 'rule of thumb'), which we paraphrase:

- Suppose there are n people on a network, and the value of the network to them grows proportionally to the number of people they can communicate or interact with on the network.
- Let's say that for each person, the value of the network to that person increases by v cents/pence for each extra person added to the network – that extra person gives new trading opportunities, potential for fascinating communications, romantic opportunities, or whatever.
- Each of the n persons on the network can communicate (interact, trade, date) with the other $n - 1$ persons. Therefore the value of the network to each person is $(n - 1)v$.
- The total value of the network is the value for each individual multiplied by the number of persons accessing the network (which is n).
- Therefore the total value of the network is $n(n - 1)v = v(n^2 - n) \approx vn^2$ (since n^2 is much bigger than n for large values of n).
- If v is a constant, then Metcalfe's Law is supported.

However, pretty obviously, v is not a constant (it most likely behaves as an 'S' curve. For the eBay trader, profit opportunities are not increased linearly by adding potential bidders to eBay: once a critical mass of bidders has been garnered, bids will not rise appreciably when extra bidders are added (especially if that critical mass includes some bidders who may be arbitraging between eBay and bidders without internet access). Even for teenagers, there are only so many hours of idle chatter that can be enjoyed. Most people prefer to only have one romantic partner at a time, thus cutting themselves off from many of the network benefits! Network effects reach saturation, and the value of the network to each user $(n–1)v$ tails off as n rises, so v must fall.

The second problem, which we alluded to at the start of the chapter, is that even if the network has value, that value may not accrue to the corporations playing in the market. For an illustration of this, Bennahum (2000) points to the fax network. It has enormous number of users, and is very valuable – many firms would not be without it. But who is making money? The production of fax machines (most of which now use commoditized plain paper as their main consumable) is extremely competitive; and basic telephone service provision is also very competitive. The value has gone to the *users* of the technology, not to the firms.

Shapiro and Varian shed some light on this. The key issue preventing firms from extracting value from the fax network is that the fax network uses open, widely accepted standards. In this, and many other industries such as telephone handsets, personal computers and ISP provision, companies can compete by adhering to those standards. If there is an accepted standard that is proprietary, then the company owning that standard can extract some of the value that people get from the expanded network – think of Microsoft and its Windows operating system.

However, when there are multiple standards in an industry, which often occurs early in an industry's life, positive feedback (of which network effects are a consequence) can cut both ways, and can exaggerate the effects of small differences in early rates of adoption. The most famous example of this type of 'tippy' market is the battle between Betamax and VHS video tape formats. The adoption of the tape formats required consumers, tape machine manufacturers, producers of movies, and stores (electronics and video rental) to make separate decisions to back one or more standards. Leaving aside the consumers for a moment, many of the costs for these companies are fixed.

For example, consider the costs of developing a video player. A company spends a few hundred million yen testing the technology, and once it has arrived at the final specification, trained the assembly line, and started production, the incremental video player comes out fairly cheaply. That means that if one video system has a two-thirds share, and one has a one-third share, the manufacturer of the player with the leading system can price much more cheaply (because he or she has twice as many video machines over which to spread development costs) while still making a profit. At best the following manufacturer will leave the old player on the market, meaning that the players with the leading system (whose manufacturers can afford to keep developing new models for the larger user base) will have more features to attract users, and will increase their lead. More likely, the following manufacturer will look to the fixed costs inherent in the manufacturing process itself (costs of machine changeovers to start each batch, and costs of maintaining an extra SKU in inventory) and think about throwing in the towel. Electronics stores, where each inch of shelf space has to make a return, will be even more ruthless in delisting low-volume players. Because the key firms in the industry are all making decisions based on profit functions that are inherently very sensitive to volume, a losing standard or product will quickly suffer at the hands of a winning one, even when the differences between the two are relatively modest. And because a small difference in volume at a crucial time can make a big difference, the industry is unstable and can be envisaged as prone to 'tip' over one way or another from one standard to another. This is the intuition for the term 'tippy'.

In order to try and figure whether network effects are likely to be important to internet businesses, we need to think about three fundamental questions:

1. How does v (the value added to each existing network user when someone new joins the network) behave? Do the users really care if an extra person is added to the network?
2. If the internet business depends on the support of other players (for example, software or content providers), how sloping (sensitive to volume) are the profit curves of the other key players in the industry? If the curves do not slope much, then the players may not mind supporting two or more standards.
3. How high are the switching costs between networks? If they are not high (and there is no other barrier to switching), then when the leading firm tries to monetize its dominance, lower-price networks will gain share again.

For network effects or positive feedback to occur, either 1 *or* 2 (or both), *and* 3 must be answered positively. Let us survey the areas of the internet where network effects were anticipated, and ask how they have worked out (see Table 13.1).

To summarize, network effects are far more difficult to achieve than might at first be envisaged. The key issue is that someone (either the customer or needed business partners) must lose out if the network's volume declines; and the network must be able to monetize that, so it cannot be easy for customers to switch. In the case of Amazon, benefits to the user from extra users in the network are low. It is nice to see an extra review on the website, but it is unlikely to affect the buying decision – people will buy on the basis of value and service. Also, publishers and distributors, whose businesses are tuned to dealing with many small retailers, will be neither pleased nor concerned by the appearance of a leading player. By contrast eBay customers gain from having extra auctions to view (1), and will not happily switch to sites with far fewer auctions (3). Merchants cannot effectively switch to another auction site, because volumes at the other auction sites are too low (2). However, recall our caveat on the valuation of eBay in Chapter 3. Stocks with network effects can still be over-priced.

THE AUCTION ECONOMY AND THE QECAP MODEL

The *auction economy* represents a picture of the world where all purchase

Table 13.1 Network effects on the internet

Company	Value of extra user, to the existing users	Slope of other firms	Customer switching costs	Network effect value
Book retailing (for example Amazon)	Close to zero	Low	Low	No
Ebay	High, but declining in *n*	High	High	Yes
AOL	Low, now AOL is linked to the internet	Low	Medium	No
AOL Instant Messenger	High	N/A	Low (can have both AOL and MSN chat applications)	No[1]
B2B exchanges	Medium	High	Low[2]	No[2]
B2B software	Medium	May be high	No standard yet	Possible
Windows *vs.* Macintosh	Low	High[3]	High	Yes
Homepage providers, for example Geocities	Low (can access homepages even if not on Geocities)	Low	Low	No[4]

1 AOL Instant Messenger may perform a defensive role in dissuading defection from the AOL flagship internet service
2 Because no B2B exchange ever reached critical mass, switching between exchanges did not appreciably affect how many trading partners could be found
3 Software developers, hardware developers
4 No network effects, but can sell advertising on the homepages

requirements by businesses are put out for offers using the internet, instead of being filled using established relationships. This would allow businesses access to the maximum possible number of suppliers. Eventually, as Hamel and Sampler (1999) suggested, even 'your weekly grocery shopping [could be put] out to bid.'

This model of the world represents the extreme of the 'competitive wasteland' view that we advanced in Chapter 12. As a rule of thumb, firms make 80% of their profits from the 'top' 20% of their customers. Typically the profitable customers are large-volume customers who buy consistently. The large volumes these customers buy mean that batch costs of preparing, packing and shipping the order are minimized on a per unit basis. The fact that these are long-term customers means they are not on the phone every day asking how to use the product because they have never seen it before. This again means they cost less to serve. The auction economy implies that this model of relying on these 'gold' customers may not operate in the future. Larger volume buyers will be able to receive prices which reflect the lower cost of dealing with them; low-volume buyers may suffer, but at the same time suppliers' revenues are likely to be negatively impacted across the board.

There is a trend to competitiveness in all markets, which the internet has helped to speed up. The auction economy has not yet come about, because of the lack of standardization in communications between merchants, but progress will continue towards it. However, it will never be completely achieved. Value-adding intermediaries will continue to be a feature of new markets and the markets for new products and services. Let us consider the example of the futures markets for corn and other grains. These have been 'auction economy'-style markets for hundreds of years, mediated by leading commodity exchanges such as the Chicago Board of Trade (CBOT). They lent themselves superbly to the auction economy model, since uniform specifications could be easily defined in terms of the weight, quality, colour and size of the grains. The internet's effect will be to expand the number of goods that can be traded in this way. But for some types of good, the auction economy is a long way off. For example, imagine selecting a lettuce purely on the basis of the cheapest offer: we imagine the salad might not taste too good (and we are inordinately fond of a good salad). The issues are similar to those we discussed in the section above on 'Consumer propensity to buy'. Consider the continuum shown in Table 13.2.

Even if, as Table 13.2 suggests, the auction economy is not around the corner, it still has lessons for online businesses. Many online businesses attract customers on the basis of low prices, in the case of B2C shops or B2B commerce operations, and on the basis of favourable interest rates or charges, in the case of financial institutions. As Higson and Briginshaw (2000) note, too often the assumption is made that these customers, disloyal to their previous supplier and clearly price-sensitive, will remain loyal to their new supplier! 'Sticky' websites and strong online brands are intended to ensure that rivalry is conducted on the basis of website features and the desire to be part of the online community, rather than on the basis of price. Perhaps not. While any action of switching between suppliers is never without effort, it is to some extent true that, once a defector, always a defector.

Let us look ahead for a moment and consider how the auction economy may work. The concept of management focus will be key in maximizing efficiency. Consider the auto insurance industry, and how focus is achieved. There are insurance brokers or agents, who face the customer. And there are insurers themselves, who price risks. The insurers may also possibly invest insurance premia to maximize value but, in line with our desire for management focus, let us assume this has been outsourced to a specialist investment house. The

Table 13.2 Suitability for auction vs. information needed to describe product

Information needs	Example good or service	Information to specify	Can communicate by	
Very Low	Foreign exchange Grain (CBOT specification)	Single figure (price)	Open outcry	↑ Auction now
Low	Movie tickets Airfare	Time, location and price	Telephone or web	
Medium	Temporary staff	Name, past experience, time needed, wage rate	Personal interview Telephone and fax	
High	Lettuce Car/auto	Price, colour, feel, freshness, 'quality'	Personal, physical experience	↓ Auction never

insurers have a pricing model, which in the traditional way of doing business may be a mainframe or AS400 (or similar) system, a set of spreadsheets or even a paper manual setting down rates for different autos in different post-codes/zipcodes with different ages of driver. In response to a customer query to the broker, the details are transmitted by telephone to the insurer, the model is queried, and the priced risk is communicated back to the broker by telephone, and then to the client. In the future the system will be automated, but will work in a similar way. Each insurer will code its risk pricing model into a quoting engine. The quoting engine will accept input of a person and car/auto specification, defined within an open standard such as *XML* (*eXtensible Markup Language*). Quoting engines (to prevent spoofing) will only accept queries from accredited customer acquisition portals. The customer acquisition portal will be charged with gathering customer data to fill the details of the XML person specification and auto/car specification. The portal will then query the available quoting engines.

Currently, it is often necessary for comparison sites to store much of the pricing model of many insurers on their own servers, but this is inefficient and requires frequent rechecking of the insurers' policies. Only a small subset of the insurer's risk model should be stored on the portal (to avoid unnecessary queries), such as 'we do not insure in Alabama' or 'we do not insure drivers under 23'. However, most customer enquiries will result in pricing by a number of quoting engines in real time. Insurers will focus to their strengths.

- Some insurers have had great success in directly facing the customer, for example Progressive in the USA and Direct Line in the UK. Their quoting engine will sit on their servers, and can interface with a customer acquisition portal on their website, a portal which can also be accessed by their telephone-based customer service centre staff. However, the customer service portal will also query other insurers' quoting engines sitting on the other firms' servers, but only in response to end-customer queries.

- Other insurers will simply evolve quoting engines, and add these as a communication medium to their existing channels opened with brokers. As internet-based volume grows, they will allow their telephone and fax communications to undergo atrophization and focus only on adjusting and fine-tuning the risk model incorporated in the quoting engine.
- Leading brokers will concentrate on customer acquisition, and will optimize their telephone and web processes so that each call or homepage visit is converted into the XML records needed to initiate a query of the quoting engines, as a route to the gaining of a commission.

As unnecessary telephone and fax communications are eliminated, costs for insurance will tend to decrease. The quality of risk pricing, which will increasingly be done by companies focused on risk pricing and unconcerned about customer acquisition, will rise. The performance in terms of customer acquisition will similarly rise as a result of focus on that by the relevant firms.

Similar systems of *quoting engine and customer acquisition portal* (QECAP model) will be evolved in other industries. Some early models of the customer acquisition portal already exist. The ecompare.com portal claims to use proprietary technology to query merchant price lists and inventory on books and other products. However, it is likely that this system must carry out extensive post-processing due to the non-standard interfaces with the various merchants. In general, proprietary technology is not the way to go here, for two reasons. First, although a portal or comparison engine would be in a very strong position if it could persuade all merchants to adopt its proprietary standard for price queries, merchants are unlikely to allow this, precisely because of the power this would give the portal. Second, emulating large parts of the pricing model at the portal server is very expensive, requiring frequent rechecking of inventory and prices at a large number of supplier servers.

In summary, many price-comparison engines are having difficulty surviving. This is for two reasons. First of all, it has proved difficult to negotiate terms with merchants to reflect the type of sales-lead that the comparison engines provide. The lead is highly 'qualified', in that it is more likely to lead to a sale than other clickthroughs. But it is also highly price-sensitive, and may hit the merchant's loss leader offers without purchasing any higher margin products, lowering average margins and possibly causing stock-outs of the loss leaders. These features of the portal-based leads are somewhat unavoidable. The second and key problem is that the standardization of query format has not reached a stage where the customer acquisition portal model is viable in terms of cost. The portal systems need to be of fairly low complexity and low cost, focusing on generating customer queries, not on mimicking pricing engines. Until standardization is achieved, the comparison engines have an uncertain future.

CHAMELEONIZATION

In their paper on the auction economy, Hamel and Sampler conclude that the internet will enhance competitive forces, but will not fundamentally change the critical factors needed for business success, but rather will accentuate the need for them. In the new economy, success will go to companies with 'relentless innovation, unparalleled service and … products with real performance advantages'.

The main difference then, will be a matter of speed. While in the past firms could rely on competitive advantages remaining for a period, internet commerce will make this more difficult. Therefore the successful companies will be somewhat like chameleons, able to change not only colour, but also shape and behaviour to exploit rapidly changing niches. General Electric, Inc. is not successful because of a single patented discovery or secret: it is successful because of a long track record of taking its opportunities in a wide range of markets, and once it has a position, reacting quickly to change and challenge, and defending its position successfully.

For the new economy, companies which can

- change rapidly
- compete aggressively
- keep close control on costs and value

will survive, and some new-economy companies may become the GEs of tomorrow. But it will be a far longer process than many commentators envisaged in the heady days of 1999.

Notes

1 Ronald H. Coase (the winner of the Nobel Prize for Economics in 1991) and Oliver E. Williamson are two of the pioneers of transaction cost economics. See, for example, Coase (1980) and Williamson (1999).
2 We wish to acknowledge that this discussion of Tesco was greatly informed by Kathy Hammond's presentation on the London Business School eExperts executive programme.
3 *New York Times*, 5 October 2001, pp. W7.

CHAPTER 14

The Outlook for Internet Business Segments

THE STRATEGIC MODELS WITHIN THE INTERNET CLUSTER

The strategic models we use for analysing the internet cluster are broad groupings, based on customers addressed and the type of business model. The framework in Figure 14.1 is based on that of Steve Harmon (www.Marketsnap.com) with the addition of a content category and of delivery vectors. As it shows, there are seven *fundamental sectors* (shown down the page), which play in three *delivery vectors* (shown left to right).

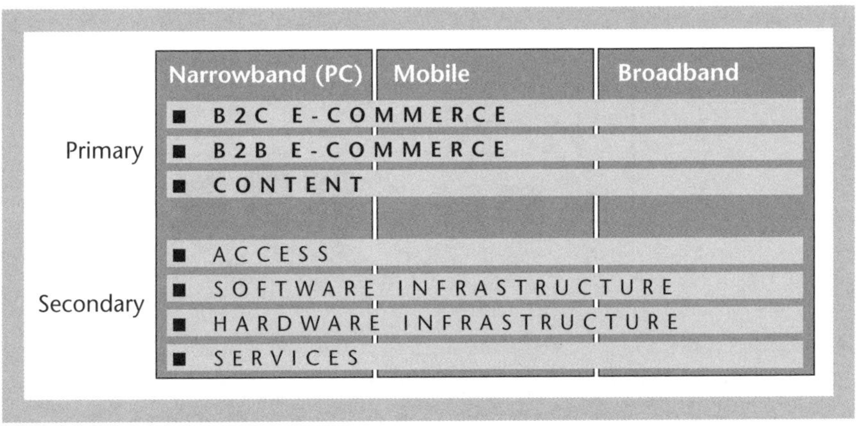

Figure 14.1 Strategic models within the internet cluster

We make a distinction between primary and secondary internet business models:

- *primary models* bring people to the web by providing useful goods and services, and interesting content (shown in **bold** type)
- *secondary models*, which are usually business-facing, support the effort of primary firms or their customers – these models are dependent on the success of the primary in driving usage (shown in plain type).

Market valuations by sector: May 2000–May 2001 (pure play only)

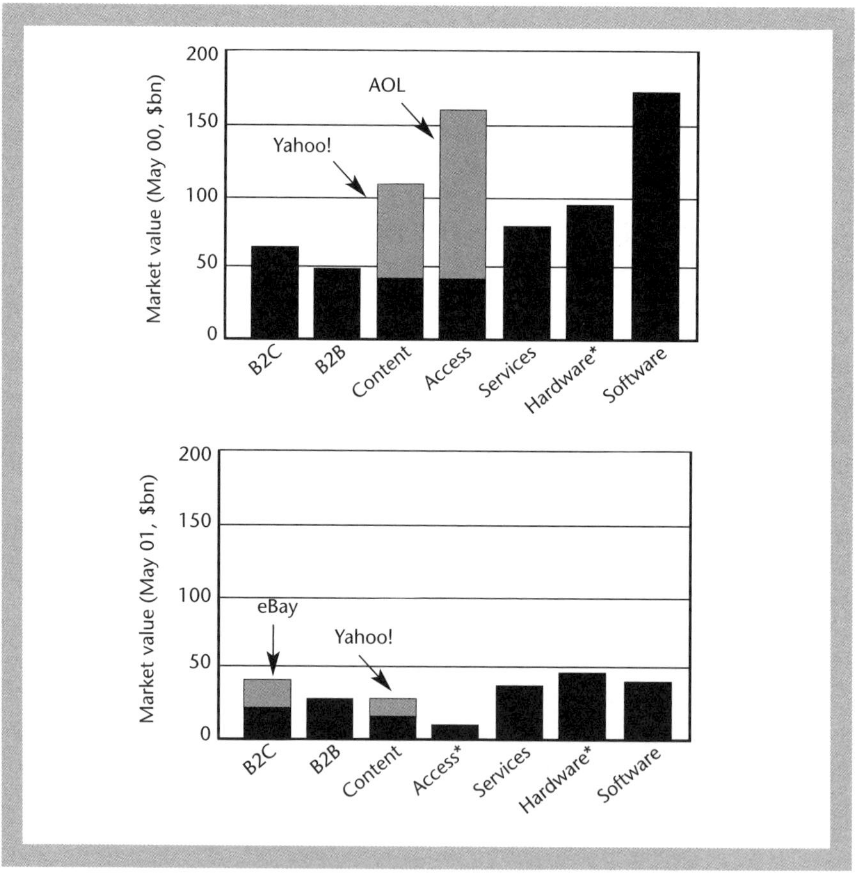

Figure 14.2 Strategic models within the internet cluster

**Note:* For clarity, the May 2000 chart excludes Cisco ($420bn) from hardware infrastructure and the May 2001 chart excludes AOL Time Warner ($221bn) from Access and Cisco ($139bn)

The seven fundamental sectors[1]

The seven sectors shown in Figure 14.1 are described in Tables 14.1–14.7.

Table 14.1 B2C e-commerce

Definition	*B2C e-commerce*: companies directly or indirectly involved in the buying and selling of products and services over the Internet to consumers.
Examples	USA: Amazon.com, CDNow/Columbia House, E*Trade, eBay. UK: QXL, iii.
Key threats	Threat of new entrants and rivalry: ■ from bricks and mortar retailers ■ from shopping bots (mySimon, dealtime). Economics may not work for physical e-tailers. Extreme difficulty of obtaining further funding for marginal models.
Key tasks	Build brand as barrier to entry: it's not surefire, but it's the only game in town.
Outlook	Most pure-play merchants will go out of business; or partner with, or be acquired by, physical retailers. eBay has the best chance for success, but is likely to remain a relatively small business.

Table 14.2 B2B e-commerce (exchanges)

Definition	*Business-to-business* (*B2B*): companies that engage in or provide portals for corporate commercial transactions via the internet.
Examples	US: Covisint. Europe: cpgmarket.com.
Key threats	As discussed in Chapter 14: power of buyers, power of suppliers – simple intermediaries will be glorified commodity exchanges, but with higher cost structures.
Key tasks	Become added-value intermediaries – do it better than existing brokers or communication structures.
Outlook	The B2B pure plays have been pretty much wiped out because of their extremely weak strategic position. Companies have transitioned to services and software infrastructure, or have gone out of business. There is still an opportunity for NLBs (nice little businesses) which have industry-specific knowledge and a lot of patience. However, there is much potential for value creation by 'clicks and mortar' plays and 'plain old mortar' (POM) customers and suppliers of the exchanges. We will discuss this further in Chapter 20, regarding procurement savings.

Table 14.3 Content

Definition	*Content*: companies engaged in providing non-commercial content to users, supported by advertising (many of these are transitioning to B2C e-commerce).
Examples	US: Yahoo!, Internet.com, CNET. UK: UKPlus.
Key threats	Threat of substitutes: we used to say that the 'jury is out' on whether internet advertising is effective – well now it's back, and banner ads are priced accordingly, at very low rates. Surviving fall-off in banner revenues (see Figure 14.3).
Key tasks	Transitioning to fee-based from banner-supported model. The quicker websites face up to this challenge, the better.
Outlook	From the consumer perspective, we are probably seeing the end of the golden age of free content on the web. Many of the current pure-play websites will close down; old-economy media firms will either close down their websites or streamline them to use a feed from the print edition, with little customization for web. *Bundling* will become important: to avoid subscribing to 1000 different sites, people will look to subscribe to a bundle of sites from MSN or Yahoo! *Micropayment* does not seem workable (although it may be on mobiles – see the section on mobiles below).

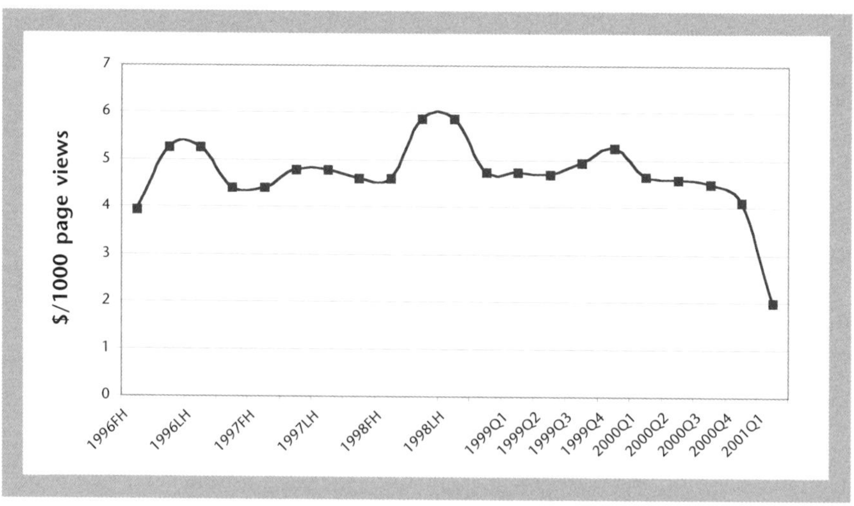

Figure 14.3 Yahoo! revenue per page view

Source: Yahoo! financial reports and releases

Table 14.4 Access

Definition	*Access*: internet service providers (ISPs) and companies that enable access to the internet (including hosting providers).
Examples	AOL, Netzero (United Online).
Key threats	Strong supplier power of the telcos make it very difficult for ISPs to negotiate a satisfactory split of interconnection revenues.
Key tasks	Outsource everything to do with being an ISP: ■ servers to IBM and so on ■ customer support to India ■ telecoms operation to telcos. Move to *Content* business model? Concentrate on sales and service?
Outlook	AOL is likely to be the world's only financially successful ISP. Independent ISPs outside the USA are vulnerable to telcos' 'light grip on the throat' of the telecoms market; and to competition, unless they are: ■ genuine innovators and top content providers ■ closely protected by telecoms regulators (for example, regulators must abolish local call charges). It is hard to see a scenario whereby most ISP revenue does not end up with the telcos. Business-aimed ISPs – a temporary sweet spot until supply catches up with demand.

Table 14.5 Software infrastructure

Definition	*Software infrastructure*: developers of applications that enable a variety of internet business activities, including, for example, electronic commerce, communications, content provision and web development.
Examples	Verisign, Baltimore Technologies.
Key threats	Threat of new entrants: entrenched competitors with consumer trust (for example, banks in financial services) or large software companies (for example, Oracle, IBM, or Microsoft). Threat of substitutes if price gouging occurs. Overvaluation of some players (many niches will turn out to be NLBs).
Key tasks	Erect barriers to entry by proprietary or superior technology. Defend ferociously against entry (unless the entrant is too big – in which case, look for partnership). Tailor marketing to 'clicks and mortar' plays.
Outlook	Good in parts, however many players will turn out to be NLBs.

Table 14.6 Hardware infrastructure

Definition	*Hardware infrastructure*: computer, digital and electronic products designed and developed to enable internet business activities, products and services.
Examples	Cisco, Broadcom.
Key threats	Threat of new entrants or substitutes: someone with a better mousetrap (entrant), or a mouse gun (substitute).
Key tasks	Maintain technological lead.
	Reap benefits from high costs of entry by firms at same technological level.
	Tailor marketing to 'clicks and mortar' plays.
Outlook	Good in parts; most successful small or medium players will be acquired.

Table 14.7 Services

Definition	*Services*: firms that provide corporations with professional and information services related to the internet (that is, 'everything else').
Examples	Doubleclick, MediaMetrix, Razorfish.
Key threats	Many of the business models just do not work, or have problems with cost structure and/or management ability.
	Some of the businesses have little operating leverage (for example, web-based consulting), and do not look like new economy businesses at all.
Outlook	A mixed bag, but generally poor.

BROADBAND

Broadband is a generic term for any access faster than the fastest readily available modem technology. At the time of writing, the fastest modem technology working on a non-upgraded copper-wire telephone line is 56 kilobits per second. There are two types of commonly available residential and SME (small-to-medium enterprise) broadband connections, which give significant speed advantages over 56 kb/s (see Table 14.8).

ISDN (*Integrated Services Digital Network*) is a technology giving 128 kb/s[2] download/upload using a dedicated phone line. It received some adoption in the USA and especially in the UK. However, with the advent of 56 kb/s narrowband modems, ISDN no longer provides significant advantages.

Digital cable internet requires a fibre-optic connection into the home. Many US consumers already possess this because they have cable TV. DSL

Table 14.8 Common residential broadband connections

System	Speed
Digital cable internet	up to 3000 kb/s peak
DSL (Digital Subscriber Line)	between 400 and 2000 kb/s peak

can be used for twisted-pair (copper) connections, so homes do not require additional cable. However, DSL is only available for a subset of homes, less than approximately two miles from an appropriately equipped switch.

Take-up of broadband has been disappointing, and the leading company focused on cable internet access (Excite@Home) has recently sought bankruptcy protection. Our view is that broadband will become ubiquitous, but probably at the $20 (£10–£15) per month price point. At the time of writing, the rate is approximately $40–$50 per month. There are disadvantages to both broadband systems. Both DSL and digital cable internet systems frequently have upload limited to approximately 128 kb/s (roughly twice the maximum speed available from narrowband modems); however, since internet browsing is usually dominated by download activity, this is not particularly serious, unless the user is uploading graphic attachments or other files to a mail server or web server. More serious for cable users is the possibility of deterioration of download speeds during peak times. The main technical problem for DSL users is the non-availability of the DSL service in many areas. Poor customer service and frequent billing problems also seem to be common complaints in dealing with broadband providers.

However, technical problems are not the major issues limiting take-up of broadband services. The main issues are problems of supply availability (especially for DSL service) and the lack of a clear reason why users should adopt the broadband technology. There is no 'killer app'.[3] The main suggested application is video-on-demand television. So far *true video on demand* (*TVOD*) is unavailable. This would give consumers the ability to order any movie and view it immediately. Currently *limited video (nearly) on demand* (*LNVOD*) is available on digital cable television, allowing users to view a limited number of movies, at staggered start times. This usage simply uses the multiple available channels on the digital cable system, arranging a popular movie at 5- to 30-minute intervals.

True video on demand would require digitization of all filmed entertainment, possibly some upgrading of the internet backbone, and the installation of a large number of high-capacity servers which would store frequently demanded movies close enough to the user that the *quality of service* (*QoS*) implications of internet transport would not interrupt playback. An alternative solution is for individual households to purchase local data storage to which movie files could be downloaded. These would be similar to the *TiVo* box, which allows the storage of several hours of TV on a hard disk, for playback at user convenience. However, security concerns would have to be conquered so that the downloaded movie files would not be copyable, or copyright holders will be leery about supporting the technology.

The QoS issues associated with internet transport are key. The internet protocol concerned with transport of data is the *TCP* (*transport control protocol*). The transport control protocol maximizes the efficiency of data transfer by splitting up data files into small *packets*. Each packet is tagged with information about its destination, the file of which it is part, and its position within the file. This header information ensures that the file goes to the correct destination computer, and that the individual packets can be reassembled into the complete file at the destination. This is necessary because the packets may not necessarily arrive in the right order. Packets will be routed via various routes and, although TCP aims to maximize speed, some packets will encounter unexpected, random data congestion and may be held in 'queues' (small local data stores) while

Table 14.9 Levels of video on demand (VOD)

Level of VOD	Description	Requirements
Limited video nearly on demand (LNVOD)	Limited selection available at predetermined times.	Uses cable TV infrastructure. Available now.
Limited video on demand (LVOD)	Limited selection available on demand.	Installation of high-capacity local servers. Servers will be pre-uploaded with popular titles ahead of LVOD release. Then available for download to local machines. Available 5–10 years.
Near video on demand (NVOD)	Wide selection of movies available. Some delay or available only at predetermined times.	Most likely implementation is set-top high-capacity disks. Download of the video files would be ordered, and the movie would start after a brief delay, after the file (or a large buffer segment) has been loaded to the local disk from a central server. Would also require digitization of a large number of undigitized movies. Available 5 years+ to a limited number of users.
True video on demand (TVOD/VOD)	Wide selection of movies available immediately.	Would require high QoS for end-to-end data transfer. Requires upgrade of internet architecture, or some elements of the internet to be dedicated to video transport. Available possibly never; certainly not any time soon.

waiting for capacity in the onward link. Movies need to be watched sequentially, naturally, so packet loss (or packets out of order) causes delay or picture loss. This is why *streaming video applications* on narrowband buffer data at the client.

There are enormous costs for each of the options, and the benefits to the user have to be analysed rigorously. It is instructive to compare the user who has one of the types of VOD with the non-user who has to make a trip to the local 'Blockbuster'. It is clear that LNVOD or LVOD provide no advantages, NVOD provides modest advantages, and TVOD provides advantages (in selection and convenience), but would require changes to the way the internet operates. Unless another killer app can be found that gives concrete step-gains for the user, rather than the incremental gains of faster internet downloads, broadband internet is unlikely to become a mass product unless priced at approximately the same rate as narrowband.

MOBILE/M-COMMERCE

Mobile is exciting, but overhyped. As we will see in the NTT Do Co Mo case (Chapter 15), much of the demand for high-tech phone services is based not on cutting-edge e-commerce applications, but on simpler services such as voice and short messages.

Location sensing is a technology for which high hopes were held out. Location sensing has the potential to enhance mobile e-commerce (*m-commerce*) by allowing cellphone providers to locate where individual cellphone subscribers are to a 50–300-metre tolerance. Currently cellphones 'roam' between base stations, selecting the base station antenna with the strongest signal (usually the nearest); subscribers can be located only approximately (especially in rural areas) if at all. Location sensing will allow cellphone providers to triangulate between the three nearest base stations to locate users, or to use in-phone *GPS* (*global positioning system*) chips to locate the user. Location sensing was planned to be adopted starting in October 2001 and with all new US cellphones having the facility by end 2002, with necessary network upgrades taking place also. However, in October 2001 the US FCC (at the request of the mobile phone companies) extended the timeline, and the process may not complete until 2005 under the new timetable.[4] This is because network adjustments (needed for triangulation) proved very costly and time-consuming, and the GPS-based system that now looks like being the main system took some time to plan. While much discussion has taken place about the possibilities for e-commerce, the primary use of the technology in the USA will be to allow emergency operators (911/999) to locate cellphone emergency callers. Approximately 30% of emergency calls emanate from mobile phones and, unlike calls from fixed line phones, these cannot be instantly located with existing exchange technology.

The promise of LBS (location-based services) for e-commerce is to feed focused advertising directly onto the mobile phone screen, according to the user's location. The ideal way of operating, for example, would be as follows. Imagine that a user has expressed an interest in buying a computer: when he or she walks near a Circuit City or Dixons where there is a sale, the mobile phone would beep and perhaps offer a downloadable money-off coupon. A nice idea to sell to some investors ... but perhaps a trifle annoying for the user. Most likely what the future holds is a permission-based marketing approach. As location sensing phones slowly become available worldwide (they are already available in Sweden and other parts of Scandinavia, for example), some users will sign up for an advertising test application, in return for reduced subscription and/or call time rates.

SCREEN AND KEYBOARD LIMITATIONS

Forrester (a leading market research firm) estimates that 33% (220m) European consumers will be using mobiles to access the internet by 2004. Another consultancy, Ovum, estimated that there will be 684m wireless web users worldwide by 2006. But Ovum states that if networks and appliances do not improve soon, customers will be put off by poor experiences.

The problem with internet access using cellphones is the small size of the screens on most devices. Five lines, or sometimes as few as three. Broadband access is being rolled out in some nations, but the true demand is for reliable narrowband access, and a wider choice of webpages adjusted for the low capacity of cellphone screens.

While mobile internet is still at an early stage, we can anticipate some trends. Communication (short messages and email) and simple entertainment (ring tones and games) are likely to be the major non-voice applications for some time. Voice will be a very large part of the traffic until mobile Palm-type devices gain acceptance. The Palm-type devices, which combine *PDA* (*personal digital assistant*) functionality and mobile phone capability, have the potential to make far more use of wireless web capability, since their screens will be much larger (although still far smaller than a PC). Until then the emphasis will be on *parsing* (converting) webpages (which usually consist of 2000–30,000 bytes) into the kind of small snippets of content that the user needs on the go (many cellphones have a 30-byte – 3 lines of 10 characters – screen view!): the address of the restaurant that one has searched for, rather than the wine list. This parsing must be carried out at the mobile provider's side (that is, not in the handset), to avoid high download times. Porting big websites lock, stock and barrel is a loser.

Many telcos also stand to lose, because of the crippling licence fees agreed for third generation networks. This is despite the fact that they, if anyone, are at the choke point of the industry value chain, because the network auctions set them up as duopolies or oligopolies. However, even a place at the choke point is not of infinite value. Question: can't telecom companies just raise prices to recoup the fees? No. Think about Porter's five forces again, and of where mobile telephony fits into people's everyday experience: part communication, part entertainment. If prices rise a great deal, substitutes elsewhere in the entertainment and communication 'macrocategories' (for example movies, internet chat, fixed-line telephony, non-3G mobile) will start to exert their pull and to steal revenues away from 3G mobile. Also, projections for 3G are not universally optimistic; for example, Sony Ericsson announced in 2001 that they expect only 30% of handsets to be 3G-capable by 2005 (source: www.3gnewsroom.com).

NAVIGATING THE 3G JUNGLE

In terms of data download, the WAP system is a 9.6 kb/s network, with NTT Do Co Mo's initial I-mode system operating at about the same speed (NTT Do Co Mo has now rolled out its faster 'FOMA' service around Tokyo; this had approximately 10,000 subscribers at the end of 2001). However, these are peak speeds, and often unavailable because of network congestion and download delays. If the connection is not 'always-on' call connection time is also a problem. (For example, WAP is not always on. I-mode (pre-FOMA) is not always on either, but has a quick latency which makes it look always on to the user.) One other possible reason for delays is that while many HTML pages are cached close to the user on narrowband, this is perhaps not the case with wireless internet.

When data transport rates do increase – what will the killer apps be? Several ideas have been advanced. Certainly, ring tone download has been

Table 14.10 Levels of mobile network speed

System	Speed	Availability
WAP/I-mode	9.6 kb/s	Now
HSCSD (Orange)	14.4 kb/s	Experimental
NTT PHS (mobile modem)	32 kb/s, (64 kb/s some areas)	Now
GPRS (over GSM network)	50–100 kb/s	Experimental
NTT Do Co Mo FOMA	300 kb/s	Tokyo area only
Edge	150–384 kb/s	Experimental/concept
3G (expected)	144–2000 kb/s	Concept

extremely popular in initial networks. We can expect music download to be popular. Snippets of video content (soccer highlights, or baseball 'home runs') are likely to be popular. However, relatively old technology is capable of supplying cheap mobile TVs, so pricing will have to be kept in check. Cellular modem technology is potentially a key application although the market is uncertain, as demonstrated by the failures of small-scale rollouts in the Bay Area, and the weak financial performance of NTT Do Co Mo's PHS offering. Computer usage in cars is not extensive, thank goodness. For other potential cellular modem applications, such as connectivity in airports, coffee shops and offices, WiFi/802.11b wireless LAN technology is an effective competitor in the macrocategory of connectivity.

Finally, video mobile telephones were one of the concepts suggested by NTT Do Co Mo. One worry about this idea is the low take-up of fixed-line video telephony. However, as observed in the NTT Do Co Mo case, many up-to-the-minute handsets have been bought because they are status symbols. If a 3G handset with video phone is released, many trendsetters will buy it, even if bad hair days prevent extensive use. It may be that the future of 3G is a constant feverish process of keeping the 'punters' replacing their handsets by constantly updating features. Arguably pre-3G mobile has followed this pattern and 3G is likely to do the same.

Notes

1 Examples in each sector are selected to be large, well-known companies. Comments in 'Key threats', 'Tasks' and 'Outlook' are not and should not be viewed as comments on example companies.
2 A 'blistering speed' according to BT's (the UK telecoms company) webpage describing its Home Highway ISDN service.
3 'Killer app' means killer application, in other words an application of (or use for) a technology which is viewed as very important to consumers – consumers' need for the application then drives adoption of the technology. For example, the killer apps driving the initial adoption of PCs were word-processing and spreadsheeting. Technology by itself, without applications and uses, is not attractive to the mass market.
4 'Deadline set on cellphone emergency calls', *New York Times*, 6 October 2001.

CHAPTER 15

CASE STUDY
NTT Do Co Mo:
Mobile Telephony in Japan

INTRODUCTION

The following case study gives information about NTT Do Co Mo, the dominant Japanese mobile telephony operator, to assist in study of the firm. The main body describes the business of the firm. The appendices provide pricing, usage and financial accounting data. Readers are asked to construct an Excel spreadsheet to value the company.

BACKGROUND

NTT Do Co Mo (the second part of the name stands for 'Do Mobile Communication') was spun off from NTT, the Japanese telecoms company, in 1992. NTT retains a 64.1% stake in the spin-off. NTT Do Co Mo introduced its I-mode mobile internet service on 22 February 1999. In a country where internet take-up was quite low (about 13% of households online by early 2000), the service accelerated to 20m users by March 2001, and was the leading exemplar of a successful mobile internet service. At November 2001, the company had 39.2m

The case study has been prepared entirely from publicly available information as a basis for discussion rather than to illustrate either effective or ineffective handling of an administrative situation.

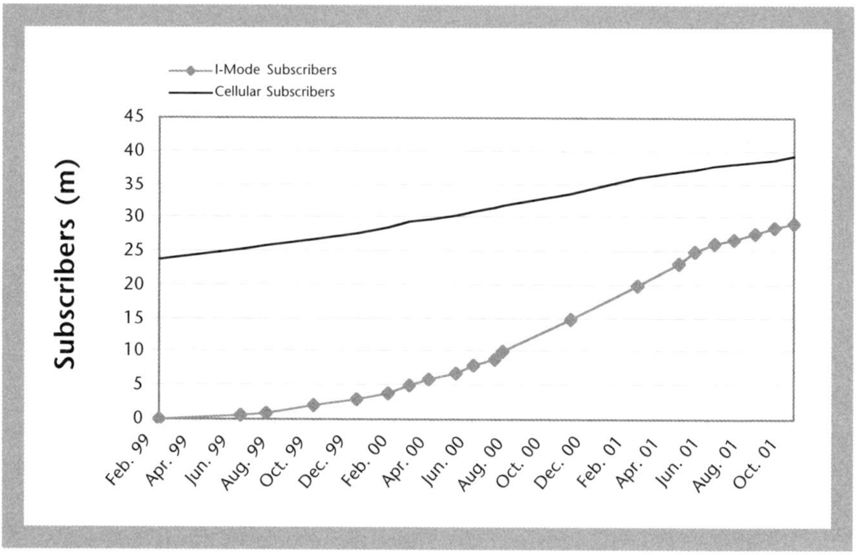

Figure 15.1 NTT Do Co Mo: growth in subscribers to I-mode
Source: NTT Do Co Mo

cellular customers, including 29.3m customers of I-mode. Figure 15.1 shows a chart of the increase in I-mode subscribers since the inception of the service.

THE I-MODE SERVICE

The *I-mode service* is a packet-switched service which uses an overlay of Do Co Mo's *personal digital cellular* (*PDC*) system. The PDC is capable of carrying signals at 28.8 kb/s, but currently the overlay network is set to run at 9.6 kb/s, since this is viewed as adequate given the small size of most screens and therefore the limited bandwidth required.

The I-mode service is portal-based, giving the user access to a number of sites that have been written in the I-mode language, cHTML. cHTML stands for *compact hypertext markup language*, and is a subset of the HTML language used for webpages. I-mode pages are therefore not compatible with the WAP/WML standard widely used in Europe. At October 2001 there were 1953 Do Co Mo menu sites (cHTML websites registered with Do Co Mo), up from 600 in early 2000. Websites being accessed by users receive a share of airtime fees.

Table 15.1 NTT Do Co Mo: revenues (half year to September 2001)

Business area	% of revenues
Cellular voice	62.9
Packet data (I-mode)	12.9
PHS (personal handy system)	1.7
Other mobile telephony	0.7
Other revenues	21.8

Charging is based on a per-packet usage measure. The charges were kept low to encourage usage, an email costing approximately 1–4 yen to send and 1–2 yen to receive, depending on size. Mobile email messages are restricted to 500 characters. The exchange rates for yen at March 2000 were ¥129/$1 and ¥182/£1 (exchange rates can be updated at www.oanda.com). A full pricing table is shown in Appendix 15.1. Data on the types of site available and user accesses by type of site are shown in Appendix 15.2.

BUSINESS AREAS

The company's segmental breakdown in percentage revenues for the half year to September 2001 is shown in Table 15.1.

Cellular voice

Revenues from cellular service and the sale of equipment. NTT Do Co Mo's cellular mobile service has 39.2m subscribers and accounts for approximately 60% market share. Its main competitors are KDDI (16m mobile subscribers) and Japan Telecom (9m mobile subscribers). (Vodafone owns 67% of Japan Telecom.)

Packet data

This includes the short latency I-mode 9.6 kb/s telephones, and will include revenue from the third-generation FOMA system which has been rolled out commercial within the 30 km radius of Tokyo in October 2001, and is scheduled for commercial launch in Osaka and Nagoya in December 2001. To September 2001, the company had not reported any revenues for the FOMA service, which had 150,000 trial subscribers at September 2001. Packet data revenue includes revenue from packet data equipment sales.

PHS

This is a 32 kb/s system designed for use with cellular modems, but also available for voice use and for music downloading. Revenue comes from service and equipment.

Other mobile telephony

These are revenues from mobile telephony not covered in the categories above.

Other revenues

'Other revenues' comprise international dialling services, revenues from the provision of system development services, and other miscellaneous revenues.

STOCK PRICE AND FINANCIAL PERFORMANCE

Financial performance data is shown in the appendices. These include outline historical financial data (Appendix 15.3) and detailed balance sheets and income statements (Appendix 15.4).

In the half year ended September 2001, the company suffered a writedown of ¥300Tr in its investment in KPN Mobile N.V., a Netherlands-based mobile operator. This was due to permanent dimunition in value of the shares.

Share price performance is shown in Figure 15.2. At the end of September 01, the company reported that it had 10,036,000 shares in issue. Market capitalization of the company peaked at ¥42,000Tr (about $330bn or £225bn) in March 2000. Market capitalization at December 2001 (¥1.44m per share) was ¥14,500Tr. The annual eps reported in March 2001 was ¥38,000 /share, giving a PE ratio of 38 (historical) at December 2001.

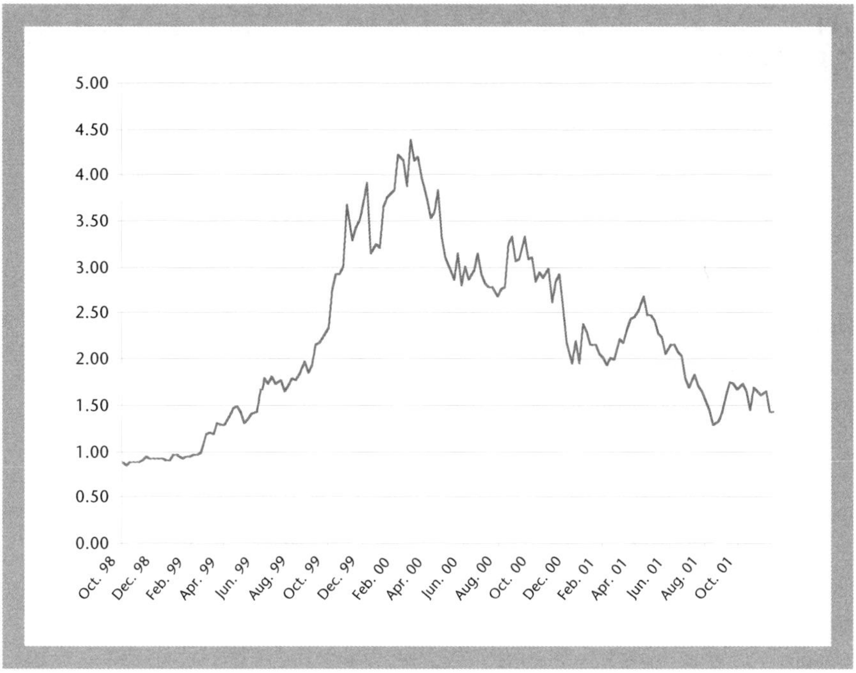

Figure 15.2 NTT Do Co Mo share price 1998–2001

COST OF CAPITAL

Risk-free rates and interest rates in Japan were extremely low at December 2001. Short-term risk-free rates were approximately zero (the Bank of Japan's official discount rate was 0.1%) and long bonds were in the 1–2% range. To illustrate this, NTT Do Co Mo issued ¥100Tr of 10-year bonds in October 2001 at a coupon yield of 1.5% basis selling price. Dimson et al. (2001) estimated that the historical MRP in Japan was at 6.8% for 1900–2000 over short-term bills and 6.3% over bonds.

APPENDIX 15.1: NTT DO CO MO: I-MODE SERVICE

Table 15.2 Guideline costs

	(¥)
My Menu[1]	2–3
What's New!! –	
Menu list	3–4
News	17–18
Mobile banking (balance confirmation)	20–21
Mobile banking (funds transfer)	59–60
Share prices[2]	26–27
Airline seat availability	24–25
Restaurant guide	37–38
TOWNPAGE (NTT telephone directory)	35–36
Do Co Mo charges information[3]	10–11
Tokusuru Menu	6–7
Options –	
Centre inquiry (when no messages are stored)	0.4–1.3
Image downloading[4]	7–8
i-melody[5]	18–19
i-anime[6]	10–11
i appli[7]	25–26

i-mode mail transmission charges (approximate)

Characters	Sending (¥)	Receiving (¥)
20	0.9	0.9
50	1.5	0.9
100	2.1	1.2
150	3.0	1.5
250	4.2	2.1
Centre inquiry	0.4–1.3	

1. Depending on the number of sites registered.
2. Transmission charge for searching by issue code.
3. Transmission charge for inquiring about dialling charges or packet transmission charges (up to the previous day).
4. Transmission charge for downloading one still image the size of the display.
5. Transmission charge for downloading one 16-chord melody approximately 45 seconds long.
6. Transmission charge for downloading one moving image the size of the display.
7. Only for downloaded i appli.

APPENDIX 15.2: NTT DO CO MO: TYPE OF USE DATA

Table 15.3 I-mode accesses: email vs. I-Menu vs. non-I-menu sites

	September 2000 (%)	March 2001 (%)
Mail	36	41
I-menu sites	32	25
Voluntary websites	32	34

Table 15.4 I-menu site breakdown by category

Type of website	September 2000 (%)	March 2001 (%)
Ring tone/screens	32	35
Games/horoscopes	19	18
Other entertainment	19	19
Information	17	14
Transaction	9	9
Database	4	4

Table 15.5 I-mode accesses: hits by category (Do Co Mo premium websites)

Hits by category	July 2000 (%)
Entertainment	64
Information	21
Database	6
Transaction	9

Source: NTT Do Co Mo

APPENDIX 15.3: NTT DO CO MO: OUTLINE FINANCIAL DATA

Table 15.6 Financial data

Y Tr	Y/E Mar. 99	Y/E Mar. 00	Y/E Mar. 01	HY/E Sep. 98	HY/E Mar. 99	HY/E Sep. 99	HY/E Mar. 00	HY/E Sep. 00	HY/E Mar. 01	HY/E Sep. 01
Operating revenues	3118.3	3718.6	4686.0	1462.8	1655.5	1762.3	1956.3	2217.4	2468.6	2613.0
Total telecoms	2525.9	2986.9	3599.3	1204.1	1321.8	1450.3	1536.6	1725.5	1873.8	2043.8
Total voice	2447.7	2907.2	3219.8	1158.1	1289.6	1420.7	1486.5	1594.1	1625.7	1694.3
– cellular	2380.4	2796.9	3103.5	1136.8	1243.6	1361.4	1435.5	1535.9	1567.6	1643.2
– PHS	30.1	80.2	84.1	0.0	30.1	41.5	38.7	40.4	43.7	45.0
– other	37.2	30.1	32.2	21.3	15.9	17.8	12.3	17.8	14.4	6.1
Total data	68.6	71.6	370.2	40.1	28.5	25.0	46.6	127.1	243.1	342.6
– packet svc	0.2	38.5	353.4	0.0	0.2	5.7	32.8	117.2	236.2	336.8
– paging	68.3	33.1	16.8	40.0	28.3	19.3	13.8	9.8	7.0	5.7
– other	0.1	0.0	0.0	0.1	0.0	0.0	0.0	0.1	–0.1	0.2
Other telecoms	9.5	8.0	9.1	5.7	3.8	4.5	3.5	4.2	4.9	6.9
Rounding in telecoms	0.1	0.1	0.2	0.2	–0.1	0.1	0.0	0.1	0.1	0.0
Other revenues	592.4	731.7	1086.6	258.6	333.8	311.9	419.8	491.8	594.8	569.0
Rounding/other	0.0	0.0	0.1	0.1	–0.1	0.1	–0.1	0.1	0.0	0.1
Operating income	508.5	545.7	777.1	307.0	201.5	351.4	194.3	412.0	365.1	550.4
Recurring profit	350.3	477.7	686.9	233.1	117.2	332.5	145.2	397.2	289.7	482.5
Earnings	204.8	252.1	366.5	154.1	50.7	178.0	74.1	217.5	149.0	103.9
Revenue growth	**99–00** (%)	**00–01** (%)		**Sep. 98–Mar. 99** (%)	**Mar. 99–Sep. 99** (%)	**Sep. 99–Mar. 00** (%)	**Mar. 00–Sep. 00** (%)	**Sep. 00–Mar. 01** (%)	**Mar. 01–Sep. 01** (%)	
Growth telecoms (annualized)	18	21		21	20	12	26	18	19	
Growth I-mode (annualized)	19,150	818			81,125	3,211	1,177	306	103	
Growth other (annualized)	18	18		28	13	20	19	13	4	

Table 15.7 Segmental data

NTT Do Co Mo does not split out the profitability of its packet data (I-mode: FOMA) operations from cellular telephony operations. The following segmental data were published in the most recent reports.

	Year ended		Six months ended	
Revenues	**31 Mar. 01**	**31 Mar. 00**	**30 Sep. 01**	**30 Sep. 00**
Mobile phone business	45,299	35,716	25,369	21,454
PHS business	1,130	1,029	582	556
Quickcast business	185	366	59	111
Miscellaneous business	244	75	118	52
Consolidated operating revenues	46,860	37,186	26,129	22,174
Operating income				
Mobile phone business	8,891	6,957	5,811	4,687
PHS business	−916	−996	−276	−469
Quickcast business	−211	−491	−35	−108
Miscellaneous business	8	−11	5	11
Consolidated operating income	7,771	5,457	5,504	4,120

APPENDIX 15.4: NTT DO CO MO: DETAILED FINANCIALS

Table 15.8 Balance sheets

ASSETS	30 Sep. 00	30 Sep. 01	31 Mar. 01
Fixed assets			
Fixed assets for telecommunication businesses			
Property and equipment	2,176,394	2,479,827	2,288,878
Machinery and equipment	1,033,073	1,098,403	1,046,896
Antenna facilities	326,506	374,001	355,710
Satellite mobile communications facilities	6,762	5,234	5,900
Terminal equipment	3,504	2,734	3,160
Buildings	243,756	284,885	265,810
Tools, furniture and fixtures	175,969	184,818	187,051
Land	148,157	166,341	151,366
Construction in progress	183,785	295,223	206,316
Other fixed assets	54,878	68,184	66,664
Intangible fixed assets	297,999	372,177	337,407
Computer software	234,727	311,661	270,396
Other intangible fixed assets	63,271	60,515	67,011
Total fixed assets for telecommunication businesses	2,474,394	2,852,004	2,626,286
Investments and other assets			
Investment securities	658,453	1,566,194	1,928,426
Deferred income taxes	73,749	230,559	89,614
Other investments	57,281	67,711	66,369
Allowance for doubtful accounts	–791	–998	–928
Total investments and other assets	788,693	1,863,465	2,083,481
Total fixed assets	3,263,087	4,715,470	4,709,767
Current assets			
Cash and bank deposits	76,979	112,704	116,065
Notes and accounts receivable, trade	755,932	827,015	908,251
Securities	299	300	199
Supplies	129,442	181,100	125,237
Deferred income taxes	22,068	32,190	24,408
Other current assets	56,400	71,584	50,283
Allowance for doubtful accounts	–22,072	–23,484	–22,974
Total current assets	1,019,050	1,201,409	1,201,472
TOTAL ASSETS	4,282,138	5,916,879	5,911,239

continued

Table 15.8 *continued*

LIABILITIES	30 Sep. 00	30 Sep. 01	31 Mar. 01
Long-term liabilities			
Bonds	133,000	448,000	296,000
Long-term borrowings	369,174	566,049	367,282
Liability for employees' severance payments	105,579	132,978	124,595
Reserve for point loyalty programs	–	54,461	24,999
Other reserve	92	105	147
Other long-term liabilities	846	3,434	3,368
Total long-term liabilities	608,692	1,205,029	816,393
Current liabilities			
Current portion of long-term debt	211,916	184,544	175,685
Accounts payable, trade	282,419	305,572	364,350
Short-term borrowings	533,800	59,160	543,700
Accrued income taxes	171,205	248,712	203,815
Accounts payable – other	227,116	270,049	377,024
Other current liabilities	33,248	193,795	80,669
Total current liabilities	1,459,706	1,261,833	1,705,246
TOTAL LIABILITIES	2,068,398	2,466,862	2,521,639
MINORITY INTEREST			
Minority interest	65,549	89,005	74,754
SHAREHOLDERS' EQUITY			
Common stock	474,499	949,679	949,679
Additional paid-in capital	817,205	1,292,385	1,292,385
Consolidated retained earnings	855,987	1,097,552	999,488
Net unrealized gains on securities	716	978	47,670
Foreign currency translation adjustments	–217	20,417	25,621
TOTAL SHAREHOLDERS' EQUITY	2,148,190	3,361,012	3,314,845
TOTAL LIABILITIES, MINORITY INTEREST AND SHAREHOLDERS' EQUITY	4,282,138	5,916,879	5,911,239

Table 15.9 Income statements

	6 months 30 Sep. 00	6 months 30 Sep. 01	Full year 31 Mar. 01
Recurring profits and losses			
Operating revenues and expenses			
Telecommunication businesses			
Operating revenues	1,725,570	2,043,938	3,599,329
Selling expenses	719,017	803,500	1,537,100
Maintenance	70,775	89,404	168,409
General expenses	19,400	21,167	37,853
Administrative expenses	56,318	59,128	122,966
Research costs	21,305	25,948	60,554
Depreciation	257,555	281,159	570,086
Loss on disposal of fixed assets	15,968	13,219	68,119
Communication network charges	163,838	213,182	287,144
Taxes and public dues	13,777	13,858	25,159
Rounding adjustment	4	4	4
Operating expenses	1,337,957	1,520,569	2,877,394
Operating income from telecommunications businesses	387,613	523,368	721,935
Other businesses			
Operating revenues	491,896	569,025	1,086,674
Operating expenses	467,457	541,986	1,031,446
Operating income from other businesses	24,439	27,038	55,227
Total operating income	412,052	550,407	777,162
Non-operating revenues and expenses			
Non-operating revenues	3,984	4,277	11,217
Interest income	362	82	863
Dividend income	108	59	112
Gain on sale of investment securities	475	668	-
Lease and rental income	789	1,052	1,434
Miscellaneous income	2,247	2,414	8,806
Non-operating expenses	18,778	72,163	101,461
Interest expense	10,282	9,722	22,950

continued

Table 15.9 *continued*

	6 months 30 Sep. 00	6 months 30 Sep. 01	Full year 31 Mar. 01
Equity in losses of affiliated companies	2,329	59,293	31,845
Loss on write-off of inventories	4,159	1,943	16,786
Miscellaneous expenses	2,007	1,203	29,878
Recurring profit	397,258	482,521	686,918
Special profits and losses			
Special losses	–	262,712	–
Write-down of investment in affiliated companies	–	262,712	–
Income before income taxes	397,258	219,808	686,918
Income taxes – current	170,911	248,281	322,522
Income taxes – deferred	–2,040	–146,792	–21,911
Minority interest	10,870	14,450	20,802
Net income	217,516	103,869	365,505

Table 15.10 Cash-flow statements

	6 months 30 Sep. 00	6 months 30 Sep. 01	Full year 31 Mar. 01
I. Cash flows from operating activities:			
Income before income taxes	397,258	219,808	686,918
Depreciation and amortization	262,651	287,485	582,167
Loss on sale and disposal of property and equipment	12,369	10,023	48,260
Interest and dividend income	–471	–141	–976
Interest expense	10,282	–	–
Interest expense and discounts on commercial paper	–	9,764	23,119
Equity in losses of affiliated companies	2,329	59,293	31,845
Write-down of investment in affiliated companies	–	262,712	–

continued

Table 15.10 *continued*

	6 months 30 Sep. 00	6 months 30 Sep. 01	Full year 31 Mar. 01
Decrease (increase) in notes and accounts receivable, trade, net of allowance for doubtful accounts	–289,399	81,236	–435,546
Increase in inventories	–40,137	–56,225	–40,747
Increase in liability for employees' severance	17,068	8,382	35,495
Increase (decrease) in accounts payable, trade	55,652	–71,550	161,198
Decrease in accrued consumption tax	–10,269	–2,892	–3,146
Other – net	7,420	6,082	79,438
Subtotal	424,753	813,979	1,168,027
Interest and dividends received	499	157	988
Interest paid	–10,738	–9,459	–24,455
Income taxes paid	–185,762	–203,384	–305,249
Net cash provided by operating activities	228,751	601,293	839,311
II. Cash flows from investing activities:			
Purchase of property and equipment	–436,275	–480,742	–800,133
Purchase of intangible fixed assets and other investments	–64,207	–92,771	–149,274
Purchase of investment securities	–596,711	–14,195	–1,828,173
Advances on loans, deposits and other investments	–2,501	–1,422	–4,363
Proceeds from collection of loans, deposits and other investments	41,734	2,436	43,274
Other – net	–63	1,083	1,557
Net cash used in investing activities	–1,058,025	–585,612	–2,737,112

continued

Table 15.10 *continued*

	6 months 30 Sep. 00	6 months 30 Sep. 01	Full year 31 Mar. 01
III. Cash flows from financing activities:			
Net change in short-term borrowings	533,800	–484,540	545,800
Net increase in commercial paper	10,000	107,400	60,500
Proceeds from long-term borrowings	242,000	76,000	
Repayment of long-term borrowings	–115,496	–62,373	–246,619
Proceeds from issuance of bonds	–	199,180	179,272
Redemption of bonds	–	–20,000	–
Issuance of common stock	–	–	930,006
Cash dividends paid	–4,978	–5,189	–9,766
Net cash provided by (used in) financing activities	423,325	–23,522	1,535,194
IV. Effect of exchange rate changes on cash and cash equivalents	–2	–1	27
V. Net decrease in cash and cash equivalents	–405,950	–7,842	–362,579
VI. Cash and cash equivalents at beginning of the period	481,003	118,424	481,003
VII. Cash and cash equivalents at end of the period	75,052	110,581	118,424

PART IV

Applications

CHAPTER 16

Valuing Start-up Firms

MANY START-UPS WORTHLESS

The period between June 1999 and Spring/Summer 2000 was an exceptional time in venture capital. Many marginal or completely unsustainable business plans attracted venture capital support. Many banks and groups of rich private individuals ('angels') entered the venture capital (we will use the abbreviation VC for 'venture capital' and 'venture capitalist', according to context) business for the first time, attracted by the extremely high returns on VC funds in 1999 (estimated at 140% by VentureOne). Much of this was 'dumb money', keen to take advantage of high IPO valuations by executing an 'IPO pipeline' of start-up 'enterprises' which would transition from concept to prospectus in short order, and then be sold to the voracious public market for high valuations. Ted Dintersmith of the established VC firm Charles River Ventures sums it up with a baseball metaphor: 'there were a lot of pop-ups that suddenly were home runs.'[1] Dintersmith is perhaps generous – at the height of the mania, there were quite a few groundouts that were treated as home runs.

Fortunately or unfortunately, depending on one's point of view, those days are gone. At the time of writing, financing for start-up businesses is hard to come by under any circumstances, and even credible business plans with experienced entrepreneurs at the helm will find the financing process fraught. Even when money was easiest to come by at around end 1999/early 2000, the 'man in the street' had an extremely hard time taking advantage of the relatively easy availability of capital. Although most venture capitalists make a point of at least glancing at every business plan that is sent to their offices, in practice only plans which had been sent via some kind of referral or had received a recommendation had any reasonable chance of gaining detailed consideration. This is not an example of an 'old boys' network', but simply a sensible way of rationing time. VCs will expect a plan that has the recommendation of a previously successful entrepreneur or fellow VC to be of higher quality than a non-recommended plan. In an environment of time famine, they simply cannot give full consideration to each and every business plan they receive (many of which are of extremely poor quality). Other avenues to gain VCs' attention were business plan competitions, meetings and organizations such as those run by leading business schools (for example, London Business School's Foundation for Entrepreneurial Management and the Haas Business School's Berkeley Entrepreneurs' Forum), but these avenues are mainly open to alumni and current students of the relevant institutions.

Therefore if you are sitting at home with a business plan and this book, and wondering how much venture capital your idea might attract, the answer is probably zero. Depending on how good the quality and quantity of a VC's supply of business plans and opportunities is, he or she will invest in between 2 in 100 and 1 in 1000 of the plans received. A very small proportion of business plans are funded, and an infinitesimal proportion of ideas scribbled on the back of a napkin make the long journey from napkin to plan to business. In the 'Get rich quick via venture capital' strand of business literature that has found a wide readership recently, you will only read about the ones which *do* make that journey, never the 99.9% that don't. Our advice is: put this book down, try and sell the book to someone else if you can,[2] and go out and start your business on a small scale. This is the only way out of the 'no funding = no value' conundrum. If you can prove your business on a small scale, you will be in a far better position to attract needed capital later. If you are prepared to give up your job before receiving venture funding, this will be further evidence of your commitment.

It is possible that, after developing the business for one or two years, you may find that it is a poor business, and be forced to wind it up at a cost of two years of your time and some personal or 'friends and family' funding. (This is a high cost, and if you are not prepared to bear it, you should not go any further.) On the other hand, you may be able to create an NLB (nice little business) of your own, which supports comfortably yourself, your family and a workforce, and does not require any funding other than internally generated cash – that is not to be sniffed at. Or you may require further funding to grow your (probably already profitable) business two years out, possibly a loan from your bank, maybe venture capital – before your business grows into a huge success. It is cold comfort, but the *second* time you build a business (when you will be termed a 'seasoned entrepreneur'), you will be in a better position to raise VC funds. This is the historical pattern, and it is returning. There will always be exceptions: but don't bank on being one. (For example, you may be able to bend or break these rules if you have a truly innovative piece of hardware or software technology – particularly if you partner with an experienced entrepreneur or business person. A successful 10- or 15-year career in a leading related corporate – Cisco, Intel, Microsoft – may also make the VCs sit up and take notice.)

CLEARING THE QUALITY BAR

The process of valuing a start-up business for VC purposes breaks down into two stages:

- determining whether the business will clear the 'quality bar' and attract venture capital interest
- valuing the business on the assumption that it clears the quality bar.

Before the commencement of the funding search process, the business idea should be translated into a *business plan*. If one is a Jim Clark or a Steve Jobs, a 'one pager' may well attract funds from investors who know your pedigree. Otherwise a formal document will be required setting out key details and financial projections for the business. A business plan will consist of at least the following elements:

- executive summary
- business description
- outline financials and assumptions with justification
- market scope (customers, competitors)
- marketing plan (how to get to them)
- operations plan and timeline
- management team
- detailed financials.

These are a minimum listing, and other elements may be required. For a business plan based on a technological advance an extensive technical description, written at layman and detailed level, will be essential, and a major part of the plan. Other relevant elements will be added to these.

Financial data will be a key part of the plan, both at a headline level and at an extremely detailed level. The detailed financials will specify the cash flows out for each month by line item. If the lease that the firm will take on for its premises has a large up-front payment, then this will be reflected in the cash flow statement in the appropriate month. Staff costs are a key element of the costs of a start-up business, and the cash flows to pay each type of staff member, including employers' National Insurance or social security contributions and any benefits, and the headcount of that type of employee, must be included in the financials. If the manager knows that three webmasters will be required from April 2003, but does not know the salary for a webmaster, then this must be determined before the business plan is completed. Revenue forecasts will also be the subject of intense scrutiny, and should be detailed and supported by sufficient back-up in the form of market and sales forecast data.

Time should be spent fine-tuning the executive summary. An executive summary which

- gains the reader's attention
- gets across the attractions of the business and team
- lays out the financial return to investors

is an essential part of any successful plan. There are many sources on the topic of writing business plans, so we will not dwell more on it here.

The initial action of the funding search process is that the potential entrepreneur will identify the appropriate venture capitalists to which the plan will be sent. The first stage is to peruse VC websites and other corporate information to check that the business plan is in a sector and of an investment size which will appeal to the VC. There is no point sending a business plan requiring seed investment of £250,000 to a VC fund which only deals in series C (or immediate pre-IPO) investments of over £20m. Similarly, some VCs specialize in biotechnology projects and will not respond to an internet-related business plan. The basic searching process may be carried out using online sources such as VentureSource, or by perusing the annually published *Pratt's Guide to Venture Capital* (Securities Data Publishing) which has coverage of US (75–80%) and Rest of World (20–25%) venture capitalists, indexed by industry and stage of investment. However, at this point aggressive networking is required to get the plan in front of contacts of the relevant venture capitalists. A recommendation will not ensure funding, but the appropriate recommendation will enhance the chance of funding.

A sample list of criteria for a VC fund is shown below:

- Is the investment in the VC's target industry sector?
- Is the investment at the correct stage (or correct size) for this VC?
- Is the market attractive (five forces, and the like)?
- Does the business have potential to grow into a substantial public company or trade sale?
- Is the business the first mover?
- What is the potential competition in the space?
- What is the quality of management team?
  - previous business success (especially in a relevant sector)
  - technical knowledge
  - management and control skills
  - determination and passion.
- What are the results of risk assessment? Does management have the capability and plans in place to manage risk effectively?

If the business plan meets the VC fund's set of criteria, initial interviews with management are scheduled; and if these are successful, the progress towards a *term-sheet* (an agreement between the VC and the entrepreneur/team) commences.

VALUATION BASED ON TRIANGULATION

The first valuation which will be obtained for a business will be as a result of the initial VC projection for the term-sheet. VCs are unlikely to value a business in which they have no interest. Valuations by managers of the business, or by consultants or accountants engaged by the managers of the business, are not likely to figure in this process. Such valuations may still be viewed as guidelines for negotiation by entrepreneurs, but are only likely to become relevant if the business plan attracts substantial demand by multiple VCs.

Since valuation of start-up businesses is such a difficult task, venture capitalists will (and indeed, should) get the benefit of a number of calculation methods, and will use sensitivity analysis within those methods to calculate values. Then they will estimate the final value by *triangulation* between these individual estimates, and will offer this to entrepreneurs, or possibly a smaller amount to allow negotiation, depending on the firm's policy. (Many VCs have a policy of avoiding negotiation, but will, of course, bend this policy anyway for a particularly attractive opportunity.) *Triangulation* means that a number of valuations are obtained (ideally three or more, hence the name), and a final valuation is selected using a weighted average of the valuations, based on the likelihood that the operating parameters on which the valuations are based will occur, and on the perceived reliability of the different valuation methods.

There are five basic methodologies for valuing a start-up firm, one or more of which may be used in valuing any given business plan or investment opportunity:

- comparable-deal-based (how is a company of this type/maturity/projected revenue valued in typical VC deals?)
- cash-flow projection-based (or a – usually simpler – variant)
- public market multiple-based (for example, multiple of sales or predicted sales versus public market comparables)
- discounted expected flotation proceeds
- discounted terminal value (earnings multiple).

PRELUDE TO VALUATION: CHECKING AND TESTING THE PLAN

Before the valuation process begins, the VC has to be confident of the values in the financial projections that are contained in the business plan. This does not mean that he or she has be convinced that the numbers are what will actually *occur* in the future – such a level of confidence about the uncertain future is unobtainable. But he or she has to be confident that the numbers are as good a prediction of the future as can be obtained. The VC has first of all to determine that the numbers have some basis in fact or are a reasonable estimation of uncertain quantities (they are not plucked out of the air, or from somewhere even less salubrious). They should not be tainted with undue optimism. This is a difficult task, since both entrepreneurs and (to a lesser extent) VCs are naturally optimistic people.

The task for the VC is to turn the data in the business plan into information which he or she can use to value the business. Sometimes 'data' is too generous a term for what is in the business plan. One dictionary definition of 'data' is 'Factual information, especially information organized for analysis or used to reason or make decisions'. Many of the numbers in business plans are just that: numbers.

One key example of 'numbers' in the business plan where there should be 'factual information' is the '5% of a large market' type of revenue projection. Large markets are, almost invariably, groups of smaller market segments. Segments may be geographic or based on consumers' interests. The '5% of a large market' which entrepreneurs are projecting to secure will almost certainly turn out to be 20–50% of the addressable niche, and that means that a very strong and focused appeal to that segment will be needed.

For this reason, revenue forecasts should be 'bottom up', not 'top down'. They should be based on an extremely attractive appeal to one or more smaller segments, tested by market research in this segment. For start-ups addressing business markets, Frederick J. Beste III (a frequent speaker at the Venture Capital Institute graduate training program) suggests that entrepreneurs should talk to at least a dozen prime customer targets before committing to a product strategy. For a business targeting a consumer market, detailed tailored surveys will be necessary to give third-party confirmation of entrepreneurs' sales projections. Some entrepreneurs demur from surveying and questioning, with the declared reason that they are concerned about giving secrets away to potential competitors. This is a risk that can be limited by the correct line of questioning. Also, the desire to avoid competition, while wise, cannot be the be-all and end-all. An attractive business model will attract competition in short order, however careful the pre-planning and 'stealth mode' preparation has been.

A better attitude to competition is to be prepared for it and to plan for it. The issue of risk assessment is key, and this should be in the form of planning and worst-case projections. What is the fallback, and what is the effect of the fallback on the cash funds that the company will possess at key junctures?

Entrepreneurs' cost projections can and should be tested in two ways: bottom-up and top-down. Bottom-up testing can be a process as simple as checking the salaries of webmasters in the locale of the business and confirming that these are in line with the business plan. What office rental per square foot has the company assumed? Has this been confirmed by local commercial estate agents or real estate brokers?

Costs of personnel and property are a large part of many business cost structures, but the price of these is not the only way cost projections can go wrong: the business plan may also mis-predict the quantity required. The development of technology, whether hardware or software, is expensive and time-consuming. At what stage is the technology of the business at the time of seeking capital? Where does it need to be? What is the plan to get there? Is the plan reasonable or is it too optimistic? Many VC valuers are qualified in electronic engineering or are experienced technologists in their own right, and will use their own knowledge to evaluate the feasibility of technological plans. If the valuer is operating within the environment of a large VC company with experience of a number of start-ups, he or she can get second opinions from VCs who have previously shepherded companies through the technology development process. In the absence of these sources of information, a senior technologist at another portfolio business (somewhat related but not directly in competition) should be tapped for some consultancy, in return for either cash or options in the new firm.

The top-down method of assessing whether costs are reasonable is to look at mature companies in a similar business, and to see what margins and returns on capital they are making. This provides an estimate of whether costs are reasonable, relative to revenues. The statement from entrepreneurs that 'There's nobody like us' is generally a turnoff for VCs. If a team can't see who the competition is, it just means they haven't found them yet. For instance music download-based businesses are in a new and uncertain business, but can look towards other entertainment industry companies to discover comparable margins. One potential issue with this approach is that new-economy companies may have very low assets employed, so achieving industry-level margins will give them very high returns on capital. In fact, low operating assets may well be a signal of low margins. This is because the process of competition forces returns on capital to lower levels, down to the opportunity cost of capital when full competition comes into the marketplace. If a business is assuming high margins and high asset turnover (asset turnover = sales/operating assets: that is, high asset turnover means efficient use of operating assets), this means a very high return. In sense-checking cost assumptions that lead to such high returns, only one question needs to be asked: 'When people see these high returns they are going to enter this market like crazy: how is the company going to stop them?' Without strategic barriers to entry, such as a patent or a wide technological advantage that is difficult for competitors to match (think of Intel's chip-fabrication expertise), new entrants will quickly erode the high returns. (For further discussion of the return on capital and competition, see Chapter 6; and for further discussion on the concept of 'barriers to entry', see Chapters 11 and 12.)

COMPARABLE-DEAL-BASED VALUATION

Basic data

Once the soundness of the data has been checked, we move on to the valuation process. One of the main methods of valuation in pre-IPO companies is that of *private market comparables*. This is the same method that we feel is unsuitable to use as a valuation metric for public market companies. However, VCs use private market comparables because they feel:

- that there is often insufficient information to construct an accurate DCF forecast
- that comparables can allow the incorporation of a wider range of value-relevant information
- that valuation based on comparables reacts more quickly to changes in the private equity and VC marketplace
- more confident in making a 'market-based' valuation than one based on assumptions
- that valuation is not particularly important once the decision to back the business has been made.

Basic data on comparable deals is obtained from online sources such as VentureSource (Reuters' VentureOne), VentureEconomics, Venturewire, vcbuzz.com and so on. The valuer starts with the basic data on the business being valued, which will be the stage of the investment and the industry segment that the investment will be in. The VentureSource database can be searched on the following criteria:

- company name
- VC/investor name
- executive
- service provider (for example, law firm)
- location (city, state if in USA, country, world area if outside USA)
- industry
- internet category
- total raised (range)
- date of financing (range)
- valuation amount (range)
- financing round

- company stage (start-up, product development, shipping product, profitable or restart)
- current status (independent, acquired, public, out of business, and so on)
- date founded (range)
- number of employees (range).

The VentureSource database outputs data on deals, and basic data on the individual companies – that is, a one- or two-line business description, financing status, internet focus, names of key executives, and so on. The round data is in Figure 16.1.

The *round number* is the numerical index of the round in the VentureSource database. The meaning of *round type* is as shown below. Round types are sometimes described in terms of the *series*, which is the label of the preference stock issued. Stock issued in the first major funding is labelled *series A stock*, in the second funding is labelled *series B stock* and so on. Ordinarily, series C stock will have liquidation seniority to series B stock and so on. Post-valuation is the valuation immediately after the round. Unfortunately this information is frequently missing.

Median pre-money amounts for high-tech deals during 1993–97 by development stage[3] are as follows:

- start-up: $1m
- development: $5m
- shipping: $27m
- profitability: $64m

Money raised at each round type is shown in Table 16.1. Note that the figures given are illustrative. There is a lot of variation in the size of deals, and a tendency for funding to come in 'dribs and drabs' rather than in the clean progression of seed, series A, series B, and so on.

Post-money is the value immediately after the payment of VC cash, and is calculated based on the value of the investment received and the percentage sold for that investment. For example, if a VC investor pays $350,000 for 20% of a pre-seed investment in a company, the post-money value of that company is

Figure 16.1 Format of round data

Round number	Round type	List of investors	Funding raised ($m)	Post-valuation $m (if known)	Company stage

Table 16.1 Characteristics of funding rounds

Round type	Series	Purpose of funding	Median investment[4] ($m)
Pre-seed*	Usually common stock	Early-stage feasibility study	0.2–0.5[5]
Seed*	Usually common stock	Solidifying business plan; recruitment of some core staff	1
1st	A	Funding firm to the shipping of product (if applicable); building operational website; recruitment of sizeable staff	2.6
2nd	B	Further funding to scale up the business: likely to include expanded facilities and staff	3.8
3rd	C	Necessary funding to bring the business to cash self-sufficiency and to make it suitable for public market or trade sale	2.8
Mezzanine*		Funding to continue operations until an already-scheduled IPO	4.5

* Note that at the time of writing pre-seed, seed and mezzanine funds are particularly hard to raise. Pre-seed funds should be raised from entrepreneurs' personal funds, friends and family, or incubators such as those associated with higher education institutions. Government small business loans and community organizations should also not be forgotten as a potential source of funds. In the absence of available series C or mezzanine funding, entrepreneurs should plan on achieving cash self-sufficiency based on the series B cash funding.

\$350,000/0.2 = \$1.75m. The *pre-money* value is the value immediately *before* the payment of the VC cash: that is, \$1.75m – \$0.35m = \$1.4m. It is an accounting reality that the activity of the cash payment by the VC only adds precisely the cash value paid to the business. It is true that in the week leading up to the agreement, the negotiators' perceptions of value may have suffered wild fluctuations, although generally on an upward trend! But at the instant before cash payment, the deal has been agreed and only the value of the cash is added.

Another type of round that may occur is a *'rescue' round* (sometimes called *restart*, *cram-down* or *burnout*), whereby a business is running out of cash before it can reach cash self-sufficiency or a liquidity event (for example, an IPO or a trade sale for cash), but the VCs still feel it has the potential to succeed. Possible reasons why a business may require a rescue round are that:

- the business has not reached its targets because of operational problems which are fixable with some changes to strategy or personnel

- the public market will not support an IPO of the business now, but is expected to do so in the near future
- VCs feel that a trade sale is possible to preserve some value, but need some time to source potential buyers and negotiate a price: the rescue round supports the business until then.

Rescue rounds may be conditional on the resignation of the CEO or founder, and may involve down-valuing of the business and large amounts of the equity being sold to the rescue-round investors (heavily diluting early investors and 'sweat investors' (managers), hence the terms *cram-down* and *burnout*). Because of the cash shortage, entrepreneurs requiring a rescue round will be in a very weak negotiating position.

After examining the VentureSource data, the valuer has obtained perhaps 2–5 deals which appear to be in the same industry sector and the same series or round of funding as the opportunity he or she is valuing. The next stage is to gather more detailed data on these comparable companies, and finally to use these data to calculate comparable ratios, which enable us to value the firm being studied.

Obtaining detailed data

Having obtained a shortlist of comparable companies, we now have to attempt to extract further relevant data. We have a lot of data about the company we are valuing. Ideally we would like to have the same data about the comparable companies. We would like their revenue projections and indeed the whole financial projections of management, together with VCs' projections and how they arrived at their valuation. Obviously, we will not obtain all that data, but may be able to obtain some of it. Softer data is often easier to obtain and can be extremely relevant. For example, if we are attempting to value a three-person seed-stage start-up in wireless networking, we need to know how comparable are the comparable companies suggested by our initial examination of VentureSource. Are they in the same field? Do they have more key staff? How far along the road towards commercialization of their technology were they when the funding occurred?

Although the VentureSource data are not very detailed, they do give us the name and address of the funded company and of the VC funding it. The website of the funded company can be a useful first port of call. This will almost certainly have a basic description of the funded company's product, to allow us to judge how comparable it is to the product of our subject firm. The company may have a pack of financial information for potential investors, either available for download (ideal) or available by email request. The number of staff in a firm may be something that the telephonist will divulge without difficulty, since it is a number that is often requested by local governments, local service businesses and other bodies.

A 'bio' page for the founders and key staff is also frequently found, and can be extremely useful. The bio page will allow us to cross-reference the key staff and to find out more about their activities, as a further aid to determining how comparable the products of the subject and comparable companies are. This is particularly true if the start-up is one based on a technological innovation. If some of the key personnel have previously been working at a university, or a corporate environment that allows or encourages publication of results such as Xerox PARC (Palo Alto Research Center), we may find that the staff have published papers on the technology of the company. A patent search using a patent information agency can also be instructive. If the valuer is acting on behalf of the venture capitalist, this is also an excellent opportunity to see whether the company being valued has a technological lead over the competition or vice versa. Conference appearances by the key staff may also provide useful information about their products and plans.

At this point it should be noted that the valuer is likely to be acting as an employee or a consultant to the company seeking investment, or as an employee, a partner or a consultant to the venture capitalist who is potentially an investor in that firm. Therefore the questioning of the comparable company is questioning of a potential competitor, and falls within the realm of *competitive intelligence*. As such, satisfactory ethical practices should be maintained.

Using the data

Once the data on comparable companies have been obtained, how should they be used? We will want to take advantage of as much value-relevant information as possible to determine relative valuations against comparable companies. The most reliable financial figures we possess will be early-stage revenue predictions from the management's plan, but we may or may not have early-stage revenue projections from comparable companies. For a *very* early-stage company, we will also be looking at more uncertain concepts such as the 'size' of the business we are taking a stake in, using proxies such as the number of patents, the size of the innovation, the number of technologists, and the amount of progress that the managers have made in developing their product pre-VC funding.

The basic methodology is to take an operational parameter of the business, for example the number of personnel, and to use this to value the business by taking that parameter as a proxy for the 'size' of the business. If we are valuing an eWidgeting company called Business B, and we have a known value concluded in a financing of Business A (a very similar type of business to B), which has twice as many employees as business B, then these data suggest that Business B is half as valuable as Business A:

$$\text{value per eWidgeting employee (VPE)} = \frac{\text{Business A value}}{\text{Business A employees}}$$

$$\Rightarrow \text{Business B value} = \text{Business B employees} \times \text{VPE}$$

To maximize the modest reliability of this method, we want to calculate multiple value-based parameters. Other possible operational parameters are:

- historical revenues
- predicted revenues
- number of patents
- number of customers
- number of employees holding PhDs.

The method requires careful use. For example, if the entrepreneur running Business B knows that the VC is valuing a business based on number of employees, what is the surefire method of increasing value? Hire more people, even if they are in the mailroom! This is the problem of incentives that we mentioned when discussing the valuation of publicly held internet companies. Therefore, multiple parameters, backed by strategic insight, must be utilized.

To take a slightly more detailed example, suppose we have obtained some data on a comparable company in Atlanta, Georgia, which is a seed-stage start-up in 802.11b wireless networking software with a post-money valuation of $2m. The comparable company has four key founders, whereas our company (in New York or London) has three key founders. Therefore this suggests a value of $1.5m for our company ($2m/4 = $500,000 per key founder), if we assume that the key founders (sources of technical, scientific or management ideas) are each the source of profitable ideas, and that the number of these capable people predicts the future size of the business. This is not a great method of valuation – we cannot 'test' the quality of either firm's personnel's ideas, or tell how quickly each set of ideas will translate into profits – but, if there are few other data, we will want to enter it in our mental valuation model. However, continuing the example, if one of our company's key founders is the doyen/ne of 802.11b networking, with twice as many ideas and potentially profitable contributions as other executives at both companies, then he or she should be valued as double the 'normal' key person, and the suggested valuation would be $2m. The point to make here is that some judgement is required.

Now, let us suppose that the company we are valuing has projected revenues of $1.5m in 2003, and that we have obtained 2003 projected revenue for the Atlanta company (this would be somewhat miraculous, admittedly). If the Atlanta projected revenue is $2m ($1 of 2003 revenue per $1 post-money), then this would suggest a post-money valuation of $1.5m for our New York or London firm. On the other hand, if the three New York/London founders say that they need $400,000 to do the key research and feasibility studies for the next stage, and will not issue any more than 20% of equity for it, then many VCs (having taken the decision to back the business already) will not wish to lose the opportunity on the valuation issue, especially if there are other VCs 'sniffing around'. If the gap was wider, as it often currently is for firms which took their last financing at the boosted levels of early 2000, the VC would probably walk away.

We might also have obtained a comparable figure for a Boston start-up, which has six key individuals, and has recorded a seed round at a $2m post-money valuation. This would suggest a much smaller valuation for our firm, and would suggest somewhere between $330,000 and $500,000 per key person. However, our detailed research has revealed that this is a 'bluetooth' software start-up. We might believe bluetooth (the cheap, low-power, short-range wireless technology) to be more of a wireless remote-control technology than a wireless networking strategy; if so, we would dismiss this comparable. Or we might enter it in our mental model, but with a low weighting.

To summarize, private market comparables will be a useful indicator, but will require research, some judgement and, as in all the valuation methods, some flexibility if the business is attractive. (And, if it wasn't attractive, it would not have got to the valuation stage.)

CASH-FLOW PROJECTION-BASED (OR SIMILAR) VALUATION

DCF in venture capital

Most VCs believe that in an ideal world, DCF (discounted cash flow) is the superior form of valuation. Due to lack of data, however, valuation of internet start-ups is *not* an ideal world. Lower risk private equity deals, such as management buy-ins or buy-outs, and funding of established businesses as part of leveraged buyouts, make extensive use of DCF valuations.

In response to the shortage of data, there are several alternative courses of action for the VC believing that DCF is a superior method. The most sensible approach is to use a simple DCF, one with fewer line items and one which does not go far out into the future, 2–5 years of projections being standard. This is a tool for valuation, but also a tool for checking that the business has sound economics going forward. We include in the 'Cash-flow projection or similar' method any 'economically based' value-forecasting method, by which we mean any method that models value by future cash flows or profits. This will include simple projected P&L/income statement-based valuation and cash-flow forecasts using *decision trees*.

In our section above entitled 'Prelude to valuation: checking and testing the plan', we discussed in some detail the need to check data in the business plan to ensure their veracity. If this process has been completed to the VC's satisfaction, then producing a DCF forecast is fairly straightforward with two exceptions:

- the determination of the cost of capital
- the determination of the ending multiple.

We discussed the methodology of DCF in Chapters 1–4; readers are referred to those chapters for a review. The simple DCF for valuation should proceed by adding together many of the line items which will be broken out in the detailed financials listed in the business plan. It should also show the yearly or half-yearly (rather than monthly) cash flow or profit. (Some VCs prefer an income statement or P&L framework, because businesspeople are used to talking in terms of profits, and because, as per our discussion in Chapter 3, the profit calculation smooths out some large capital spending to give a more intuitive measure of profitability.) The simple DCF or P&L should be seen as an alternative view of the detailed financial data in the business plan, useful not only for valuation but also as a helicopter view of where trends in staff costs and levels of other costs are headed.

The determination of the cost of capital

VC cost-of-capital determination by the CAPM is problematic because the CAPM assumes that investors hold the market portfolio. This is thought not to be the case for VCs, although an argument can be made that a VC investment represents an element of an end-investor's diversification strategy. Recent research by Berk et al. (1999) suggests that higher cost of capital is justified even if the investors do hold the market portfolio, because the sequence of decisions and resolution of uncertainty in an R&D or start-up project has option-like characteristics, which carry higher systematic (undiversifiable) risk.

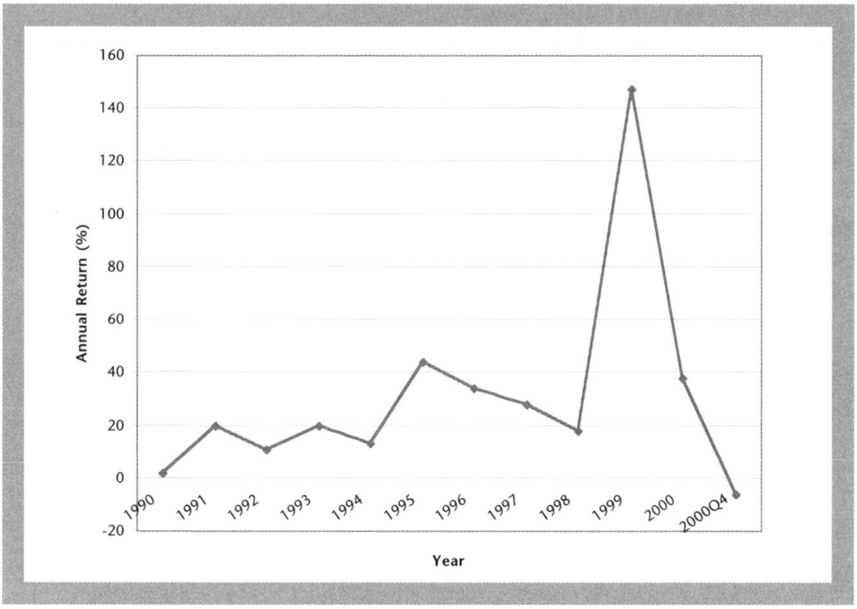

Figure 16.2 Venture capital returns: 1990–2000

However, we can use the more general method of calculation of cost of capital by looking at expected returns for the same risk-class, and using long-term past returns as an estimate of these. Note that we restrict the asset class to venture capital as defined in the USA, in high-tech or early-stage companies, as opposed to venture capital as it is defined in the UK, which includes lower risk investments such as MBOs (management buyouts, in which management buy shares in their (usually mature) business, with the help of private equity investors). The UK high-tech venture capital industry has too short a history for long-term past returns to be reliably calculated; and in the brief period it has existed, returns have been disappointing, of the order of 8–10%.[6] Looking at the United States, VentureOne (reported in *The Economist*) reports average high-tech venture returns of about 20% (nominal). Figure 16.2 shows the history of recent returns. It can be seen that the extreme performance of 1999 (over 140%) was aberrant, although it is fresh in the mind of many VCs. Venture returns for the first half of the 1990s were in single figures.

In contrast to the 20% that would be suggested by observation of long-term VC returns, observed VC costs of capital are considerably higher than 20%, normally between 30–80%. Intuitively we would expect the required returns

Table 16.2 Venture capital required returns

Stage	Discount rate range (%)
Start-up	50–70
First stage	40–60
Second stage	35–50
Third stage	35–50
Fourth stage	30–40
IPO	25–35

for start-up stage investments to be higher than for later stage, so the 20% average perhaps conceals a pattern of higher achieved returns trending down to lower returns in the later stages. However, this still cannot explain the distribution of venture capital required returns observed by, for example, Plummer (1987) (see Table 16.2).

The reasons advanced for these high discount rates are as follows:

- 'VC is very risky: if firms cannot deliver 50% per year we don't want to back them.'
- 'Investors demand 35% per year, and we need to find companies that can provide it.'
- 'A higher cost of capital sets a higher benchmark for our companies.'
- 'If we price our money expensive, we get a bigger piece of the pie.'
- 'We need a higher IRR to adjust for liquidity.'
- 'We need to adjust these optimistic management projections *somehow*.'

The first three explanations make no sense, in fact. Setting a 50% cost of capital does not deliver ex post returns of 50%: it simply delivers a sky-high heap of plans with financial projections *suggesting* a rate of 50% appreciation on VC money. Spreadsheeting is easy, it's business that's difficult! Similarly, a high cost of capital will not help deliver high returns to investors: it is picking the right businesses that will do that. The claim that a high cost of capital sets a high benchmark and incentivizes entrepreneurs is also wrong. In fact, the effect of a high cost of capital may be precisely the opposite, because it gives entrepreneurs less of a stake in future success.

To see why this is true, consider a business that an omniscient valuer would value at £100m (in today's money) using a cost of capital (determined using omniscient powers of calculating risk-adjusted cost of capital) of 20%. For simplicity let's assume that the business consists of one cash flow in three years of 100×1.2^3 = £172.8m. Further suppose that the business requires £25m of funding, which would secure the VC 25% of the business – that £25m would appreciate at an expected rate of 20% per annum. Now consider how much stake a VC who imposed a 50% cost of capital would get. He or she would value the business far more lowly than the correct value (£51.2m instead of £100m), and £25m would correspond to a much larger share (over 50%). The VC would have invested £25m in a business which would be correctly valued at £75m pre-money, and would have obtained a 50% stake! Now that may be good negotiating, but is it motivational? In reality, the net effect is that the VC gets a bigger piece of the pie.

The issue of liquidity is important, but the 20% returns on past VC investments include a premium for the lack of liquidity in these types of investments. Since we are comparing like with like, we should not tack on another premium for liquidity over and above these historical returns – that would be double-counting.

The final reason is probably the most important. If profit forecasts that managers come up with are too optimistic, a 'fair' cost of capital will systematically overvalue start-up businesses. The effect will be the reverse of the 'bigger piece of the pie' argument above – VCs using a fair, risk-adjusted cost of capital will price businesses too high and, because the investment requirements of the business are usually a predetermined amount of cash, will end up accepting too small a share of equity. Adjusting the cost of capital upwards will not correctly value the business (except by incredible coincidence), and this is why this 'fudge factor' approach is counselled against by every finance text from Brealey and Myers to Higson's *Business Finance*. But many VCs feel that it's better than nothing, and hope that the errors (optimistic profit forecasts and excessive cost of capital) roughly even out. Also, the fudge factor approach avoids the 'fights' with entrepreneurs that occur if VCs try to get them to change their revenue forecasts to make them more realistic. These conflicts can often be extremely emotional, and can create such enmity between entrepreneurs and VCs that investment is effectively forestalled.

Anyway, we counsel against the 'fudge factor' high discount rate approach. Instead, move towards a more suitable cost of capital of 20–30%, and work aggressively to make management projections more reasonable. If necessary, introduce a 'haircut' (a multiplier of perhaps 0.5 or 0.75 which is used to adjust management projections downwards) (even a secret one, to safeguard the VC–entrepreneur relationship) for optimistic management revenue and profit forecasts, and then discount the adjusted figure. Also, use several scenarios and a simple decision-tree format to make sense of downside cases. A simple implementation is to use a similar format to that in Part I of the book, working out worst-case, continuing-case and best-case scenarios – estimate probabilities, but do not evaluate the probability weighted value yet; for now, simply note the scenario values. And *don't* use a sky-high ending multiple …

The determination of the ending multiple

For any forecast where a limited number of years is forecast, the value at the end of the forecast period has to be calculated. This is then discounted back to the current period, and added to the discount period cash flows:

$$V = \Sigma C_i + \text{TV}$$

where C_i = cash flows between years i and the end of the period
TV = the terminal value.

TV is normally calculated as a multiple of cash flow or earnings. In order to smooth large cash flows, earnings are more suitable as a basis for calculation of terminal value.

Given that the forecast is a short-term forecast of up to five years, the choice of terminal value multiple is important in determining total valuation. There is no 'rule of thumb' for the terminal value multiplier, but there are some guidelines that can be used:

- minimum: multiple-based on long-term economy growth rate ($1/(r\text{–}4\%)$), where r is the cost of capital
- staging posts:
  - market multiple (long-term average) (≈12)
  - market multiple (recent average) (≈20)
  - industry multiple (average for quoted companies in the industry)
- maximum: industry multiple for high-growth companies.

Provided that a sensible cost of capital has been utilized, a multiple towards the low end of the range should be used. The guiding factors for the final choice of the value are as follows:

- What earnings growth rate do we expect the business to achieve at the end of the forecast period? (High prospective growth ⇒ high earnings multiple.)
- What cost of capital do we expect the business to have at the close of the forecast period? (High cost of capital ⇒ low earnings multiple.)

For a more detailed discussion of the logic underlying the calculation of multiples, see the section on the Gordon growth model in Chapter 9.

PUBLIC MARKET MULTIPLE-BASED VALUATION

Of the numbers available in the financial plan, probably the ones that both entrepreneurs and VCs have most confidence in are the revenue projections for the first two years. Therefore, one of the key inputs into the valuation triangulation process is the valuation based on the two-years-ahead revenue and adjusted market multiples.

The basic method is as follows:

$$\text{Public market-comparable P/R ratio (PPR)} = \frac{\text{Market value of company (average over last 6 months)}}{\text{Forecasted revenues for current year}}$$

An average or median PPR should be selected using the 4–6 most comparable public market companies. Then the implied value of the (private) company being valued is as follows:

$$\text{Private company value} = \text{PPR} \times \text{2 years ahead projected revenues of private company} \times \text{adjustment multiplier}$$

The *adjustment multiplier* is a multiplier used to adjust for the higher projected growth of the earlier-stage private companies (which would tend to increase the private company value), the lower liquidity of the private market company (which would tend to decrease the private company value), and the embedded optimism in the prediction of two-years-ahead revenues (decrease). The multiplier value is usually between 0.5 and 0.8, depending on the growth rate of the private firm relative to the public market comparables, and on the level of optimism embedded in the forecast. However, often VC firms fix a ratio as a policy, in order to limit effort on the valuation task.

Comparables based on number of employees and other operating parameters may also be calculated. However, this is not usually done, because number of employees is hardly at all comparable between an early-stage company (which will have a majority of development and managerial staff) and a public firm (which will have a broad range of staff, many in lower-level positions).

While private market comparables are more comparable, public market company data are more available. The problem with public market comparables is fivefold:

- companies in the public market may differ from the company being valued, in geographical reach or product scope, or other issues of *potential scale*
- even if the scale is the same, companies in the public market may be at *different stage of growth* than the company being valued
- the public market may have different characteristics from the private market (for example liquidity, transparency of information)
- the public market may be in a bubble state
- the public market may be in a depressed state.

(The latter two issues are two 'flavours' of the same problem.)

The potential scale issue is relevant, for example, when comparing multiples between US and European firms. US firms have an addressable consumer market of about 250m people in the continental United States. Geographical distances are huge, and local ways of doing business may differ, but there is a common language, a common legal framework, and nationwide logistics providers. By contrast, a European company seeking to address a market of 250m people has to produce online and offline content in 12 languages and to secure multiple national agreements. Jeremy Reffin of Apax estimates that start-up costs for a European business are of the order of three times that of a US business, for a target addressable marketplace of 250m people. Unfortunately, since value is determined not just by start-up cost but by its comparison to revenue and the operating leverage issue, this does not translate into a rule of thumb for comparing US and European revenue multiples. Also, the market may reward businesses for the greater costs in terms of higher revenues. However, in general multiples for European businesses should be expected to be lower than those for similar US businesses at the same stage of growth.

The reason why two-years-ahead revenue is used is that this revenue number is the most likely one to have commensurate growth with the public market firms. Why is growth important? Let us consider a company which has a value of $100m (independently and correctly determined by an omniscient valuer), whose revenue growth proceeds along exactly the expected path (that is, no surprises). The company returns 15%, which is also its cost of capital, per year. Its first-year sales are $1m, at the end of which it is worth $115m (historical sales multiple of 115). Its second-year sales grow to $5m (exactly as expected by the omnipotent valuer), while value grows to $132.2m (historical sales multiple of 26). Obviously, if we use the second-year multiple of 26 to value a start-up company which is only at the first-year stage, we run the risk of undervaluing the company. The solution to this problem is to observe market valuations and their variation with company growth rates for the comparable, and to track these back to a time when the prospective growth rate of the public market comparable was as similar as possible to the private market company's two-year-ahead growth rate. Then the revenue multiple will be closest to what is required. There will still be inaccuracies, because market-wide factors that influence pricing may have changed in the interim period.

How attractive is liquidity? We understand that liquidity *is* attractive, but not *how* attractive it is, or even precisely how to measure liquidity between private and public markets. Rules of thumb used by VC investors suggest that private market businesses are viewed as between 50% and 100% as valuable as public market businesses (even without a hot market for IPOs). It is difficult to believe that private businesses are only 50% as valuable as identical publicly quoted businesses; if they were, this would cause extensive arbitrage. In other words, financial intermediaries could make profits simply by purchasing privately held businesses and issuing their stock on the public markets. This did indeed seem to be occurring in 1999–early 2000, but it is not a sustainable long-term model.

Misvaluation is a problem for the investor assessing an opportunity. The public market comparable is most relevant to the valuation process when the relative valuation is *constant* between the time of valuation (early in the subject company's life) and the time of the liquidity event (IPO or trade sale). In the event that the valuation is being done at a time of high stock market volatility, an *average* market value over time should be taken as the denominator of the market side of the comparable. For example, rather than using a snapshot sales multiple (P/R ratio) at March 2002, a sales multiple based on sales divided by the average market value over the six months September 2001–March 2002 should be used.

In summary, then, the public market comparables are likely to be less valuable per dollar of sales because they are at an earlier stage of growth. On the other hand, their stock is more liquid than the stock of the private firm; and their financial parameters, being historical rather than predicted, are far more reliable. Finally, most publicly quoted comparables are US firms, making them less suitable if one is valuing a non-US firm. For this reason an adjustment factor (usually of 0.5–0.8), as noted above, is used to attempt to mitigate these problems.

DISCOUNTED EXPECTED FLOTATION PROCEEDS VALUATION

The *discounted expected flotation proceeds* valuation model was used by some VC firms at the height of the internet valuation 'mania', but is now less important because the number of firms being IPO'ed has declined precipitately. This method views the VC's investment as a purely financial 'trading' investment, where stock is bought in the early stage firm, to be liquidated when the IPO occurs, and the financial return between purchase and sale is calculated.

The basic method requires the estimation of two parameters:

- the *valuation of the company at liquidation*, VLU at IPO plus the lock-up period)
- the *time to liquidation*, T years.

The current value is then calculated by applying the NPV formula:

$$\text{current valuation} = \frac{\text{VLU}}{(1+r)^T}$$

where r = the cost of capital (customarily an extremely high cost of capital of 75%–100% per year was used in these calculations).

VLU is calculated using similar methods to that detailed above in the calculation of public market comparables. Projected revenues at the time VCs can liquidate are forecast, then multiplied by PPR. An adjustment multiplier may be used for valuation, but typically is not, since a high cost of capital is used to 'fudge' the numbers down to a suitable current valuation.

For the calculation of T, the key issue is when the VC will be able to liquidate his or her investment in the firm. Typically, VCs and other insiders (such as management) agree a lock-up period of at least 180 days from the IPO. This is fundamentally a measure intended to protect non-insider investors in the IPO: since the non-insider investors are at a severe information disadvantage at the IPO time, the lock-up period is intended to prevent insiders from 'getting out' quickly before any bad news is revealed by the more strict disclosure required for public companies.

The implication for this valuation method is that value cannot be liquidated until the lock-up period expires, so this is the key time and gives the value of T. Under US securities rules (SEC rule 144), the selling of VC stock must be done at a limited rate. Insider sellers cannot sell more than the average weekly volume (in the four weeks preceding the sale) or 1% of stock outstanding (whichever is greater) in each three-month period. A more precise measure of T will factor in this delay.

The decline in the number of IPOs, which as been referred to by many commentators as the 'shuttering of the IPO market', has led to the abandonment of this method. Since it is almost impossible to conduct an IPO or a float for an internet company, the implicit assumption that an IPO will take place is no longer sensible. To illustrate, *Business Week* reports that from January to October 2001, there was only one internet-related IPO, compared to 129 taking place in the calendar year 2000. That IPO, of LoudCloud, Netscape co-founder Marc Andreessen's internet operations services company, had a post-IPO return of –77% to October 2001.

At some point the market for technology IPOs will become more friendly. However, valuation methods based on fundamental value will still be superior to the discounted IPO method, which emphasizes financial arbitrage.

DISCOUNTED TERMINAL VALUE VALUATION (HYBRID METHOD)

One method which finds a good deal of use is the discounting of the terminal value. This takes the analysis of profitability from the DCF method, and uses it to form a terminal value, which is then discounted back to the present. All intermediate cash flows up to the terminal point are ignored. The method is very similar to the discounted flotation proceeds method, but the emphasis is on estimation of value driven by fundamentals, in particular future profitability, not predicted market sentiment. The terminal value is seen as the potential sale proceeds for the firm (based on an earnings multiple) in year T, and this is then present-valued and compared with the investment required.

As with discounted flotation proceeds, the method requires the estimation of two parameters.

- the valuation of the company at T years, V dollars
- the time to valuation, T years.

The current value is then calculated by applying the NPV formula:

$$\text{current valuation} = \frac{V}{(1+r)^T}$$

where r = the cost of capital. 'Standard' VC costs of capital (as shown above in Table 16.2) are used in the calculation.

V is calculated using the projected cash flow or income statements. These statements are projected forward until such time as the company is in a profitable position (3–5 years), and the profit or earnings at that point is multiplied by a terminal multiplier calculated as discussed in the section on DCF valuation.

For the calculation of *T*, the key issue is when the firm will be mature enough so that profitability has been achieved, and also mature enough that a somewhat pedestrian multiple will give a sensible value.

This valuation method is preferred because it is fairly intuitive (unlike a full-blown complex DCF calculation) and because it can be used to set achievable long-term objectives for management. A common condition of investment is that managers are required to meet certain targets of revenues, development progress and/or profitability. This valuation method assumes that valuation is dependent on three-years-ahead earnings, so this can form a well-defined target for management.

PUTTING IT ALL TOGETHER: TRIANGULATION

Once the valuer has concluded his or her estimates based on one or more of the methods outlined, the task remains to put these together into a final summary estimate of valuation. This is a process which requires art as well as science. Results from the different methods should be arranged in order, from the highest valuation to the lowest. Methods which are inherently unreliable (that is, discounted expected flotation proceeds), and/or methods with data availability problems or which are felt to have given unsuitable valuations, are discarded. On the other hand, there may be multiple scenarios from the DCF-type valuation and multiple outputs from the comparable-based deal valuation method (for example, valuation based on number of PhDs and valuation based on sales revenues). These should not be aggregated but should be incorporated in the valuation range.

The triangulation or averaging process may be simple or difficult, depending on the dispersion of the valuations. After discarding valuations which are thought to be extreme or unreliable (for example, because of incomplete or questionable data), the remaining valuations may be averaged. To determine the final valuation, the constituent valuations should be weighted by the valuer, according to their reliability, their relevance, and the likelihood that the operating parameters assumed will occur. (For example, if an identical company had been funded the previous week for $20m this private market comparable would receive a very high weighting.) The average of the constituent valuations, however weighted, is the valuation.

Value and the negotiation process

Negotiation is key in the valuation process. Valuations by both parties can clearly be only a first step towards the final agreement. Also the monetary valuation is not the only part of the negotiation. Terms of agreement or the precise capital structure can impose draconian consequences on the unwary entrepreneur, and an attorney or lawyer who is expert in the field should be engaged before proceeding.

On the other hand, if the entrepreneur's idea is sufficiently attractive, and if he or she has networked well to create multiple interested VCs, then this can exert upward pressure on valuation.

Kane (1989) estimates the following breakdown of futures for VC deals:

- Total loss 40%
- 'Living dead' 30%
- 2–5 times return 20%
- 5–10 times return 8%
- 10+ times return 2%

If VCs feel they have detected a 'ten-bagger' they will go after it, pushing up the price. In this scenario – a happy but recently a rare one for entrepreneurs – the entrepreneur will seek to secure the optimal combination of valuation and 'smart money': the most helpful VC, with the best network to help secure potential partners and high-level employees, and the VC most able to guide and mentor the entrepreneur and his or her board.

On the other hand, many companies which received funding at the peak values of early 2000 are finding negotiation of follow-on capital difficult. This is because public market comparable-based valuations which seemed sensible at that point now seem unsupportably high. Values have fallen across the board, and this is a bitter pill to swallow, especially for entrepreneurs who have agreed anti-dilution provisions for their early VC investors (see below).

Conditions and terms

Writing about venture capital structuring in 1974, John R. Dominguez stated that 'Venture capitalists prefer that the financial structure be as simple as possible, with only one class of common stock. Experience has shown that in a small company, a variegated capital structure increases the risk of failure.' Oh, to have those simpler happier days again! Unfortunately current capital structures are a morass of securities, with venture capitalists normally only agreeing to invest in securities that give them additional rights in various scenarios.

In the simplest case, where all parties are happy to accept common equity (a situation that may well pertain, for example, at the 'friends and family' stage), the funds to be raised are divided by the calculated value, and the result is the share of common equity to be owned by the investing shareholders (the remainder to be retained by the existing owners, the entrepreneurs in the case of the first fund-raising). However, given that the type of stock issued to venture capitalists invariably has additional rights in various scenarios, it therefore has a higher value per share. Therefore the stake to be given to the venture capitalist, if his or her shares are convertibles or participating preferred, is less than the share that would be suggested by the simple calculation. This difference depends on the precise terms of the stock, but is particularly large in the case of participating preferred stock. We discuss convertible stock and participating preferred stock in the following paragraphs.

The traditional venture capital security is the *convertible preference share*. This is a combination of a preference share, which looks like debt, and a 'warrant', which is a form of long-term call option. In the event that the performance of the company is good the VCs will convert the convertible preference shares into equity, as the contract with the entrepreneurs allows them to do. Indeed this is the expected outcome that everyone hopes for. If the company performs poorly the convertible preferred shares will not be converted, and will behave as preference shares, which are similar to debt in that they pay dividends which are fixed at the outset (so they look more like the coupon payments on debt than the variable, profit-linked dividends on common equity). In other words, if the business does badly the convertible preference shares will behave as debt (and VCs will quickly end up controlling the firm if the capital value declines), and if the company does well the stock will behave like equity (because the VCs will convert the stock). The convertible is therefore more valuable than debt alone (because if things go well it can convert to equity) and more valuable than equity alone (because if things go badly it receives some liquidation preference). For further detail, see the discussion of the pricing of convertibles in Chapter 7.

The use of convertible preferred stock by a VC is sensible and addresses the incomplete information problem that he or she faces – that is, the entrepreneur knows much more about the business than the VC, however careful the VC's analysis. Using the convertible preferred the VC leverages the entrepreneur's return, especially for bad states of the world. To take an example, suppose that the VC invests $3m of convertible preferred (convertible into $3m of stock at the initial post-money valuation on a liquidity event) for a post-money valuation of $10m. Therefore on equity equivalent, the entrepreneur and early investors owns 70% and the VC owns 30%. If the final valuation is $100m, the VC converts and now has $30m of stock, and the entrepreneur and the rest have $70m. However, if the final value is $4m, the VC does not convert and keeps his or her $3m of preferred stock. The entrepreneur and his early investors have only $1m of common stock (because in a liquidation, the preferred stock is preferred and gets the first sale proceeds of the firm's assets). This is intended to encourage the entrepreneur to give at least enough return that the VC will find it worthwhile to convert. If the business performs very badly, this capital structure may also give the VC another chance to salvage matters by taking control before the business fails, using the preference shares. Also some preference shares have a coupon (a schedule of cash interest payments from the firm to the VC) that forces entrepreneurs to make some intermediate payouts to VCs, which imposes some discipline and also gives some intermediate liquidity for the VCs to invest in other projects.

However, the participating preference share is rapidly becoming more common. This is the VC equivalent of the 'gift that keeps on giving', since under certain circumstances the stock converts into both a common share (equity) and a preference share (debt-like). The participating preferred share is effectively a convertible, but with a low or even zero exercise price for the warrant element. A call with a zero exercise price is stock, plain and simple. While entrepreneurs commonly value the convertible preferred using the implied amount of common equity, this method should not be used for the participating preferred. This latter type of stock should be valued as shares plus debt. As Bartlett (2000) suggests, '… the choice between participating and convertible preferred should be heavily bargained. The form of the transaction is a significant money issue, one that goes directly to the ultimate rate of return.' Participating preferreds are clearly attractive to the VC and highly unattractive to earlier shareholders.

VCs will usually insist on *anti-dilution terms*: if a funding round results in a down-valuation, they will insist on receiving shares to maintain the book value of their investment, even if they do not put in any money. These extra shares can rapidly dilute non-preferred investors (usually management and 'friends and family') so this is again a value issue for initial investors. However, Bartlett (2000) estimates that VCs receive anti-dilution privileges in over 90% of deals. Therefore, the usual riposte to this is the 'pay or play' provision, where investors who do not invest any cash in a round suffer the loss of their anti-dilution protection – this limits, but does not eliminate, the dilution of ordinary investors.

In summary, the precise nature of the securities sold to the VCs can substantially increase their 'share of the pie'. While the main concern of the valuer should be the determination of the enterprise value by triangulating between the methods discussed above, the valuer should be cognizant (especially if operating from the entrepreneur's perspective) of the potential of the precise terms to abstract more value for one participant or the other.

Notes

1 Reported in *New York Times*, 21 October 2001, p. BU3-1, by Amy Cortese. The equivalent cricket metaphor might be 'there were a lot of singles that looked like sixes'.
2 Since skill in selling is so important for an entrepreneur, this will be a far better exercise than just returning the book!
3 Houlihan Valuation Consultants and VentureOne (2000).
4 These monies raised are for deals in 1993–97 and are taken from Houlihan Valuation Consultants and VentureOne (2000) 3rd round numbers seem anomalous and may include some rescue rounds, although the authors do not discuss this.
5 Author's estimate.
6 Returns of 8.4% on UK 'Early Stage' funds over the 10 years to 1998 are reported in Nelson (2001).

CHAPTER 17

CASE STUDY Trendybop.com: Fashion for the e-Generation

INTRODUCTION

Trendybop.com is a pan-European and US fashion portal, which will use the internet to transform the fashion-buying process for young internet-savvy Europeans and Americans. The company's founders, Andrew Lanes and Annabella Fioretta, have assembled a capable team of technical and marketing experts, and two excellent lead investor groups. However, the opportunity exists for further investors to back the group. At the time of our case study it is *early June 2000.*

THE TRENDYBOP CONCEPT

The Trendybop concept has four elements:

- a market-leading website which will provide a 360° view of the fashion item, full information on sizing and patterns, and the ability to order individually tailored styles and garments

Disclaimer: This case study is fictional and discussion of individuals or firms within the case study or case presentation does not imply any information or judgements about their historical or future actions.

The case study has been prepared entirely from publicly available information. It is not endorsed and has not been checked by any company, and does not constitute a statement of strategy or a statement about valuation for any firm or individual, past or present.

This case study has been written to encourage discussion and not to demonstrate effective or ineffective handling of an administrative situation.

- a market-leading brand-image, based on concepts from the BBLL agency, which recently won the Prix D'Or advertising award of the European Advertising Association
- a Europe-wide launch and branding, calling on the experience of the lead investors
- a unique sourcing strategy, building relationships with exclusive and up-and-coming designers, while outsourcing supply-chain risks.

TRENDYBOP STAFF AND INVESTORS

Andrew Lanes (co-founder, joint CEO), 29

Andrew is an expert in internet technology, having graduated from the University of Sussex in Computer Science. Prior to co-founding trendybop.com, he co-founded the pan-European bookstore readbooks.eu in 1997 with Annabella Fioretta. Readbooks.eu was extended from Italy to Spain and Portugal, and reached an annual revenue of $12.5m in 1999, representing a 50% share of the online bookstore market in its target countries. Readbooks.eu had 200,000 cumulative clients as of 1999. Readbooks.eu was sold to leading media company Kamazalam.com in 1999 for an undisclosed sum.

Annabella Fioretta (co-founder, joint CEO), 28

Annabella is an expert in fashion and internet technology. Immediately previous to founding Trendybop.com, she co-founded and sold readbooks.eu (with Andrew Lanes, see above). Prior to her work with readbooks.eu, she was a leading young actress, starring in several French and Italian films. She also worked as a fashion model for leading Milan houses.

Gianni Asperge (co-founder, CFO), 31

Gianni is a finance specialist, having worked for Fratelli Strachiatella Investment Bank in Milan for three years. He will serve as chief financial officer of the company.

Adam Mallory (technical director), 27

Prior to joining trendybop, Adam was the managing director of Adam Mallory Consultants, which carried out successful e-commerce buildout projects for several UK and French retailers. He will lead trendybop's website development effort, working with in-house and contracted staff.

Michael Simons (director of marketing), 33

Michael is an expert in branding and consumer marketing, having been stores director for Hannes & Mauboussin Stores UK (a mid-price fashion brand) during 1998–2000. During that time, he achieved like-for-like sales increases of 20% against an industry average of 4%.

Anders Jarrensen (director of procurement), 41

Anders was in charge of international purchasing for Pipeline Jeans (a high-end branded fashion jean company) during 1998–99 before joining Trendybop. During that time, he enhanced supplier and customer satisfaction, and decreased delivery lead times by 30% by promoting closer supplier–customer relationships.

Lead investors: Luigi Andresani and Andrew Walven

Luigi Andresani is the founder and chairman of Andresani, a company which sells couture clothing and accessories, as well as owning several *cru classé* Bordeaux châteaux. The company has grown from one shop in Milan in 1957, to a business with a turnover of US$3.2bn in 1998.

Andrew Walven is the CEO of International Look, a highly successful multinational fashion brand. International Look has stores in all 50 states of the USA, and international operations in Latin America and Spain.

Funding has also been secured from the leading investment banks Golden Stanley and J. P. Sorghum.

THE TRENDYBOP BUSINESS MODEL

Market-leading website

Trendybop.com will address the key issues currently preventing the adoption of online buying for fashion goods, by providing:

- a 360° view of the fashion item
- a close-up zoom to see patterns, colour and stitching
- full information on sizing and patterns
- the ability to order individually tailored styles and garments
- a 'trendybop try-on' virtual mannequin
- a 'trendybopper-style counsellor' – intelligent agents to aid clothes search
- a no-quibble money-back guarantee.

The 'trendybop try-on' feature will allow users to mix and match fashion items on a virtual mannequin, so that combinations of clothing can be tested.

The mannequin will be adjustable to reflect different body shapes of customers, and will use detailed data on the garment dimensions to show exactly how clothes will hang on the body.

The 'trendybopper style counsellor' intelligent agent will use an interactive quiz to suggest clothing and fashion gift ideas to users. It will also provide a user-friendly search function for the website.

In keeping with the pan-European nature and vision of Trendybop.com, the website will have full functionality in seven European languages.

The Trendybop.com website will represent a major step forward in e-commerce design, and will provide a substantial competitive advantage for the company. In an environment of rapidly increasing broadband access to the internet, trendybop will give consumers the full benefit of high-speed access and upcoming *ADSL* (*Asynchronous Digital Subscriber Line*) links.

To manage the substantial technological risks inherent in any such development, Trendybop.com plans to outsource the major website design effort to a leading systems development company, while exercising strategic control and constantly quality-checking output. Advanced discussions are taking place with two leading players in this industry, Arnoldson Consulting and Logicon.

Preliminary development of the website is proceeding using the founders' own financial resources (from the sale of Readbooks.eu and so on). The founders expect the site to launch in time for the Christmas 2000 season.

Market-leading brand image

The Trendybop brand image will be hip and yet laid back. Young and attractive role models are being recruited from a variety of European and African countries to model the Trendybop clothing in a 'Trendybop.com: The New European Union' advertising campaign, which will play on the increasingly Eurocentric identity of young continental Europeans. As Trendybop expands worldwide, this advertising campaign can be re-strapped as 'Trendybop's World Union'.

The media to be used will be a full range of offline and online media. Extensive use of television advertising and sponsorship will be carried out, as well as outdoor and print. The company is also negotiating revenue share partnerships with leading online portals, such as the leading worldwide portal Yahoo!, and leading portals in France, Germany and the UK.

The attractiveness of the brand will be further enhanced by the supplier partnerships Trendybop has formed with leading fashion brands such as Gucci, DKNY, Gianni Versace and Ralph Lauren, together with leading youth and sport goods brands such as Fred Perry, Converse, New Balance, Cosmic Girl and FUBU.

Europe-wide launch and branding

It is considered to be vital to have a co-ordinated launch Europe-wide and in the USA, in order to maximize brand impact from the extensive marketing spend. In this respect, the company will call upon the international branding skills of the lead investors, Luigi Andresani and Andrew Walven, as well as the experience of the management in creating a multinational company.

In order to ensure that the company remains close to its consumers, the company has concluded lease agreements on offices in New York, Paris, Stockholm, Amsterdam and Munich. These offices will report to the company's head office in central London.

Unique sourcing and distribution strategy

The company's aggressive sourcing activity will have a two-pronged approach:

- form agreements with key volume suppliers
- source new suppliers with trend-setting products.

To eliminate distribution risk and to allow Trendybop to 'stick to the knitting' where most value can be added, international distribution has been outsourced to Federal Parcel Service (FPS) in the USA and to DutchPost in Europe.

FUNDING REQUIREMENTS FOR TRENDYBOP

Trendybop had originally planned to issue 25% of equity for Ecu80m, valuing the firm at Ecu320m. However, in view of the recent downturn in technology stocks, there may be the potential to issue a larger amount of equity for the required Ecu80m startup-funding. This is one of the issues to be discussed by investors and the management team.

OUTLINE FINANCIAL PROJECTIONS FOR TRENDYBOP

Financial projections for Trendybop are given in Table 17.1. (Comparator figures for net working capital: The Gap = 5% of sales, Amazon = –25% of sales, Nordstrom = 20% of sales. Fixed assets are assumed to be not material, since offices and distribution centres will be leased.)

Table 17.1 Trendybop.com: outline financial projections

	Year ending 31 December			
	2000	2001	2002	2003
Revenues	20	100	270	520
Cost of goods sold	9	42	108	208
Gross profit	11	58	162	312
Distribution costs	2	10	27	52
Selling and marketing	20	15	25	35
Website development	30	15	10	10
General and administration	10	30	40	50
Operating profit	–51	–12	60	165
Taxation	0	0	6	58
After-tax profit	–51	–12	54	107
Net working capital	1	6	16	31

THE EUROPEAN FASHION MARKET

The Western European fashion market was estimated to have a total value of ECU203bn in 1998, having grown by an average rate of 1.8% over the period 1994–98. The breakdowns by broad sector are given in Table 17.2. Countries included are Austria, Belgium, Denmark, Finland, France, Germany, Greece, Ireland, Italy, Netherlands, Norway, Portugal, Spain, Sweden, Switzerland and United Kingdom. In addition, the US and Canada market had grown from ECU130bn in 1993 to ECU155bn in 1998. This corresponds to growth of 2.7% per annum (when growth is measured in home currency).

At the time of writing, in March 2002, the proportion of the marketplace occupied by online retail is small. However, Forrester (a leading market research consultancy) estimate that online clothing sales worldwide will reach $US20bn by 2003. (The ECU/$US exchange rate is $US1 = ECU1.048.)

COMPETITORS AND COMPARABLE COMPANIES

Some available online and offline comparator companies are listed in Table 17.3.

Table 17.2 The fashion market in Western Europe

Value sales (ECU m)	1993	1994	1995	1996	1997	1998
All clothing	184,149	189,924	190,182	194,013	198,031	202,480
Clothing accessories	10,402	10,767	10,921	11,337	11,793	12,386
Footwear	39,563	39,884	38,829	40,062	41,616	42,451
Knitwear	25,721	26,107	26,377	27,305	27,357	28,039
Men's outerwear	47,338	48,046	47,979	48,448	49,322	50,543
Socks, stockings and tights		9,831	10,024	9,927	9,876	9,945
Underwear and nightwear	22,998	25,035	23,757	24,474	24,839	25,383
Women's outerwear	68,087	70,139	71,124	72,522	74,845	76,184

Source: Euromonitor

HOW TO USE THIS CASE STUDY

This case study can be used for self-study or group work. If used for self-study, readers should evaluate comparables versus cash-flow valuations of the firm, as well as the management plans and forecasts. The case can also be used for groupwork and negotiation. If used for negotiation, participants are assigned roles as either:

- Bellyworks Papax Fund (potential investors), or
- management team.

Participants should assume that, such is the respect in which Bellyworks Papax is held in the venture capital community that the other investors have elected to await Bellyworks Papax's successful negotiation on pricing of the business. In other words, the participation of Andresani, Walven, Golden Stanley and J. P. Sorghum is certain, but they have no pricing input into the negotiation.

Participants should value the business, negotiate an investment in the business of approximately 10% of the ordinary equity, and conclude heads of terms for the conditions of the investment.

Advanced issues of the capital structure of the company (for example, convertibility or preferred status of equity, debt/equity mix) should not be discussed: concentrate instead on the pricing of the enterprise as a whole.

Table 17.3 Trendybop.com: comparator companies

Company	Speciality	Revenue (last)	Revenue (previous)	Earnings (last)	Market cap. (June 00)	Market cap. (Feb. 00)
Bluefly	E-tail – fashion (discount)	5.0	0.2	–13.2	14.8	120
Fashionmall.com	Vertical fashion portal	3.7	2.06	–6.3	17.8	24
Ashford	E-tail – luxury goods	39.9	5.9	–72	139.5	310
Amazon.com	E-tail – general	1,640	610	–720	18,226	24,200
Women.com	Vertical portal	13.4	4.2	–15.5	207	680
CNET	Vertical portal	112.3	56.4	416.8*	2971	4510
Alloy.com	Portal – youth	31.2	10.2	–14.8	182	271
The Gap	Fashion retail	11,635	9,054	1,127	29,327	42,300
Nordstrom	Fashion retail	5,124.2	50,27.8	202.6	3,360	2,800
Donna Karan	Fashion	661.7	622.5	10	144.3	151
Polo Ralph Lauren	Fashion	1,955.5	1,713	143.5	1,381	1,620

* Includes exceptional of 735.2 pre-tax, pre-exceptional pre-tax= –61.2

CHAPTER 18

Issues in Internet M&A Valuation

EVIDENCE ON THE RETURNS TO M&A ACTIVITY

Before we assess valuation issues, we discuss the related issue of returns from *mergers and acquisitions* (*M&A*) activity. In considering returns to M&A (internet as well as other M&A activity), there are three separate perspectives we can take on the topic:

- society's perspective: does M&A enhance the wealth of society as a whole?
- an acquiring shareholder's perspective: is the investment made by buying a firm (as opposed to buying separated assets and building a business) likely to provide economic profits?
- an acquired shareholder's perspective: if an offer to purchase the stock in a target is received, what criteria should guide the decision as to whether or not to sell stock?

The standard view of M&A is that the activity constitutes the working of a market for corporate control, where the control of productive assets passes from poor managers to better managers. Disparate shareholders in target companies, because they each have only a small shareholding, do not have sufficient incentive to act to rein in profligate or incompetent managers, because of the free-rider problem. To illustrate, suppose a shareholder owns 1% of a company. If he or she decided to organize a majority of shareholders against current management, he or she would expend a substantial effort, but would only receive 1% of the benefit, as the other 99% of shareholders would 'free-ride' on the effort made. Even if the value freed up is substantial, there will be a lot of inertia as shareholders wait for each other to act.

Acquisition provides a way around this, since the acquirer makes effort to enhance efficiency only after purchasing the company, and therefore gets all the benefits, eliminating the free-rider problem.

A large amount of research has revealed generally accepted facts about the value effects of M&A activity:

- M&A activity increases value: it is beneficial for shareholders in aggregate
- substantially all of this value is abstracted by target shareholders, who receive returns variously estimated between 25% and 50% in a short period after the announcement of the deal[1]
- acquiring shareholders receive little or no reward in terms of increasing equity value.

The first bullet point does not precisely answer the first question posed above regarding whether M&A is beneficial to society. The main *externality* (occurrence or consequence external to the fortunes of shareholders) of M&A deals is that often many staff lose their jobs when companies are acquired. A subsidiary externality is that tax revenues to government may fall because acquiring firms frequently increase debt to fund acquisitions, and debt receives more favourable tax treatment in a company's capital structure than equity. This is because interest on debt is tax-deductible at the corporate level, whereas equity dividends are not. Externalities are important in determining societal impact, because if M&A activity simply *transfers* wealth from employees or government to shareholders, then it is not beneficial to society as a whole. This may not seem important to shareholders, but in the long run regulators will treat M&A activity more sympathetically if it is beneficial to society as a whole. If the labour market in a country is fairly efficient, especially in terms of providing opportunities for laid-off workers to rejoin the workforce quickly, the effect of the externality on laid-off workers is not too severe, and M&A is seen as beneficial in aggregate. This situation is thought to exist in the US and UK, and labour-market efficiency is thought to be on the rise in most other nations. However, it is difficult to break out the effect of economic growth (which will increase jobs available to laid-off workers, but only as long as the economic growth persists) from improvements in underlying labour-market efficiency (which will have a more permanent effect).

Skipping ahead, the last question is the simplest to answer. Normally, an offer to purchase stock by acquisition provides a rapid return of 25–50% to the target shareholders. This return is unlikely to be achieved as rapidly in any other way, although the announcement of cost-cutting initiatives or the conclusion of *leveraged buyouts (LBOs)* has sometimes given similar returns to investors.

It is unclear why acquiring shareholders tolerate acquisition activity, which is of negligible benefit to them. It is possible that a 'free-rider' problem exists that prevents individual shareholders from reining in acquisitive managers. Alternatively, the opportunity to engage in acquisition spending may be seen as a necessary perquisite (perk) to attract the highest calibre of manager to large firms. It should be noted that acquisitions financed by stock are particularly poor for acquiring shareholders; some research has shown a negative value effect for these (although not usually a statistically significant one). In contrast cash-financed acquisitions have sometimes been shown to provide a (once again, usually insignificant) positive return to acquiring shareholders. The explanation researchers have proposed for this is that stock acquisitions, since they result in the issuance of a lot of stock, are more likely to occur when the acquiring company management believe that the stock is overvalued.

THE DIFFICULTY OF DETERMINING RETURNS TO INTERNET M&A

Within the subset of internet firms, there is not yet enough data to break out the positive or negative returns from M&A activity from the rapid swings in value in the underlying sector. Clearly, if we had observed all acquiring internet firms between January 1999 and March 2000, their stock would have appreciated compared to commonly used market benchmarks such as the S&P 500. This is despite the fact that most (if not all) of these deals were financed by stock, and would be in contrast to the experience with non-internet M&A as detailed above. However, this rise simply reflects a rise in price of internet stocks compared to the general market, a rise mainly due to overvaluation at that time. Therefore it is not sensible to form conclusions about internet firm acquisitions being 'different', just from evidence gathered over this time period. We believe it is more sensible to assume that the general pattern of returns discussed above (positive returns for acquired shareholders, close to zero returns for acquiring shareholders on average) will persist for internet acquisitions.

However, *average* zero returns will be made up of some positive returns (successful acquisitions) and some negative (unsuccessful acquisitions). We now go on to discuss the general valuation drill for each participant in the acquisition process. We then consider the opportunities and pitfalls of internet acquisitions, and the indicators that will help determine whether acquisitions are successful or unsuccessful.

VALUATION METHODOLOGY FOR INTERNET M&A

The basic methodology for valuing companies is as per the previous parts of the book:

- DCF basis for public companies
- triangulation basis for private companies (see Chapter 16).

The drill for valuing a target company is as follows:

1. Value the target company as it stands, using the above methods: value 1.
2. If the company is quoted, note the market value: value 2.
3. Value the target company with efficiency gains and revenue increases from merging with the acquirer: value 3.
4. If the company is quoted, multiply the market value by 1.35 (assuming that the market has not factored in the possibility of acquisition): value 4.
5. The greater of value 1 and value 2 is the lower end of the negotiation range: value 5.
6. The greater of value 3 and value 4 is the higher end of the negotiation range: value 6. (However, a value greater than value 3 is not predicted to provide economic benefit to the acquirer.)
7. The agreed value will probably be closer to value 6.

Clearly, value 3 is a key calculation. In assessing potential cost cutting and synergies, valuers have to assess the attractiveness of new markets and the feasibility of serving existing markets with combined resources. Analysis of customer needs to ensure that they can be served using smaller resources, and analysis of the attractiveness of new niches using industry analysis techniques such as the five forces framework, can be helpful here. In an increasingly common situation, the target internet company may have not been supportable as a standalone business, but may have some technology or expertise that a potential acquirer can integrate into his or her business. In this case, careful analysis should be carried out to determine the potential synergies. However, target management must bear in mind that the acquirer always has the potential to refuse to buy the firm, instead waiting to 'pick up the pieces' from the administrator after a possible liquidation.

Almost invariably, the target and acquiring companies will arrive at different values for the bounds of the negotiation range. Partly this will reflect a bias in the forecasts reflecting the goals of each company in the negotiation process. However, it also reflects differences in the information known by each company. The target company will have more information about the detail of its operations; the acquiring company (although at a disadvantage in terms of total information) will have more information about its own operations, and therefore about the synergies that it can take advantage of should it acquire the target. These information advantages and disadvantages should be used strategically by the negotiators.

Shareholders with substantial, influential stakes in either company should conduct a similar analysis. Shareholders in the target may decide to vote against merger if they conclude from their analysis that the standalone target is more valuable than the offer that has been made by the acquirer. They may also demur if they feel the premium over previous share price in the merger arrangement is not sufficiently large, and that there should be an attempt to wait for or actively attract a competing bid. Shareholders in the acquiring company may choose to influence management if they feel the price being paid for the target is higher than the value including synergies. On the other hand, they may 'vote with their feet' by selling the stock.

The decision for shareholders with *small* stakes in target or acquiring firms is slightly different. Both of these groups, in the normal case of a stock for stock acquisition, will end up with stock in the combined entity. History suggests that, on average, both groups would do best to immediately sell the stock in the combined entity, because a stock acquisition presages (on average) below-market performance for the combined entity. However, the way to test whether this is wise or not is to attempt to value the combined entity, and to compare it to the post-acquisition share price and equity market capitalization. If the share price overvalues the combined firm, the stock should be sold, and vice versa.

ASSESSING MOTIVATIONS FOR M&A

Motivations for merger activity may be:

- economic
- quasi or non-economic.

Merger for economic reasons (for example, to maximize shareholder wealth) is preferable to merger for non-economic reasons, of which the most extreme case is perhaps mergers concluded because acquiring company managers want a 'bigger empire'.

The types of sensible economic rationales are as follows:

1. A belief that the target is undervalued:
   - the market cannot correctly value the target firm, but the acquirer can.
2. The acquirer believes that he or she can extract value from the target on a standalone basis:
   - by eliminating inefficiencies
   - by enhancing marketing or sales
   - by introducing more appropriate management information systems
   - because the target firm has undervalued tax shields or other assets (for example, undervalued pension assets).
3. The acquirer believes that exceptional synergies can be obtained by integrating the target into the acquirer:
   - economies of scale
   - economies of scope
   - economies of vertical integration
   - complementary resources.

These are arranged on a continuum of the need for management action by the acquirer, which also corresponds to the level of integration needed by the target into the acquirer, and therefore to the risks of the acquisition.

- In the extreme of case 1, the acquirer may need to do nothing to the target but wait for the market to value it correctly. In this case, the skills needed by the acquiring firms are valuation skills and possibly superior knowledge of product markets, to support their valuation viewpoint.
- As we move to case 2 (the model of the UK's Hanson plc in the 1980s and to some extent the model of Berkshire Hathaway in more recent times), some integration is necessary – perhaps new MIS, management structures or reporting structures may be introduced – but the target is left pretty much to its own devices, rather than being integrated into the acquirer. The skills needed by acquiring management in this case might be referred to as

'general business management skills', such as cost cutting, the ability to motivate existing staff, and the ability to detect which markets to exit from.

- Model 3 is the most relevant for internet acquisitions (although the synergies that have been advertised have sometimes been illusory). This requires genuine merger between the firms. Strategic assets of one or the other firm are leveraged across the businesses of both. Activities which have limited scope or scale in acquirer or target become more economic when executed across the combined firm. These can be opportunities to decrease costs or increase revenues. For many internet company acquisitions, the main opportunity was *cross-selling* (that is, selling target products to the acquirer's customer base, and vice versa), and at the time of the AOL–Time Warner merger, this was one of the main reasons given for the deal taking place. Model 3 requires the highest level of skill and carries the highest risks of integration problems. The skills needed might loosely be described as 'integration skills', the ability to form quickly one coherent and operational organization out of two. Often 'vision' of the potential to cross-sell and to leverage intellectual assets of the two firms may also be important in creating and capturing value from the acquisition.

Non-economic or quasi-economic reasons for mergers are not as healthy. We have mentioned the example of the acquiring managers who wish to build a 'bigger empire': this is termed the *size maximization* goal, and may get in the way of *value maximization* which shareholders require. The diversification motive for acquiring another company, perhaps in an unrelated industry to spread risk, seems at first sight attractive, but it is not a wise motive. This is because shareholders themselves can diversify much more cheaply by buying an unrelated stock, and thereby avoid the high costs of concluding an acquisition. The most common unsound quasi-economic reason given for recent acquisitions was old economy companies acquiring internet companies to obtain 'a new economy valuation' or multiple. However, if the market is operating somewhat efficiently, it will see through this and value the firm as the weighted average of the internet company and the old economy company, irrespective of the corporate 'wrapper'. For some small firms, nevertheless, this tactic did seem to pull the wool over the eyes of investors for a time. However, Purdue University's Rau et al. (2000), suggest that there was a cheaper way to do this than acquiring an internet company – they document large risk-adjusted returns to non-internet companies changing their name to '.com' during 1999–2000, even without any change to their business. (This paper can also be seen as illustrating the breakdown in the use of sensible valuation techniques at that time.)

Moving specifically to internet companies, we can discuss some rationales suggested for individual acquisitions and how they relate to the strategic and valuation issues. Motives include:

1. gain of synergies
2. cost reduction (economies of scope or scale)
3. establishment of standards
4. M&A to gain control of scarce resources or skills
5. creation of a monopoly or cartel
6. private/public market valuation arbitrage
7. crystallization of value (internet or non-internet valuation arbitrage)
8. growth
9. diversification.

Motives 1–5 fit into sensible economic frameworks (although motivation 5 may attract the ire of anti-trust or competition regulators). Rationales 6 and 7 are concerned with taking advantage of the public market's misvaluation at the time of the acquisition. In case 6, companies bought privately held businesses in 1999–2000 with the aim of making a company large enough to get market attention as an IPO. Then the equity holders attempted take advantage of inflated public market values for the merged company. In case 7, internet companies with high valuations attempted to buy companies with tangible assets or consistent profit potential, to crystallize the inflated equity value into 'real assets'. Motive 8 came from the need for managers (valuing partly on PR ratios) to generate growth, including by acquisition, to maintain revenue growth since this was a key parameter for the market's valuation of their equity. Motive 9 has been discussed above.

However, even correct motivation (such as rationales 1 to 5) is not a guarantee of acquisition success.

KEY THREATS TO SUCCESSFUL ACQUISITION

The key difficulties that prevent value being generated from acquisitions are these:

- overpaying (the 'winner's curse')

- difficulty with integration
- cost
- time
- elapsed time (slower to reap benefits)
- management time (being distracted from the core business)
- regulatory issues.

Overpaying is common in any auction-based sale. Let us suppose that three acquirers are attempting to buy company A, and each submits a sealed bid. Let us further assume that the acquirers have all conscientiously estimated the value of company A from available data, and their bids are distributed with an average of the true value. Should acquirer 1 win with the highest bid, we know for sure that acquirer 1's bid is above the true value (unless all the firms bid exactly the true value), because acquirer 1 would not have won if its bid had not been above the average. This problem with auctions is called the *'winner's curse'*, since if we win an auction, this indicates that our estimate of the value of the purchase was higher than those of the other auction participants. Assuming that all participants are trying to determine the true value with random measurement or estimation error, the winner will be the participant with the most unfavourable error.

In 1999–2000, an even more significant, but transient, reason for overpaying was the high level of the market. Managers focused on growth were prepared to pay high amounts to maintain the rate of increase in revenues. Also the 'story-based' valuation arguments caused excessive sums to be paid for purchased businesses. We discussed elsewhere an example of this in the purchase of Bluemountain.com by Excite.

Customarily, acquisition integration takes longer, absorbs more management time, and costs more than is initially predicted. Investors should be careful to include 'integration costs' in their reckoning of the benefits to acquisition. Since these are an incremental cost of acquisition (that is, we would not need to integrate if we did not acquire), they should be factored into future cash-flow analysis, even though companies may classify them as non-pro forma costs.

Finally, the regulatory aspects should not be forgotten. For example, regulators were concerned that the combination of Time Warner and AOL would threaten competition for high-speed internet services by the combination of Time Warner's cable assets and AOL's internet business. Therefore arrangements were required to mitigate this threat.

THE FUTURE OF INTERNET ACQUISITIONS

In the environment of shake-out, as many internet firms run out of money prior to reaching profitability, large firms will continue to 'bargain hunt' for failing firms if these have some useful assets (such as brand or technology). This is especially true of B2B technology firms. Although the strategic position of B2B intermediaries is weak, there is tremendous potential for cost savings using more efficient purchasing of which the internet will be a part. Therefore there will be demand for expertise and technology in these areas, albeit at low values. Finally, we would expect mergers for the purposes of establishing standards to be a continued feature of the landscape.

Notes

1 Palepu, Healy and Bernard (2000) use Mergerstat data to show mean acquisition premia of 40% and median premia of 30% during 1989–98.

CHAPTER 19

CASE STUDY
AOL and Time Warner

INTRODUCTION

The following case study gives some information about AOL and Time Warner Incorporated. The case study summarizes data about the company, to assist in study of the performance and valuation of the company. Readers are asked to construct an Excel spreadsheet to value the company.

BACKGROUND

AOL is by far the largest internet service provider in the world, with 34 million subscribers. The company was founded in 1985 as a provider of online community using a proprietary interface. It now provides its customers with access both to its own content (not available direct from the web) and to content on the World Wide Web.

Time Warner is one of the world's largest communication companies, with interests ranging from *Time* magazine, through major movie studios such as Warner Brothers and New Line, to the company's cable channels (notably

The case study has been prepared entirely from publicly available information as a basis for discussion rather than to illustrate either effective or ineffective handling of an administrative situation.

CNN and HBO) and cable infrastructure. The company's cable infrastructure passes 21.3m homes and has 12.6m customers.

MERGER BETWEEN AOL AND TIME WARNER

In January 2000, AOL and Time Warner announced a merger.

Despite the larger size of Time Warner (twice AOL's revenues), AOL was worth roughly twice as much as Time Warner prior to the merger. Under the merger terms, AOL shareholders owned just under 54% of the combined company. Time Warner shareholders received 1.5 new company shares for each of their Time Warner shares, while AOL shareholders received one share for each share of AOL stock.

The stocks began to track each other shortly after the merger announcement. However, the merger was only consummated on 11 January 2001. The company reported on its first year in January 2002. Accounting data on the merged company is shown in Appendix 19.1.

ACCOUNTING FOR THE MERGER

The transaction was accounted for as a purchase of Time Warner by the smaller company, AOL. AOL announced in February 2000 that it expected to amortize intangibles totalling roughly $190bn. Since January 2000 the company has reported depreciation and amortization of $8.65bn in the full year ending December 2000 (pro forma) and $9.67bn in the full year to December 2001 (actual). This compares to depreciation and amortization of $4.82bn in the full year ending December 1999 for standalone Time Warner, and $363m in the full year ending June 2000 for standalone AOL. Prior to the merger AOL reported on an end-June fiscal year, but following the merger the combined company adopted a calendar-year fiscal year end.

PROSPECTS FOR THE COMPANIES AND MOTIVATION FOR THE MERGER

AOL's large size and healthy cash flow from its mainly subscription-paying customers has enabled it to develop its offering aggressively. However, the firm lacked an alliance with a cable operator, and the threat of cross-platform migration to cable was seen as a major threat to the company's ongoing growth.

Time Warner's prospects in its conventional businesses seem good. However, these are businesses with relatively pedestrian growth prospects, as evidenced by the company's revenue growth rate of 19% during 1993–98. The company's efforts to set up businesses using new communications and interactive technology have met with little success, examples being their Full Service Network trial of interactive TV in Orlando, Entertaindom.com and the Pathfinder website. Merrill Lynch estimate that Time Warner has committed $200m per year to these initiatives, including management time and capital resources, in the run up to the merger.

Furthermore, Time Warner's reliance on relatively traditional distribution routes for its product (such as movie theatres and videotapes) is seen by the market as a weakness. Although rollout of broadband services has been relatively slow, it is thought that video on demand and interactive television will enhance the customer experience without increasing costs, and will therefore be attractive. AOL's internet presence will also provide Time Warner's TV and paper-based content with a new distribution channel.

Table 19.1 shows the projected growth rate and future size of key markets for AOL Time Warner.

AOL also operates in the internet advertising industry. This industry has suffered decline in revenues during 2001 and the prospects (and even the current performance) are somewhat uncertain. The Interactive Advertising Bureau (reported in Bossong-Martines 2001) reports that first half 2001 revenues were approximately 8% down on 2000 revenues (2000 revenues were reported to be $8.2bn by IAB, but another source, Competitive Media Reporting Interactive, estimated that revenues were less than half that). 2002 revenues are predicted at between $4.1bn (*Business Week*/Universal McCann, February 2002) and $13.4bn (Forrester, March 2001).

Table 19.1 AOL Time Warner: projected figures for growth and key markets

Market	Projected growth (annual to 2004)	Projected US market size ($bn 2004)
Consumer internet service provision	27%*	60.5*
Internet shopping (total)	40%**	184**
Cable TV	6.6%	30.2
Film production	2.2%	7.1
TV networks	1.7%	66.1
Recorded music	3.1%	16.1
Periodicals	4.2%	35.5

Source: Quick & Baldwin (2001) except *Kessler (2001), **Forrester Group (2001)

POSSIBLE SYNERGIES

Management had predicted synergies in the following areas:

- revenue opportunities and synergies in areas such as advertising, by providing 'one stop' shopping for companies for their online as well as print- and broadcast-media buying campaigns
- increased subscriber growth through cross-promotion and marketing opportunities between Time Warner's brands and content and America Online's brands and interactive services
- efficiency in marketing across various platforms and distribution systems, including cable, publishing and interactive services
- cost synergies in areas such as technology and network infrastructure, direct mail and interactive marketing, use of billing systems, sales forces and other corporate services
- cost efficiencies in launching and operating interactive extensions of Time Warner brands.

Management of the combined companies had estimated that synergies from cost savings and revenue increases (from cross-selling and so on), together with new businesses, would generate $1bn in EBITDA in 2001. Management anticipated that the company would have a revenue base of approximately $40bn in the first year of operation as a combined company, and an EBITDA of $11bn including synergies (source: AOL Time Warner proxy statement). However, performance fell short of these levels due to the economic downturn.

POTENTIAL THREATS

The regular pressure to innovate, high risks attached to successful filmed entertainment product, and high costs of establishing cable infrastructure are the main threats affecting the former Time Warner units. The internet and communications improvement may also introduce a stronger threat of piracy and bring the issue of copyright protection into focus.

The former AOL units, as we have mentioned, are threatened by competitors using faster broadband technologies. The firm is also threatened by generic low-cost ISPs in the USA; and some branded ISPs, principally MSN, a service of Microsoft Corporation. AOL's international growth has been retarded by differing pricing structures for telecoms in other countries (specifically, the absence of free local-rate calls) and by different regulatory structures (which allow some countries to give an 'inside track' to their home telecoms company's internet subsidiary).

INTEGRATION AND SUCCESSION

These threats still exist for the merged company; one of the tests of whether the merger will create value is whether it enables the combined company to fight these threats more effectively. One major additional threat is the issue of integration costs and the difficulty of integration.

AOL's largest previous acquisition of note was the acquisition of Netscape in 1998. The company's efforts in integrating the new businesses were lengthy; in 2000 AOL announced a thousand job losses in its Enterprise solutions business, split evenly between AOL and Netscape departments.

Time Warner was formed by the merger between Time, Inc. and Warner Communications in 1989. The integration process, although ultimately successful, occupied extensive amounts of management time and effort for approximately five years. The more recent acquisition of Turner Broadcasting in 1996 (CNN, TNT, Superstation) was seen as a success, and the acquired company was quickly integrated as a division of Time Warner.

As the process of integration moved toward completion one year after the consummation of the merger, AOL Time Warner's CEO, Jerry Levin, announced his retirement effective from May 2002. He was to be succeeded by Richard Parsons, formerly of pre-merger Time Warner, who was to be promoted from co-Chief Operating officer (co-COO); while Robert Pittman, formerly of pre-merger AOL, becomes sole COO in the new management structure. Steve Case, formerly president of pre-merger AOL, remained as chairman. This change has been seen by commentators as possibly indicative of a decline in the influence of the AOL side of the business.

POST-MERGER PERFORMANCE

Stock price performance since the merger is shown in Figure 19.1.

In the year immediately prior to the merger (1998–99), revenues of AOL grew 84% from \$2.6bn to \$4.8bn, and Time Warner grew its revenues 4% from 26.2bn to \$27.3bn. The weighted-average revenue growth for the companies during 1998–99 was just over 11%. In its post-merger period the company reported revenue growth of 13% for 1999–2000 (pro forma) and 12% between 2000 and 2001 (actual/pro forma).

Further financial information is presented in Appendix 19.1 (income statement, segmental breakdown, and balance sheet).

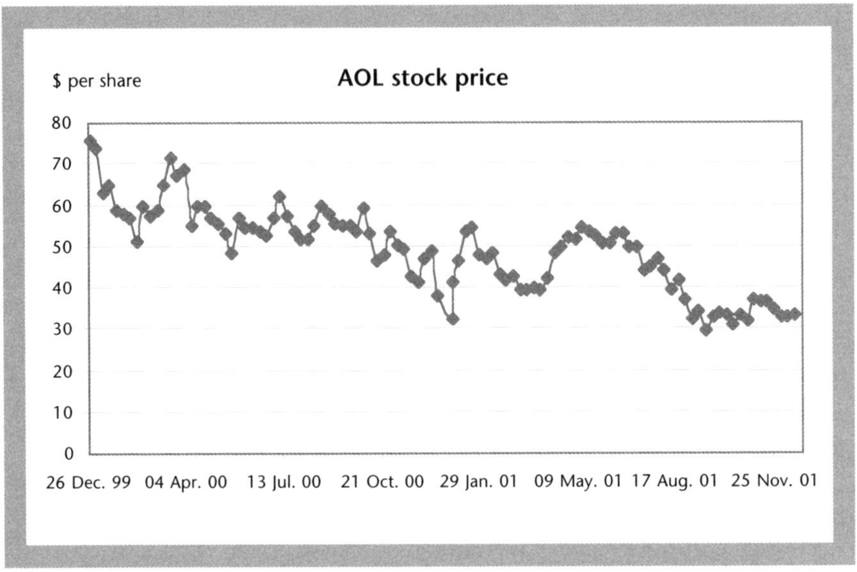

Figure 19.1 AOL stock price performance since the merger announcement

In terms of highlights, the company's film studios were achieving substantial success in the year 2001. AOLTW's Warner Bros unit had just completed the extremely successful release of the film of the first Harry Potter book, *Harry Potter and the Sorcerer's/Philosopher's Stone*. The company's New Line cinema unit was to release the first part of the *Lord of the Rings* trilogy at the end of 2001, a film which had received excellent advance reviews. However, growth in the AOL unit had slowed. According to the 2001Q3 10-Q form, the AOL unit had achieved growth of only 14.4% between the first 9 months of 2000 and the first 9 months of 2001 (actual/pro-forma).

APPENDIX 19.1: ACCOUNTS FOR AOL TIME WARNER

Figure 19.2 AOL Time Warner: income statement

	Pro Forma 1999 (a)	Pro Forma 2000 (a)	Actual 2001	Growth 1999–00	Growth 2000–01
Revenues:					
Subscriptions	$ 13,044	$ 14,733	$ 16,543	13%	12%
Advertising and commerce	7,029	8,744	8,487	24%	-3%
Content and other	12,452	12,736	13,204	2%	4%
	----------	----------	----------	----------	----------
Total revenues	32,525	36,213	38,234	11%	6%
	======	======	======	======	======
Consolidated operating income before depreciation and amortization ("EBITDA")	8,175	8,267	9,656	1%	17%
Depreciation and amortization	(8,414)	(8,650)	(9,203)	3%	6%
	----------	----------	----------	----------	----------
Operating income	(239)	(383)	453	60%	N.M.
Interest expense, net	(1,333)	(1,373)	(1,379)	3%	0%
Other income (expense), net	1,235	(1,356)	(3,539)	–210%	161%
Minority interest	(475)	(264)	(310)	–44%	17%
	----------	----------	----------	----------	----------

continued

Figure 19.2 *continued*

	Pro Forma 1999 (a)	Pro Forma 2000 (a)	Actual 2001	Growth 1999-00	Growth 2000-01
Income (loss) before income taxes, and other items	(812)	(3,376)	(4,775)	316%	41%
Income tax provision	(1,570)	(551)	(146)	−65%	−74%
	----------	----------	----------	----------	----------
Loss before other items of effect	(2,382)	(3,927)	(4,921)	65%	25%
Extraordinary loss on other items	(12)[1]	(443)[2]	–	N.M.	N.M.
	----------	----------	----------	----------	----------
Net loss	(2,394)	(4,370)	(4,921)	83%	13%
Preferred dividend requirements	(52)	(14)	–	−73%	−100%
	----------	----------	----------	----------	----------
Net loss applicable to common shares	(2,446)	(4,384)	(4,921)	79%	−6%
	======	======	======	======	======

1. Extraordinary loss on retirement of debt
2. Cumulative effect of accounting change

Figure 19.3 AOL Time Warner: segmental breakdown

Revenues	1999Q1	1999Q2	1999Q3	1999Q4	2000Q1	2000Q2	2000Q3	2000Q4	2001Q1	2001Q2	2001Q3	2001Q4	Trendline growth (annualized)
AOL	1,259	1,384	1,463	1,618	1,814	1,885	1,945	2,059	2,125	2,138	2,196	2,259	23%
Cable	1,296	1,330	1,342	1,406	1,447	1,502	1,511	1,594	1,625	1,711	1,769	1,887	14%
Filmed Entertainment	1,697	1,783	2,208	2,387	1,896	1,804	2,008	2,411	2,212	1,893	2,112	2,542	8%
Networks	1,379	1,607	1,468	1,732	1,610	1,796	1,603	1,793	1,699	1,828	1,663	1,860	8%
Music	956	843	876	1,258	934	1,001	949	1,264	881	895	939	1,214	4%
Publishing	908	1,072	1,029	1,333	939	1,196	1,081	1,429	966	1,187	1,122	1,535	10%
Intersegment elimination	(255)	(257)	(323)	(274)	(324)	(276)	(339)	(319)	(428)	(450)	(481)	(665)	N.M.
Total revenues	7,240	7,762	8,063	9,460	8,316	8,908	8,758	10,231	9,080	9,202	9,320	10,632	11%

EBITDA	1999Q1	1999Q2	1999Q3	1999Q4	2000Q1	2000Q2	2000Q3	2000Q4	2001Q1	2001Q2	2001Q3	2001Q4	Trendline growth (annualized)
AOL	243	322	358	412	506	583	609	652	684	801	742	718	49%
Cable	582	1,311	1,073	656	694	685	713	767	768	777	791	863	-2%
Filmed Entertainment	378	235	276	112	185	213	215	183	113	250	307	347	1%
Networks	273	361	329	447	335	376	348	443	449	444	450	454	16%
Music	91	110	98	198	101	129	110	178	94	87	87	151	1%
Publishing	91	215	148	267	94	224	139	290	113	271	196	329	25%
Corporate	(65)	(65)	(65)	(83)	(84)	(76)	(70)	(74)	(74)	(71)	(74)	(75)	3%
Merger-related costs	(103)	(15)	0	(5)	(46)	(41)	(52)	(16)	(71)	0	(134)	(45)	N.M.
Intersegment elimination	12	1	(23)	0	(8)	(16)	(4)	(18)	(1)	(22)	(36)	(27)	N.M.
Total EBITDA	1,502	2,475	2,194	2,004	1,777	2,077	2,008	2,405	2,075	2,537	2,329	2,715	12%

Figure 19.4 AOL Time Warner: consolidated balance sheet

	31 Dec. 01 Actual	31 Dec. 00 Pro Forma(a)	31 Dec. 00 Historical(a)
	----------	----------	----------
	($m)	($m)	($m)
ASSETS			
Current assets			
Cash and equivalents	719	3,300	2,610
Short-term investments	-	886	886
Receivables, less allowances of $1.533B, $1.725B and $97m	6,054	6,033	613
Inventories	1,791	1,583	47
Prepaid expenses and other current assets	1,710	1,908	515
	----------	----------	----------
Total current assets	10,274	13,710	4,671
Noncurrent inventories and film costs	6,853	6,235	-
Investments, including available-for-sale securities	6,886	9,472	3,824
Property, plant and equipment	12,684	11,174	1,041
Music catalogues and copyrights	2,927	2,500	-
Cable television and sports franchises	27,109	31,700	-
Brands and trademarks	10,684	10,000	-
Goodwill and other intangible assets	128,338	128,927	816
Other assets	2,804	2,329	475
	----------	----------	----------
Total assets	$ 208,559	$ 216,047	$ 10,827
	======	======	======

continued

Figure 19.4 *continued*

	31 Dec. 01 Actual	31 Dec. 00 Pro Forma(a)	31 Dec. 00 Historical(a)
	----------	----------	----------
	($m)	($m)	($m)
LIABILITIES AND SHAREHOLDERS' EQUITY			
Current liabilities			
Accounts payable	2,257	2,125	105
Participations payable	1,253	1,190	-
Royalties and programming costs payable	1,515	1,488	-
Deferred revenue	1,456	1,660	1,063
Debt due within one year	48	45	2
Other current liabilities	6,443	6,163	1,158
	----------	----------	----------
Total current liabilities	12,972	12,671	2,328
Long-term debt	22,792	21,318	1,411
Deferred income taxes	11,260	15,165	-
Deferred revenue	1,054	1,277	223
Other liabilities	4,819	4,050	87
Minority interests	3,591	3,364	-
Mandatorily redeemable preferred securities of a subsidiary holding	-	575	-
Shareholders' equity			
Series LMCN-V Common Stock, $.01 par value, 171.2 million shares	2	2	-
AOL Time Warner (and America Online, as predecessor) Common Stock $.01 par value, 4.261, 4.101 and 2.379 billion shares outstanding	42	41	24
Paid-in capital	155,172	155,796	4,966
Accumulated other comprehensive income (loss), net	49	61	61
Retained earnings (loss)	(3,194)	1,727	1,727
	----------	----------	----------
Total shareholders' equity	152,071	157,627	6,778
	----------	----------	----------
Total liabilities and shareholders' equity	$ 208,559	$ 216,047	$ 10,827
	======	======	======

CHAPTER 20

Issues in 'Clicks and Mortar'

THE PROMISE OF 'CLICKS AND MORTAR'

The internet's early boosters were too ambitious. Put very simply, they expected the internet to transform business and to change the identities of the people running it! The pure-play internet superstars are in retreat, but the transforming power of the internet itself is not entirely dissipated. Some industries will still undergo discontinuous change. This is the promise of *clicks and mortar*, in which internet commerce and e-business ('clicks') are incorporated into the strategies of old-economy companies ('mortar').

We have already hinted at where the most likely sites for change are. Industries which produce an intangible product, such as travel, insurance, financial services, are likely to see delivery methods changing quite quickly – progress in travel has already been rapid. In B2B, procurement of direct materials may not change as quickly as initially was thought, but procurement of administrative supplies such as stationery and non-critical equipment such as desks and filing cabinets will shift to internet-based procurement more rapidly. During the internet boom, commentators erred in underestimating the resilience of the old way of doing things – recall the case of car dealers, 'sitting ducks' according to Evans and Wurster (2000), but change here has been slower than expected; and Narayandas' survey of Freemarkets' users (mentioned near the end of Chapter 11). Going forward, the error is likely to be in thinking that, with internet stocks in the doghouse, the *threat* from new ways of doing things based on internet technology has also disappeared. There are three reasons why this is not true:

- The internet is getting bigger and better: peak values of internet stocks assumed growth rates of traffic and revenue that were never on the cards, but the actual rates of traffic and revenue have been steadily rising.
- The internet is getting cheaper: while internet consumers are likely to receive some shocks over the next year (the end of free content, and increases in ISP fees) as underpriced services regain touch with economics, business is looking at a glut of connectivity. Bandwidth capacity has never been cheaper, and may fall to new lows before consolidation kicks in.
- All that money 'wasted' on start-ups was not entirely wasted:
  - It enhanced the available technology, and especially the software, enormously. Amazon had to build its storefront from scratch. Now companies can pay a couple of thousand dollars to buy one of the shelf. It won't be as good as Amazon's, but it will allow the firm to shift product if it can get customers.
  - It trained and skilled an enormous number of people in web-design skills, especially in the West Coast US and other e-commerce centres, such as London. These people are available for employment by clicks and mortar teams, their training already paid for by the VC backers of their first business.

Discontinuous change doesn't always come from outside an industry. In fact, *frequently* it doesn't. One can recall the examples of Peter Wood's work at Direct Line, which changed insurance in the UK, and Sam Walton's influence in changing the US retail business. Even in the travel industry, where pure-play web companies such as Expedia and Priceline have had a good deal of success, phone-based travel company Cheaptickets is still an effective web-based competitor.

SEAMLESS SUPPORT FOR THE CUSTOMER

Offline competitors entering the internet space have four potential advantages over pure-play internet firms:

- physical location near the consumer
- greater experience in dealing with customer problems
- sounder business models, so that they are more likely to be 'still around' to provide continued support

- in current market conditions, easier access to capital.

Physical location close to the customer is the most important of these advantages. Both businesses and consumers frequently have last-minute needs that are only fillable through an 's-commerce' application – that is, visiting the shop! In the USA, the initial strategy of many B2C firms set up the online business completely separately from the offline, because this enabled the online business not to charge sales taxes (up to 10%). This strategy is now giving way to integration between online and offline, to prioritize the quality of the consumer experience. The integration strategy means that website, the shop or store, and possibly the catalogue offer the same products, and customers who require service or other assistance can use whatever channel or means of contact is most convenient. Each channel requires access to the customer's information on transactions with the firm.

PRACTICAL ISSUES IN VALUING CLICKS AND MORTAR

The clicks and mortar valuation should start from a sound valuation model for the company being studied. This can be constructed in a similar way to that outlined in Part 1 of the book, to allow easier integration of the internet part of the business.

The addition of an internet business, or increased involvement in internet procurement or selling, may have one or more of the following results:

- Higher costs in the short term:
  - website construction
  - cost of integrating the website with back-end inventory control.
- Higher revenues in the medium to long term, especially if a leadership position is established or if the product is particularly suitable for internet sale:
  - wider geographical reach from the internet compared with offline selling
  - customers select businesses that provide a seamless service.
- Lower costs in the medium to long term:
  - selling on the web:
  - avoiding the costs of physical facilities in new markets served
  - decreasing staff costs by meeting customer information requirements at the website
  - purchasing on the web:
  - lower cost resulting from access to a wider range of suppliers
  - lower inventory resulting from closer contact between contract partners.

- Higher margins in the medium term, eroded as other firms catch up technologically:
  – as competitors catch up technologically, their costs will decrease
  – this will be reflected in lower market prices.

B2E applications (*business-to-employee* applications, internal to the company) can also save costs and enhance efficiencies. These can be concerned with issues such as facilitating teleworking, facilitating communication (for example, top management communications at Ford are mediated by B2E), HR applications (such as expenses, hiring, transfers), and training.

There are no rules of thumb for revenue increases from selling online: these are dependent on the effectiveness of the online marketing strategy and the suitability of the market for online selling. For the latter point, there is a discussion of the relative suitability of goods for online sale in Chapter 13. However, research does indicate some guideline savings from online procurement, which we discuss below.

PROCUREMENT SAVINGS[1]

While opportunities for enhancing businesses by selling on the web are important, one of the most significant areas for potential advantages is in *e-procurement*, buying and sourcing from the internet. The benefits of e-procurement are of two types: decreased costs and increased asset efficiency. Due to the cost of establishing dedicated e-procurement systems, these are only economical for companies with cost bases of $1bn or more. However, smaller businesses can become members of *e-procurement networks* or *eMarketplaces*, which will deliver cost benefits of approximately 5% of costs (gross). The most suitable products for purchase in eMarketplaces are indirect supplies. The US company UTC secured savings of 10% on its indirect supplies. For small to medium-sized businesses, the task of taking the purchase of vital direct raw materials online is not so straightforward, because there are often hidden benefits of customization which bind firms to existing suppliers (as briefly discussed in Chapter 11).

For companies that set up an e-procurement system, savings of 7–14% of costs are likely. The savings in cost are driven by the complexity of the product purchased. Commodity-type products are already likely to be fairly efficiently priced, whereas manufacturers of more added-value products potentially can discount more deeply because they have higher margins. After the costs of the e-procurement system, the net savings to the firm are usually between 3–5% of costs per year. As part of this, purchasing costs are substantially decreased.

Boston Consulting Group has estimated that purchase orders decrease from \$100 to \$10 per purchase order under e-procurement. Through automation, time taken for the purchasing process can also be drastically shortened from 2–4 weeks to 1 day. Another benefit is that far more purchases are within the purchasing system, for example purchased from suppliers with which the company has pre-negotiated prices and terms. In the case of IBM, in-system purchases increased from 70% to 99.4%, decreasing costs and increasing control, as well as optimizing the company's position for the next round of procurement by maximizing volume and demonstrating the purchasing function.

As a further step, businesses may set up *eSCM* supply-chain management systems. These are e-procurement systems that are highly integrated with suppliers' systems. They facilitate two-way communication of real-time demand by customers back to suppliers, and of supply and production issues forward to the company from its suppliers. These systems have the potential to secure cost savings higher than 5%, but require extensive work in changing business systems and culture to reach the highest savings.

EAuctions produce possibly the highest percentage savings. EAuctions are one-time Dutch auctions for provision of a single bundle of service or product. Savings of as much as 15–20% of revenues have been achieved, but some suppliers have withdrawn from the process, citing the impossibility of receiving rewards for quality and service in the eAuction format. This suggests that these savings may be transient. If high-quality suppliers withdraw from company-purchasing processes, this may presage problems for the future. For example, one large industrial company which put its legal services out to the eAuction format found that suppliers reacted badly and refused to tender. However, GE, which has been one of the pioneers in using eAuctions, reports cost savings of 5–50% on supplies, and a 50% decrease in purchasing cycles and lead times.

ASSET EFFICIENCY

Advanced e-procurement or eSCM systems also have the potential to substantially decrease operating assets and to optimize speed of supply. We can consider the example of the computer industry, where Dell's e-procurement system is thought to be more advanced than Compaq's system. This is reflected in lower inventory levels for Dell. In 2000, Dell's inventory of components was approximately 7 days of supply, whereas Compaq's was 35 days. This has benefit in terms of limiting the cash flow needed to maintain inventory. Since most computer components (such as CPUs, memory and hard drives) are subject to deflation at a rate of approximately 1% per fortnight, it also gives a raw material price benefit. On average Dell could purchase its supplies 28 days later than Compaq, thus taking advantage of a further month of price decline in the deflating components.

Valuing this benefit for Dell is fairly straightforward:

- Dell cost of goods sold (COGS) = \$20,045m.
- This means 1 stock day is worth \$54.9m.
- One-off cash flow of \$54.9m per stock day, so 25 stock days = \$1,373m.
- Regular avoidance of 1% per fortnight deflation.
- Dell pays on average 2% less on deflating materials (30 days).
- Assume 50% of the inventory is deflating.
- Saving per annum is \$20bn × 2% × 50% = \$200m.
- Perpetuity is worth \$1336m at 15% cost of capital (=200.45/0.15).
- Total present-value benefit ≈ \$2.7bn.

LIMITED TIMESCALE

It should be noted that most of the benefits of e-procurement should be seen as temporary. This is not because costs will rise again, but because as competitors see the same cost savings from *their* adoption of the e-procurement technology, they will lower prices to compete, and customers will take up the slack. Recall that benefits to shareholders are only realized if there are increased margins: decreased costs are not sufficient. Typical timescales for competitors to update their systems will be 2–3 years. Let us revisit the Dell example, using the assumption that the benefit to shareholders will last for 3 years before it has to be 'paid back' in terms of lower prices:

- One-off cash flow of \$54.9m per stock day, so 25 stock days = \$1,373m.
- Received by Dell in year 0, paid back in year 3.
- Value = $1373 - 1373/1.15^3$ = \$470m.
- Saving per annum due to deflation is \$20bn × 2% × 50% = \$200m.
- Value (years 1, 2 and 3) = $200/1.15 + 200/1.15^2 + 200/1.15^3$ = \$458m.

- Annuity is worth \$458m at 15% cost of capital.
- Total present-value benefit ≈ \$0.9bn.

The valuer projecting benefits forward should bear in mind that the competitive process will limit the timescale of the benefits from e-business projects within companies, and therefore the value of these will be limited. However, the alternative of *not* doing the e-business and making e-procurement enhancements if competitors are considering them may mean loss of market share, lost of profitability, and possible risk to survival of firms.

THE BUSINESS RISKS

Business risks of increasing reliance on internet channels include the following:

- fear of cannibalization (cheaper online sales may not increase total sales)
- channel conflict
- distribution systems of clicks-and-mortar firms are unsuited to supplying the newly gained customers (for example the systems may be optimized for large orders).

Cannibalization was discussed in the customer time economics example in Chapter 13. Companies which give customers incentives to purchase via the web should be wary of the potential of existing offline customers switching simply to take advantage of the incentives. The solution for firms is to price the web-based service appropriately in terms of its expected long-term costs. This does not mean ignoring the set-up cost of the web interface, but rather amortizing this cost in the pricing of the web service. However, the long-term benefits to the firm (for example, by eliminating value-subtracting intermediaries as discussed in Chapter 13) must also not be forgotten, and some of these must be passed on to the consumer to encourage the change to the more efficient mode of delivery.

Channel conflict is another potential consequence of increasing the proportion of web-based business. We discussed the case of online brokerage in Chapter 13. These firms, together with pre-existing discount telephone-based brokerages such as Charles Schwab's phone operation, have caused problems for traditional full-service brokerages such as Morgan Stanley. Morgan Stanley wished to introduce a web-based interface to forestall defections from its lucrative client base. However, the full service brokers who work for the firm are very valuable employees and a powerful channel, even if a channel that may be becoming somewhat obsolete. A channel conflict could have resulted if the firm had opened the web function and therefore eroded brokers' commissions. Its highest-producing brokers, with the closest relationship to wealthy clients, could have defected to other brokerages. Therefore the company's solution was to introduce the web interface after concluding an agreement with its broker staff that guaranteed their brokerage commissions for a transitional period of 1–2 years. Morgan Stanley faced a classic problem of a business that is successful in one channel that has to change quickly as the business shifts to a more efficient channel, or face severe consequences. Morgan Stanley's prompt action was sensible. In comparison, Encyclopedia Britannica (EB) failed to shift channels from commission salesmen under the threat from CD-ROM encyclopedias such as Encarta due (partly at least) to fear of channel conflict, and found its business devastated.[2]

The final business risk is in attempting to serve web-based (possibly smaller order-size) customers when the company's production and/or supply chain is better suited to serving larger customers. Since many costs of selling goods are 'batch-based', a company's cost structure can deteriorate markedly if it increases the number of orders filled, and it can find profitability eroding even as revenues increase.

All three of these business risks are ones which probably need to be *managed* rather than avoided. Companies in industries that are shifting to the web to save costs will also need to shift, even if this causes channel conflict. Cannibalization may be unavoidable, and it is better to have your customers lured away by another department of your own firm than by another company. Finally, if a company has a distribution or production unsuited to producing and delivering small and/or customized orders, it will most likely be sensible to update this technology or methods, or both, provided that customers are prepared to pay a sufficient premium to make it worthwhile. In all cases, competitor action may leave firms with little choice.

SUMMARY

In summary, cost savings of the order of 5% are available for firms shifting procurement to web-based systems. This is because the web-based systems enhance efficiency and also because they provide a signal that a buyer is becoming more price-sensitive – the suppliers in such a forum are self-selecting as those which are prepared to meet that need for lower prices. The purchase of indirect goods is particularly suitable for simple web-based procurement systems such as eMarketplaces, which are run by trusted third parties such as banks or advisory companies. Sophisticated eSCM systems can also provide asset efficiency improvements. However, from the valuation perspective, the benefits of the e-commerce initiatives will be temporary, lasting 2–3 years. Competitors will then catch up. Of course, if a firm has the ability to innovate in its corporate 'genes', by that time it will have come up with another valuable innovation. In this case, incremental cash flows will persist for longer periods.

Notes

1 We wish to acknowledge that this discussion of eProcurement was greatly informed by Mark Frohlich's presentation on the London Business School eExperts executive programme.

2 The story of the encyclopedia industry is told in both Evans and Wurster's *Blown to Bits* (2000) and Shapiro and Varian's *Information Rules* (1999). To be fair to EB, there is some doubt whether any action they could have taken on channels and so on could have forestalled the threat of the CD-ROM encyclopedia, as these authors state.

Conclusion: Back to Value

Markets are prone to periodic bouts of misvaluation, and the rises in internet stocks 1998–2000 were an example of this. The precipitous fall in values of pure-play internet stocks does not mean that the internet is unimportant, however. There will still be opportunities, both for pure play and for existing firms. Pure-play firms are likely to be most valuable if they concentrate on areas where they can erect barriers to entry, such as in infrastructure. The internet also has the potential to support an increase in small business activity, as it gives specialist merchants access to a wider marketplace. However, this type of 'Mom and Pop' store will never gain substantial value.

From the valuation perspective, investors should concentrate on value as calculated using DCF techniques. Real-option value is important only for a small number of companies, and is eroded very quickly as competition in an industry increases. Comparable methods of valuation are unwise. They impose the wrong incentives on management, have poor historical performance and, since they do not give absolute valuation messages, are unsuitable if the valuation of an entire sector is uncertain.

The type of value analysis we advise takes careful note of past financial history, and of a company's strategic position. Alterations to the 'traditional' method of calculating cost of capital (the single-factor CAPM) are needed, but no better theory is available at present. Certainly, we should not let high equity prices (some of which persist, for example among the US blue chips) persuade us to decrease the cost of capital to 'make the numbers work'.

In start-up valuation we see a period of extreme uncertainty coming to an end, and investment gradually increasing in the most attractive areas of providing e-commerce to existing businesses. However, many potential entrepreneurs would be well advised to consider alternative sources of funding, or funding from personal resources, since the availability of venture capital (VC) funding is unlikely to return to 2000 levels in the foreseeable future. Valuation paradigms in VC should be based on future profitability.

In conclusion, we should reiterate our belief that the internet still has the power to transform. It will be most able to do this if internet businesses are valued on a sensible profit-based model, with full cognizance of the strategic issues in each company's sector. We hope that this book is helpful in establishing such a model, and commend this model to the reader.

References

Abreu, Dilip and Brunnemeier, Marcus K. (2001) 'Bubbles and crashes' (Princeton University, Department of Economics: working paper (preliminary)).

Aldrich, D. (1999) *Mastering the Digital Marketplace* (New York: John Wiley & Sons).

Altman, Edward I. and Vellore, M. Kishore (1996) 'Almost everything you wanted to know about recoveries on defaulted bonds', *Financial Analysts Journal*, Nov/Dec, pp. 57–64.

Bainbridge, J. (1999) 'The world's biggest brands', in *Marketing Online* (http://www.marketing.haynet.com/leagues/brand99/index.htm).

Barber, Brad and Odean, Terrance (2000) 'Trading is hazardous to your wealth: the common stock investment performance of individual investors', *Journal of Finance*, **55**(2): 773–806.

Bartlett, Joseph W. (2000) 'Negotiating the best valuation and terms for early-stage investment', in Lake, Rick and Lake, Ronald (eds) (2000) *Private Equity and Venture Capital* (London: Euromoney Books).

Bennahum, David S. (2000) 'The biggest myth of the new economy', *Strategy & Business*, **18**: 15–17.

Berk, J., Green, R.C. and Naik, V. (1999) 'Valuation and return dynamics of new ventures' (University of California: working paper).

Bernard, Victor (1995) 'The Feltham–Ohlson framework: implications for empiricists', *Contemporary Accounting Research*, **11**(2).

Black, Fischer and Scholes, Myron (1973) 'The pricing of options and corporate liabilities', *Journal of Political Economy*, **81**: May/June.

Brav, Alon and Gompers, Paul (2000) 'Insider trading subsequent to IPOs: evidence from expirations of lock-up provisions' (Duke/Harvard: working paper). Available on ARN (www.ssm.com).

Brealey, Richard A. and Myers, Stuart C. (2000) *Principles of Corporate Finance* (Boston: Irwin McGraw-Hill).

Campbell, John Y., Lettau, M., Malkiel, B. and Xu, Y. (2001) 'Have individual stocks become more volatile? An empirical exploration of idiosyncratic risk', *Journal of Finance*, **56**(February): 1–43.

Cantillo, M. (1997) *BA234 Reader* (Berkeley, CA: University of California).

Carpenter, Jennifer N. (2000) 'Does option compensation increase managerial risk appetite?', *Journal of Finance*, **55**(5): 2311–31.

Claus, James and Thomas, Jacob (2001) 'Equity premia as low as three percent? Evidence from analysts' earnings forecasts for domestic and international stock markets', *Journal of Finance*, **56**(5): 1629–66.

Coase, Ronald H. (1990) *The Firm, the Market and the Law* (Chicago, IL: University of Chicago Press).

Copeland, Tom, Koller, Tim and Murrin, Jack (2000) *Valuation: Measuring and Managing the Value of Companies*, 3rd edn (New York: John Wiley).

Core, J., Guay, W.R. and Buskirk, A.V. (2001) 'Market valuations in the new economy: an investigation of what has changed' (University of Pennsylvania: working paper).

Damodaran, Aswath (2001) *The Dark Side of Valuation* (Upper Saddle River, NJ: Prentice Hall).

Dash, Mike (1999) *Tulipomania* (New York: Three Rivers Press (Random House)).

Davis, Angela (2000) 'The information content of earnings and revenue announcements for internet firms: Does reporting grossed-up or barter revenue make a difference?' (University of Washington Business School: working paper).

Demarzo, P.M. (1998) *Finance Seminar 238A* (University of California, Berkeley).

Dimson, Elroy, Marsh, Paul and Staunton, Mike (2001) *Millennium Book II: 101 Years of Investment Returns* (London, UK: ABN Amro/London Business School). See also (by same authors): *Triumph of the Optimists: 101 years of Global Investment Returns* (2002) (Princeton, NJ: Princeton University Press).

Dominguez, John R. (1974) *Venture Capital* (Lexington, MA: Lexington Books).

Evans, Philip and Wurster, Thomas S. (2000) *Blown to Bits* (Boston, MA: HBS Press).

Fama, Eugene, and French, Kenneth R. (1992) 'The cross-section of expected stock returns', *Journal of Finance*, **47**(June): 427–65.

Feltham, G.` and Ohlson, J. (1995) 'Valuation and clean surplus accounting for operating and financial statements', *Contemporary Accounting Research*, **11**(2).

Fogarty, Tim G. (1999) 'Amazon.com, Inc. Building an E-commerce Superstore', (New York: ING Barings) (23 Dec).

Forbes, Scott Woolley (2000) 'Lying' eyeballs,' *Forbes* (7 August).

Foster, G. (1986) *Financial Statement Analysis* (Englewood Cliffs, NJ: Prentice-Hall).

Ghemawat, Pankaj and Baird, Bret (1998) 'Leadership online: Barnes & Noble vs. Amazon.com' (Boston, MA: HBS (Case Study)).

Glasner, Joanna (2001) 'When pro forma is bad form', Wired.com (6 December).

Grenadier, Steven (2000) *Game Choices: The Intersection of Real Options and Game Theory* (London: Risk Books).

Grenadier, Steven (2002) 'Option exercise games: an application to the equilibrium investment strategies of firms', *Review of Financial Studies*, forthcoming.

Hamel, Gary and Sampler, Jeff (1999) 'The E-corporation: more than just web-based, it's building a new industrial order', *Fortune*, **138**(11): 80.

Hand, John (2000) 'The role of economic fundamentals, web traffic, and supply and demand in the pricing of US internet stock' (UNC: working paper). Available on ARN (www.ssrn.com).

Harmon, S. (1988) 'Home improvement, web style: inside the internet valuation tool chest', internetnews.com (14 July).

Healy, Paul, Palepu, Krishna and Bernard, V. (2000) *Business Analysis & Valuation: Using Financial Statements* (Cincinnati: South-Western College Publishing).

Higson, Chris (1995) *Business Finance*, 2nd edn (Oxford: Butterworth).

Higson, C. and Briginshaw, J. (2000) 'Valuing internet companies', *Business Strategy Review*, **11**(1): 10–20.

Hof, Robert D. (2001) 'Is Amazon out of its depth?', *Business Week Online* (6 August).

Houlihan Valuation Consultants and Ventureone (2000) 'The pricing of successful venture capital-backed high tech and life-sciences companies'. In Lake, Rick and Lake, Ronald (eds) *Private Equity and Venture Capital* (London: Euromoney Books).

Ibbotson Associates (annual) *Stocks, Bonds, Bills, and Inflation Yearbook* (Chicago, IL: Ibbotson Associates).

Jagganathan, Ravi and McGrattan, Ellen R. (1995) 'The CAPM debate', *Federal Reserve Bank of Minneapolis Quarterly Review*, **19**(4): 2–17.

Kane, Edward W. (1989) 'Understanding the venture capital market'. In Institute of Chartered Financial Analysts (1989) *Investing in Venture Capital* (Charlottesville, VA: ICFA).

Kieso, D. and Weygandt, J. (1998) *Intermediate Accounting* (New York: John Wiley).

Mauboussin, Michael J. and Hiler, B. (1998) *Cashflow.com: Cash Economics in the New Economy* (New York: Credit Suisse First Boston (Desk Note)) (February 1998).

McCarty, E. Jerome and Perrault, William D. (1997) *Essentials of Marketing* (Chicago, IL: Richard D. Irwin).

Meeker, Mary (2000) *Inflection! Amazon.calm!* (New York: Morgan Stanley Dean Witter) (3 February).

Nelson, James (2000) 'Overview of UK venture capital'. In Lake, Rick and Lake, Ronald (eds) (2000) *Private Equity and Venture Capital* (London: Euromoney Books).

Palepu, Krishna, Healy, Paul, and Bernard, V. (2000) *Business Analysis and Valuation using Financial Statements* (Cincinnati: South Western College Publishing).

Penman, Stephen H. (1998) 'A synthesis of equity valuation techniques and the terminal value calculation for the dividend discount model', *Review of Accounting Studies*, **2**: 303–23.

Penman, Stephen H. (2000) *Financial Statement Analysis and Security Valuation* (New York, McGraw-Hill).

Plummer, James L. (1987) QED Report on Venture Capital Financial Analysis (Palo Alto: QED Research). Quoted in Sahlmann, William (1990) 'The structure and governance of venture capital organizations', *Journal of Financial Economics*, **27**: 473–521.

Porter, Michael (1980, 1998 (reprinted)) *Competitive Strategy: Techniques for Analyzing Industries and Competitors* (Boston, MA: Free Press).

PricewaterhouseCoopers (1999) *Manual of Accounting: The Definitive Guide to UK Accounting Law and Practice* (London: PricewaterhouseCoopers).

Prudential Securities (1999) *Amazon.com* (New York: Prudential Securities (Research Note)).

Rau, Raghavendra P., Cooper, Michael L. and Dimitrov, Ortin (2000) 'A rose.com by any other name', *Journal of Finance*, **56**: 2371–88.

Robinson, Peter (2001) 'Understanding Digital Certificates and Secure Sockets

Layer (SSL)', http://www.entrust.com/resources/pdf/understanding_ssl.pdf (Addison, TX: Entrust Inc).
Roll, Richard (1994) 'What every CFO should know about scientific progress in financial economics: what is known and what remains to be resolved', *Financial Management*, **23**: 69–75.
Rubenstein, M. (1998) *Derivatives* (Corte Madera, CA: www.in-the-money.com).
Shiller, Robert J. (1989) *Market Volatility* (Cambridge, MA: MIT Press).
Shiller, Robert J. (2000) *Irrational Exuberance* (Princeton, NJ: Princeton University Press).
Skinner, Doug and Sloan, Richard (1999) 'Earnings surprises, growth expectations, and stock returns: don't let an earnings torpedo sink your portfolio' (University of Michigan Business School: working paper).
Stires, David (2000) 'Cashing in on the January effect', *Fortune*, 27 November, pp. 279–80.
Trigeorgis, Lenos (1996) *Real Options: Managerial Flexibility and Strategy in Resource Allocation* (Cambridge, MA: MIT Press).
Von der Porten, Eric (2000) 'Lifetime customer value analysis: comments on the revised DLJ model' (San Carlos, CA: Leeward Investments LLC (June)).
Wang, Ko, Yuming Li and John Erickson (1997) 'A new look at the Monday effect', *The Journal of Finance*, **52**(5): 2171–86.
Welch, Ivo (2000) 'View of financial economists on the equity premium and other professional controversies', *Journal of Business*, 73(4): 501–37.
Williamson, Oliver E. (1999) *The Mechanisms of Governance* (Oxford: Oxford University Press).
Young, C.K. (1993) What's the right Black–Scholes value? *Financial Executive*, Sep/Oct, pp. 57–9.

Index

Note: 't' suffix indicates reference to table or figure rather than text.